A SOCIAL AND RELIGIOUS HISTORY OF THE JEWS

INDEX

TO VOLUMES I-VIII

A SOCIAL AND RELIGIOUS HISTORY OF THE JEWS

By SALO WITTMAYER BARON

Second Edition, Revised and Enlarged

INDEX

TO VOLUMES I-VIII

COLUMBIA UNIVERSITY PRESS 1960

New York

LIBRARY OF CONGRESS CATALOG CARD NUMBER: 52-404

PUBLISHED IN GREAT BRITAIN, INDIA, AND PAKISTAN
BY THE OXFORD UNIVERSITY PRESS
LONDON, BOMBAY, AND KARACHI

MANUFACTURED IN THE UNITED STATES OF AMERICA

CHRONOLOGICAL TABLE OF PRINCIPAL EVENTS AND PERSONALITIES

NOTE. Dates given for rulers indicate years during which they reigned. Dates followed by an asterisk (*) are approximate.

B.C.E.		
2000*–1500*	Middle Bronze Age	
1700*	Hammurabi	
1675*–1560*	Hyksos period	
1650*–1500*	Age of Patriarchs	
1500*–1300*	Israel's sojourn in Egypt	
1500*–1200*	Late Bronze Age	
1490*–1436*	Thutmes III	
1413*–1360*	El Amarna Age	
1377*–1360*	Akhenaton (Amenhotep IV)	
1300*	Exodus from Egypt	
1225*–1020*	Period of Judges	
1200*–1000*	Early Iron Age	
1020*–1004*	Saul	
1004*–965*	David; 1004*–998* in Judah only	
965*–926*	Solomon	
882*–871*	Omri of Israel	
872*–852*	Jehoshaphat of Judah	
871*–852*	Ahab of Israel; 853*–852*, participates in battle of Karkara. Elijah	
800*–785*	Amaziah of Judah	
793–753	Jeroboam II of Israel. Amos	
746–737	Menahem of Israel. Hosea	
785–747	Uzziah (Azariah) of Judah	
742–725	Ahaz of Judah	Isaiah. Micah
725–697	Hezekiah of Judah	
733–732	Assyrian invasions of Israel (Tiglath Pilesser)	
721	Fall of Samaria	
701	Assyrian invasion of Judah (Sennacherib)	
696–642	Menasseh	
663–609	Psammetichos I of Egypt	
663* (586?)	Foundation of Elephantine Colony	
639–609	Josiah	
621	Deuteronomic Reformation	Jeremiah
608–593	Jehoiakim	
598	Nebukadrezzar's first invasion	
598–597	Zedekiah	Ezekiel
587	Nebukadrezzar's second invasion	
586	Fall of Jerusalem	
586–516* (538?)	Babylonian Exile	
549–528	Cyrus the Great of Persia; 539, conquers Babylon	Deutero-Isaiah
538	First return of exiles to Palestine	
522–486	Darius I	
520–516	Zerubbabel completes Second Temple. Haggai	
500*	Malachi	
486–465	Xerxes (Ahasuerus)	

465–425	Artaxerxes I	
458* (397?)	Ezra the Scribe. Second return of exiles to Palestine	
445–433	Nehemiah governor of Judaea	
419	Passover decree (Darius II)	Men of the Great Synagogue
411–410	Destruction of Elephantine Temple	
340*	Aristotle meets Jew of Coelesyria	
336–323	Alexander the Great; 332, in Palestine. Simon the Just. Samaritan schism deepens	
323–283	Ptolemy I of Egypt	
312–311	Battle of Gaza and Egypt's rule over Palestine. Beginning of Seleucid Era	
312–280	Seleucus I of Syria	
260*–200*	Tobiads (Tobiah, his son Joseph, his grandson Hyrcanus)	
247	Rise of Parthia	
223–187	Antiochus III of Syria	
221–203	Ptolemy IV of Egypt; allegedly persecutes Jews (III Macc.)	
200*–100*	Letter of Aristeas; beginnings of Greek translation of Scripture (Septuagint)	
200–198	Antiochus III conquers Palestine and grants charter to Jews	
180*	Joshua ben Sirach	
175–163	Antiochus IV of Syria; Samaritans and Hellenizers collaborate with his regime.	
167	Outbreak of Maccabean Revolt	
165	Rededication of Temple (Ḥanukkah)	
160	Death of Judah Maccabeus	
160*	Onias IV founds temple in Leontopolis, Egypt	
160–142	Jonathan Maccabeus	
143–134	Simon Maccabeus; 141, named prince	
143	Palestine orders Egyptian communities to observe Ḥanukkah	
140–139	Rome's recognition of Judean independence; expulsion of Jews from city of Rome	
134–104	John Hyrcanus; his conflict with Pharisees	
128	Destruction of Samaritan temple on Mt. Gerizim	
103–76	Alexander Jannaeus	
76–67	Salome-Alexandra and her brother Simon b. Shetaḥ	
66–63	Aristobulus II	
63	Pompey's conquest of Palestine. Hyrcanus II, high priest	
59	Cicero's defense of Flaccus	
54	Crassus despoils Temple	
55*–43	Antipater, Idumaean unofficial ruler of Palestine	
49–48	Break between Julius Caesar and Pompey. Caesar's Jewish privileges	
44	Caesar's assassination	
40–38	Parthians conquer Jerusalem. Antigonus, high priest	
39–4	Herod the Great. Hillel and Shammai	
31–C.E.14	Augustus	
C.E.		
4	Judaea divided between Archelaus, Herod Antipas, and Philip	
6	Judaea under Roman procurators	
14–37	Tiberius. Ministries of John the Baptist and Jesus	
37–41	Gaius Caligula; 39, riots in Alexandria; Philo's mission to Rome	
40*–60*	Paul's missionary activities	
41–44	Agrippa I	

41–54	Claudius; edicts of toleration	
48–53	Agrippa II (reigned in Jerusalem only to 53, but remained ruler of adjacent lands to his death in 100)	
54–68	Nero	
66–70	Roman-Jewish War; 66, Christians withdraw to Pella; 69, surrender of Joseph b. Matattiah (Josephus Flavius); 70, burning of the Second Temple	
69–79	Vespasian; 70, allows Johanan b. Zakkai to establish academy at Yabneh (Jamnia); 73, closes Temple at Leontopolis	Eliezer b. Hyrcanus and Joshua b. Ḥananiah (69–117)
79–81	Titus. Princess Berenice	
81–96	Domitian; 95, Gamaliel I and associates visit Rome	
98–117	Trajan	
115–17	Jewish revolts in Egypt, Cyrenaica, Cyprus	
117–38	Hadrian. 'Aqiba begins compilation of Mishnah	
132–35	Revolt of Bar-Kocheba. Death of 'Aqiba	
134	Jerusalem renamed Aelia Capitolina	
135	Fall of Bethar	
138–61	Antoninus Pius. Reconstitution of Sanhedrin in Usha. Simon b. Gamaliel appointed patriarch. Simon b. Yoḥai. Meir continues work on Mishnah. Judah b. 'Ilai. Jose b. Ḥalafta. Jose the Galilean	
161–80	Marcus Aurelius	
170–217	Judah I, patriarch. Final redaction of Mishnah	
180–92	Commodus	
193–211	Septimus Severus	
212	Caracalla's *Constitutio Antoniniana* universalizes Roman citizenship	
217–25	Gamaliel II, patriarch	
219–47	Abba Arikha establishes academy at Sura. Mar Samuel in Nehardea. Johanan and Simon b. Lakish in Tiberias	
222–35	Alexander Severus	
224–42	Ardashir I founds Sassanian empire of Persia	
225–55	Judah II, patriarch	
242–73	Shapur I	
254–99	Judah b. Ezekiel founds academy of Pumbedita	
255–75	Gamaliel IV, patriarch	
263–72	Odenath and Zenobia of Palmyra	
275–320	Judah III, patriarch	
284–305	Diocletian	
300*	Council of Elvira	
309–30	Rabbah b. Naḥmani	
310–79	Shapur II	
311–37	Constantine the Great	
313	Edict of Toleration and victory of Christianity	
320–65	Hillel II, patriarch	
321	Constantine's edict to Jewish community of Cologne	
325	Council of Nicaea	
337–61	Constantius II	
338	Death of Abbaye	
358*–359* (344?)	Hillel II proclaims perpetual calendar	
361–63	Julian the Apostate	
365–85	Gamaliel V, patriarch	

375–427	Ashi of Sura begins redaction of Babylonian Talmud
379–95	Theodosius I
385–400	Judah IV, patriarch
395	Beginning of barbarian invasions
399–420	Yazdegerd I, of Persia, and his Jewish wife
400–429	Gamaliel VI, patriarch; 425*, suppression of patriarchate
408–50	Theodosius II; 438, Theodosian code
409–12	Vandal and Visigothic invasions of Spain
438–57	Yazdegerd II
459–84	Perez (Firuz) Shapur
471	Exilarch Huna Mari executed
474–99	Rabina II completes redaction of Babylonian Talmud
476	Odoacar ends Western Roman Empire
481–511	Clovis
485–507	Alaric II
488–531	Kavadh I. Rise and fall of Mazdak
491*–518*	Mar Zuṭra II's execution; end of his Jewish principality. Mar Zuṭra III emigrates to Tiberias
493–526	Theodoric the Great; 500, confirms Jewish privileges
500–650	Age of Saboraim
516*–25	Dhu Nuwas, Jewish king of South Arabia
527–65	Justinian I; 553, *Novella* 146
529	Samaritans declared a Christian sect
531–79	Khosroe I
555	Italy conquered by Belisarius
566	Lombard occupation of Italy
569–632	Mohammed; 622, hejira to Medina; 627–28, destroys Jewish tribes
575	Persian penetration of southern Arabia
586–601	Reccared I of Spain; 587, converted to Catholicism
590–604	Gregory I, pope
590–628	Khosroe II
604–30	Perso-Byzantine wars; Persian conquest and loss of Palestine; Jewish uprisings
610–41	Heraclius, Byzantine emperor; 632, forces conversion of Jews
612–20	Sisebut of Spain; 613, forces conversion of Jews
628–38	Dagobert I of France; 629–33, forces conversion of Jews
633	Fourth Council of Toledo
634–44	'Umar I, caliph; conquers Syria, Egypt, and Persia
638	Sixth Council of Toledo attempts to suppress Judaism in Spain
641*	Bustanai, exilarch
649–72	Recceswinth of Spain enacts *Leges Visigothorum*
650–1038	Age of Geonim
661	Perctarit's forced conversion of North Italian Jews
673	Kairuwan founded. Temporary suppression of Judaism in Narbonne
685–705	'Abd al-Malik, caliph
687–702	Egica
692	Trullan Council (Quinisext)
693–94	Sixteenth and Seventeenth Councils of Toledo
701	Dahya al-Kahina defeated in North Africa
711–15	Muslim conquest of Spain
717–20	'Umar II, caliph
717–41	Leo III, the Isaurian; 723, forces conversion of Byzantine Jews
730*–740*	Bulan of Khazaria; 740, converted to Judaism

732	Battle at Tours and Poitiers
752	Death of Aḥai of Shabḥa
754–75	Al-Manṣur, caliph
755	Abu 'Isa dies in battle
755–88	'Abd ar-Raḥman I of Spain
760–64	Yehudai Gaon of Sura
763–66	Baghdad becomes capital of Caliphate
767	'Anan's schism
768–814	Charlemagne; 787, sends Isaac to Harun ar-Rashid; 800, crowned emperor
772	Exilarch Naṭronai b. Ḥabibai in Spain
786–809	Harun ar-Rashid, caliph
813–33	Al-Ma'mun, caliph
814–40	Louis the Pious
820–29	Michael II
820*–40*	Agobard of Lyons, archbishop
825*	Simon of Qayyara's code
827–1061	Sicily under Muslim rule
830*	Benjamin an-Nahawendi
839	Bodo's conversion to Judaism
842–58	Palṭoi Gaon of Pumbedita
843	Treaty of Verdun
846–61	Al-Mutawakkil, caliph; 849–50, issues anti-dhimmi decree
853–56	Naṭronai b. Hilai Gaon of Sura
853–953	Isaac b. Solomon Israeli
856–74	Amram Gaon of Sura
867–86	Basil I; 873–74, forces conversion of Byzantine Jews
875–76	Expulsion of Jews from Sens, France
878	Palestine is part of Tulunid Egypt
880*	Ḥivi al-Balkhi's Bible criticism
882–942	Saadiah b. Joseph; 928–42, gaon of Surah
885*	Eldad ha-Dani's appearance in North Africa
886–912	Leo VI
892*–930*	Neṭira and his children
895	Magyar occupation of Hungary
900*	Daniel al-Qumisi
908–32	Al-Muqtadir, caliph
910–70	Menaḥem b. Saruq
912–59	Constantine VII
912–61	'Abd ar-Raḥman III of Spain
913–82	Shabbetai b. Abraham Donnolo
916–40	David b. Zakkai, exilarch
919–44	Romanos I
920*–90*	Dunash (Adonim) b. Labraṭ
921–22	Saadiah–Ben Meir controversy
932	Doge Petrus II promotes forced conversion of Jews in Germany
937–38	Pope Leo VII permits expulsion of Jews from Mayence
940*–66	Ḥisdai ibn Shapruṭ; 958, negotiates treaty with Ordoño III
941–43	Jews of Tibet mentioned
960*	Moses b. Ḥanokh arrives in Cordova
960–1028	Gershom b. Yehudah, "Light of the Exile"
963–92	Mieszko I of Poland
965	Sviatoslav's occupation of Kertch (Panticapaeum)
968–98	Sherira Gaon of Pumbedita; 987, writes Epistle

969	Faṭimid conquest of Egypt and Palestine; Jauhar-Palṭiel (?)
980–1015	Vladimir of Kiev; 989, adopts Christianity
980*–1053	Ḥananel b. Ḥushiel
985–1040	Jonah ibn Janaḥ (Abu'l Walid ibn Merwan)
987	Capetian dynasty established in France
993–1056	Samuel b. Joseph ibn Nagrela ha-Nagid
996–1021	Al-Ḥakim, caliph of Egypt; 1012–20, persecutes Jews and Christians
998–1038	Hai Gaon of Pumbedita
1000*–1050*	Nissim b. Jacob ibn Shahin
1012	Expulsion of Jews from Mayence
1013–1103	Isaac b. Jacob Alfasi
1021*–58	Hezekiah, exilarch; 1038–58, also Gaon of Pumbedita
1021–69	Solomon b. Joseph ibn Gabirol
1035–1106	Nathan b. Yeḥiel of Rome, 1101, writes dictionary *'Arukh*
1038–73	Badis of Granada
1040–1105	Solomon b. Isaac (Yiṣḥaqi or Rashi)
1056–1106	Henry IV, emperor; 1090–97, enacts privileges for Jews of Spires, Worms, and Ratisbon
1061–73	Alexander II, pope; 1063, praises Spanish Church for defending Jews against Crusaders
1065–1109	Alphonso VI of Castile; 1085, conquers Toledo
1065–1136	Abraham b. Ḥiyya Savasorda
1066	Massacre of Granada Jewry
1066–87	William the Conqueror in England
1070*–1130	Yehudah b. Barzillai of Barcelona
1070*–1139	Moses ibn Ezra
1077–1141	Joseph b. Meir ibn Megas
1084	Invitation of Jews to Spires; first formal Jewish quarter
1086–1141	Yehudah b. Samuel Halevi
1089	Death of Yehudah b. Isaac ibn Ghayyat
1092–1167	Abraham ibn Ezra
1096–99	First Crusade; 1099, establishment of Latin Kingdom of Jerusalem
1100–1135	Henry I of England
1101–54	Roger II of Sicily; 1147, transplants Jews from Balkans
1103	Imperial "peace" for Jews and others
1106–42	'Ali, Almoravid ruler of Spain
1109	Anti-Jewish riots in Castile and Leon
1110*–80	Abraham ibn Daud
1119–24	Calixtus II, pope; enacts first *Constitutio pro Judaeis*
1120–90	Yehudah b. Saul ibn Tibbon
1125–86	Abraham b. David of Posquières
1126–57	Alphonso VII of Castile
1130–38	Anacletus II, pope
1135–1204	Moses b. Maimon; 1180*, completes *Mishneh Torah;* 1195*, completes *Guide*
1137–80	Louis VII of France
1144	First Blood Accusation, in Norwich
1145–53	Eugenius III, pope
1146–47	Second Crusade; massacres of Jews; intervention by St. Bernard of Clairvaux; Peter of Cluny attacks Jews
1146–48	Almohades conquer Muslim Spain; force conversion of Jews and Christians
1148	*Decretum Gratiani*

1152–90	Frederick I, "Barbarossa"
1154–89	Henry II of England
1158–1214	Alphonso VIII of Castile; 1205, Pope Innocent III censures his pro-Jewish policies
1159–81	Alexander III, pope
1160–73	Benjamin b. Jonah of Tudela's journey
1170	Death of Joseph Qimḥi
1171	Blood Accusation at Blois. Death of Jacob b. Meir Tam
1179	Third Lateran Council
1180*	Petaḥiah b. Jacob of Ratisbon's journey
1180–1223	Philip II of France; 1182, expels Jews from royal France; 1198, recalls them
1187	Saladin recaptures Jerusalem
1189–92	Third Crusade
1189–99	Richard Lion-Heart; 1189–90, anti-Jewish massacres in England; 1195, English chirograph offices established

INDEX

INDEX

A

Aaron, I, 318; "Death of Aaron," midrashic apocryphon, VIII, 278; priestly descent from, V, 173
Aaron, Egyptian priest, *Pandects,* VIII, 242
Aaron, scholar of Baghdad, V, 56 f.
Aaron, *see* Abu Aaron
Aaron b. Amram, III, 152
Aaron b. Asher, *see* Ben Asher
Aaron b. Elijah, V, 261, VIII, 195
Aaron b. Jacob ha-Kohen of Lunel, VI, 74
Aaron b. Joseph the Elder, V, 234
Aaron b. Meir, *see* Ben Meir
Aaron of Lincoln, IV, 79, 82, 84, 214; home, IV, 85; *scaccarium Aronis,* IV, 203 f.
Aaron of Toledo, VII, 139
Ab, *see* Ninth of Ab
Abacus, VIII, 353
'Abar Nahara, I, 377
'Abassids, III, 198; feud with 'Umayyads, III, 107; period of transition to rule of, III, 121 ff.; policy toward minority groups, III, 120 f., 140
Abba, R. (Amora), II, 249
Abba, R. (Tanna), II, 227, 230
Abba, R., identified with R. Abbahu, VIII, 21; *see also* Raba
Abba, surgeon, VIII, 233
Abba, Mar, patriarch, VI, 4
Abba Arikha, *see* Rab
Abba b. Memel, R., II, 311
Abba b. Zabda, R., II, 309
Abba Benjamin, II, 281
Abba Eliyahu, Palestinian sage, VI, 402
Abbahu, R., VI, 155, 181; Caesarean academy, II, 175, VI, 248; friendly to Greek studies, II, 142; on Graeco-Roman vaudeville, I, 264; political attitudes, II, 178, 197; on prayers by proselytes, I, 376; relations to Gentiles, II, 430; sayings, II, 123, 138, 309, 310, 311, 313, 409; uncertain identification, VIII, 21
Abba Mari Astruc of Lunel, VIII, 145
Abba Saul, II, 314
Abbaye, II, 251, 278
'Abd al-Ḥaqq, Jewish convert to Islam, V, 85 ff.; attack on Jews, V, 97
'Abd Allah, emir, III, 103
'Abd Allah, Spanish king, III, 170
'Abd Allah ibn 'Ali, III, 121 f.
'Abdallah ibn Saba, V, 168; 'Ali's Jewish adviser, VI, 12
'Abd al-Latif, Saladin's court physician, VIII, 346; on the *Guide,* VIII, 314
'Abd al-Malik, caliph, III, 88, V, 182, VI, 153, VIII, 224; construction of mosques, III, 134; employment of Jew as fiscal adviser, III, 150; monetary reform, IV, 210; re Muslim-*dhimmi* relations, III, 146; *see also* Mosque of the Rock
'Abd al-Masi'h, VIII, 246
'Abd al-Mu'min, Almohade ruler: and "original" Almohades, III, 127; religious persecution in Fez, III, 124 f.
'Abd ar-Raḥman III, Spanish caliph, III, 107, 155, 183; gift from Romanos II, VIII, 246
'Abd as-Salam, astronomer, III, 133
Abdera, Spain, *see* Adra
Abdiḥipa of Jerusalem, I, 34
'Abd Isho ('Ebedjesu) b. Berikha, Syriac poet, VIII, 260
Abel, I, 22, 230, II, 136, 382
Abelard, Peter: apologia of Christianity, VIII, 67; biblical studies, VI, 272 f.
Abenalazar, *see* Ibn Eleazar
Abgar IX of Edessa, II, 165
Abiathar, priest, I, 149, 330, 340
Abiathar b. Elijah ha-Kohen, V, 33, 38, 306; vs. David b. Daniel, VI, 215 f.; Scroll, V, 31, 37, VI, 215; on moon's first nativity, VIII, 203
Abiathar family, II, 343
Abimelech, I, 75
Abin, R., II, 284
Abin the Levite, R., II, 424

Abisha Scroll, V, 372
Abjuration, converts' oath of, III, 41 f., 184, 194, 322
Ablution: ritualistic, V, 29 f., VI, 14, 182; conversion through, IV, 187 f., 334; general hygiene, VIII, 262
'Abodah, service, VII, 91
Abraham, patriarch, I, 34-38 *passim,* 136, 203, 301, 376, II, 82, 364, V, 137, VIII, 134; alleged falsification of story of, V, 88; Apocalypse of, VIII, 20; Arab traditions re customs introduced by, III, 273; astrology and, VIII, 176; bilingualism, I, 20; contribution to astral sciences, II, 16; dependence on lunar month, I, 44; descent from, II, 31, III, 201, V, 99; Egyptian sojourn, I, 304; formulation of monotheism, VI, 229; God's blessing of, V, 99 f., VI, 300; God's visit to, VI, 302 f.; importance to Mohammed, III, 81, 85 f., 266; journey "toward the South," V, 329; Judeo-Christian rival claims, II, 137 f., 383; and Lot, VI, 39; at Mamre, V, 106 f., 121; and Melchizedek, I, 312; missionary activities, I, 51, 315; names of family, I, 44, VI, 170; "religion of," III, 201, VIII, 124; religious league organized by, I, 51; revelation to, V, 93; role of, in mysticism, VIII, 20
Abraham (Ibrahim) Abu Sa'ad, Jewish banker, III, 158
Abraham b. David of Posquières, II, 408, VI, 101, 179 f., VIII, 24; commentaries, VI, 62; correspondence with Zeraḥiah, VI, 87 f., 118; criticism of Maimonides, VI, 105 f., 380 f., VIII, 40 f., 100 f.; on influence of the stars, VIII, 181; monographs, VI, 73 f., 354, 385; and mysticism, VIII, 39 f.; on the Tosafists, VI, 56, 350
Abraham b. Hillel: re Saladin, IV, 116; vs. Zuṭṭa, VI, 215
Abraham b. Ḥiyya, *see* Bar Ḥiyya
Abraham b. Isaac, "Father of the Court," VI, 73; and Yehudah b. Barzillai, VIII, 38
Abraham b. Isaac b. Meborakh, Hebrew poet, VII, 118, 139, 192
Abraham b. Maimon, R., VII, 311; *see also* Abraham Maimonides
Abraham b. Nathan ha-Yarḥi of Lunel, VI, 129 f., 391 f.
Abraham b. Nathan ibn Aṭa, V, 40
Abraham b. Samuel ibn Ḥisdai, *see* Ibn Ḥisdai
Abraham b. Shabbetai, VI, 57, 256
Abraham b. Sherira, V, 15
Abraham b. Solomon of Torrutiel, VI, 209
Abraham ha-Kohen, Baghdad scholar, VI, 119, 127
Abrahamites, ancestors of, I, 44
"Abraham Judaeus," name denoting Ibn Ezra and Bar Ḥiyya, VIII, 170
Abraham Maimonides, Nagid, V, 47 f., 72, 366, VI, 104, 313, 401, VIII, 63; and Aggadah, VI, 412 f.; on bans, V, 48; biblical authorship, I, 308; biblical law, VI, 143; categories of midrashic lore, VI, 180 f.; on eschatological folklore, V, 165; and his father, VI, 120, 297, VII, 120 f., VIII, 70; re Karaites, V, 281; on local customs, VI, 127 f., 131; marriage contract issued by, VI, 138; on masoretic text, VI, 293; on *piyyuṭim,* VII, 102 f.; on segregation and autonomy, V, 4
Abraham of Saragossa, IV, 48 f.
Abraham the Babylonian, grammarian, VII, 46
Abraham Zuṭra of Thebes, VI, 278
Ab-Ram, see Abraham
Abram, meaning, I, 311
Abravanel, Isaac: condemnation of Martini, VI, 172; on rational law, VI, 144
Abrogation, of biblical law, V, 91, 124, VI, 145 f.
Absentee landlordism, I, 72, 277, II, 246
Abtalyon and Shemaya, II, 346
Abu Aaron (or Aaron), Babylonian mystic, VIII, 44
Abu 'Ali ibn Fadhlan, *see* Ibn Fadhlan
Abu Bakr, caliph, III, 122, VI, 151; death of, V, 294; suppression of Jews, III, 76
Abu Bakr al-'Attar, scholar, VI, 243
Abu-Bekr, *see* Ibn Bajja
Abudarham, David, VII, 105 f.
Abu Dulaf, III, 115
Abu Ḥanifa, Muslim jurist, V, 210, 211, 213, VI, 107, 325; re expression of condolence to a *dhimmi,* III, 147; re property of a convert, III, 144
Abu Huraira, VI, 13
Abu Ibrahim b. Joseph ibn Benveniste, *see* Ibn Baron

Abu-'Imram al-Tiflisi, *see* Za'frani, Musa al-
Abu 'Isa al-Isfahani (Obadiah), V, 182, 185, 191 f.; seven daily services instituted by, VII, 64
Abu-Isḥaq of Elvira, III, 158, V, 93
Abu Kathir of Tiberias, VI, 265
Abulafia, Meir ha-Levi, R., jurist-poet, VII, 164
Abulafia, Ṭodros b. Yehudah, VII, 147, 196
Abu'l 'Ataluj, Baghdad court poet, VII, 169
Abu'l Barakat Ḥibbat Allah ibn Malka al-Baghdadi, Jewish philosopher, III, 158, VI, 477, VIII, 63, 141, 249; doctrine of impetus, VIII, 223
Abu'l Fadail ibn an-Nagid, Jewish eye-doctor, VIII, 237, 254 f.
Abu'l Fadhi, *see* Ibn Ḥisdai, Abu'l Fadhi
Abu'l Fadl, Muslim scholar, VII, 87
Abu'l Faraj Harun, Karaite grammarian and exegete, V, 233, VII, 3, 26, 38 f., VIII, 60; commentaries, VI, 206; grammatical works, VI, 290
Abu'l-Fatḥ, chronicle of, II, 29, 340, V, 175 f., 367, 371, VI, 212
Abu'l Kamal Tamim, Moroccan rebel, III, 108, 122
Abu'l Ma'ali ibn Hibbat Allah, Jewish court physician, VIII, 249
Abu'l-Ma'ali Juwayni (Imam al-Haramein), VIII, 333
Abu'l Mina ha-Kohen al-'Attar, VIII, 257
Abu'l Walid ibn Merwan, *see* Ibn Janaḥ
Abu Manṣur adh-Dhamari, VI, 181
Abu Manṣur al-Baghdadi, V, 327
Abun (or Bun), R., II, 13, VIII, 34
Abu Saliḥ, Christian chronicler, III, 136, 297
Abu Shuja, vizier, III, 141
Abu Tahir, Qarmatian chief, V, 104
Abu Tahir ibn Shibr, Jewish leader, V, 295
Abu 'Ubaid, III, 168
Abu Yusuf, fiscal authority, III, 162, 295, 299, 302, 309, 310, IV, 181, VI, 112
Abu Zakariya Yaḥya ibn Daud Ḥayyuj, *see* Hayyuj, Yehudah b. David
Abyss, meaning of, VI, 285
Abyssinia, *see* Ethiopia
Academies, ancient, II, 120 f., 205, 206, 207, 399, 425; Babylonian leaders of, in Palestine, II, 208; Caesarea, II, 175; calendar proclamations issued by, II, 198; decline of, and growth of synagogue, VII, 62; funds, II, 194; Ḥira, III, 61; *kallah* gatherings, II, 245, 247, 276, 277; leadership, II, 196, 197, 403; Pumbedita, II, 207; Sura, II, 207; Tiberias, II, 196; Usha, II, 126, 378; Yabneh, II, 115, 120, 126, 377
—— medieval Babylonian, IV, 215; V, 10, 16, 282; at assemblies, V, 19 f.; authority of, V, 13-20, 51, VI, 22, 26 ff., VII, 147 f.; and Caliphate, V, 14; courts, V, 20, VI, 9 f.; decline of, VI, 119, VIII, 4; differences between Sura and Pumbedita, VI, 389; and evolution of law, V, 22, VI, 16 ff., 25; and the exilarchate, V, 6; explanations of talmudic terms, VI, 27 ff.; guardians of oral tradition, VI, 427; hereditary principle of leadership, V, 50, 300; investiture of gaon, V, 24; *kallah* gatherings, VI, 111, 154; Karaites and, V, 230 ff., 237, 274; legal decisions, V, 22 ff., 211, VI, 55, 301, 384; on local customs, VI, 124 ff.; loss of archives, VI, 112; mystics among leaders, VIII, 7 ff.; neglect of Hebrew philology, VII, 19; and proclamation of leap year, VIII, 194 ff.; re prophets and sages, VI, 202, VIII, 130; revenue of, III, 154, V, 19, 23 f., 33, 40, 51 f., 237, 306, VI, 111; on ritualistic innovations, VII, 64 f., 78; titles awarded by, V, 52; use of Arabic, VII, 6; work on biblical texts, VI, 238 ff., 248 f., 253, 261
—— medieval Palestinian, IV, 215, V, 32 ff.; aggadic studies, VI, 153; calendar proclamations, VI, 216, VIII, 193 f.; homiletical and biblical studies, VI, 152 ff., 245; controversies over regional leadership, VI, 214; halakhic monographs, VI, 63 ff.; talmudic commentaries, VI, 56 f.; vernacular versions of Bible, VI, 239
—— medieval, Western, IV, 26, 45, 215, VI, 56; founded by captive scholars, V, 46; ordinance re communal establishment of, VI, 140 f.; responsa, VI, 117 ff.
—— Muslim, VII, 138
Accadian dialect, I, 20
Accents: masoretic, VII, 126, 283; musi-

Accents (*Continued*)
cal, VII, 126 f.; in punctuation, VI, 237, 249, 259 f.
Acco, Palestine, I, 255, IV, 116, VIII, 249; *see also* Ptolemais
Accursius, VI, 55
Achaemenids, dynasty, I, 107, 341; and Babylonia, I, 355, II, 206; and chronology, II, 26; effects of, I, 131, II, 317; and Egypt, I, 354; *see also* Persia, Achaemenid
Achillas Rufus, II, 98
Acmonia, synagogue in, II, 24
Acoustics, and music, VII, 209
Acre, *see* Acco; Ptolemais
Acropolis of Athens: burned, I, 348; statue to Herod, I, 262
Acrostics: alphabetic, VII, 88, 91; double, VII, 92; list of words for, VII, 14; on names, VII, 99, 141, 144, 289; related to Haduta or Ḥaduta, VII, 259
Active Intelligence, VIII, 115, 128, 338
"Acts of Pilate," II, 379
Acts of the Apostles, Ebionite, II, 75
"Acts of the Heathen Martyrs," I, 190, 381, II, 108
Adalbert (Wojtech), bishop of Prague, III, 219
Adalbert, bishop of Worms, IV, 99
Adam, VIII, 203; allegorical meaning of, VIII, 86, 338; "Book of Adam," VI, 17, 197; dualist critique of story of, V, 106; and Eve, V, 235, VI, 283; and future ideas, I, 10, 52; midrash on the speech of, VI, 269; sin and punishment, VI, 303; sons and daughters, VI, 170; years of life, VIII, 149
Adam of Bremen, VIII, 224; re Kiev, III, 217
Adam zakhar, phrase, VIII, 149 f.
Adda, R., talmudic sage, VIII, 189, 193, 198 f., 358
Adelard of Bath, VIII, 174
Aden, Arabia, III, 115; dynasty of communal officials, V, 51
Adfuwi, al-, commentator on the Qur'an, VI, 282
Adharbaijan, Khazar invasion, III, 199
Adhémar de Chabannes, IV, 57
Adhémar de Monteil, bishop of Le Puy, IV, 98
Adiabene, kingdom, I, 168, II, 213
Adiabene, royal house of, I, 173, 183, 210, III, 63, VI, 257; opposition to Trajan, II, 371; tombs, II, 333
Adjectives, multiplication of, VIII, 14
Adler papyri, I, 261
Administration, communal, *see* Communal control; Communities, Jewish
Adon, king of Ascalon, I, 334
Adonai, divine name, I, 244, II, 18, 361, VI, 449; *see also* Names, divine; Yahweh
Adonim, *see* Dunash b. Labraṭ; Ibn Tamim
Adoniram, servant of Solomon, III, 244; alleged tombstone of, III, 34
Adonizedek, I, 45
Adora, I, 224
Adoram, I, 74
Adra (Abdera), Spain, III, 34
Adrianeion of Tiberias, II, 108, 400
Adult education, II, 275 f., 421 f.; *see also* Education
Adultery, V, 240 f., VI, 324; Muslim law on, III, 142 f.; punishment for, I, 361, II, 222, 228; *see also* Sex
Adventure stories, VII, 183 ff., VIII, 211 f.
Aelia Capitolina, Jerusalem renamed, II, 107, III, 269
Aelius Gallus, III, 64
Aeon, cosmic, II, 60, 351, 436
Afdhal, Abu'l Hasan 'Ali al-, sultan, VIII, 260 f.
Afdhal, Abu'l Qasim al-, vizier, V, 203
Afendopolo, Caleb b. Elijah, V, 234, 410
Afghanistan, VI, 299; inscription, III, 282; Jews in, III, 110
Africa: Christians in, II, 165, 188, 393; commercial relations with Rome, I, 410; gold and silver mines, IV, 211; Jewish communities, I, 262, III, 106 f., 116, IV, 174; Semitic civilization, I, 64, 176, 374; size of, VIII, 215
Africa, North: abandonment of Aramaic Targum, VI, 264; Arab expansion in, III, 90 ff.; Canaanite-Phoenician antecedents, III, 214, 271; Graeco-Roman linguistic heritage, VII, 12; Jewish communities, V, 25; Karaite settlement, VII, 226; resistance to Belisarius, III, 7; *see also* individual countries
Africanus, (Sextus) Julius, *see* Julius Africanus
Agag, the Amalekite, III, 63

Agapios of Alexandria, VIII, 241
Agapius (Mahbub) of Menbidj, III, 98, 236; re forced conversion to Christianity, III, 176 ff.; re sack of Damascus, III, 121 f.
Agathias Scholasticus, III, 54; quoted, II, 183, 399
Agde, Council of, III, 36, 245, IV, 241
Agents: business, IV, 180; merchant travelers as, IV, 174 ff.; slaves as, IV, 196
Age of maturity, II, 219, 421 f.
Agga, name, I, 120
Aggadah, I, 205, II, 293, 298, 429; on Abraham, VI, 39; III, 71, 273; anthropomorphism in, VI, 178, 268, VIII, 99; debates recorded in, II, 310; doctrine of the Exile, V, 101; on Elijah, V, 195; form of transmission, II, 65; re fasting, VI, 14; German students of, VI, 422, VIII, 44 f.; on God's love, VIII, 114; handmaid of the Halakhah, II, 298, 429, VI, 178; on the Hereafter, VIII, 105; historical outlook, VI, 231; on humility, VIII, 121; liturgical poets and, V, 151, VII, 83; messianic concepts, V, 139, 164, 185; mixed reactions to, VI, 43, 152 ff., 160 f., 175-81; Mohammed's familiarity with, III, 83, 265; Palestinian and Babylonian positions on, II, 316 f.; reappraisal of older teachings, II, 362; secular stories and romances, VI, 181 ff.; "seventy nations," VIII, 216; source of philosophic speculation, VIII, 4 ff.; transition from mystical to rationalist, II, 426; Yosephon III, 240; *see also* Ethics; Midrash; Rabbis and rabbinate; Talmud
Aggadic Midrash, *see* Midrash
Aghlabids, Moroccan dynasty, III, 108
Agnosticism, VIII, 79; in the Renaissance of Islam, V, 103 ff.; views on matter and space, VIII, 88
Agobard, archbishop of Lyons, IV, 14, 18, 26, 51 f., 220, VI, 153, VIII, 26; anti-Jewish writings, IV, 263, V, 123, 126 f.; dilemma re canon law, IV, 263 f.; on *magister Judaeorum,* V, 63
Agriculture: ancient, I, 42, 250-55, 406-7; in Babylonia, II, 244, 246, 257, 414; changing attitudes and laws, II, 263 f., IV, 151; effect of antisemitism, II, 244; Essenes' occupation, II, 48; evolution from nomadic life to, I, 55 ff.; exiles engaged in, I, 109; laborers, I, 70, 281; in Palestine, I, 277, II, 245, 246; rate of production, I, 65, 251, 253, 265
—— medieval: Jewish contributions to, III, 70 f., 197, 260, IV, 161; Jewish settlements, IV, 29; Jewish share in, IV, 151 ff.; Karaites and, V, 272 f.; laws, V, 257
—— *see also* Farmers; Land; Peasants
Agrippa I, king, I, 66, 219, 236, 246, 261, 264, 372, II, 131; economic blockade of Tyre and Sidon, I, 277; family's statues, I, 401; letter to Caligula, I, 218; no right to be king of Judaea, I, 223
Agrippa II (Marcus Julius Agrippa), II, 82, 91, 105, 123; imaginary arguments by, II, 99, 101
Agrippa, Marcus Vipsanius, I, 215, 218, II, 17, 402; protection of temple funds, I, 215, 393
Agrippenses, congregation of, II, 402
'Agunah, II, 238, IV, 184
Agur b. Jakel, VI, 160
Aḥa, R. (Amora), II, 392
Aḥa, R. (Sabora), VI, 20 f.
Aḥa, R., "the fort commander," II, 259
Ahab, king, I, 68, 77, 78, 93, 318, 327; chariots, I, 332; and Jezebel, I, 322; in battle of Karkara, I, 67
Aḥa b. Adda, R., VI, 238
Aḥa b. Jacob, R., prayer of thanksgiving, VII, 109
Aḥa b. Ḥanina, R., II, 287
Aḥai of Shabḥa, R., V, 15, 32, 212, VI, 22 f., 81, 156; juridico-homiletical work, VI, 37 ff., 169, 174, 202, 336 ff.; on liturgical problems, VII, 68, 110; weekly homilies, VI, 91
Ahasuerus-Xerxes, I, 354
Ahaz, king, I, 326, VIII, 361
Aḥimaaz, ancestor of Aḥimaaz of Oria, V, 376 f., VI, 216 f.
Aḥimaaz of Oria, III, 180, IV, 23, VIII, 44; chronicle of, III, 154, IV, 157, 216 f.; re Palṭiel, V, 40 f.
Aḥiqar story, I, 187; VII, 183
Aḥmad, numerical equivalent of, V, 86
Aḥmad as-Ṣinhaji al-Qarafi, *see* Qarafi
Ahuramazda, I, 130, 348, II, 316
Aḥwaz, city, IV, 201, 340
Ai, city, I, 299

'Ain Fashkha cave, *see* Dead Sea Scrolls
Air, cosmic principle, VIII, 22
Aix-en-Provence, IV, 58
Ajal, doctrine, VIII, 259
Akhenaton unodeistic reform, I, 45 f., 53
Akko, *see* Acco
Alabarch, office of, I, 261, 409, 410
Alaçar, IV, 39
Alans, III, 98, 203; Jewish influence on, III, 200, 208
Alaric II, *Breviarium,* III, 35, 49
Al-Balia, *see* Isaac b. Baruch
Alban, Saint, shrine of, IV, 84
Albert of Aix, IV, 111
Albertus Magnus, VIII, 167
Albigensian Crusade, IV, 61, 132, VIII, 32
Albigensianism, IV, 9
Al-Biruni Ḥamza al-Isfahani, Arab historiographer and astronomer, V, 13, 327, VI, 199, 307, 437, VIII, 148; chronological computations, VIII, 189 f., 194, 209; Chronology of Creation, VIII, 377; collector of scientific material, VIII, 370; Table, VIII, 368
Albo, Joseph, VII, 207, VIII, 99
Alcaeus, poet, I, 184
Alcala de Henares, Spain, IV, 32 f.
Alchemy, VIII, 223 ff.
Alcuin, IV, 26, 44 f.
Alduin, bishop of Limoges, IV, 57; conversion of Jews, IV, 284
'Alenu, prayer, IV, 138, VII, 75 f., 89
Aleppo (Ḥaleb; Ṣobah), Syria, III, 104 f.; biblical manuscript, VI, 447; exilarch, V, 311; Rabbanite community, V, 50, VI, 247
Alexander, *alabarch,* I, 261, 265
Alexander II, pope, IV, 94, 122, 131; crusade against Spanish Islam, IV, 284; intervention for Spanish Jewry, V, 361; against forced conversion, IV, 236
Alexander III, pope, IV, 14, 434; re Christian nurses, IV, 15; re Jewish officials, IV, 15; re Judeo-Christian litigation, IV, 16, 240; and St. Augustine monastery, IV, 84; re tithes, IV, 153 f.; welcomed by Jewish elders, V, 59
Alexander Jannaeus, king, I, 167, 215, 218, 221 ff., 235 f., 276, II, 13, V, 255, VI, 207
Alexander b. Moses, IV, 119
Alexander of Aphrodisias, VIII, 76
Alexander Severus, emperor: donor to synagogues, II, 87, 191, 402; religious syncretism, II, 390
Alexander the Great, II, 4, 311-12; Alexander Romance, VIII, 306; alleged conversion of, VIII, 306; conquest of western Asia, I, 184, 228, 338; *Du'l Qarnayim,* V, 329; encounter with Simon the Pious, VI, 207; era of, VIII, 205; established communities, II, 34, 341; Hebraic paraphrase of Romance, VI, 192; and Jewish quarter, I, 188; Samaria, rebuilt by, II, 27; and Temple of Bel, I, 168
Alexandria, ancient: antisemitism, I, 188, 191, 216, 219, 246, 372, 381, II, 159, 189, 365, 402, *see also* "Acts of the Heathen Martyrs"; center of trade with India and China, II, 249; Claudius' edict, I, 240, 403; early capitalistic system, I, 201, 411; intellectual center extinguished, II, 163; intermarriages in, II, 233; largest Jewish community, I, 185, 188, 393; necropolis, II, 286; omitted from Paul's journeying, II, 84, 365; Phoenician ghetto, I, 176; population, I, 171, 371; religious customs, I, 200, II, 306; shipowners' guild, II, 261; a "sister" of Jerusalem, I, 219; status of Jews, I, 190, 221, 240, 248, 403, II, 419; uprising suppressed, II, 95
—— medieval, III, 271, VIII, 57, 241; Arab conquest, II, 402, III, 90; Coptic church, III, 9; Jewish community, II, 402, III, 106; medical treatise concerning, VIII, 226; prohibition of new synagogue, III, 9; schools of, VIII, 61, 76
—— *see also* Egypt
Alexis Comnenus, Byzantine emperor, III, 186; and the papacy, IV, 95
Aleyan Epic, I, 312
Al-Fasi, *see* David b. Abraham al-Fasi
Alfasi, Isaac b. Jacob, Spanish jurist, II, 295, 425, IV, 213, VI, 27, 48; on Babylonian Talmud, VI, 25; birthplace, VI, 367; re celebration of the New Year, V, 29, 49; compilation of laws, VI, 84-90; influence in southern France, VIII, 292; legalization of drafts, IV, 213; Maimonides and, VI,

59; manuscripts, VI, 368; prohibition of Arabic tunes, VII, 205; on ransom of captives, IV, 178; responsa, VI, 117; on Saadiah's Book of Pledges, VI, 69
Al-Fellaḥi, vizier, III, 158
Alfonso, Spanish kings, *see* Alphonso
Al-Gasum, *see* Ibn al-Jasus
Algebra, VIII, 153 ff.
Algeria: dialect of Berber tribes, VII, 12; preservation of Saadiah's texts, VI, 296
Al-Ghazzali, *see* Ghazzali, al-
Al-Haitham, *see* Ibn 'Adi
Al-Hajjaj, governor, III, 120
Al-Ḥakim, caliph of Cordova, VI, 61
Al-Ḥakim bi-Amrillah, Egyptian caliph, III, 122 ff., 289, VIII, 248
Al-Ḥanbali, Abu 'Ali, V, 296
Al-Ḥaqir an-Nafi', court physician, VIII, 248
Al-Ḥaqq, *see* 'Abd al-Ḥaqq
Al-Ḥarith, Khaibar leader, III, 87
Al-Ḥarizi, Yehudah b. Solomon, poet and traveler, VII, 155, VIII, 64, 306 f., 340; on cantor-preachers, VII, 58 ff., 81; linguistic feats, VII, 191; on medical quack, VIII, 238; original Hebrew work, VII, 185 f.; paraphrase of Hariri's *Maqamas,* VII, 184 ff.; poem reading backward and forward, VII, 151, 197; on R. 'Uzziel of Ḥamat, III, 159; translations into Hebrew, VI, 60, VII, 7
Al-Ḥijr, city, III, 64
Al-Ḥimyari, re Granada, III, 109
'Ali, Mohammed's son-in-law, V, 168, VI, 12; greeting from Jews of Mosul, III, 276; marriage of his son Ḥusain, III, 89; violent death, III, 122
'Ali aṭ-Ṭabari, *see* Ṭabari, 'Ali at-
'Ali b. Israel Alluf, V, 298 f.
'Ali b. Suleiman, VI, 287 f.; dependence on Rabbanite exegetes, VI, 291
'Ali b. Yehudah 'Alan of Tiberias, VII, 34
'Ali b. Yusuf, Almoravid ruler, III, 145
'Alides, Muslim faction, V, 375, VI, 12
"Alien law," theory of, and "serfdom," IV, 262
Aliens: resident, I, 179, 325, 375; status in Carolingian Empire, IV, 50
'Ali ibn 'Isa, vizier, III, 146, 153, 158; and his Jewish bankers, IV, 201, 208
Al-Idrisi, *see* Idrisi, al-
Al-Isfahani, *see* Abu 'Isa al-Isfahani
Aliturus, actor, II, 9
Al-Jaḥiẓ, VIII, 67 f.; on bilingualism, VII, 10; on his lack of success, VIII, 237; on interfaith animosities, V, 108; on intermarriage, III, 143; study of zoology, VIII, 386
Al-Jauhari, Arab lexicographer, VII, 26
Al-Jubai, Jewish rationalist, VIII, 67
Al-Khwarizmi, Mohammed ibn Musa, Muslim mathematician, VIII, 147; *Algebra,* VIII, 149, 153
Allegory: in biblical interpretation, I, 205-7, II, 144, 158, VI, 297, VII, 167 f., VIII, 100; harmonization of revelation and logic, VIII, 85 f.
Allodia, hereditary, IV, 47
Al-Malik az-Azhir Khoshkadem, Mameluk sultan, V, 268
Al-Ma'mun, caliph: decree re sects, V, 9 f., 222; expulsion of many Jews from Baghdad, III, 100; founder of libraries, VII, 138; Judeo-Christian debates, V, 83, 85, 110; promoter of scientific studies, VIII, 162, 167, 198
Almanac, Latin treatise on, VIII, 362
Al-Manṣur, caliph: building of Baghdad, III, 99, IV, 170, VIII, 148; employment of non-Muslims, III, 126, 152; stamp of tax receipts, III, 168; transplanting of Armenians to Syria, III, 98
Al-Manṣur, Muslim regent of Cordova: decree re clothing of Jews, III, 141; and Ibn Jau, V, 44
Al-Mas'udi, VI, 192, 199; on differences between Hebrew and Arabic, VI, 453; on Saadiah's Bible translation, VI, 458
Al-Mawardi, VI, 150
Almeria, city, IV, 332
Almohades, Berber sect, III, 173; conquest of Spain, IV, 21; influence on Jewish theology, VIII, 96; Jewish refugees, III, 291, IV, 3 ff.; mass conversions, III, 127, 176; religious persecution by, III, 108, 111, 124, 132, 281; Saladin's appeal to, IV, 298
Almoravids, Moroccan dynasty, III, 108, 124 f., 289; conquest of Spain, VII, 153, 186; persecution of *dhimmis,* IV, 3, V, 200
Alms, *see* Charity
Al-Mu'izz, Faṭimid caliph, III, 154, VI, 325, VIII, 167

Al-Muqammiṣ, David ibn Merwan, III, 295; classification of the sciences, VIII, 141 f.; commentary on Genesis, VI, 284; on eschatological retribution, VIII, 104; quoted on oneness of God, VIII, 97 f.; "Twenty Tractates," VIII, 58
Al-Muqtadir, caliph, III, 88, 158; characterized by Suyuti, III, 153; decree re public office, VIII, 236; eunuchs of, IV, 191 f.
Al-Musta'in, ruler of Saragossa, VIII, 248
Al-Mustanṣir, Faṭimid caliph, III, 190
Al-Mu'tadhid, caliph, III, 152 f.; re taxation of Jews, III, 167
Al-Mu'tadhim, caliph, III, 166
Al-Mu'tamin, III, 158
Al-Muzaffar 'Umar ibn Nur ad-Din, VIII, 251
Alphabet: Cyrillic, III, 208 f.; Glagolitic, III, 209, 330; Hebrew-Phoenician, I, 307; Ugaritic, I, 307; Western Slavonic, III, 218; *see also* individual alphabets, e.g., Arabic alphabet
"Alphabet of Ben Sira," VI, 159, 169
Alphonsine tables, VIII, 161
Alphonso I, king of Aragon and Navarre, IV, 30; godfather of Petrus Alphonsi, V, 116; marriage to Doña Urraca, IV, 252 f.; privilege for merchants, IV, 179; *see also* Alphonso VII
Alphonso II, king of Aragon, IV, 159
Alphonso III (Alphonso the Great), king of Asturias, IV, 35
Alphonso VI, king of Castile and Leon, IV, 9, 36, 254; re moneylending, IV, 207; re Mozarabs, III, 127
Alphonso VII, king of Castile and Leon: amnesties, IV, 39 f.; and Christian merchants, IV, 179 f.; coronation, IV, 28; egalitarian policy, IV, 254; *see also* Alphonso I
Alphonso VIII, king of Castile: egalitarian policy, IV, 254; Jewish mistress, IV, 37; papal threats, IV, 42, 188 f.
Alphonso X, king of Castile and Leon, IV, 37, VIII, 161
Alqabeṣ, Solomon, VII, 251
Al-Qali, Armenian philologist in Cordova, VII, 19, 20
Al-Qasim ibn Ibrahim, a Zaidite, V, 7, 12 f.
Al-Quds, Muslim name of Jerusalem, IV, 109
Al-Qumisi, Daniel, *see* Qumisi, Daniel al-
Alroy, David (Menahem b. Solomon Al-Roḥi), III, 204; messianic movement, V, 202 ff.
Altars: of the patriarchs, I, 48; prohibited outside of Jerusalem, I, 128; *see also Bamot*
Al-Tell, city, I, 299
Altercatio Jasonis et Papisci, II, 133
Altercation (Theophilus), II, 138
Al tiqri, formula of, VI, 166
Al-Zarqali, Muslim scientist, VIII, 358; Ibn Ezra and, VIII, 173; "Toledan Tables," VIII, 171
Amadia, city, V, 203
Amah, see Slaves and slavery
Amalekites, I, 57, 317, III, 63
Amalfi, Italy, IV, 24
Amalfitans, in Cairo, IV, 331 f.
Aman, see Passport
Amarna Age, *see* El-Amarna age
Amaziah, king of Judah, VII, 313
Amaziah, priest of Bethel, I, 86
Ambrose, Saint, II, 172, V, 133; and Gregory I, III, 243; victory over Theodosius, II, 189, 192, 401, III, 30
Amel-Marduk (Evil Merodach), I, 115, 116; pacific policy, I, 132
Amen: congregational chant, VII, 125; repetition of, VI, 130
Amen-em-ope, I, 363, VII, 165
'Am ha-areṣ, I, 278, 280, III, 263; discrimination against, discontinued, II, 272; enmity of scholars, II, 242, 282, 286, IV, 167, V, 178, 284, VI, 342, VII, 109; and Karaites, V, 219, 394
Amida, Mesopotamia, Church of, III, 10; contributions of Jews to, III, 231
'Amidah, prayer, I, 186, 351, 376, II, 61, 112, 115, 282, 351, V, 26, 248, 303, VI, 14 f.; accuracy of oral transmission, VII, 112; benedictions, VII, 66 ff., 244, 247; date of, II, 40, 61, 345; definitive form, II, 119, VII, 101; *Musaf,* VII, 107 f., 127, 172; prayer against heretics, II, 135, 381; prayer for peace, II, 115; substitution of new prayers for, VII, 69, 95 f.; *targum* of, VII, 67; texts, II, 376, VII, 105 f.; *see also* Prayers
Amittai b. Shefaṭiah, poet, V, 152, VII, 176 ff., VIII, 30, 60

Amixia, II, 223; *see also under* Marriage
Ammi, R., VI, 441
Ammianus Marcellinus, II, 257
'Ammiel, name of Messiah's father, V, 153
Ammon and Ammonites, I, 55, 56, 156, 162, 190, III, 61; endogamous exclusion of, II, 232, VI, 303
Amnesty, general, in Castile, IV, 39 f.
Amon, king, I, 78, 155
Amorai, R., VIII, 35 f.
Amoraim, I, 386, II, 295, 296, VI, 17 ff., 30, 65, 240, VIII, 21; and ancient Babylonian traditions, II, 207; authority of, VI, 201; debates, V, 180 f., VI, 63; end of age, VI, 17; and geonim, VI, 334, VII, 108; mystics among, VIII, 6; ritualistic autonomy, VII, 65; status of first generation, VI, 29; support of synagogue, VII, 62; tombs of, VI, 436; and written midrashim, VI, 158; *see also* Talmud
Amos, prophet, I, 79, 94, 128; expelled from Bethel, I, 86; sycamore grower, I, 87, 89; teachings of, I, 25, 72, 340, 360
Amphictyonies: Greek, I, 319; Israelitic, I, 61
Amram b. Sheshna, gaon of Sura, IV, 187; anti-Karaite bias, VII, 70; on congregational leaders, VII, 80; letter to Barcelona community, V, 19 f.; prayer book, V, 28, 248, VI, 15, 69, 112, 264, VII, 69, 81, 111 ff.; re prayers, V, 26, VII, 65, 250; on thanksgiving for education, VII, 109
Amraphel, king of Shinear, I, 301
Amulets, protective, II, 20, 336, 337, 390, 435, VIII, 29
Amulo, French churchman, IV, 14, 18; antisemitism, IV, 53, 54; appeal for obedience to canon law, IV, 54
Amun hymns, Egyptian, I, 52
Anacharsis, the Scythian, I, 228
Anacletus II, pope, IV, 121; family background, IV, 10 f.; and Roger II, IV, 21
Anagrams, in poems, VII, 49 f.
Analogy: approach to philology, VII, 34, 52, 58; in biblical interpretation, V, 213
'Anan b. David, founder of Karaism, II, 221, III, 161, 202, V, 181, 210-22; approach to Jewish law and life, V, 216-22; Book of Commandments, V, 212, 219 f., 227, 231; claim re his copy of Deuteronomy, VI, 243 f.; conflict with brother Ḥananiah, V, 9; genealogy, VI, 200 f., 446; and his successors, V, 256 f.; Ibn Daud's discussion of, VI, 481; liturgical reforms, VII, 64, 72 f., 110 f.; on medical practice, VIII, 247; observation of new moon, VIII, 194; in Persia, V, 183; predecessors of, VI, 363; reading vs. spelling of biblical words, VI, 243; on the soul, VIII, 107; on the Talmud, V, 276; writings hidden in caves, V, 255; Yannai as legal source, VII, 94
Ananel, I, 216
Ananias, general, I, 215
Ananias, high priest, I, 272
Ananias, merchant-missionary, I, 173, 183
'Ananites: attitude toward Jesus, V, 262; doctrine of catenation, VI, 69; *see also* Karaites
Ananus, high priest, II, 131
Anapa, *see* Gorgippia
'Anaqim, biblical giants, III, 63
Anarchy, in Roman society, II, 234
Anastasios the Sinaite, III, 175, VI, 304; anti-Jewish dialogues, V, 350
Anastasius, Byzantine emperor: and Antioch, III, 6; capture of Yotabe, III, 69 f.
'Anat, 'Anati, 'Anat-Yahu, goddess, I, 128
Anathema, *see* Curse; Excommunication
Anatoli b. Joseph, Sicilian judge and poet, VII, 176
Anavim, I, 152, 364, II, 269
Anbari, 'Ubaid Allah al-, Muslim philosopher, VI, 472
Ancestor worship, I, 148
Anchorets, VIII, 119 f.
Andalusians: in Fez, III, 145; quotation re children and Jews of, III, 148
Andreas, archbishop of Bari: alleged conversion to Judaism, III, 189 f., IV, 294
Andrew II, king of Hungary, III, 213
Angelos stones of Thera, II, 25
Angels, I, 139, 140, II, 17 ff., 32, 44, 335, VII, 180, 275; antagonism to man, VII, 251; Babylonian-Persian, in Arabia, III, 82; in Book of Jubilees, II, 43; heavenly family, II, 317, VIII, 23; as intermediaries, V, 228, 259, VI, 469, VII, 76, VIII, 3 ff., 93 ff.; intervention

Angels (*Continued*)
of, II, 67; knowledge of Aramaic, VII, 193; in messianism, V, 142; ministering, VII, 66, 193; in magic formulas, VIII, 8 f., 21; in poetry, VII, 181 f.; on Sinai, VIII, 6; singing, VII, 77; winged, II, 332; *see also* Heavenly hosts
Angers, France, IV, 182
'Ani, I, 152, 364, II, 269
Anilaeus, principality, I, 168, III, 63
Animal figures in art, II, 9, 10, 13, 15, 154, 402
Animals, VI, 103; castration of, V, 174, compensation for suffering of, VIII, 103 f., 230; consumption of, V, 92 f., VIII, 227; first-born, V, 53; life-endangering illness of, VIII, 228, 387, names of, VIII, 226; ritualistic slaughtering, II, 306; in stories, VI, 182 f.; VII, 189; tithe of, V, 399; *see also* Meat; Monsters; Slaughtering
Animal sacrifice, V, 123, 273, 249, VI, 125, VII, 78 f., VIII, 228; in Armenia, III, 110; in Khazaria, III, 202; *see also* Paschal lamb; Sacrifices
Animal worship, Egyptian, I, 199, 402
Annona, I, 410
Anointed priest, term, I, 152, 364
Anomaly, approach to philology, VII, 34, 58
Ansegisus, archbishop of Sens, IV, 56
Anselm, Saint: treatise on incarnation, V, 115; motto, VIII, 113 f.
Ansuvannam, India, III, 114 f.
Anthropomorphism, V, 249; in aggadic works, VI, 178, 268, 342; biblical, I, 196, V, 90, 106, 197, 226, VI, 267 f., 300 ff., VIII, 99 ff.; defense of, I, 13; and divine attributes, VIII, 97; Karaite and Muslim charges, V, 121, 258 f.; in mystic literature, V, 258, VI, 175, VIII, 25 ff., 29 ff.; Rashi and, VI, 51; rejection of, I, 49, 335, VI, 45 f., VIII, 57 ff.; in Septuagint, I, 383, VI, 258 f.
Anthropopathism, VIII, 98
Antichretic transactions, II, 302, 431
Antichrist, *see* Armilus; *Dajjal*
Antifeminism, VIII, 53
Antigonus of Socho, II, 41
Anti-intellectualism, VIII, 17
Anti-Jewish riots, *see* Antisemitism
Antimonarchical trends, I, 91-93, 336-38
Antinomianism, V, 80, 122, 194, 235, VI, 3, 143, VIII, 49; Jewish attitude toward, II, 310, VIII, 17 ff., 295; in magic arts, VIII, 11; Qur'an and, VI, 7
Antinoupolis, I, 410
Antioch: antisemitism, I, 188, II, 189; archaeological excavations, III, 230; cemeteries, II, 286; Christians, II, 188, 189, 366, 401, III, 38, 161; Crusaders in, IV, 243, 285; decline, III, 105; earthquake, III, 234 f.; Hannah and sons buried in, VI, 417; Herod's work in, I, 236; Jerusalem named after, I, 229, 398; Jews in, I, 216, 248, III, 3, 58, 73; loot from Temple in Jerusalem, I, 217; Persian conquests of, II, 178, III, 19, 56; political and religious riots, III, 6, 21, 38, 161; *see also* New Antioch; Syria
Antiochians: in Jerusalem, I, 399; vilification of Jews and Judaism, I, 192
Antiochus, renegade, II, 3
Antiochus III (Antiochus the Great), king of Syria, I, 239, 369, 373, 397; charter extended to Palestine Jews, I, 216
Antiochus IV (Antiochus Epiphanes), king of Syria, I, 166, 185, 220, 244, 369, II, 30, 81, 98, 100; conflict with Jews, I, 193, 216, 217, 230, VI, 189; desecration of Temple, I, 192; homily on, VIII, 278; identification with Zeus, I, 229, 398; oppressive measures, I, 229, 398; story of ritual murder, I, 193; *see also* Maccabees, revolt by
Antiochus V, king of Syria, I, 216
Antiochus, Scroll of, *see* Hasmoneans, Scroll of
Anti-oriental sentiment, I, 212
Antipater, king VI, 192
Antirationalism, and progress of medical science, VIII, 248
Antisemitism, ancient: in Alexandria, I, 188, 191, 209, 216, 219, 381, II, 189; in Asia Minor, I, 283; Christian teachings and, II, 353; and economic motivations, I, 194, 383, II, 241; in Egypt, I, 381, 383, II, 89, 159; fountainhead of literature, II, 427; Hellenistic, I, 188-95, 283, 379-83, II, 55, 170, 401; and historic beliefs, II, 55; Marcionite, II, 167 f., 394, VIII, 288; in Persia, I, 116; pogroms, I, 191, 266, II, 189, 402; in Syria, I, 283, II, 89

—— medieval, III, 3 f., 91-94; accusation of demonic powers, V, 132; characterizations of Jews, V, 131 ff.; of clergy, IV, 14 ff., 53 ff., 121 ff.; economic basis, III, 194, IV, 85, 206, V, 96 ff.; imperial oppression, VII, 94 f., 266; of Jewish converts, V, 115 f.; and Jewish legalism, VIII, 52; liturgical, V, 352, VI, 42, VII, 85; millenary movements and, IV, 91 f.; of Nicetas, IV, 166; in periods of crisis, V, 111 f.; of Peter the Venerable, IV, 122; of Petrus II Candiano, IV, 25; popular, IV, 67, 69 f.; and protected minorities, III, 170 ff.; Qarafi on Christian, V, 108 f., 346; reaction of poets to, VII, 177 ff.; and royal protection, IV, 79 f.; social, III, 139-49, V, 96 ff., 125-34; tanners as targets of, IV, 166 f.

—— *see also* Massacres; Persecution; Pogroms

Antitalmudic movements, II, 264

Antonia, fortress, I, 239, II, 284

Antonines, dynasty, II, 109

"Antoninus," friend of R. Judah, II, 187, 374, 400

Antoninus Martyr, II, 355, 412

Antoninus Pius, emperor, II, 107, 108, 110, 126, 132, 187, 193, 374, 400; encouragement of scholars, II, 243

Antonius, Marcus, I, 237

Apamaea, surname, II, 338

Apamaea, city (Asia Minor), I, 393; coins, II, 24

Apamaea, city (Syria), II, 199

Aphraates, bishop, II, 149, 191, V, 109 f., 114, 358; anti-Jewish polemics, VI, 322; censure of Judeo-Christian relations, VI, 241

Aphrodite, I, 374

Apion of Alexandria, I, 192, 233, 242; antisemitism, I, 195, II, 170

Apiphior, equation with pope, IV, 241

Apiru, *see* Ḥabiru

Apocalypses and apocalyptic writings, I, 153; Baruch, II, 60; collection, V, 353; Daniel, III, 179, 183, 315; Elijah, III, 16, 19; and messianism, V, 139-50; and the supernatural, II, 17, 335

Apocrypha: biblical, I, 385, II, 145, VI, 159; contribution to mysticism, VIII, 5; glorification of martyrs, IV, 95 f.; messianic speculation, II, 59, 60, V, 139; parallels in Yosephon, VI, 419 f.; Pharisaic acceptance, II, 17, 44; Slavonic translations, III, 211; source of folk tales, VI, 186 f.

—— other: Falasha books, II, 212; *Megillat bene Ḥashmona'i,* VI, 269; midrashic, II, 296, 426; pseudo-Philo, VI, 421 f.

Apocryticus, II, 391

Apoios, I, 389

Apokatastasis, term, II, 360

Appollinopolis Magna (Edfu), Jewish quarter, I, 188, 380

Apollo, I, 61, 119

Apollonius Molon, I, 194, 195

Apollonius of Tyana, II, 175

Apologetics, Jewish, I, 195-99, V, 83 ff., 110 ff.; and Christian polemics, II, 130 ff., V, 109 ff., 114 f.; and Jewish philosophy, VIII, 135 ff.; major themes, V, 117

Apostasy, I, 172; departure from orthodoxy as, II, 292; from Islam, III, 132; and magic, VIII, 47 f.; and relapse of a convert, III, 14; *see also under* Convert

Apostates, treatment of, II, 253, 287

Apostolé (*aurum coronarium*), II, 194

Apostolic Constitutions, I, 186

Apothecaries, V, 96

Apries, king of Egypt, I, 110, 346

Aqabiah b. Mahallalel, II, 41, 346

'Aqedot, in Mayence, VI, 193, 218

'Aqiba, R., I, 231, II, 46, 116, 118, 125, 204, 220, 230, 287, 314, 319, VI, 181; Alphabet of, II, 426, V, 259, VIII, 11 ff., 191; buried in Caesarea, II, 371; compilation of tannaitic law, VI, 107; disciples of, I, 190, IV, 145; encounter with ghost, VI, 23, VII, 245 f.; fervor of prayer, VII, 74 f.; on free will, VIII, 109; intellectual leader, II, 98, 100, 121; letter symbolism, VIII, 15; on marriage relations, II, 221, 228, 409, 410; martyrdom, II, 100, IV, 96, 104; mishnah, unnamed, VI, 204; priestly blessing, II, 282; on the revelation of the Torah, V, 93; on transmigration of souls, VIII, 36

'Aqri'el, angel, VIII, 8 f.

Aquila, proselyte, II, 143, 147; Greek fragments, II, 17; literalness of, VI, 271; quoted, II, 153

Arabia: archaeological excavations, III, 256 ff.; cultural and economic contributions of Jews, III, 70, IV, 161; destruction of Jewish communities, VII, 191; Jewish inscriptions, III, 61, 66, 82, 258; Jewish refugees from, V, 180; Jews in, I, 169, 372, II, 211, III, 60 f., 63 ff.; messianic movements, V, 168; Mohammed's treaties with Christians and Jews, III, 163; a province of Rome, II, 369; role of kings, III, 61; urban settlements, III, 71

Arabia Felix, III, 71

Arabic alphabet: adopted in Persian language, VII, 5; Muslim view of use of, VII, 190; weak consonants in, VII, 43

Arabic classics, translations: Hebrew, IV, 3; Latin, IV, 32, 248

Arabic language: Aramaic displaced by, II, 387, VI, 255; borrowings from Hebrew and Aramaic, III, 81, VII, 10, 89; dialects, VI, 407, VII, 4 ff., 10, 221; diminutive forms and biblical parallels, VII, 16; glorification of, V, 330, VI, 168; grammarians and lexicographers, VII, 5 ff., 20; in Hebrew alphabet, V, 112, VIII, 75, 140 f.; influence on Hebrew speech, VI, 250; latitude in punctuation, VI, 243; like-sounding words, VII, 8; liturgical use, VII, 67; masoretic monograph, VII, 33; medical writings, VIII, 242 ff.; numerical values, VIII, 150; plant and animal names, VIII, 229; in poetry, VII, 150; refinement of, VII, 59; Saadiah's purism, VI, 268 f.; spread of use of, IV, 21, VII, 6 ff., 33, 45, 59 f.; translations of sacred writings into, VI, 263-72; transliteration of names and terms, VIII, 172, 174; unifying force in expansion of Judaism and Islam, III, 118 f.; use of, in explaining Hebrew terms, VII, 18; use of, by Jews, III, 118, 170, IV, 3, 36, V, 110, VII, 7, 59 f., 191 ff.

Arabic numerals, VIII, 150

Arab-Jewish relations, III, 60 ff.; and the Berbers, III, 90 f.; occasional violence in, III, 122 f.; in Spain, III, 157 f.; *see also* Judeo-Muslim relations

Arabs: ancient: Ammonites and Moabites overrun by, I, 190, VI, 308; Mesene occupied by, II, 405; penetration into Palestine and Babylonia, III, 60, 89 f.; pressure upon Edomites, I, 106; relations with Jews and Romans, II, 92, 114, 369, 375, seminomadic southern, I, 57

—— medieval: alliance with Jews against Mohammed, III, 78 f.; attitude toward agriculture, IV, 152; conquest of Alexandria, III, 90; cultivation of self-esteem, III, 98; familiarity with Scripture, III, 82; ignorance of Hebrew, V, 328; rhyming technique, VII, 88; *see also* Berbers; Muslims; Muslim-Christian relations; Judeo-Muslim relations

—— modern: multiple marriages, II, 227

Aragon: *fueros,* IV, 13; rabbinic manuscripts, VI, 171; royal flour mills, IV, 318; *see also* Spain

Aramaeans, I, 55, 67, 322

Aramaic deeds, I, 111, VI, 66 f., 357; *see also* Deeds

Aramaic language: Abraham's, I, 20; areas of use, I, 121, 159, 185, II, 146 f., 405, VI, 27 ff., VII, 5; biblical, VII, 26, 39; biblical translations in, II, 146, 387, 411, III, 72 f., VI, 239 f., 255-63, 312 (*see also* Targum); decline in use, VI, 56, 63, VII, 20; eastern dialect, VII, 29; Hebrew and, II, 142, 147, VI, 240; of Jesus and disciples, II, 66, 67, 145, 355; loan words, III, 70, VI, 13; magic formulas in, VIII, 9; in Palestine, I, 187, V, 227; plant and animal names, VIII, 229; prayers in, VII, 66 f.; repudiated by some Jews, II, 145, 146; supplanted by Arabic, II, 387, III, 119, VII, 5, 101; transliterations, VI, 248; use by Hebrew authors, VII, 192 f., 195

Ararat, Mount, location of, VII, 18

ARB, ARD, number, III, 315

Arbitration, courts of, II, 266, 267

Arc, measurement of, VIII, 355

Arcadius, Roman emperor, II, 191; re Gaza, III, 8

Archaeology: Palestinian, II, 10 ff.; 'Ain Fashkha cave, II, 52; *see also* Dead Sea Scrolls; Qumran; and ancient art, II, 330; Bethshan, II, 28; Beth She'arim (*q.v.*), II, 398; coins, II, 28, 369; Gerasa, II, 174; lack of evidence for Christianity, II, 63, 74, 353, 361; ossuaries, II, 63; paucity of extant sculptures, II, 9; Philippopolis, II, 175; search for churches, II, 392; synagogues

discovered, II, 241, 284, 285, 423; Third Wall in Jerusalem, II, 108, 369, 377
—— other: Antioch, III, 230; Arabia, III, 256 ff.; Khwarizm, III, 326; magic bowls in Euphrates Valley, II, 23, VIII, 8 ff., 274 ff.; Russia, III, 213, 333 f.; and spread of Jews in Europe and the Orient, II, 210 f., 406 f.; at Vatican, II, 74; *see also* Inscriptions
Archelaus, king, I, 263, II, 21, 33; banishment to Vienne, III, 47
Archevolte, Samuel, VII, 207
Architecture: impact of Greek, II, 9; unimportant to synagogue, II, 284; Jewish, in England, IV, 281 f., VIII, 159
Archives: ancient, II, 265, 266; geonic, VI, 112 f., 383
Archontes, I, 274
"Arch Presbyter," in medieval English Jewry, V, 319
Ardashir I, Persian emperor, II, 174, 176, 317, III, 55; Mesene conquered by, II, 405
Ardea Viraz, II, 229
Areopagus in Athens, Paul's speech, II, 79 f., 362, 363, 389
Aretino, Pietro, VII, 149
Areus, king, I, 185
Argabadh, title, II, 196, 403
Arians, sect, II, 134, 188, III, 7, 25, 35, VI, 6 f.; *see also* Arius
Aribert, bishop of Narbonne, IV, 47
Aristarchus of Hippo, VIII, 163 f.
Aristeas, Letter of, *see Letter of Aristeas*
Aristobulus, philosopher, I, 196, 204, 207, 396
Aristobulus II, high priest, II, 13, 54, 349
Aristocracy: caste system of Persia and Rome, II, 176; lay, I, 73 f., 274; priestly, I, 149, 272, 274, *see also* Priests; sins and abuses, I, 126; *see also* Classes, social
Aristotle, I, 174, 283; basic concepts, VI, 146, 396, VIII, 76, 90 f., 92 f., 98, 114; commentaries on, VIII, 65 f.; division of sciences, VIII, 143, 146; ethical system, VIII, 117, 120 ff.; influence on Jewish philosophy, VIII, 63 ff., 324; and Judaism, VI, 230; legend of conversion, VIII, 77, 306; meeting with Jew of Coele-Syria, I, 377; quoted, I, 184; spurious "Theory" of, VIII, 91; translations of, VIII, 316
Arius, V, 379, VII, 128; *see also* Arians
Arks, built into synagogue, V, 247 f.
Ark of the Covenant, I, 49, 59, 314
Arles, France, III, 250, IV, 55 f.; corvée labor by Jews of, IV, 56; custumal, IV, 60 f.; defense of, II, 179, 398; Jewish community, IV, 59
Armenia: Christianity in, II, 165; deportees from, II, 204, 404; and Edessa, IV, 114, V, 203; families of Jewish descent, I, 169, 283; forced Jewish purchase of churches, III, 160; Jews in, I, 372, II, 405, III, 110, VIII, 288; Persian invasion, III, 18; and Syrians, III, 98
Armenian Code, VI, 4
Armillary sphere, VIII, 166 f.
Armilus, III, 19, V, 144 ff., 152, 160, 358 f., 364, VI, 481
Armoricus, William, IV, 62
Arms, *see* Weapons
Arms, Assize of, IV, 126, 141
Army, *see* Military service
Army camp, Jewish, *see* Elephantine
Arnulf, patriarch, IV, 114
Aroer, city, VI, 293
Arpad, Magyar chief, III, 211
Ar-Radi, Baghdad caliph, VI, 214
Arras, Flanders, IV, 57
Ar-Rashid, *see* Harun ar-Rashid
Ar-Rawandi, *see* Rawandi, ar-
Arrian (Flavius Arrianus), II, 157
Arroyo de los Judíos, Spain, IV, 33
Arsham, governor, I, 347
Arsinoe, city, II, 199
Arslan Tash, Syria, I, 329
Artabanus, Parthian king, II, 20, 177, 316
Artapanus, historian, I, 198 f., 207, 304, II, 16, 31, 334
Artaxerxes I, king of Persia, I, 130, 245, 349
Artaxerxes II, I, 130, 349, II, 229
Artaxerxes III (Ochus), I, 131
Artisan guilds, *see* Guilds
Arts: alien motifs and techniques assimilated, II, 11; Christian, II, 11, 84, 154 f., 165, 365; Graeco-Oriental music and, II, 6-15, 146, 154, 330-34, 402; representation of Jew in medieval, V, 132; "seven," VIII, 145; *see also* Architecture; Figurines; Mosaics; Music; Painting; Pottery; Sculptures
'Arukh, dictionary, VI, 28
Asa, king, I, 322

Asaph Judaeus, Jewish medical writer, III, 240, VIII, 235, 241 f., 256, 258, 393; on medical ethics, VIII, 238; on ritualistic ablutions, VIII, 262
Asarhaddon, king, I, 96
Asatir, Samaritan book, II, 29, 339, VI, 212
Ascalon, city: burning of St. Mary's Church, III, 137; Jewish captives in, IV, 110 f.; refuge of Jews from Palestine, IV, 111, 113, 296
Ascension: of human soul, VIII, 21 f., 23; of Mohammed, VIII, 284 f.; of Moses, VIII, 6
Asceticism, VIII, 119 f.; Christian, VIII, 53; of Essenes, II, 48, 49; and love of God, VIII, 116; and traditional Judaism, II, 256, 435, VIII, 53
Asclas, Gaius Julius, I, 404
Asenath, daughter of Potiphar, VI, 170
Ash'ariya (Ash'arites), school of Islamic theology, V, 90 f.; VIII, 103, 109, 113, 248; doctrine of divine Speech, VIII, 343
Ashdod, city, I, 361
Ashema, II, 28
Asher, "the great Sheikh," VI, 245
Asherah worship, I, 78, II, 13, 332
Asher b. David, VIII, 42
Asher b. Yeḥiel, VI, 55, 136 f.; on book lending, VII, 287 f.; laws of phylacteries, VI, 65; and tax exemption, V, 77
Asherites, generations of, VI, 446
Ashi, R., II, 14, 134, 179, 247, 261, III, 3, VI, 100; advocate of proselytism, II, 149; assumed title Rabbana, II, 198; date of death, VI, 202; as redactor of the Talmud, II, 295, 296, 425, VI, 17
Ashkenazi author of anonymous grammatical work, VII, 54 f., 241
Ashkenazi, Bezalel, VI, 348
Ashkenazim, III, 174, IV, 3 f., 345, V, 61, 275, VI, 75, 87, VII, 144; conversions to Christianity, VII, 304; dynamic approach of, VII, 123; ethical literature, VII, 180; formula for confession, VII, 80, 92; Hebrew pronunciation, VI, 250; influence of Tam, VI, 55; and Khazars, IV, 235, VII, 18; liturgy of, VII, 105, 175, 183, 282; poetry of, IV, 309, VI, 422, VII, 175, 199; and Saxony, IV, 4; and Sephardim, IV, 3 f., 43, 235, VI, 25 f.; talmudic commentary, VI, 344
Aṣhor, I, 113, 114
Ash-Shafi'i, *see* Shafi'i
Ashshur, V, 162; *see also* Assyria; Mosul
Ashur, province, I, 326
Ashurbanipal, king, I, 96
Asia Minor: Christian art in, II, 165; Crusaders in, IV, 106 f., 309; deportations to, I, 373; Jewish rights threatened, I, 401; Jews in, I, 169, 170, 216, 283, III, 182; Marcionism, VIII, 288; religious situation, II, 3, 166, 393; *see also* Near East
Asinaeus, principality, I, 168, II, 213, III, 63
Asklepios, god of healing, II, 336
Asma, poet, VII, 191
"Assassins" (*sicarii*), II, 47, 347
Assault and battery, IV, 70; punishment for, III, 49, IV, 69, 129 f., VIII, 231
Assi, R., II, 113, 208, 270, 275, 283
Assidaioi, I, 237; *see also* Ḥasidism
Assimilation: ancient, I, 118-21, 349; to culture of conquered population, I, 56
—— modern, I, 27; Aryan opposition to, I, 19; and survival, I, 30
Assize of Arms, IV, 126, 141
Associations, professional, I, 257; *see also* Guilds
Assumption of Moses, II, 47, 59, 346
Assyria: banking, I, 108; expansion, I, 67; fall, I, 96; imperialism, I, 95, 108, 345; interest rate, I, 69; Israelitic settlement, I, 107, II, 27; price fixing, I, 85; protection of masses by law, I, 84; revenge for conquest of Israel by, I, 210; "rod of God's anger," I, 90
Assyrian code, I, 327
Astafortis, Hungarian tax collector, III, 188; conversion, III, 319
Astarte, goddess, I, 49, 57, 146, 318, 374; figurines of, I, 59, 329
Astrabadh-Ardasher (Mesene), II, 405
Astrolabe, VIII, 166 f., 170, 173
Astrology, VIII, 175 ff.; alleged Jewish origins of, II, 16 f., 334 f., VIII, 176; appeal of, VIII, 225; and astronomy, VIII, 145, 181 f., 367; and biblical interpretation, VI, 298; computation of dates by, VI, 231, VIII, 25, 206 f.; and interpretations of history, V, 143, VIII, 62; Maimonides and, V, 384; and man's fate, VIII, 111; in messianic computations, V, 146, 162 f., 200 f.,

204 f., 384; and music, VII, 210 f.; natural and judicial, VIII, 169 f., 175, 182; and occult sciences, II, 15 f., 44, 334; parallels for seven "kings," VII, 241; and poetic themes, VII, 162; practical applications, VIII, 160
Astronomy: Aristotelian-Ptolemaic approach, VIII, 93; and astrology, VIII, 145, 181 f., 367; Babylonian, I, 6, II, 16; computations, II, 206, 209, V, 246, 279, VI, 269, VIII, 26 f., 160 ff.; Gentile writers, VIII, 175 ff., 366 f.; Latin translations of Arabic works, VIII, 167; opposing doctrines, VIII, 173 f.; research in, VIII, 166 ff., 359 ff.; tables, VIII, 139, 171 ff.; 362 ff.; talmudic age, II, 306; Yeraḥmeel's knowledge of, VI, 422
Asturlabi, al-, quoted, VIII, 139
Asylum, institution of, I, 145, 276, 360, 414
Asylums for homeless and aged, II, 285
'Atar, meaning, I, 124
Atheism and atheists, I, 179, 234, VI, 298, VIII, 72; attacks on Islam, V, 104
Athens: exclusion of Jews from, III, 232; Paul's work in, II, 79 f., 362; philosophic academy, III, 11, VIII, 241
Athinganoi, Judaizing sect, III, 178, 181
Athos, city, I, 304
Athos, Mount, III, 232
Athtar, god, I, 57, 318
Atlantic Ocean, VIII, 214 f.
Atmosphere, of earth, VIII, 213
Atomist hypothesis, VIII, 88, 222, 323
Aton, god, I, 46, 311
Atonement, V, 217; *see also* Day of Atonement
Atrocities, IV, 109 f., 133 ff.; *see also* Burning; Massacres; Murder
Attaleia, Byzantium, V, 413
Attalus III, king, II, 25
Attire, *see* Clothing
Attributes, divine: in Judaism, I, 312, VIII, 95 ff., 326 ff.
Auch, France, inscription, III, 251
Augustine, Saint, I, 191, II, 138, 166, 188; on Easter controversy, VIII, 195; on Jewish dispersion, II, 168 f., 395; on Jewish serfdom, V, 129; on Latin Bibles, VI, 292; on Roman law, II, 299; sermon on the prodigal son, III, 31 f., 244
Augustus, Roman emperor, I, 236, II, 57, 151, 175, 198, 237; complaints before, against Herod's regime, I, 263; pro-Jewish attitude, I, 404; and Sebastes, I, 236; subsidized sacrifice, I, 245, 404; western orientation, I, 246, 404
Aurelian citizens, II, 109
Aurelius Dionysius, Tiberian Jew, III, 207
Aurum coronarium (*apostolé*), II, 194, III, 191
Authority, governmental, V, 77 f., *see also* State; Karaite doctrine of, V, 235; *see also* Power
Authorization, letters of, IV, 212 f., V, 27, 52 f., 303; re non-Muslim cemeteries, III, 137
Authors, Jewish, bilingual and trilingual, VII, 6 ff.; creative upsurge, VII, 39-46; influences on, VII, 193 ff.; and Arabic script, VII, 191 ff.; volume of production, VII, 138 f.; *see also* Literature; Poetry
Autobiography, VI, 219
Autonomy, *see* Self-government
Auxerre, bishop of, IV, 13
Avaris (Tanis), I, 35, 37, 38
Avars, tribe III, 239
Avempace, *see* Ibn Bajja
Avendeath, John (Johannes Hispalensis or Hispanus), V, 214, VIII, 61 f., 178 f.; apocalyptic vision, V, 146
Aven gilyon, term, II, 133
Averroës (Ibn Roshd), V, 85, VIII, 66; books banned, III, 133; on heretics, VIII, 310 f.; "Outline of the Almagest," VIII, 358
Averroists, "double truth" theory, VIII, 80
Avicebron (or Avicebrol), *see* Ibn Gabirol
Avicenna, VIII, 63, 387; *Canon,* VIII, 249
Avitus, bishop of Clermont, III, 52
Azariah, martyr, I, 116
Azariah de' Rossi, *see* Rossi, Azariah de'
'Aziz, al-, Faṭimid caliph, III, 154
Azizus of Emesa, king, II, 21
Azriel, Gerona mystic, VIII, 286
Azulai, biographer, VI, 50 f.

B

Baal, I, 13, 37, 48; Egyptian counterpart, I, 304; Elijah's struggle against priests of, I, 87; inscription to, III, 66; names

Baal (*Continued*)
compounded with, I, 78; temple, moneylending, I, 86; worship of, I, 57, 59, 146, 334 f.
Ba'alah, I, 43
Ba'ale batim, term, II, 276, 422
Baal Hammon, deity, I, 374
Ba'al marriage, I, 310
Baalshamem, I, 87, 374
Baal Zaphon, I, 347
Baalzebul, I, 63
Baal-Zeus, coins dedicated to, II, 28
Baba Raba (Rabbah), Samaritan leader, II, 33, 340, III, 9, 62, V, 170
Babel, I, 107, 134; *see* Babylonia; identification with Baghdad, III, 100; Tower of, VII, 15
Babli, *see* Talmud
Babylonia: ancient and Achaemenid, I, 108, 282, 355; conflicting influences in, I, 105, 118; deportations to Asia Minor, I, 373; and deported nations, I, 108; economic, ethnic, and religious structure, I, 282; economic changes, I, 68, 85, 108-11, 132, 346; festivals taken over from, I, 5; houses rented, I, 109, 346; Jewish population, I, 108, 115, 168, 170; a leader of house of David, I, 116; legal structures, I, 142; mythology, VIII, 10 f.; purity of family valued in, I, 125; religion, I, 44, 45, 105, 107, 197, 311, 373, VIII, 175, seven-day week, I, 360; ten genealogical classes returned from, I, 275; use of numerical principle, VIII, 284; *see also* Exile, Babylonian; Persia, Achaemenid
—— Hellenistic and Sassanian, VI, 402; agriculture, II, 244, 246, 257, 414; ancient traditions, II, 205 f., 207; astral and astrological influences, II, 15 f., 206; Christianity's slight advances, II, 164; class position of Jews, I, 281, II, 279, 320; compromises upset by religious fanatics, II, 213; exilarchate, II, 195 ff., 200 f., 205, 291, 403; family records, reliability of, II, 234; immigration to, II, 164, 173, 204, 208, 210, 404, 405; intergroup relations, II, 190; joyfulness, II, 113; Julian's Persian campaign, II, 179; leadership, economic and intellectual, II, 204 f., 206 f., 247, 320; leaders of Jews, II, 196, 204 f., 206 f., 247, 320 f., 403; learning, II, 205, 206, 207, 405; marriage customs, II, 226, 232; Media's association with, II, 205; mortgages and interest, II, 251, 414; official control of Jewish settlements, II, 196, 403; Palestinian rivalry, II, 205, 207 f.; Parsiism checks other religions, II, 150; Pharisaism's dominance, II, 36; pilgrims sent to Jerusalem, I, 213; proselytism, II, 149, 150; ritualistic divergences, II, 7; supremacy, II, 204-9, 405; theocracy, II, 279; world-duration computations, II, 318; *see also* Persia, Sassanian; Talmud, Babylonian; *and* individual localities
—— medieval, IV, 161; academies (*q.v.*), V, 13 f., 25, 34, VI, 133 f., VIII, 76; Arab penetration, III, 62, 89 f.; Aramaic speech, VI, 255 f., *see also* Aramaic language; communal leadership, V, 5, 50, VI, 214; decline of state revenue, III, 311; exilarch's letter on intercalation, VIII, 194, *see also* Exilarchs and exilarchate; influence on Spanish Jews, V, 61; intellectual supremacy, VI, 262; Jewish agriculture in, IV, 151; Jewish population, III, 99, VI, 224; legal institutions, VI, 4 ff., 133 f., *see also* Judges; liturgy, VII, 100-105, 266; Karaites, V, 271; religious observances, V, 246; and Sefardim, IV, 4; sexagesimal system, VIII, 373; welfare of city dwellers and farmers, V, 304; *see also* individual localities
Bachelors, II, 225
Bacon, Roger, VIII, 215
Badges, III, 139 ff., 159, 298, V, 133, 202
Badis, Berber ruler of Granada, III, 157, V, 311 f.
Baghdad: academy, III, 195, VI, 105, 112, 224, VI, 17; 'Adhud Hospital, VIII, 389; 'Ananites, V, 221; bankers, III, 153 f., 167, IV, 202, V, 10 f., VI, 214; building of, III, 99 f., IV, 159, 170, VIII, 148, 159; burning of books, III, 133; cantorial family, VII, 80, 144; capital of caliphate, III, 120; center of philological learning, VII, 5, 19, 21; chief *ḥazzan,* VII, 80; delegation from Meshekh, III, 202; exilarchate, V, 43; and Fusṭaṭ, III, 105; influence of Ar-Rawandi, V, 103; Jewish community, III, 99, 159, V, 50; Jewish quarters, III, 100, 145; Jews in government employ, III, 151; messianic

movement, V, 202 ff.; musical accompaniment to psalms, VII, 129; Muslim riots, III, 133, 165; Nizamiya Academy, VI, 468; oppressive decrees, III, 141; philosophers' assemblies, VI, 198 f., VIII, 55 f.; physicians, VIII, 237; population, III, 276; public debates, V, 83; Rabbanite center, V, 269; seat of *catholicos* and exilarchs, V, 7; Shi'ites, III, 123, 133; synagogues, III, 135; taxation of Jews, III, 169; wedding ordinance, VI, 140; *see also* Exilarchs and exilarchate

Bagohi (Bagoas), Persian governor, I, 129, 353 f.

Bagratids (or Bagratuni), Armenian family, I, 169, III, 110; genealogy, III, 282

Bahir, Sefer, VIII, 32-37, 55, 289 ff.

Bahram I, king of Persia, VI, 428

Baḥram Tshubin, Persian general, III, 17, 58

Bahrein Islands, III, 65

Baḥya ibn Paquda, V, 366, VI, 95, VIII, 39, 224 f.; appeal to the masses, VIII, 71; on asceticism, VIII, 120; on biblical law, VI, 143, 148; biblical semantics, VI, 296; on creation *ex nihilo,* VIII, 89; dialogue between Soul and Intellect, VIII, 105 f.; on divine attributes, VIII, 97; "Duties of the Heart," VII, 10, 222, VIII, 62, 68 f.; duties of the "limbs" and "heart," VIII, 113; on emigration, IV, 221; evaluation of sciences, VIII, 143; on humility, VIII, 121; on love of God, VIII, 116; on necessity and justice, VIII, 109 f.; prayers, VI, 175; *see also* Pseudo-Baḥya

Baihaqi, scholar, VII, 4

Bailiffs, Jews as, IV, 267

Bakhtawi, Abu Ya'qub (Joseph) al-, Karaite grammarian, VII, 16

Bakri, Abu 'Ubaid 'Abd Allah al-, geographer, III, 65, 217, VI, 221 f., 434

Balaam, I, 46, 312, V, 192, VIII, 133; oracles of, I, 320

Baladhuri, III, 168; re capture of Caesarea, III, 88; on Mohammed's statement of religious rights, III, 131; re Tripolis, III, 104

Baldicus, *see* Baudri

Baldwin, archbishop of Canterbury, IV, 125

Baldwin I, king of Jerusalem, IV, 112; biblical manuscript redeemed from, VI, 247, 447 f.

Balfour Declaration, I, 200

Bali Yama, I, 349

Balkans: civil law re Jews, V, 57; Crusaders in, V, 200; invasions of, III, 24 f.; Jewish communities, I, 169, 283, III, 189, 206 ff., IV, 173, V, 54 ff.; Jewish literature, VI, 187; Karaites in, VIII, 195; proselytes, I, 283; tax farmers, IV, 153; *see also* Byzantium

Balkh, Persia, Jewish community, III, 109

Balsam, I, 252, VIII, 253

Baluqiya, legend of, V, 367

Bamberg, bishop of, IV, 98

Bamot, I, 332, 353

Banco di San Giorgio, IV, 209

Banking and bankers, I, 132, 255, 261, 410, II, 431, IV, 197 ff., 338 ff., VI, 68 f.; in Assyria, I, 108; *dhimmis,* IV, 199; entry of Jews, I, 108 f., 346, IV, 197 ff., 338 f., V, 10; holdings in convertible commodities, VIII, 224; laws, IV, 198 f.; prominent Jewish family, III, 152 f., 158, 167, IV, 202, V, 10 f., VI, 214; ramifications, IV, 207-15, 344 ff.; and tax farming, IV, 201 f.; varied enterprises, IV, 349; wealth, IV, 214, *see also under* Merchants; Moneylenders and moneylending

Bannus, Essenian hermit, II, 49

Banu Hishna, tribe, III, 65

Banu Nadhir, tribe, III, 64, 79

Banu Qainuqa', tribe, III, 64, 78 f.

Banu Quraiẓa, tribe, III, 64, 79, 264, V, 179

Baptism, I, 179, II, 75, 361; of children with parental consent, III, 10; fees for, III, 249; freedom of slaves through, III, 14; inviolability of, IV, 6, 117; of Jews, III, 23, 182, IV, 100; Pope Nicholas I re, III, 209; and relapse of faith, III, 320; worldly inducements to, III, 28; *see also* Conversion; Converts

—— enforced, III, 20, 28, 38, 51, 52, 184, 240 f., 254, IV, 104 f.; Leo VII re, IV, 6; suicide as alternative to, IV, 96

Baptists, pre-Christian, II, 348

Baqillani, Abu Bakr al-, Asharite, V, 84

Barabbas, II, 72, 359

Baraita de-Niddah, VI, 181 f.

Baraita de-Shemu'el, VIII, 147, 171, 192 f., 253
Baradani, al-, family, VII, 144
Baradani, Nahum b. Joseph al-, cantor, V, 296
Baraitot, I, 270; compilation of, VI, 204
Barcelona, Spain, IV, 29; Jewish community, III, 281, IV, 34, 159; Montjuich cemetery, IV, 33, 249; ownership of land, IV, 161; population, III, 281; public baths, IV, 37; rights for Jewish litigants, IV, 41 f.
Bardeisan, heresiarch, VII, 128
Bards, I, 141
Barhebraeus, Gregory, Syrian scholar, I, 170, 372, III, 16, 177, V, 9, VIII, 249
Bar Ḥiyya, Abraham (Savasorda), Spanish-Jewish astronomer and mathematician, IV, 37, V, 146, 162 f., VI, 149, VIII, 69, 148 f.; ambivalence toward astrology, VIII, 169 f., 182 f.; astrological interpretation, VI, 231 f., 298, 440, VIII, 170, 176, 182; astronomic works, VIII, 158, 169 f., 183, 360 ff.; on biblical synonyms for sin, VI, 296; calendar computations, VIII, 204, 207 f., 209 f., 361; categories of man's souls, VIII, 110 f.; classification of sciences, VIII, 142 f., 347 f.; collaboration with Plato of Tivoli, VIII, 148 f., 266, 351 f.; on divine government of the universe, VIII, 86; doctrine of creation, VIII, 94; doctrine of repentance, VIII, 105; on ethical conduct and free will, VIII, 119; ethical works, VIII, 62, 304; on existence of time, VIII, 88; geographic observations, VIII, 214 ff.; on Hipparchus, VIII, 372; justification of scientific studies, VIII, 219; letter to Yehudah b. Barzillai, VI, 149, 439; mathematical works, VIII, 155 ff., 351 ff.; quoted in the book of the Bright Light, VIII, 33; on scriptural guidance, VIII, 119, 335 f.; sources, VIII, 356, 360 f.; style, VIII, 74; on superiority of Israel, VIII, 133; theological context of scientific data, VIII, 201 f.; *Yesode ha-tebunah,* VIII, 347 f., 352
Bari, Italy, III, 281, IV, 24, V, 46, 56, VI, 119, 421
Baridi, al-, emir, III, 165, IV, 208 f.
Bar Kocheba (Koziba), Simon, I, 231, V, 188, VI, 239, 241, 430, VII, 244; messiahship, II, 121, 126, 132; military measure against Christians, II, 132; rebellion led by, II, 97 f., 101, 102, 106, 107, 121, 371, 372; rebellion's aftermath, II, 130, 142, 169, 271
Barley, I, 251, 252
Barnabas, Saint, II, 86, 366; Epistle of, II, 137, 167, 382
Bar Qappara, VIII, 161
Bar Satia, Joseph b. Jacob, VI, 483
Bartenora, Obadiah, VII, 120
Bartholomew, bishop of Exeter, V, 136
Baruch, I, 334, 341; apocalypse of, II, 60
Baruch b. Samuel of Mayence, VII, 179
Bashyatchi, Elijah b. Moses, V, 229, 234, VII, 220; re candle lighting, V, 403; Code, V, 405 f.
Bashyatchi, Moses b. Elijah, V, 214, 390
Basil I, Byzantine emperor, III, 179; and conversion of Jews, III, 183, 193; *Epanagogé,* III, 186; *Procheiros Nomos* (Legal Handbook), III, 186
Basil II, Byzantine emperor, III, 184, IV, 24 f.; edict on Venetian shipping, IV, 24 f.
Basilika, Byzantine code of, III, 181, 186 ff., 190, 319
Basil the Great, Saint, VII, 65
Baṣra, VI, 245; commercial and intellectual center, VI, 81, 153, 364; contribution to Sura academy, V, 14; Jewish banker in, IV, 202; Jewish community, III, 90; local customs, VI, 124 f.; school of Arabic philology, VII, 11, 15, 19, 34, 58
Bastards, II, 218, 222, 276, 409, V, 267
Baths, public, II, 400; in Barcelona, IV, 37; decrees re, III, 142, 175, 194, 299
Bathsheba, I, 127
Baṭlanim, title, V, 50 f.
Battani, al-, VIII, 201, 360; astronomical tables, VIII, 139, 170, 376 f.
Baudri (Baldicus) of Bourgueil, IV, 107
Bavaria, IV, 65 f.
Bayyit, term, VII, 199
Bazaars, IV, 179 f.; *see also* Fairs
Becket, *see* Thomas à Becket
Bede, Venerable, VI, 279
Bedouins, I, 33, 71, 301, 335; assaults on Palestine, I, 57, II, 246
Beena marriage, I, 310
Beer, II, 249
Beersheba, I, 167, 344; pilgrimages to, I, 94, 338

Beggars, I, 275, 282, II, 272, 274
Behemoth, V, 148
Beirut, law school, III, 11
Beja, Spain, V, 298
Bekhor Shor, Joseph, VI, 295
Bel, Temple of, I, 168; *see also* Baal
Belgium, Jewish physicians in, VIII, 390; *see also* Flanders
Belisarius, Byzantine general: conquest of Naples, III, 25; suppressive measures, III, 230; trophies from the Temple of Jerusalem, III, 11; western campaigns, III, 7
Ben Asher, family chronology, VI, 445 f.
Ben Asher, Aaron, Tiberian Masorite, VI, 245 f., VII, 32 ff., 126; biblical manuscript, VI, 246 f.; effect of mysticism on, VIII, 15; masoretic monograph, VI, 252; punctuation, VI, 445; as Rabbanite, VI, 447
Ben Asher, Moses, VI, 246, 445, 446
Ben 'Azzai, Simon, II, 221
Ben Bag Bag, II, 220; re the Pentateuch, V, 212
Benedictions, II, 333, 361, VII, 66 ff., 96 f., 120, 244; deviations in, VII, 279; differences on, in ancient sources, VII, 109, improvisations for, VII, 86; the hundred, VII, 110 f.; at meals, VII, 81; Samuel b. Ḥofni's classification of, VI, 70; seven-word, VII, 244; *see also 'Amidah;* Blessing
Benedict of York, IV, 125
Bene-Israel, in India, III, 115
Bene Moshe, V, 192
Benevento, Italy, IV, 236
Bene Yisrael, I, 41
Benjamin, tribe of, I, 65, 321
Benjamin b. Ḥiyya, Hebrew poet, IV, 288
Benjamin b. Jonah of Tudela, Jewish traveler, III, 185, VI, 222 ff., VIII, 379; reports on: Baghdad, III, 100; Bohemia, III, 214; Byzantine taxes, III, 192 ff.; communal officials, V, 50 f.; Damascus, III, 104; the exilarchate, V, 11 f.; Fusṭaṭ, III, 106; Jerusalem, IV, 113; Jewish communities in Germany, IV, 73; Jewish population, III, 113 f., 283 f.; Narbonne, IV, 47; Paris, IV, 60; Rome, IV, 13 f.; Samaritans, V, 176; sectarians in the Orient, VI, 475; Slavonia and Canaan, III, 214
Benjamin b. Moses Nahawendi, Karaite leader, V, 182, 223 ff., 227, 363, VIII, 58, 91, 297; biblical exegesis, V, 225, VI, 276, 283 f.; Book of Commandments, V, 231, 259, 401; calendar reform, V, 224; on double holiday, VIII, 374 f.; re Jesus, V, 344; theory of divine government of world, V, 259
Benjamin of Tiberias, III, 23
Ben Mashiaḥ, Karaite, V, 277, VIII, 204 f.
Ben Meir, Aaron, V, 32 f., 223; letter to Babylonian leaders, V, 49; month of creation, VIII, 197; struggle with Babylonian chiefs over calendar, V, 30 f., 212; *see also under* Saadiah Gaon
Ben Naphtali, Moses (b. David), Masorite, VI, 247
Ben Sira, alphabet of, VI, 159, 169; *see also* Sirach, Jesus
Ben Tabal, I, 155
Ben Zoma, Simon, II, 218, 248
Berakiah b. Naṭronai the Punctuator, VII, 189 f.
Berbers, I, 176; antagonism to Arabs, III, 91, 107; attacks against Solomon, governor of Africa, III, 230; dialect, VII, 12; in Granada, III, 156 f.; IV, 29; and Judaism, II, 212, III, 7, 90 f., 272; mass conversion to Islam, III, 132
Berditshevski, Micah Joseph, I, 11
Berenice, Jewish princess, II, 92, 369
Berenice inscription, II, 202 f., 404
Bereshit rabbati, medieval midrash, V, 146; *see also* Moses the Preacher (ha-Darshan)
Bernard, hermit, IV, 61
Bernard of Clairvaux, Saint, IV, 11; injunction to Cistercian monks, IV, 299; on Jewish serfdom, V, 129; letter in behalf of Jews, IV, 121; on usury, IV, 206, V, 128
Beroea (Verria), city, II, 79
Berossos, historian, I, 197, 345
Beruriah, scholar, II, 239, 275, VI, 408, 415
Bet 'almin (house of eternity), II, 289; *see also* Cemeteries and catacombs
Beth-Alpha, synagogue, II, 138, 285, VIII, 367
Bethel: city, I, 129, 346; images erected, I, 66; excavations, I, 106
—— deity, I, 128; theophorous names connected with, I, 352
Bethlehem, V, 147, 153
Beth-shan (Scythopolis), I, 225, II, 27, 392

Beth She'arim, cemetery, II, 10, 14, 174, 272 f., 286, 333, 336; destruction of, II, 179, 398; inscriptions, I, 378, II, 289, 424; Palmyrene and Arabian Jews buried in, II, 211, III, 68, 258, 260
Beth-shemesh, pottery, I, 320
Beth-Zur, city, I, 184, 369
Betrothal, V, 29 f., 401 f., VI, 391; forms of, VI, 98; ring without stones, VI, 130; *see also* Marriage; Wedding
Bet-Zabdai, city, II, 52
Bezalel, I, 14, VIII, 7
Bezalel Ashkenazi, VI, 348
Béziers, France, IV, 55 f., 132
Bible: allegorical vs. literal interpretation, I, 202, II, 144, 386; in Arabia, III, 82, 265; authorship of books, VI, 159, 307 f.; books and manuscripts ransomed from the Crusaders, IV, 111 f., 296 f.; canonical recension by Jewish scholars, VI, 312; Catalan, with musical notation, VII, 282; Christian students, and Jewish scholars, VI, 272; contradictions in, V, 87, VI, 305 f., 474 f.; early versions of parts of, III, 82; exegesis, II, 141-47 *passim*, 385-87, *see also* Exegesis; fictional use of narratives, VII, 183 ff.; and history, I, 42, 295, VI, 306 ff.; Justinian's decree re versions of, III, 12 f., 233, V, 209, VII, 94 f., 263; Khazars and, III, 202 f.; loan on copy of, IV, 340; marriage relationships mentioned, II, 230, 411; masoretic accents, VII, 126; Masoretic text, III, 72, V, 176, 195 f., VI, 236 ff., 441 ff.; Mohammed's knowledge of, III, 81 ff.; Muslim criticisms of, V, 87 ff., 97, 174, 175 f., VI, 8 f., 242, 254, 274, 291 f., 307; narrative in sacred poetry, VII, 180 f.; new philological approaches, VI, 268; persecution for possession of, VII, 86; poetic allusions to, VII, 193 f., 201 f.; popularity of hermeneutical sermons, VI, 153; Porphyry's criticisms, II, 158, 391; preoccupation with each letter of, VIII, 14 f.; in Rabbanite community of Cairo, VII, 137; reading of, III, 12, 189, 253, V, 218, VI, 248 f.; references to God's love, VIII, 114; restudy of, VI, 235-313, 441-86; revealed word of God, VI, 294, 307 ff., VIII, 127; rules of cadence in reading, VI, 237; Samaritan, II, 30, 340, V, 262, VI, 236; scarcity of copies, III, 201; study of, III, 72 f., V, 229, VI, 11, 34 f., 123 f., 142 f., 234, VIII, 5, 84; tannaitic law on acquisition of, VII, 135; use of different texts in computing chronology, VIII, 206; use of historical data from, VI, 437; zoological and botanical names in, VIII, 226 f.;
—— translations, III, 211, V, 39, 83, 85; Arabic, III, 82, 265, V, 85, VI, 263-72, 459-61; Aramaic, II, 146, 387, 411, III, 72 f., VI, 239 f., 255-63, 312, 453-57; *see also* Targum; books other than the Pentateuch, VI, 260 f.; Christian, VI, 271; *see also* Vulgate; Greek, III, 189, 211, V, 39, 89; *see also* Aquila; Septuagint; Latin, VI, 272-74, 292, 462 f.; *see also* Jerome, Saint; *Vetus Latina;* Syriac, VI, 241; *see also* Peshiṭṭa; Western, VI, 272 ff., 462 f., VII, 222
—— *see also* Apocrypha; New Testament; Old Testament; *also under* names of sections, books, and ancient or medieval versions
Bida', Arabic term, VIII, 65
Bigvai, I, 119
Bilingualism, I, 19, VII, 4 ff., 222 f.
Bilshan, I, 119
Biography, VI, 203, VIII, 223
Biology, VIII, 225 ff.
Birth control, II, 209
Bitruji, al-, Arab astronomer, VIII, 162
Black clothing, III, 140, 153
Black Sea, III, 197
Blasphemy, I, 92, V, 335; against king, V, 237; of Mohammed, III, 94, 132; punishment for, III, 295; *see also* Curse
Blessing, priestly, II, 282, VI, 178, 182, 336; omission of, VII, 249; ritualistic, VI, 123 f., 359; *see also* Benedictions
Blessing of Moses, II, 31
Blois, France: blood accusation, IV, 137 f., 307 f., VII, 179; suffering of Jewish community, V, 131, VI, 219
Blood: circulation, VIII, 242; and soul, VIII, 107
Blood accusation, I, 193, IV, 80, 83, 135-39, 306 ff.; origin of myth of, I, 192, 382
Blood money, fine for murder, III, 132
"Blood of the covenant," V, 390
Blood ritual, I, 51; *see also* Ritual
Boaz, house of, V, 295
Bodleian Library, I, 347
Bodo (Botho), IV, 9, 52f., 264, V, 126

Body, human, VIII, 229 f.; "humors" of, VII, 210; and soul, VIII, 36 f., 226; well-being of, VI, 142; words as, VII, 51
Boethos, I, 221
Boethosians *or* Boethuseans, II, 342, V, 255, 280
Bogoljubov, duke of Kiev, III, 216
Bogomils, III, 209, IV, 132, VIII, 31, 56
Bohemia: Benjamin of Tudela re, III, 214; Jewish resistance to Crusaders, IV, 291; jurisdiction of local rulers, IV, 72
Bohemund I, Crusader in Macedonia, IV, 107
Bohemund III, of Antioch, IV, 114
Bologna, Italy: expulsion of Jews, IV, 27; university, VI, 54
Bondage, of debtors, I, 69
Bondage, Egyptian, V, 167, VI, 303, VII, 181, 290
Bones, number of, in human body, VIII, 230
Bonfils, Joseph, *see* Tob 'Elem
Bonn, Germany, IV, 306
Book of Adam, VI, 17, 197
Book of the Bright Light, *see Bahir*
Book of the Dead, I, 50
Books: acquisition of, VII, 135 f.; banned or burned, III, 133, IV, 32; in codices, II, 156, 390; collected at synagogue, VII, 139; decorated with signs of Zodiac, VIII, 184; introduction of paper, VI, 184; lists of, VII, 139; 287; production and distribution, VII, 136; reverence for, VII, 139; shortage of, VI, 181
Boppard, Germany, IV, 133, 143
Bordeaux, France, IV, 55
Borion, city, III, 8, 230
Bosporus, III, 197
Botany, VIII, 226 f.
Botho, *see* Bodo
Bowls, magical, II, 336, VIII, 8 f., 277
Boycott: of *dhimmi* physicians, V, 97; of Judeo-Christian trade, IV, 13
Boys, *see* Children
Bracteates, Hebrew, III, 218, 339
Bratislav, duke of Prague, IV, 100
Braulio, bishop of Saragossa, III, 40
Bray-sur-Seine, France, IV, 62, 128 f.
Bread: blessing of, VI, 123; thrown into the water, III, 241; unleavened, V, 217, 239, 247, 346
Brethren of Purity, VII, 206, VIII, 15, 112, 345, 347
Breviarium Alarici, III, 35, 49
Bribery, I, 263; *see also* Tribute
Bride: homecoming of, and moon's conjunction, VIII, 375; laws re, VI, 63; substitution for, VII, 188; *see also Kallah*
Bridegroom: astral forces and, VIII, 182; hymn for, VII, 143
Bristol, England, IV, 80
Bronze Age, I, 60
Brotherhood, II, 4
"Bryson," *Oikonomikos,* IV, 349 f.
Buddha, Gotama Siddhartha, I, 315
Bug, river, III, 333
Building industry: ancient, II, 334; medieval, IV, 170
Bukhari, al-, III, 87; compilation of traditions, VI, 78
Bulan, ruler of Khazars, III, 198, 199, 326
Bulgaria, II, 210, 406, III, 209, V, 210
Bun (or Abun), R., II, 13, VIII, 34
Bureaucracy, II, 186; *see also* Public office
Burghers: Caen charter, IV, 205; and the clergy, IV, 99; economic rivals of Jews, IV, 60, 65, 141 f.; Jews and, IV, 67 f., 69, 74 f., 85; and protection of Jews, IV, 100; status of, IV, 23, V, 319
Burgos, Spain, IV, 250
Burgus Judaicus, IV, 314
Burial, II, 287 ff.; body dressed for resurrection, II, 312; in Cave of Machpelah, III, 278; cremation replaced by, I, 382, II, 423; historical significance of, III, 335; Jewish practice of, III, 22, 297; in Khazaria, III, 202; in old graves, III, 138; Zoroastrians re, III, 22, 297; *see also* Cemeteries and catacombs
Burning: of books, III, 133, IV, 32; death by, IV, 22, 62, 138
Burnt-offering, I, 179, III, 29
Bury St. Edmunds, England, IV, 136 f.; expulsion of Jews, IV, 84; massacre of Jews, IV, 148; "Moyses Hall," IV, 282; synagogue, IV, 85
Businessmen: public discourses for, II, 275; scholars aided, II, 277
Business transactions, IV, 174; agents, IV, 180, 196; astrology and, VIII, 365; cessation of, in Alexandria, I, 266; competition, V, 68; currency ex-

Business transactions (*Continued*)
change, IV, 209 ff.; documentation, II, 266; ethics, VIII, 48 f.; of Jewish converts, III, 43; laws of, III, 45, IV, 185, VI, 71; local customs, VI, 122, 126; mathematics for, VIII, 156; mosque and synagogue as centers of, V, 67; Muslim law re, IV, 186; partnerships, IV, 37, 177, 185 f.; safeguards for secrecy of, VI, 139; *see also* Industry; Trade
Businesswomen, I, 113, II, 237, V, 243
Busrah, "house of the Jew," III, 296
Bustanai (Ḥaninai), exilarch, III, 89, V, 141 ff., VI, 19; controversy over marriage and legitimacy of offspring, III, 270, V, 8 ff., VI, 11, 200, 214 f.
Butchers, I, 275
Butter, IV, 315
Byblos, city, I, 318
Byzantine Church, VII, 68
Byzantine Empire: attitude toward polygamy, VI, 137; calendar controversy, VIII, 195; campaigns against Caliphate, III, 86 ff., 193; continuity of Jewish communities, V, 54-58, 315-17, VIII, 60; Crusaders in, IV, 107 f., 130; division between civil and religious law, VI, 3; employment of Jewish scholars, III, 184; enforced conversion in, III, 182 f.; fiscal contributions of Jews, III, 190-95, 320 f.; influence in Italy, III, 25; influence on Visigothic life, III, 246; Jewish civil judiciary, V, 57; Jewish cultural center, VI, 366; and Jewish migrations, III, 210, 220, IV, 108; Jews in military forces, III, 236 f.; Karaites in, V, 272, 399; legal codes, III, 187 f.; list of rulers, III, 317 f., VI, 211 f.; medical literature, VIII, 235; minting monopoly, IV, 210 f.; mystic literature in, VIII, 29 ff.; outlawry of Christian apostasy, VII, 256; Persian invasions, III, 17, 18, 74 f.; pig symbol, II, 152; recapture of Asiatic provinces and Egypt, III, 75; restrictions on Jewish worship, VII, 83 f., 94 f.; revival of Greek historical literature, VI, 199; scope of laws of Justinian, III, 233 f.; sectarianism and theological debates, VIII, 31; separation between Muslim and Christian worlds, IV, 44; sermons by emperors, VI, 154; slave trade, IV, 337; Slavonic mercenaries, III, 98; spread of Islam into, III, 4; status of Jewry in, III, 173-90, 199, 313-20, IV, 153; Venetian shipping rights, IV, 24

C

Cade, William, IV, 207
Caen, France, IV, 205
Caesar, Julius, I, 190, 218, 238
Caesarea, I, 225, 236, 256, 280, III, 20; academy, II, 175, VI, 248; captured by Arabs, III, 88; congregation, II, 199; population, III, 270; Samaritan stronghold, V, 171; synagogue, II, 423
Caesarea Mazaca, II, 177, 397
Caesarius of Arles, Saint, II, 398, III, 52, 244 f., IV, 265, V, 123; polemics vs. Jews, III, 250
Caesarius of Heisterbach, V, 134
Caesaropapism, II, 401
Caesars, Jewish loyalties to, I, 191
Cahorsins, IV, 207
Cain: as symbol, II, 136, 382; meaning of name, I, 60; sign of, I, 7; role in religious controversy, VI, 481
Cainites, gnostic sect, II, 137, VI, 481
Cairo: decree re public baths, III, 142; Fadhiliya mosque, VII, 138; Jewish community of Fusṭaṭ, III, 105, 160, *see also* Fusṭaṭ; Karaite community, V, 257 f., 268, 272; Katai quarter, III, 137; Nasiri Hospital, VIII, 248; observatory, VIII, 161; riot against Amalfitans, IV, 331 f.; Samaritan population, V, 177; synagogues, III, 135, VI, 247; taxation of Jewish estates, III, 169; *see also* Genizah
Calatayud, Spain, V, 298; merchant privilege, IV, 179
Calcarienses, congregation of, II, 261
Calebites, I, 57
Calendar: change in, in Mohammed's time, III, 84, 266; coincidence of Easter and Passover, II, 188, 209, 401; computation of date of Second Coming, III, 15; Gregorian, VIII, 190 f.; Jewish use of Christian, VIII, 172; Julian, VIII, 191; Muslim, V, 153 f., 191
—— Jewish, VI, 103, 269; computations, II, 306, 307; V, 404, VIII, 184; and dates of religious holidays, VI, 203; dispute over, V, 30 f., 94, VIII, 203 ff., *see also under* Saadiah Gaon; first

month of, I, 6, 294; Hebrew treatises on, VI, 307, VIII, 202-11, 377-80; inception of, VI, 227 f.; scholar Moses re, III, 184; Karaite vs. Rabbanite observances, V, 30 ff., 243 f., 273; Khazar, III, 201; lunar, I, 44; and mathematics, VIII, 147, 208; Mishawayh's approach to, V, 382; perpetual, V, 196, 212; and plant life cycles, V, 246 f.; proclamations concerning, II, 125, 198, 206, 209, VI, 216; purported Mosaic origin, V, 94, VIII, 373; reform, V, 224, 226 f., 305; sectarians and, V, 190, 195 f., 211 f., 382; stabilization, VIII, 192 ff.
—— *see also* Chronology; Year
Calf, talmudic tale of, VIII, 28
Caligula, Caius, I, 245, 284, 381, 404, II, 5, 57, 100, 368; attempt to force imperial worship on Jews, I, 218 f., 231
Caliphate, III, 75-119; concubinage with slaves, IV, 190 f.; customs duties, IV, 181 f.; expansion and dissolution of, IV, 86, V, 180; freedom of movement, VIII, 211 f.; influence of law, II, 264; international trade under, IV, 174, 178 ff.; and Jewish academies, V, 14; Judeo-Christian disputations, V, 110 f.; persecutions, III, 123; political influence of Jews, III, 154 f.; religious toleration, V, 82, 210, 264; restoration of exilarchs, VI, 200; reverence for law, VI, 11; role of Jewish communities, I, 30, IV, 225-27, VII, 107, VIII, 55; and scientific evolution, VIII, 261; Secret Profits Bureau, III, 139; sermons delivered by caliphs, VI, 153 f.; violent death of caliphs, III, 122; *see also* names of caliphs and dynasties
Calixtus II, pope, IV, 7 f., 235 f.
Calligraphy, Arabic, IV, 36 f.
Callinicum, synagogue, II, 189, III, 30
Callistus, bishop of Rome, II, 224
Cambyses, I, 129, 349
Camels, I, 301
Canaan, son of Ham, I, 335
Canaan: agriculture, I, 55; cities; I, 300; conquest and settlement, I, 16, 18, 32, 39, 308, VI, 230, 232; cult of the Sun and Moon, I, 45; figurines found in ruins of cities, I, 43, 310, 314, 318, 329; Israelitic festivals taken over from, I, 5, 72; migrations from, III, 91, 214 f.; origin of name, I, 302; and palace of Mari, I, 300 f.; political disaster, I, 53; popular religion reasserted, I, 161; term, with reference to Slavs, III, 214 f.
Canaanites: and Carthage, III, 91; circumcision, I, 6; incense altars, I, 352; incest, II, 229; influences, I, 44 ff., 63, 105, 316; injunction against marriage with, I, 38; Israelites outnumbered by, I, 40; nomadic ideals, I, 61; in North Africa, III, 91, 271; outposts of ancient race, I, 175; religion, I, 45, 49, 58, 105, 301; in Slavonic lands, III, 335, VI, 437; *see also* Phoenicia; Ras Shamra (Ugarit)
Canals, construction of, VIII, 356
Canary Islands, VIII, 215
Candelabrum, II, 11, 12, 44, 285, 333, 346; five-branched, III, 48; seven-branched, III, 11; of Temple, VII, 78
Candle lighting: Bashyatchi re, V, 403; *see also under* Light
Candles, Ḥanukkah, I, 400
Canon law, I, 182, VI, 3, 153; attitude toward Jews, III, 26 f., 33 f., 212 f., IV, 241; basic toleration, IV, 53 f., 56, 121, 141; Carolingian rulers and, IV, 51 f.; codification of, IV, 6, 17 ff.; on conversion, III, 36, IV, 6 ff., 189; difficulty of enforcement, III, 44, IV, 16 f., 54; Johannes Scholasticus, III, 187; on physicians, VIII, 231; on usury, IV, 197 ff., 338 ff.
Canons, Apostolic, IV, 18
Canterbury, England, IV, 84
Canticles, *see* Song of Songs
Cantor, II, 283, VII, 41; assistants to, VII, 125; composition of *piyyuṭ*, VII, 89-93; composition of tunes, VII, 125 ff., 144; elegies dedicated to, VII, 145; function of, VII, 81 f.; hand signals for congregational singing, VII, 127; improvisations, VII, 86, VIII, 12; latitude permitted to, VII, 79-85; liturgical handbooks for, VII, 124; name used as acrostic, VII, 141; omission of divine name by, VIII, 294; as preacher, VII, 81; professionalization, VII, 80 ff.; qualifications of, VII, 58, 129 f.; and reading of Torah, II, 283; selection of, VII, 80; *see also* Chant
Capernaum, II, 164
Capital, accumulation of, IV, 211; *see also* Wealth

Capitalism, Jews' success in, I, 261, 264
Capital punishment, I, 82, 145, II, 267, 419, V, 57, 390, VIII, 310; for adulteress, II, 222, 409; for aliens entering Temple, I, 239, 402; biblical sanctions, VI, 91 f.; in Italy, V, 316; Karaites re, V, 240 f.; perpetual excommunication as substitute for, V, 17, 280 f.; Spanish Jewry and, V, 45 f., 312; violation of biblical law, V, 235
Capitation tax, *see* Poll tax
Capito and Labeo, controversies, II, 299
Capitolina, the "God-fearing," II, 338
Capitoline Temple, II, 13, 106, 373
Cappadocia, III, 17
Capsali, Moses, V, 406
Captives: amount of ransom, V, 315; Christian, of Persians, III, 22; communal ransom of, III, 78, IV, 118, 119, 177 f.; four, story of, VI, 325, 342; Karaites and Rabbanites, V, 413; scholars, V, 46 f.; slaves, IV, 110, 192; women, problem of legitimacy of children, V, 8 f.; *see also* Piracy and pirates; Slaves and slavery
Capua, Italy, IV, 23
Caracalla, emperor, I, 244, II, 109, 110, 190
Caravans, trade route, IV, 172
Cardinals, College of, IV, 10 f.
Care (*Sorge*), I, 16
Caritas, term, II, 330
Carmel, Baal cult, I, 334
Carolingian Empire, IV, 43-53, 256-64, VIII, 42; continuity of traditions, IV, 64 f.; dissolution of, and Jewish status, IV, 53 f.; influence in Spain and England, IV, 27 f., 79 f.; *see also under* individual emperors
Carpentras inscription, II, 203, 404
Carthage, city, III, 91; Jewish proselytism, I, 176, 183, 283, 374; religion, I, 43, 374
Cassiodorus, III, 25, VI, 241
Caste system, *see* Classes, social
Castile: Jewish status in, IV, 27 ff., 245 ff., 255; *see also under* individual cities and kings
Castles as refuge of Jews, IV, 35 f., 99, 119, 125 f.
Castra Judaeorum, IV, 35
Castration, I, 147, II, 107, 219; of animals, V, 174; of humans, IV, 191 f.
Castro, Jacob R., V, 274
Castrojeriz, Spain: anti-Jewish disturbance, IV, 251; privilege, IV, 35
Catacombs, *see* Cemeteries and catacombs
Catalonia, IV, 43; *see also* Aragon; *also under* individual cities and kings
Catastrophes, I, 68; *see also* End of days
Catchwords, in liturgical poems, VII, 88
Catechisms, I, 178
Catechumenate, and enforced conversion, III, 36, 245
Catharii and Catharism, VIII, 32, 42, 46, 288 f.
Catholicoi, charter from Al-Muktafi II, V, 6, 293 f.
Cato, Marcus Portius, I, 253
Cattle raising, I, 55, 57, 60, 72, 89, 253, 254, 301, 407; change in attitude toward, II, 263; communal ownership, II, 315
Caucasus, III, 199 ff., 208
"Cause of causes," VIII, 41 f.
Cautinus, bishop of Clermont, III, 51 f.
Cave Men (*Magharians*), V, 192, 379 f.
Caves: burial in, II, 287; Dead Sea, V, 188, 378; *see also* Dead Sea Scrolls; documents preserved in, V, 188, 255, 377 f.; Machpelah, III, 278; Murabba'at, V, 188; Petcherskii Monastery, III, 215 f.; use of, for religious purposes, III, 327 f., 378
Celestine III, pope, IV, 8
Celibacy, V, 134, 351; asceticism and, VIII, 53
Celsus, philosopher, II, 36, 111, 131; anti-Christian and anti-Jewish polemics, II, 157 f., 159, 163, 391; impressed by Egyptian magic, II, 21; quoted, II, 23
Cemeteries and catacombs, I, 378, II, 25, 109, 286-90, 423 f., III, 140, V, 258; in Barcelona, IV, 33; *bet 'almin,* or house of eternity, II, 289; community owned, II, 199; cremation and catacombs, II, 12; decorative motifs, epitaphs, I, 378, II, 10 ff., 146, 284, 330 ff., *see also* Inscriptions; in England, IV, 80; joint use by Jews and Christians, II, 188; location, II, 286; Muslim, in Jerusalem, III, 297; Muslim rulings re, III, 137 f.; papal injunction re vandalism, IV, 8
Censorship, of books, V, 207, VIII, 69; under the Caliphate, III, 133
Census of Jews, Roman, I, 263, 410
Cephas (Kaipha), II, 74, 361

Ceramics, I, 257
Cereals, I, 251
Ceremonial, Jewish: appeal of, II, 149, 189, 191; *see also* Ritual
Ceremonial law, *see under* Law
Cesarius of Arles, *see* Caesarius
Ceylon, I, 321
"Chain verses," VII, 179 f., 199
Chairemon, priest, II, 55
Chajes, Zvi, VI, 158
Chalcedon, city, III, 18, 236
Chalcedon, Council of, III, 5; John Rufus re, III, 229; and Monophysite churches, III, 240
Chaldaea and Chaldaeans, I, 33, 106, 141, 338; last king of, III, 63 f.; migrations before approaching armies of, I, 105, 106; priests and magicians, II, 22; religious propaganda, I, 159; *see also* Babylonia
Châlons, Council of, III, 252; and slave trade, IV, 335
Châlons sur Saône, town, III, 253
Champagne, region: fairs, IV, 183, 329; Jewish synod, V, 70 f.; viticulture, IV, 317
Chance, Epicurean doctrine of, VIII, 103
Chansons de geste, VI, 190
Chant, synagogue, VII, 125-31; accompaniment, VII, 127 f.; Gentiles attracted by, VII, 128; improvisation, VII, 128, VIII, 12 f.; modes of, VII, 127
Characteristics of Jews, I, 20 ff.; polarity in action and thought, I, 19
Chariot, divine, VIII, 5; descenders of, VIII, 12 ff., 17, 27 f., 37, 113; discussed in the *Guide,* VIII, 73; works concerning, VIII, 11 ff.
Chariots, I, 137, 332, 357
Charity, I, 86, 275, 281, II, 269-74, 420; communal and individual, II, 273, VI, 174 f.; dependence upon, II, 256; Gentile and Jewish, II, 270 f., 420; *heqdesh* as, VIII, 240; a religious duty, I, 175; synagogue exchequer, II, 285; *see also* Poor, the
Charlemagne, IV, 44; envoy to Harun ar-Rashid, IV, 45, 174, VI, 220; influence of, in Germany, IV, 64; second embassy to Baghdad, IV, 257; trade charters, IV, 48 f.
Charles II (Charles the Bald), emperor, IV, 18; letter to Barcelona, IV, 34
Charles II, king of Navarre, IV, 30
Charles III (Charles the Simple), king of France, IV, 13, 58 f., 239
Charles Martel, ruler of Franks, IV, 43
Charms, verbal, VIII, 234
Charters: Carolingian, IV, 48 ff.; English, IV, 79 f.; merchants', IV, 48, 50; moneylending, IV, 205 ff.; Seleucid, I, 216, 369, 393; trade, IV, 48 f.
Check, prototype of, IV, 213
Chenoboskion, gnostic library of, VIII, 274
Chess, game, VIII, 160, 356 f.
Chicken, prohibition re, V, 196
Childebert I, Frankish king, III, 51
Children: compensation for suffering, VIII, 103 f.; conversion of, IV, 55, 69, V, 113; of converts, III, 43, 126, 248; education, II, 274, 275, 276, 279, 280, 421; exposure of, I, 268, II, 219, 408; illegitimate, II, 218, *see also* Bastards; of Jews, reared as Gentiles, II, 102; Karaite injunctions, V, 223 f.; legal protection for, I, 361, II, 253; legends of Christian martyrdom, IV, 80, 135 f., *see also* Blood accusation; marriages, I, 265, II, 219, 238; sacrificed, I, 51, IV, 144; slavery for debt and taxes, II, 258, 303, III, 169, 312; of slaves, II, 223, 224, III, 45, IV, 195, V, 8 f.; training in poetic arts, VII, 150, 292; *see also* Girls
"Children of Light," II, 53
Chilperic I, Frankish king, III, 52
China, Jews in, II, 212, III, 115, 173, 285 f.
Chintila, Visigothic king, III, 42
Chios, monastery of Nea Moné, III, 192
Chirograph offices, in England, IV, 280, 304, VI, 357
Choirs, church, VII, 284; use of, VII, 125
Chosen people: concept of, I, 3, 7, 11, 19, 30, 62, 88, 97, 138, 164, II, 170, V, 125 ff., 137, 285, VIII, 123 ff., 340 ff.; enhanced by individualistic doctrines, I, 276; ethics, II, 10-16; *see also* Messiah and messianism
Christ: "logos Christology" of Paul, II, 81, 364; as title with name of Jesus, II, 357; vision of resurrected, II, 71; *see also* Jesus Christ; Messiah and messianism
Christian-Arab relations, *see* Muslim-Christian relations

Christian Church: abjuration formula for converts, III, 41 f., 184, 194; aesthetic appeal, II, 154 ff., 389; antecedents, II, 86, 366; calendar, II, 125, 209, VIII, 206 f., 378 f.; collectivity of, I, 226; concessions to popular religions, II, 168; converts admitted, II, 388; decrees of anti-fraternization, III, 175; dichotomy in position of, III, 242; formation of, II, 82-88, 364-67; founders' ideal and beliefs, II, 73; growing stability and power, IV, 17, 19 f.; heir of imperial Rome, II, 87; and Judeo-Roman conflicts, II, 99, 107; language difficulties, VII, 68; on moneylending and usury, IV, 198 ff.; music, II, 155, 330, 389, VII, 130; and Nestorians, II, 164; ordination, II, 120; poetry in Syriac and Greek, VII, 98; policy of limited toleration, IV, 56, 121, 141; property, acquired by Jews, III, 230 f.; reform, IV, 10, 28; religions preeminent in, II, 165, 393; revenue from Jews, IV, 153 f., *see also* Tithes; sermons on special occasions, VI, 162; *see also* Canon law; Clergy; Judeo-Christian relations; Orthodox Eastern Church; Papacy

Christian Druthmar of Aquitania, III, 205

Christian Empire, *see* Roman Empire

Christian era, VIII, 378 f.; system of dating, VIII, 172

Christian of Stavelot, V, 131

Christians and Christianity: ancient: account of rise of, II, 62-66, 352-55, VI, 191, 258; Arian heresy, II, 134; arts, attitude toward, II, 11, 154 f.; codices and their uses, II, 156, 390; concessions, II, 168; conversion to, II, 150, 163 ff., 392, 393, *see also* Converts; declared illicit, II, 167; divorce, attitude toward, I, 114, II, 228, 410; emigration to Pella, II, 82, 99, 132; Essenes and Sadducees, II, 51, 129 f., 348; the Eucharist, I, 193, II, 71, 75; evolution of church, I, 226, II, 86 f., 366; exegetical and linguistic effects of controversy, II, 141-47, 384; expectation of redeemer, II, 57 ff., 73; fall of Jerusalem and, II, 82 ff., 364; first monarch, II, 165; and gnosis, II, 315, 435; Gospel stories of Jesus, II, 64 ff., 72, *see also* Gospels; New Testament; historical controversies, I, 296, II, 136 ff., 161; Jewish expansion checked by, II, 87; Jewish influences on worship, II, 26, 84, 365; Jewish proselytism and, I, 373; Jewish Scriptures, use of, II, 144, 145, *see also* Bible; Jews' magic powers, belief in, II, 189; Josephus' writings on, II, 131, 379; Judaism, separation from, II, 79, 82, 83, 85, 129-71 *passim,* 167, 169, 170, 183, 200, 378-95 *passim,* 399; Judaism's aid in spread of, II, 122, III, 35, 208 f.; Judaism's reaction to success in Diaspora, II, 147; Judeo-Christians, legal concepts of, II, 303, 432; leadership and community life, II, 74 f.; leadership of Hellenistic world, II, 83 ff., 163 ff.; marriage, attitudes to, I, 114, II, 224, 228, 408, 410; martyrdom, I, 400; Neoplatonists and, II, 159; pagan counterattacks, II, 156 ff.; Pauline schism, II, 76-81, 83-86, 361-67; Persia's antagonism, II, 181; pessimism and internal divisions, II, 57 f.; Pharisaism criticized, II, 343; polemics against oriental religions, II, 390; promoted by Constantine and successors, II, 150, 152; ritualistic transformation, II, 84; Roman view of, II, 86, 366; sectarian currents, II, 111; Semitic flavor of early writers, I, 187; slaves, II, 259; social background and teachings, II, 67, 356; spiritual acceptance of Roman Empire, II, 152; state religion intolerant, II, 172 ff., 180; successes, II, 151-56, 169-71, 388-90; talmudic reticence about, II, 130; term, II, 86, 356, 366, V, 119; the "third order," II, 366, 396; transformations in first century and a half, II, 25; writings in Greek and Latin, II, 156; *see also* Church; *also under* individual names, e.g. Jesus; Paul

—— medieval, V, 108, VIII, 119; Al-Ḥakim's persecution of, IV, 57; anthropomorphic beliefs, VIII, 30; Arabian, early attitude toward Mohammed, III, 78; and atrocities of Crusades, IV, 139 f.; in Baghdad, III, 276 f.; biblical laws observed, III, 83 f., V, 124; Byzantine protection of, III, 189; "Christian," as derogatory term, III, 147; class status, IV, 87; and Code of Justinian, III, 231; controversy over Jewish era of Creation, VIII, 206 f., 378 f.; conversion to, *see* Converts; in

Damascus, V, 96; debate over *filioque,* VII, 109; debate over redeemer as founder, V, 117 ff.; declaration of compliance to 'Umar I, III, 129; and divine attributes, VIII, 95 f.; eastern and western, III, 51, 176; employment by Jews, III, 30, 38, 140, IV, 15, 54, 269, 336; ethnic strains, III, 103; evacuated from Syria, III, 103 f.; excommunication for employment by Jews, IV, 269; and geographic studies, VIII, 216 f.; Hebraists, VIII, 384; icons used, VIII, 26, *see also* Iconoclastic movement; Images and symbols; intercession of Spanish Jews for, III, 156; on Jewish alliance with Satan, IV, 139 ff.; and Jewish homiletics, VI, 152 f.; on Jewish hostility, IV, 133 ff.; Jews as witnesses to, V, 135; and Judaism, III, 17, 208 f., 221, 243, V, 136, VI, 8, VIII, 51; and Karaites, V, 262; in Khazaria, III, 198, 203; Latin Bible used, VI, 292, *see also* Bible; liturgical music, VII, 128; loss of churches, III, 139; merchants, IV, 179 f.; minority status under Caliphate, III, 120; Mohammed and, III, 83 f.; moneylending, IV, 202 f.; New, III, 176 f.; as new Israel, V, 125 f., 137; and pagan practices, III, 252; and Palestine, III, 20, 103, IV, 109, *see also* Latin Kingdom; papal injunction re Jews, IV, 8 f.; penalty for murder of, IV, 39; persecutions by Almohades, III, 123 ff.; Persian captives sold to Jews, III, 22; Persian law code adapted, II, 430, VI, 4 f., 321 f.; political and religious pressures on Jews, VII, 181; religious drama, VII, 308; safety in pretending to be Jews, III, 160; sectarianism, III, 160 f., V, 189, VI, 5 f., *see also* Sectarianism; and synagogue, VII, 84, 128; Talmud condemned, II, 427

—— *see also* Judeo-Christian relations; Muslim-Christian relations

Chronica Adefonsi Imperatoris, exhortations re Jews, IV, 132

Chronicles, Books of, I, 104, 341, 343; number of verses, VI, 238; Qimḥi's commentary on, VI, 467

Chronicles, historical, VI, 212 ff., 430 ff.; Austrian, VI, 437; oral transmission, VI, 433; on persecutions of Jews in the Crusades, IV, 285 ff.

Chronology, I, 130, 294, 354, II, 73, 158; based on building of Jerusalem, V, 119, 130; biblical, II, 139, 307, VI, 307 ff., VIII, 209 f.; of book of Jubilees, V, 167 f.; computation of, VIII, 202 ff., 377 ff.; dating systems, II, 116, 118, 376; difference between Jews of East and West, VIII, 204; disregard of, in aggadic works, VI, 181 f.; increasing concern for, VI, 201 ff.; Jesus' ministry and death, II, 64, 353; of Jewish history, VI, 232; of Masorites, VI, 445 f.; misconceptions of, V, 119 ff.; Parsee and Jewish, II, 16; problems of, in Book of Daniel, V, 156 ff.; Saadiah's Book of, VI, 211; of *Seder 'Olam rabbah,* (*q.v.*), VII, 15; World Chronology (*Seder 'Olam*), II, 141, 376, 384, V, 147 ff., 256, 366, VIII, 203 f.; "World Orders," VI, 200, 233; *see also* Calendar

Chrysostom, John, Saint, II, 139, 140, 156, 188, 390, 401, V, 358, VI, 153; on Christian visitors to synagogues, VII, 84; sermons, VI, 157; and use of Syriac, VII, 68

Churches: Armenian, Jewish purchase of, III, 160; ban on building or repair, III, 129, 134, 139; built by Justinian, III, 232; conversion into synagogue, III, 136, 296; depositories of valuables, IV, 84, 208; Jews blamed for destruction of, IV, 57; Jews' possession of objects from, IV, 202, 301 f.; and land reclamation, IV, 161; pre-Constantine buildings in Holy Land, II, 392; protection of, under Byzantine law, III, 189; use of, to denounce Islam, III, 123

Church Fathers, I, 399, II, 33, 51, 309, 374, 401; method employed, II, 320; *see also under* names of Fathers, *e.g.,* Augustine

Cibetum, Asia Minor, IV, 107

Cicero, I, 174, 215, II, 5, 16; attack on Jewish plaintiffs, I, 188, 380; quoted, I, 192

Cid, The, IV, 29, 246

Cidello or Cidellus, *see* Ibn Ferrizuel, Joseph

Circle, computation of area of, VIII, 154

Circumcision, I, 6, 157, 168, 176, 179, II, 78 f., 86, 132; Aḥai on, VI, 39; Christians and, V, 122 f.; of converts, I, 183,

Circumcision (*Continued*)
V, 219; forcible, I, 235; as instituted by Abraham, II, 137, 138, 383; of Itureans, I, 396; Karaite leaders on, V, 215, 217, 223; laws of, VI, 81, 103, V, 122 f.; poem on, VII, 267; Rome's stand on, II, 97, 105, 107, 109, 374; Samaritan, II, 29, 339; of slaves, III, 36, IV, 187 f., 193, 219; symbolism, I, 388
Cistercians: and the Crusades, IV, 300 f.; nun, Jewish convert, V, 113
Cities: Greek: on Mediterranean coast, I, 255; in Palestine, I, 225, 280; in Transjordan and Galilee, I, 224
—— Israelitic: in Palestine, I, 72
—— medieval: centers of commerce and culture, IV, 44; clerical and secular jurisdiction, IV, 58; constitutions, V, 62; custumals, IV, 13, 22 f., 41 f., 60 f.; government, VIII, 348; political role, IV, 60; privileges, IV, 23, 35, 38, 42, 67 f., 71 f.; *see also* Urbanization
Cities of refuge, *see* Asylum
Citizenship, in Roman Empire, I, 240, II, 372; after Judeo-Roman wars, II, 108 ff.; Aurelian, II, 109, 374
City state, I, 55, 234, VIII, 348
Civil rights, ancient: public-office holding, II, 110, 180, 181, 375; under Persia, II, 181; in Rome, II, 106, 108-10, 180, 374 f.; *see also* Self-government
Civil service, *see under* Public office
Civitas Dei and *civitas terrena,* VIII, 18
Clan, Israelitic, I, 51, 125, 351; cohesive force in Diaspora, I, 125, 127; dissolution, I, 55, 58; religion, I, 43; ties, cause of economic and social difficulties, I, 69
Clarendon, Constitution of, IV, 77
Classes, social: ancient distinctions, I, 75, 112, 160, 277 f.; antagonisms, II, 241, 244, 277; caste system in India, I, 297; in communal charities, II, 272; and Jesus, II, 67; misfits and outcasts, I, 275, II, 46; of Persia and Rome, II, 176; priestly hierarchy, I, 274; scholarly, and masses, II, 241; social leveling, II, 242, 279; solidarity of Jews, I, 281; stratification, I, 112, 271-76, 364, 413-14, II, 176; in talmudic Judaism, II, 234; *see also* Poverty; Socioeconomic conditions; Wealth
Classics, ancient, translations of, V, 84, VI, 264
Class struggle, *see* Social unrest
Claudius I, emperor, II, 91, 110, 198; census of Jews, I, 170, 372; edicts concerning Jews, I, 239, 240, 246, 248, 402, 403; quoted, I, 189; son of a Jewess? I, 190
Claudius Tiberius Polycharmus, II, 11
Clearchus of Soli, I, 184, 377
Clement III, anti-pope, IV, 8, 98, 105, 116
Clement of Alexandria, I, 184, II, 81, VIII, 133; Christian doctrine and theories, II, 161
Cleomedes, astronomer, I, 186
Cleopatra III, queen of Egypt, I, 215, 217, 381
Clergy: antisemitism, IV, 14 ff., 83 f., 129 f.; celibacy, V, 134; corruption among, III, 249; derelictions in enforcing canon law, III, 44; disposal of consecrated objects, IV, 301 f.; importance as preachers, VI, 155 ff.; mediation offered by elevated position, II, 168; and moneylenders, IV, 83 f., 204 f.; proselytizing among Jews, IV, 54 f.; relations with Jews, III, 50, 52, 175, IV, 37 f., 53, 84, *see also* Judeo-Christian relations; tax privileges to, II, 243 f., V, 76; *see also* Jurisdiction, ecclesiastical; Priests and priesthood
Clermont, France, III, 52 f., 253 f.
Clermont, Council of, IV, 96
Climate: influence on man, VIII, 226; "seven climates," VIII, 216
Clothar II, Frankish king, III, 47
Clothing: black, III, 140, 153; decrees re, III, 96 f., 126 f., 139 f., 141, 170, 298, VII, 145; yellow badges, III, 159
Cluny, monastery, IV, 10
Cochin, state, III, 114 f.
Cocks, sacrificed, V, 196
Codes, legal, VI, 4 ff.; Bashyatchi, V, 406; Byzantine, III, 181, 186, 187 f., 319; fundamental methods of, VI, 78; Hebrew-Aramaic, VI, 94; Jewish opposition to, VI, 107 f.; systematic, VI, 90-107, 371-81; Theodosian, III, 13, 25, 49, 187, 243, IV, 50 f.; *see also* Priestly Code; *and under* names, *e.g., Halakhot gedolot;* Justinian; Maimonides
Codices, II, 156, 390
Coele-Syria, I, 377

Cognition, theory of, VIII, 79, 318
Cohen, Hermann, VIII, 117, 121
Coimbra, Portugal, monastery of Santa Cruz, III, 160
Coins and coinage: ancient: Apamaean, I, 214, 393, II, 24; crown symbol, II, 332; early use, I, 318; of Flavian emperors, II, 92, 368; Hebrew, I, 130, 353; Jesus' "Render unto Caesar," II, 77; legends of Bar Kocheba, II, 98, 371; Maccabean, I, 225, 235, 369, 401, II, 36; metallic content, II, 245; Nerva's, on abrogation of fiscal tax, II, 106; Parthian, II, 174; priests' rights, I, 130, 166, 353; Roman, II, 175, 178, 368; Schechem's, II, 28
—— medieval, VIII, 255; Arabic, in Russia and Scandinavia, III, 339; Arabic, in Spain, IV, 210; of Cabillonum (Châlons sur Saône), III, 253; gold, IV, 29; Italian, mentioned in Spires privilege, IV, 273; metallic content, IV, 210 f.; Polish, with Hebrew inscriptions, III, 218, 338 f.
—— *see also* Currency; Money
Collectio legum Mosaicarum et Romanarum, II, 301, 431
Collectio veterum canonum ecclesiae hispanae, IV, 18
Collegia, Roman, I, 258, II, 260
Cologne, Germany, IV, 72, 117; burghers and Jews, IV, 100; burning of heretic, VIII, 46; fairs, IV, 175; Jewish community, III, 48 f., IV, 119
Coloman, king of Hungary, III, 212 f.
Colonate, Roman, I, 324, II, 258
Coloni: ancient (*ḥofshim*), I, 324, II, 257; medieval, III, 31, 38, IV, 153, 155
Colophon, Karaite, on scrolls of law, IV, 112
Colossus of Rhodes, III, 16, 235
Columbus, VIII, 215
Columella, Lucius Junius Moderatus, I, 251
Commandments, biblical, II, 308; adherence to, by the masses, VIII, 81; Aḥai's interpretation, VI, 38; 'Anan's Book of, V, 212, 219 f., 227; basic equality of, VI, 143 f., 396; clarified by Oral Law, VI, 300; concerning man's attitude toward God, VIII, 115; division of, I, 80, II, 421, VI, 90 ff., 102, 372, VII, 21, 276, VIII, 20; eternal validity of, VI, 98, VIII, 20; exemption from one in performance of another, VII, 135; in Genesis, V, 214; Maimonides' Book of, *see under* Maimonides; Nahawendi's Book of, V, 231, 259, 401; Noahide, VI, 5, 145; substantive import of, VI, 267; underlying reasons for, VI, 375, VIII, 118; *see also* Decalogue; Oral Law
Commandments, Ten, *see* Decalogue
Commenda, commercial contrast, IV, 200 f., 339
Commerce, *see* Trade
Commercial colonies, foreign, I, 175
Commercial instruments: check, IV, 213; dating of, VIII, 204; development of, IV, 209; letters of authorization, IV, 212 f., V, 27, 52 f., 303; letters of credit, IV, 348; letters of introduction, IV, 177; *see also* Contracts; Deeds
Commercialization, dangers inherent in, II, 254, 260
Commercial law, *see* Jurisprudence
Commodus, Roman emperor, II, 375
"Common sense," Aristotle re, VIII, 79
Commonwealth, First, V, 255; liturgical freedom, VII, 133; *see also under* Palestine; *also* Temple at Jerusalem, First
Commonwealth, Second, III, 19, 61, V, 255; apocalyptic visionaries, V, 140; apocryphal midrash, VII, 97; chronology of, V, 119; compilations relating to, VI, 159; dependent status of, VII, 290; and the exilarchate, VI, 200; history of, VI, 191, 210; hospices, VIII, 239; messianic statements related to, VI, 310; observation of new moon, VIII, 205; predictions of Daniel, V, 156; prophecy and, V, 158; restoration of Jubilee years, VIII, 210; rulers of, V, 9, 130; Sanhedrin (*q.v.*), VI, 24; sectarianism, V, 183; *see also under* Palestine; *also* Temple at Jerusalem, Second
Communal controls, IV, 146, V, 3-81, 178, 235, 293-325; academic independence, V, 13-20; adherence to V, 100; burials supervised, II, 287; Byzantine continuity, III, 190 ff., V, 54-58; central and local, II, 198-204, 403 f., V, 38-46, 49 ff., 199 f., VI, 18; collective leadership, V, 51; collective responsibility, IV, 39 f., 134 f., 137 f., 146, V, 66; and

Communal controls (*Continued*)
decline of academies, VIII, 4; economic controls, II, 252, 253 f., 261, IV, 185; elections to boards, V, 67 f.; exilarchate vs. gaonate, V, 20-25; vs. external interference, V, 69-78, 179; forces of integration and disintegration, V, 46-54; and the individual, IV, 222, V, 65, VII, 106, 133, VIII, 120 f.; and individual rise to power, IV, 38 f.; instruments of, V, 220; leadership supplied by, II, 204, 242, III, 119; loyalty and solidarity, I, 79, II, 291, III, 132, IV, 91, V, 80, VIII, 263; officials, V, 67 f., 71, 73 f.; Palestino-Babylonian conflict, V, 47 ff.; political and economic disintegration, I, 284; primacy of scholars, V, 32-38; residence permit, IV, 71, 185; responsibility for common welfare, II, 251, 269, 270, 271, 273, 291; self-government, III, 190 ff., V, 69-81, VI, 172, 213, VIII, 109; strengthening of traditional moorings, II, 290-92; Tannaim (*q.v.*), VI, 204; weakening of, V, 179, VI, 171; in Western democracies, V, 58-69; *see also* Excommunication

Communal property, *see* Property

Communion with God, *see under* God

Communism, I, 3, 30; Essenian, II, 49, 54; Mazdakite, II, 182, 222, 251

Communities, Jewish, I, 18, 124, 132-33, 241, 283, 351, 393; accretions through slavery, III, 111; Arab influence on modes of life, III, 283; attitude toward heretics, VIII, 69; biological strength, III, 110-14; bridge between East and West, IV, 3, 94, 149; centers of learning, III, 102, 104 (*see also* Academies); and congregations, I, 123, II, 199, 286; conservatism of leaders, VIII, 67 f.; and the Crusades, III, 102, 212, IV, 89 ff., 97 f., 103, 109 f., 119, 124-28, 147-49, V, 98 ff., 398; cultural contributions, III, 189, 209, IV, 24, 29, 32 f., 38, VII, 119, VIII, 220; delegations to pope, for redress, IV, 17, 97 f.; "democratic" life, II, 200-203, 288, 424, VI, 149; development into mercantile population, IV, 150 ff.; differences in structure and outlook, VII, 175 f.; dissolution into territorial units, V, 25; diversity in local observances, VII, 63, 107 ff.; economic success, V, 126 ff., *see also under* Wealth; effect of Christian proselytizing, IV, 55; effect of individual's behavior, VIII, 254; emergence in struggle between Byzantium and Islam, III, 220 ff.; environmental pressures, VIII, 5; expansion and influence in Western Europe, IV, 86-88; expansion under Islam, III, 99-110; and the Faṭimids, III, 105 f., 154 f., 171, 184; feudalistic restrictions on, VII, 176; fiscal contributions, II, 185 f., 243, III, 161 ff., 170 f., 190-95, IV, 12-20, 23, 81, *see also* Taxation; fortified quarters, IV, 35, *see also* Castle; funereal customs, III, 22, 297; *see also* Cemeteries and catacombs; hospitality to coreligionists, V, 53 f.; influence of foreign refugees, V, 68, 179 ff.; intellectual centers, IV, 7, 26, 34, 47 f., 112; intellectual life, III, 71, 173, 195, IV, 32 f., intercommunal cooperation, V, 63 ff.; intercommunal noninterference, VI, 393; international solidarity, IV, 176; intervention in monastic quarrels, IV, 84; Judeo-Christian communalism, II, 75; Karaite propagandists, V, 269 ff., *see also* Karaites; legal continuity, III, 185-90; linked by liturgical poems and responsa, VI, 111, VII, 144 f.; linked through travelers, VI, 219; location near church property, IV, 244, 266; and magic practices, VIII, 54 ff.; medical responsibility, VIII, 239, 404; Mediterranean, need for talmudic dictionary, VII, 13; Mediterranean, reunited under Great Caliphate, VII, 107; Monophysite charges of heresy, III, 5; Muslim belief in preordained poverty of, III, 159; ownership of property by non-Jew, III, 144; papal protection of rights, IV, 8 f.; payments to avert hostile acts, IV, 38 f., 55 f., 142 f.; persecution of, III, 123, 281; personal security under the Caliphate, III, 120 ff.; pioneering services, III, 197, 222, V, 62, 319; political basis of separation among, V, 47 ff.; powers of resistance, III, 74; preponderance of males, III, 252; prestige of Hebrew language, VII, 222; property rights, III, 143 f., 300 ff.; provisions in city custumals, IV, 60 f.; ransom of members, III, 78, IV, 119, 177 f.; refugees from Arabia, V, 373; resistance to serfdom, IV, 63 f.; on Roman trade routes,

IV, 175; and royal grants of transfer of persons and property, IV, 59 f.; royal protection, IV, 40, *see also* Protection; Royal alliance; rural, and religious observances, IV, 156 f.; and science, IV, 24, VIII, 171; scriptural guidance for, VIII, 119; and sectarianism, V, 178 ff., 194; secular music, VII, 284; separate quarters, III, 11, 232 f., 301, V, 79 ff., *see also* Segregation; sociopolitical security, IV, 7 f.; solidarity among, I, 175, V, 4, VIII, 122; status of synagogue reader, VII, 130; trade associations and guilds, IV, 171; trilingualism, VII, 5 ff.; use of Arabic language, III, 118, 170, VII, 6 f., VII, 8; vitality of, in Western Europe, IV, 20; in Western democracies, V, 68 f.; world-wide leadership, V, 5-13; *see also* Communal controls; *also under* respective countries, cities, institutions, and officials

Community of women, II, 183, 222, 251

Comparative religion, VI, 301, VIII, 68 f.

Competition, communal attitude toward, V, 68

Conat, Abraham, VI, 191

Concordance, talmudic, VII, 28 f.

Concubines and concubinage, II, 224, 409, 410; Christian, of Jews, IV, 269; combated by rabbis, I, 269; and slaves, I, 71, III, 111, IV, 190, 190 f.; *see also* Harem; Slaves and slavery

Condotta, treaty, IV, 27

Condottieri, groups of, I, 34

Confession of sin: in *Musaf* service, VII, 249; liturgical formulas, VII, 79 f., 92

Congregations, *see* Communities

Conrad III, king of Germany, IV, 119, 120 f.

Conscience, II, 78, 362, V, 66

Consonants, Hebrew, VI, 242, 448; in divine name, VI, 249; double pronunciation, VI, 250 f.; Semitic, VI, 242; weak, VII, 33 f., 41 ff.

Constantine I, Roman emperor, II, 172, 181, 187, 243; anti-Jewish laws, II, 399, 401; edicts concerning Cologne Jewry, II, 210, III, 48 f.; legislation on concubinage, II, 409; as *pontifex maximus* of state religion, II, 398; promotion of Christianity, II, 150, 152

Constantine VII, (Constantine Porphyrogenitus), Byzantine emperor, III, 155 f., 183, 211, IV, 238; biography of Basil I, III, 179 f.; edict on Venetian shipping rights, IV, 24 f.

Constantine IX, Byzantine emperor, III, 192

Constantine (Cyril), *see* Cyril (Constantine)

Constantine Africanus: a founder of Salerno medical school, VIII, 245; Latin translations, VIII, 243 f.

Constantinople (Istanbul), II, 151; in the age of the Crusades, IV, 107, 130 f.; Arab assault on, III, 97, 175 f.; "Book of the Prefect," IV, 170, 321 f.; custom duties, III, 192; earthquake, III, 16; Greeks' hatred of Jews, IV, 166; Hagia Sophia, III, 174, 232, 314, V, 343; Jewish community, III, 11, 175, 195, V, 55 f., 406; Jewish quarter, III, 232; Karaite community, III, 221, V, 234, 237, 272, VI, 173; Latin Empire, IV, 130; law school, III, 11; manuscripts, VI, 7; non-Muslim cemeteries, III, 137; riot of Jews in, III, 24; sectarians, V, 267; sieges, III, 199, 239; *strategos* of the Stenon, V, 57; threat of conquest by Persia, III, 18; early use of paper, IV, 320

Constantius II, Roman emperor, II, 172, 179, 259, 398, 399; missionary efforts in Arabia and Ethiopia, III, 66

Constitutio Antoniniana de civitate, II, 109, 374

Constitutio pro Judaeis, IV, 8

Constitutio Tanta, II, 425

Contracts, I, 332, II, 258, 304; *commenda,* IV, 200 f.; *fisqa,* IV, 201; labor, IV, 170; legal, and moneylending, IV, 200 f., 205; marriage, IV, 195 f., V, 265 f.; *suftaja,* IV, 213; trade, IV, 48 f.; witnesses to, V, 56; *see also* Covenant; Deeds

Controversies, socioreligious, II, 133, V, 82-137, 326-52; antisemitism, IV, 84, V, 125-34; arguments from Scripture, V, 86-94, VI, 298 ff., VII, 223 f.; and biblical anthropomorphisms, VI, 258; in Cairo, III, 160, V, 268 f.; calendar issue, VIII, 184 ff.; Catholic-Protestant, VI, 306; over Chosen People, VIII, 123; Christology and trinitarian dogma, V, 117-22; and conversion, V, 102; gnostic-Jewish, V, 106; interfaith, III, 133, IV, 77, V, 83 ff.; Jewish law, V, 123-25; Judaic, III, 175, 179 f.; Judeo-

Controversies (*Continued*)
Christian, II, 136 ff., III, 83, 215, 336, IV, 57, 117, V, 108-22, VI, 171, 481, VIII, 29 f.; Judeo-Muslim, III, 123, 133 f., V, 172 f., 209, 374, VI, 254, VIII, 29 f.; Karaite-Rabbanite, V, 269 ff., 277 ff.; in Khazaria, III, 198; over liturgical phrases, VII, 109; on Mazdakism, III, 255; messianism in, V, 119 f., 138 ff., VII, 178 f., VIII, 295; among philosophers, VIII, 66 ff.; polemics and apologias, V, 83-94; political and economic issues, V, 95-102; predestination and free will, VIII, 333; the rebel, V, 135-37; religious liberals and Zoroastrians, V, 103-8; sectarian, V, 186; on sex ethics, VIII, 52; street brawls and riots, V, 84 f.; talmudic, III, 233, V, 180 f.; theme in Hebrew poetry, VII, 177 f.; tradition vs. innovation in, V, 109 ff.

Converts and conversion: attitude of the Church toward, III, 44, 247, IV, 5-12; baptism, III, 41 (*see also* Baptism); Catechumenate, III, 36, 245; to Christianity, III, 10, 18, 19, 23, 32, 52, 176 ff., 182 ff., 193, 203, 220 f., 230, 241, 253 f., 313, 320 f., IV, 15 ff., 93, 189, V, 112 f., 126, VI, 257, VIII, 246, 249, 295; communal condemnation of, IV, 146; communities, loss of members through, III, 182, IV, 148, V, 135; denunciation of former faith, V, 97, 115, VI, 12; disposition of property, III, 143 f., IV, 279; exclusion from public office, V, 74; fees for, IV, 42; inheritance rights, III, 10, 158, V, 18, 299; to Islam, III, 95, 112, 113, 123, 125, 126, 132, 179, 272 f., 281, 300, IV, 152, V, 88, 102, 105, 179, VII, 304, VIII, 342; Jewish resistance to, IV, 92, V, 108, VI, 193 f.; of Karaites, V, 266 f.; martyrdom, in Spain, III, 39; among minority faiths under the Caliphate, III, 131; physicians among, VIII, 246, 249; reasons for, V, 113 f.; relapsed from, III, 14, 41 ff., 123, 127, 132, 248, 259, 295, IV, 5, 61, 77, 117 f.; religious discussions, V, 116; rights, III, 144, IV, 255 f.; Samaritan, III, 14, V, 171; scientific contributions, VIII, 141, 173 ff.; of slaves, IV, 187 f., 195; suicide preferable to, VI, 193 f.; tax concessions and, III, 96, 164, 242; use of olive press, III, 180, 315; in "Vision of Daniel," III, 179

—— conversions to Judaism, I, 171-79, 181, 373-75; III, 196, VIII, 77; of Alans, III, 208; of Arabs, III, 65; of Christians, III, 10, 22, 189 f., 238, IV, 9, 47, 52 f., 66, 116, 154 f., V, 113 f., VII, 256; circumcision, V, 219; instruction, VIII, 124; Jewish attitude toward, VIII, 123 f.; *see also* Proselytes and proselytism

—— forced conversions: III, 179 f., IV, 99, 104 f., 138, 189, VII, 177; acts of retribution, IV, 291 f.; Gregory I on, III, 28; inducements to, III, 14, 158, 179 f., 193, 242, 295; inefficacy of, III, 14, 291 f.

Convocation of "all the people," I, 73, 325

Convocations, academic, V, 19 f.; *see also* *Kallah*

Coponius, I, 263

Copper, I, 64, 256, 321

Copts, V, 95 f.; black garments, III, 140; church in Alexandria, III, 9; conversion to Islam, III, 123

Copyists, economic condition, II, 422

Corbett, William John, IV, 77

Cordova, Spain: Caliphate, III, 98, 160, 183, IV, 27, 194; delegation from king of "Gebalim," III, 210 f.; Jewish intercession for Christians of, III, 156; Jews of, III, 198; library, IV, 28, VII, 138; messianic movement, V, 200 f., 384; rabbinate, V, 54; redemption of captive scholar, V, 47

Corn trade, monopoly of, I, 261

Coronation, ceremonies, VI, 420

Corporal punishment, *see* Flogging

Corporate affairs, rabbinic regulation, II, 187, 261; *see also* Communal controls; Communities

Corporate personality, sense of, I, 135

Corporate responsibility, decline of, I, 135, 136, 146

Corpses: on battlefields, V, 346; wonder-working, IV, 299 f.

Correspondence: diplomatic, VII, 149; literary quality, VII, 165; privacy of, VI, 139

Corvée labor, I, 324, III, 192, 236, IV, 56

Cosmas, bishop of Prague, IV, 100

Cosmas Indicopleustes, III, 67, 259, IV, 167 f.

Cosmas of Jerusalem, Christian poet, VII, 142
Cosmic cataclysm, II, 59, 60
Cosmic Intellect, I, 174
Cosmocrator, term, II, 394, 435
Cosmogony and Cosmology, I, 48, 358, II, 310, 311; biblical and Babylonian stories, I, 47; Jewish story, I, 138; mystic, VIII, 22 f., 35 f.; Platonic, VIII, 318; restrictions on teaching of, II, 315; sublunary and superlunary worlds, VIII, 82; *see also* Creation
"Council of all of Africa," III, 230
Council of Nicaea, *see* Nicaea, Council of
Council of the Four Lands, I, 302
Councils, ecclesiastical, IV, 10 ff., 18, V, 64 f.; Agde, III, 36, 245, IV, 241; in France, III, 50 ff.; local character of, III, 253; provincial, IV, 17; Trullan, V, 109
Councils, communal, II, 199, 201, 404
Counter Reformation, Catholic, VI, 306
Counting devices, VIII, 353
Courtiers, III, 171, 216
Court poets, of Spain, VII, 146 ff.
Courts: ecclesiastical, II, 267, IV, 17, *see also* Jurisdiction, ecclesiastical
—— Jewish, II, 137, 265 ff., 419 f., V, 56, 317; 'Anan's rules, V, 220; Aramaic formula of edict, V, 5; exilarchic, V, 16, 115 f., 300 f.; geonic, V, 16 ff.; international rulings, IV, 176 f.; *see also* Judges and Judiciary; Litigation
—— Muslim, V, 293, VI, 324
—— Western, and clerical litigants, IV, 16 f.
Covenant, between God and Israel, I, 16, 48, 89, 90, 313
Covenant, Book of the, I, 80, 85, VIII, 231
Coyanza, *see* Oviedo
"Crab poems," VII, 197 f.
Crafts and craftsmen, I, 60, 256, 257, 260, IV, 170; hereditary, I, 69, II, 260; local concentration of, IV, 171; pre-Israelitic, I, 323; prestige of, IV, 167 f.; priestly, I, 258; ratio to other occupations, IV, 171; role in industry, II, 248, 249, 408; *see also* Industry
Cranmer, Thomas, I, 9
Crassus, I, 215
Creation, V, 357; biblical story of, VI, 227, 283 f., 470, 479, VIII, 6, 226 f.; chronology of, VIII, 86, 185, 201 ff., 375 f.; continuing, VI, 268; era of, II, 376, VIII, 202 ff., 207, 380; *ex nihilo,* VI, 146, VIII, 59, 69, 73, 87 ff., 99; imperfect, and perfect Creator, VIII, 91 f., 102; month of, VIII, 197, 204, 377; of numbers, VIII, 151; principles of, VIII, 15; purpose of, VIII, 101 f., 105 f.; questions concerning, VI, 303 f.; ten elements and ten instrumentalities, VIII, 7; theories of, VIII, 78 f.; things preexistent to, VIII, 22 f., 273; through emanation, VIII, 91; works of, VIII, 11 ff.; *see also* Cosmogony and Cosmology
Creation, Book of, II, 21, VI, 241 f., VIII, 11 ff., 24, 58, 61, 147, 185, 191 f., 280, 342; attitude toward numbers, VIII, 151; authorship, VIII, 25; "book, number, and word," VIII, 15; ideas of the earth, VIII, 212
Credit, letters of, IV, 348
Creditors: debt collection, II, 262, 417 f.; right to service as payment, I, 69; treatment of, II, 303
Credit transactions, II, 302; *see also* Banking; Moneylending
Credo, Jewish, VI, 60, 102; Muslim, VII, 85
Cremation, I, 382, II, 12, 423
Crescas, Ḥisdai b. Abraham, VIII, 63, 316
Crete, messianic movement, V, 167 f.
Crime: assault, III, 49, IV, 69 f., 129 f.; blasphemy, III, 132, 295; capital, V, 17, 134, *see also* Capital punishment; heresy, III, 9; Karaite decrees re, V, 240 f.; murder, III, 132, IV, 39, 50, 127 f., 133; religious, penalties for, III, 186, 193; sexual, III, 111 f., 143, 300; tax default, III, 309 f., 312; town's responsibility for unsolved, I, 79, 327
Crimea: Byzantine invasion of, III, 198 f.; inscription, VIII, 203; Karaite communities, V, 237, 247; Khazar assaults, III, 203; sectarians in, V, 271
Crispin, Gilbert, abbot of Westminster, V, 347; *Disputatio Judaei cum Christiano,* V, 114 f., 341 f.
Criticism, biblical, new approaches, VI, 291-311, 474-86
Crops, as tribute to conquerors, III, 79; *see also* Sharecropping
Cross, ban on display of, III, 103, 140, 142, IV, 183; ban on sign of, IV, 25;

Cross (*Continued*)
Christian worship of, V, 125; "True," in Ctesiphon, III, 22 f., 238
Crowns, mystic, VII, 78; adorning letters of the Torah, VIII, 29; symbols, II, 12, 14, 332; three, doctrine of, II, 45, 346
Crucifixion of Jesus, II, 64, 70, 71 f., 358; alleged contumely of Jews for, III, 34, 47, IV, 92, 103, 257, V, 108, 118, VII, 177; belief in Jewish reenactment of, IV, 102, 139; Karaites and, IV, 112
Crusades and crusaders, age of, IV, 89-149, 283-311; attacks on Jews, IV, 101, 119, 124-29, 139 f., 212, VII, 179; background of, IV, 94 f., 102; financing of, IV, 121, 123; as holy war against Islam, IV, 95; Flemish crusaders in Constantinople, IV, 130; glorification of death in, VI, 194; Hebrew chronicles, IV, 285 ff., VI, 217 f., 433; Jewish sources of food and supplies, IV, 102 f.; Jews and Muslims vs., III, 102; Karaites and, V, 398; marauding bands, IV, 106 ff., 126 f.; meaning of, to Judaism, IV, 147; and messianic hopes, V, 199 f., VIII, 295; portent of, VIII, 46; proselytizing, V, 135 f.; psychological aftereffects, IV, 139-47, 308-11; Saladin's appeal to Almohades, IV, 298; and Saladin tithe, IV, 81, 279; Saracen victories in Syria, IV, 309; secularization of, IV, 123 ff., 131; self-sacrifice in, VIII, 44; in Spain, III, 125 f., IV, 132; spread of mysticism, VIII, 31 f.; treaties with conquered cities, IV, 30 f.
—— First, IV, 94-106, 289-93, V, 199 f.
—— Second, IV, 7, 116-23, 299-302
—— Third, IV, 123-30, 302-5
—— Fourth, IV, 130 f., 305
Ctesiphon, Persian capital, II, 196, 204, III, 99; anti-Jewish violence in suburbs of, III, 58; complex of cities, III, 255; Cross carried to, III, 22; fall of, III, 18; *see also* Madaïn
Cuenca, Spain, *fuero,* IV, 41
Cultic prophets, I, 153, 365
Cults: of the dead, I, 148; local, I, 347; primitive, I, 44 f., 311
Cultural exchanges, I, 183-87, 228, 376-79
Cummian, Saint, V, 346 f.
Currency: depreciation, II, 245; of Palestine, I, 184; *see also* Coins and coinage; Money
Curse, biblical prohibition, V, 72, *see also* Blasphemy; protective, II, 336
Cush, Noah's grandson, I, 335
Cush, city, traveler's report of population, VI, 224; *see also* Abyssinia *and* Ethiopia
Custom houses, Jewish officials of, IV, 182
Customs, local: adaptation to, VI, 10; binding force of, VI, 63 ff., 121-30, 389-92; contrary to talmudic law, VI, 391; on death of a traveler, VI, 436; differences of, in Babylonia and Palestine, V, 179; Gentile, imitation of, VI, 123; halakhic miscellanies, VI, 75; historical reinterpretation, I, 4-10; legal adjustments to, VI, 121-30; and liturgy, VII, 106, 121, 273; origin in innovations, VI, 131; records of, VI, 129 ff.; and tradition, VIII, 5
Customs duties, IV, 65 f.; ancient Roman, I, 279, 415; under Caliphate, IV, 18 ff.; in Constantinople, III, 192; discriminatory, IV, 181 f.; exemptions from, IV, 78
Custumals, city, IV, 13, 22f., 41 f., 60 f.; European, VI, 129; French, IV, 268; "of Good Conduct," IV, 310; Italian, IV, 22; Sepulveda, IV, 253 f.; *see also* Fueros
Cutheans, II, 127, V, 173, 369, 372; *see also* Samaritans
Cycles, astronomic, VIII, 188 f.; of jubilee years, VIII, 191 f., 209; Sabbatical, VIII, 208 f.
Cyprian of Palermo, III, 242
Cyprus: Christianity in, II, 165; copper mines, I, 256; Jewish settlement, I, 375, II, 102, 371, III, 19 f.; Roman war, II, 94, 95, 96, 97, 102
Cyrenaica, I, 169, III, 108; Jews in, I, 262, 375; Roman war, II, 94, 95, 96
Cyril, bishop of Alexandria, II, 189 f., 391, 402, III, 90; action against Jews, III, 9, 24, IV, 5
Cyril (Constantine), brother of Methodius, III, 198; apostle to the Slavs, III, 208; controversial tract, III, 215; conversion of Russians, III, 221; journey to Kherson, III, 209; knowledge of Jewish letters, III, 209 f.; name, III, 209
Cyrillic alphabet, II, 208 f.

Cyrillonas, Syriac poet, VII, 92
Cyrus I, the Great, I, 102, 324, 355, II, 160, 213, III, 19; decree of, I, 130 f., 161, 353 ff.; Isaiah's reference to, V, 157 f.; professions of toleration, I, 117
Cyrus (Artaxerxes), legendary king of Persia, III, 19

D

Dagobert, decree on baptism of Jews, III, 47, 53 f.
Dagon, god, I, 63
Dahriya, Muslim school of atheists, VI, 298, 311, VIII, 72, 90; attacks on Islam, V, 104
Dahya (Dehiyya) bint Tatit al-Kahina, Jewish "priestess," III, 91, 271
Dairy products, ritualist requirements on, IV, 138
Daiva temple, destruction of, I, 348
Dajjal, Muslim Antichrist, III, 109; myths, V, 358, 386; *see also* Armilus
Dalata, Palestine, burial place of Elijah Gaon, V, 37
"Dalimil," Czech chronicle, IV, 103
Dalmatia, Jewish settlement, III, 210
Damascus: ancient: antisemitism, I, 177; and Aramaean monarchy, I, 67, 322; dating of documents, II, 376; proselytes, I, 182; Samaritans in, II, 34
—— medieval, III, 20; good will of religious minorities, III, 161; Grand Mosque, III, 134; Isaiah's prophecies, VI, 293; Jewish community, III, 104, IV, 108 f., V, 103; Muslim charges vs. Christians and Jews, V, 96; Nuri Hospital, VIII, 236; sacked by 'Abd Allah ibn 'Ali, III, 121 f.; sectarian communities, V, 177, 182, 193, 266 f., 271 f.; synagogues, V, 28; traditional tomb of Moses, III, 308; treaty of surrender, III, 165; 'Umayyad capital, III, 88, 97
Damascus sect (New Covenanters), II, 52-54, 62, 130, 223, 228, 348, 351
Damietta, Egypt, III, 155; Byzantine raid on, III, 315, IV, 334
Damwah, Egypt, synagogue, III, 106, 280
Dan, city, I, 64; images erected in, I, 66
Dan, tribe, I, 95, III, 116 f.
Danel, I, 307
Daniel, prophet, I, 116, 354; apocalyptic visions, VI, 309, VII, 169
Daniel, exilarchic pretender, V, 222
Daniel, Book of, III, 179, 183, 315, V, 140, 225, VIII, 132; exegesis, V, 156 ff.; four evil beasts, II, 59; Hereafter, II, 39; messianic computations, II, 61, V, 87, 119 f., VI, 308, VIII, 206
Daniel al-Qumisi, *see* Qumisi
Daniel b. Azariah, exilarch, V, 33, VI, 215 f.; elected gaon, V, 34 ff.; sons of, V, 36
Daniel b. Ḥisdai, exilarch, V, 8, 11, 310; on calendar regulation, V, 305; on priestly leaders, V, 36
Daniel the Babylonian, VI, 279
Danube, Jewish settlers in Roman communities, III, 207
Daphne-Taḥpanḥes, I, 111, 184, 347
Dara-Izdadwar, Persian princess, III, 89
Dar al-Babunnaj, Khazaria, III, 203
Dar al-Islam, and *dar al-ḥarb,* III, 95, 119, 130
Darazi, prophet of the Druses, III, 123
Dar'i, Moses, al-, V, 201 ff., 207
Darius I, king of Persia, I, 130, 349, 353, II, 213; and local theocracies, I, 131, 149
Darius II, king of Persia, I, 131, 349, 354; decrees, I, 148, 344, 361
Darius the Mede, I, 354
Darkness and light, VI, 305 f., VIII, 22, 34
Daroca, Spain, privilege, IV, 42
Dating systems, II, 116, 118, 376
David, Hebrew king, I, 22, 63, 127, III, 63; apocalyptic vision, V, 355; devotion to religion of Moses, I, 65; and Egypt's central administration, I, 74, 326; and Goliath, I, 332; harp, VI, 343; injunction to Solomon, VII, 174; Israelitic unity made permanent by, I, 61; Jerusalem as royal capital, I, 65, 312; Melchizedek's successor, I, 322; population under, I, 29, 84, 139, 320; as prophet, VIII, 132; Psalms attributed to, I, 322, VI, 307 f.; shield of, III, 204; snake symbol, I, 66, 322; violation of tomb, I, 410
—— House of, I, 93, 130, 158, V, 35, 38; 'Anan's descent from, V, 220 f.; calendar computations and, VIII, 373; descendants of, II, 196, 205, 403, VI, 200, 207, *see also* Exilarchs and exilarchate; dual line, V, 305 f.; and exilar-

David (*Continued*)
chate, V, 7, 141, 236, VI, 200; genealogical records, VI, 423; Hillel, II, 140, *see also* Patriarchate; Messiah as scion of, I, 99, 101, II, 59, 69, V, 147, 168, 184, 202, *see also* Messiah; Moabite branch, V, 90; non-Jewish wives, I, 321; and priesthood, VI, 215, 432
David, exilarch: penitential poems, VII, 145
David, son of Daniel b. Azariah: establishment of exilarchate in Fusṭaṭ, V, 36, 38, 41; marriage to Karaite, V, 38
David al-'Adeni: *Midrash Hagadol,* VI, 401
David al-Muqammiṣ, *see* Al-Muqammiṣ
David Alroy, *see* Alroy, David
David b. Abraham al-Fasi, Karaite scholar, VI, 28, V, 233, VII, 18, 38; on prophecy of Isaiah, VI, 308 f.; use of Masorah, VI, 252
David b. Boaz, V, 231; on marriage and inheritance rights, V, 242 f.
David b. Jacob, IV, 29
David b. Maimon, brother of Maimonides, III, 115
David b. Solomon (As-Sadid ibn abi al-Bayan), Karaite physician in Cairo, VIII, 247 f.
David b. Yehudah, exilarch, V, 10, 226; controversy with brother Daniel, V, 9, 15
David b. Zakkai, exilarch, V, 11, VII, 277; conflict with Saadiah, V, 21 ff., VI, 214; Ibn Daud on, V, 178; line of descent, V, 295
David ibn abi Zimra, VI, 15
David ibn Merwan al-Muqammiṣ, *see* Al-Muqammiṣ
David of Baghdad, IV, 46 f.
Day, "cosmic," VI, 232; planetary movements and, VIII, 185
Day of Atonement, I, 5, 144, 256, II, 256, 283, III, 315, V, 30, 195 f., 245 f., VI, 86, 125; date of, VIII, 188, 195; *Kapparot* ceremony, VII, 78; and liturgy, VII, 79; *Musaf* prayer, VII, 86, 91; prayers and *piyyuṭ* for, VI, 368, VII, 90, 92, 146, 178, 245, 271, 273; recitation of "Royal Crown," VII, 171 f.; self-mortification and, VII, 122; Temple worship on, VI, 390, VII, 271; traditionally adopted by Mohammed, III, 81
Day of judgment, annual, I, 5, 144
Day of rest, *see* Sabbath
Day of the Lord, I, 94, 96, II, 58, VIII, 191; *see also* Kingdom of God
Day of Vengeance and Recompense, II, 31, 341
Dead, the: public lamentation for, VI, 14; punishment for communication with, I, 82; *see also* Burial; Funerals; Mourning
Dead Sea, I, 257; caves, V, 188
Dead Sea Scrolls, I, 331, II, 52, 349, V, 192, VI, 158, 409, VIII, 368; biblical recensions, VI, 442; Isaiah Scroll, VI, 238; Jubilee cycles, VIII, 372; liturgical poems, VII, 270; Manual of Discipline, VI, 78; phylacteries, VII, 244; *see also* Qumran sectarians
Death, I, 9; and origins of sin, I, 139; poems on, VII, 267; unnatural, for sanctuary desecration, II, 93, 369; views of cause of, VIII, 259; *see also* Immortality of the soul; Resurrection
Debates, talmudic, III, 233; VI, 141 ff.; at *kallah* gatherings, VI, 111; Alfasi's method, VI, 85; rules governing settlement of, VI, 30 f.; Tam and, VI, 55; Yehudai's summary of, VI, 80; *see also* Controversies
Debir, population, I, 321
Deborah, prophetess, I, 64, III, 91; Song of, I, 141, 317, 318
Debtors: protection of, IV, 83; treatment of, IV, 62
Debts: bondage for default, I, 69, 268, II, 303, V, 224; cancellation of, VIII, 209; of clergy, IV, 83 f., 204 f.; destruction of records of, in York, IV, 126; of foreigners, I, 156; laws of, II, 301 f., VI, 132; owed moneylenders by Crusaders, IV, 121, 123; payment of, IV, 200, 202, 204, 206; registration of deeds of, IV, 304; sabbatical cancellation, I, 261, II, 262, 417; seizure of property for, I, 412, II, 303; transferral of, IV, 204
Decalogue: ethical, I, 49, 186, 227; abrogation of, VI, 145; Christians' view of, II, 381; elaboration of, V, 229; on inscriptions, V, 370; in Jewish theology, I, 25; Mosaic origin, I, 50, 314; oral and written transmission, VI, 427; prohibition of imagery (*q.v.*), I, 314; public recitation, II, 134, 381, V, 28, VI, 127, VII, 66; Rabbanite expositors,

VI, 289; revealed character of, VI, 144 f.; Saadiah on, VI, 296, VII, 141; *see also* Commandments
—— ritual, I, 50, 314
Decapolis, I, 225
Decimus Valerius Dionysius, II, 203, 404
Decorative arts, Graeco-Oriental, 10 ff.; *see also* Arts
Decurionate, III, 187 f.
Dediticii, the "stateless" class, II, 103, 109, 372
Deeds, of debts, II, 304, IV, 304; *dioqni,* IV, 212; formulas, II, 302, VI, 66 f.; Hebrew, IV, 320 f., IV, 34; use of Greek, II, 266; *see also* Contracts; Divorce
Deeds, Book of, IV, 34; agricultural transactions, IV, 316; *prosbol,* IV, 200, VIII, 209
Deir Qunna, scribes of, III, 151
Deities, *see* Goddesses; Gods
Delos, I, 377
Delphi, manumissions, I, 259
Deluge, year of, VIII, 203 f., 378
Demetrius I, king of Syria, I, 216; promise to free captive Jews, I, 259
Demetrius II, king of Syria, I, 216
Demetrius III, king of Syria, I, 217
Demetrius, alabarch, I, 261, 265
Demetrius, Alexandrian Jewish historian, VIII, 208
Demiurge, V, 380; and "cause of causes," VIII, 41 f.; equated with "prince of the world," VIII, 19; as "little Lord," VIII, 16
Democracy, I, 75, 209; ancient Hebrew, I, 48, 325
Demography, *see* Population
Demonology, I, 139, 358, II, 17, 32, 42 ff., 436; Babylonian-Persian, in Arabia, III, 82; in German pietism, VIII, 45 f.; *see also* Exorcisms; Incantations; Magic arts
Demons, VI, 103; disguised as black dogs, VIII, 368; female, VIII, 10; as intermediaries, VIII, 3 ff.; magic formulas vs., VIII, 233; in messianism, V, 142; obsession by, III, 180; tale of, VII, 311; talmudic characterization of, VI, 342; in Testament of Solomon, VIII, 283
Dental research, VIII, 262
Denys of Tell-Mahré, V, 9
Deportations: Assyrian, I, 95; Babylonian, I, 105-6, 115, 159; expulsion from Alexandria, II, 189, 402; to Hyrcania, I, 131, 354; Samarian, I, 95, 159
Deposits, business in, IV, 208 f., VI, 68 f.
Derekh Ereṣ, tractate, VI, 63
Dervishes, VIII, 83
Descartes, and Jewish formulas of doubt, VIII, 80, 318 f.
Descriptio orbis terrae, II, 246, 414
Desert, God of the, I, 48
Determinism, II, 41, VIII, 109 ff., 333 ff.; astral, VIII, 111
Deutero-Isaiah, I, 22, 152, V, 158; God of, I, 137-40 *passim;* life and work, I, 103, 107, 135, 342; on the Sabbath, I, 144, 145, 360; on sacrifice, I, 126; "Servant of the Lord," I, 231; universalism of, I, 157
Deuteronomic reformation, I, 83, 330, 332; fugitive slave, I, 71, 85, 324; Josiah's acceptance, I, 84 ff.
Deuteronomy, Book of, VI, 302; alleged copy in Moses' handwriting, VI, 243 f.; author, I, 153; date, I, 330, 332; and history, I, 15, 25; homiletical exposition, VI, 165; on image worship, V, 125; litany of curses, VII, 179; source of *Shema',* VII, 95
Deuterosis, see Oral Law
Dew, prayer for, VII, 98, VIII, 202
Dhaḥḥak, adh-, Arab poet, III, 264
Dhimmis: in Baghdad, III, 277; discrimination against, III, 139-49, 298-303; distinguishing marks, III, 140, 159 f., 170; economic role, III, 140, 150 ff., IV, 199, 225, V, 95 f.; mutual antagonisms, III, 160, 297; physicians among, VIII, 236, 253; physique of, V, 334; property rights, III, 146; status of, III, 97, 120-72, 149, 174, 288-312, V, 200; taxation of, III, 161-70, 308-12, IV, 152; treaties with, III, 123
Dhu an-Nun, alchemy and ṣufism, VIII, 225
Dhu'l-Nun al-Misri, Muslim mystic, VIII, 116
Dhu Nuwas (Marthad-ilan Ahsan?), Jewish king, II, 211, III, 66 f., 198, V, 111, 349
Diabetes, VIII, 262
Dialectics, in talmudic commentaries, VI, 54
Dialects: local, liturgical pieces in, VII, 67; West-Semitic, I, 36; *see also* Languages

Dialogues: between God and Israel, V, 154 f.; in religious debates, V, 114 f.
Diaspora, ancient, I, 16, 18, 24, 95-96, 112, 161, 225, II, 110; and antisemitism (*q.v.*), I, 188, 285; beginnings, I, 94, 105-8, 338; Christian, I, 29, II, 62, 82, 169, 366; community, I, 121-29, 350-53, II, 198-204, 215, *see also* Communities; divisions within, I, 281; economy, I, 259-62, 409-10; effects on tradition, VI, 100 f., VIII, 5; ethnic homogeneity, I, 131, 183; freedmen, I, 269; as *galut,* I, 30, 199; Graeco-Roman, I, 170, 282, 388, VII, 84, VIII, 57; growing dispersion, I, 105-8, 168 ff., 344-45, VII, 62, 245; growth of synagogue, VII, 62; intermarriage, II, 233; Israel's unity in lands of, I, 162; and Jewish role in cultural expansion, VIII, 256; and Jewish survival, I, 118; law and the, II, 77; linguistic assimilation, I, 185 f., 196, 212; little-known Jewries, I, 165; local autonomy, II, 198-204, 403 f.; and Maccabean uprising, I, 231; migratory movements, I, 172; neglect of Hebrew in, VII, 15; and Palestine, I, 215 ff., II, 82; and pariah caste, I, 297; under Persia, I, 372; and Pharisaism, II, 56; and Phoenicians, I, 374; pilgrimages to Jerusalem, I, 213, 258, 392, II, 108, 117, 118, 374, *see also* Pilgrimages; political inactivity, I, 217, 247; population, I, 170, 371, 372; prayers for rulers, VII, 265; rationale of, I, 135, 200; and rebellions against Rome, I, 217, II, 89, 96, 102; and religion, I, 100-101; Samaritan, II, 34 f., 341, 342; slaughtering, private, I, 148; statelike features, I, 18, II, 366; and ultimate ingathering, V, 176; *see also* Exile
"Diaspora nationalists," V, 221
Dicaearchia, *see* Puteoli
Dictionaries, Hebrew, VII, 20; earliest, VII, 29; rhyming, VII, 89; to the Talmud, VI, 28; of technical terms, VIII, 227
Didaché, I, 178, IV, 18
Didrachmon, I, 215; *see also* Temple, Second, tax
Dietary laws, V, 93; breach of, V, 279 f.; Karaite, V, 249
Dietetics, VIII, 243; treatises on, VIII, 226
Diocletian, emperor, II, 151, 178, 185, 260;
Dimi of Nehardea, R., II, 249
Dinawari, Abu Ḥanifa ad-, VIII, 386
Diocaesarea, name for Sepphoris (*q.v.*), II, 108
Dio Cassius, II, 98, 101, 102, 371 f., VIII, 185
Diocletian, decree on idolatrous worship, V, 172; price edict, I, 257, II, 250, 255, 415; prohibition of polygamy, II, 226; tax system, II, 263
Diodorus Siculus, II, 16, 410
Diogenes, I, 178
Dionysius, identification with Sabbazius, II, 24
Dionysius, head of Jacobite Church, V, 9
Dionysius b. Salibi, V, 345
Dioqni, commercial deed, IV, 212
Dioscorides, VIII, 65; "Book on Simples," VIII, 393; *materia medica,* VIII, 246; popularity of work, VIII, 246
Diplostoön, I, 257
Dirges, VII, 167; for apostasy, VII, 177; in Hebrew poetry, VII, 159 ff.; on Yequtiel's assassination, VII, 163
Disasters, natural, as messianic portents, III, 15 f., V, 143 ff.
Discourses, public: by scholars, II, 275; *see also* Sermons
Discrimination, anti-Jewish, II, 216, 241; *see also* Antisemitism; Public office
Diseases, VIII, 231; communicable, quarantining for, VIII, 239; psychogenic factors, VIII, 260; *see also* Medicine
Disinherited class exalted, I, 152; *see also* Poor, The
Disloyalty, *see* Loyalty
Dispersion, *see* Diaspora
Disputations, religious, *see* Controversies, socioreligious
Disputes, extra-legal settlement of, I, 329
Disraeli, Benjamin, III, 204, V, 202
Dissection, Jewish law on, VIII, 230 f.
Dithmar (Volkmar?), count, IV, 103
Divine grace, prayer for, VII, 244 f.
Divine mediation, II, 318; prayers for, VII, 66
Divine names, *see* Names, divine
Divine right of kings, VI, 10; and authority of Church, IV, 53 f.
Divine voice, II, 139, 383
Divorce, I, 112, 113, 114, 146, II, 221, 238, 291; 'Anan on, V, 221 f.; of child-

less wife, VI, 469; compulsory, II, 222, 411; of converts to Islam, III, 142; freedom of, V, 242; Karaite, V, 266, 281; laws on, III, 112, IV, 20, V, 18, VI, 64, 132 f., 390 f.; material restraints, II, 228; of merchants, IV, 184; movement against, I, 114; of tanners, IV, 167; writs, I, 395, II, 230, VI, 133, 139, 357, 394 f.
Doctors, *see* Physicians
Documents, II, 266; dating of, II, 116, 376; *see also* Deeds
Dodona, countess of Toulouse, IV, 202
Doggerel, VII, 315
Domesday Book, IV, 277
Domination, foreign, in messianism, V, 148
Domitian, emperor, II, 92, 104, 110, 121, 368, 372; in Melitene, III, 18; taxation by, II, 105 f.
Domninus, Jewish philosopher and mathematician, VIII, 57, 241
Donkey drivers, II, 261, 417
Donkey's load, measure for manuscripts, VII, 13 f.
Donkey worship, I, 193, 383
Donnolo, Shabbetai b. Abraham, Jewish scientist in Italy, VI, 470, VIII, 60, 253; Commentary on *Yeṣirah,* VIII, 30, 185; copies of writings of sages, VIII, 171; doctrine of Microcosm, VIII, 103; medical writings, IV, 44, VIII, 243, 244 f., 258
Dosa b. Saadiah Gaon, V, 14, VI, 23, 446, VII, 116
Dositheans, sect, II, 221, V, 173, 262, 369
Dositheus, priest, I, 220
Dositheus, Samaritan messiah, II, 33, 221
"Double faith" theory, VIII, 80
"Double truth" theory, VIII, 80
Doubt, religious, justification of, VIII, 80 f.
Dove cult, II, 30, 341
Dowry, II, 221, 236; return of, IV, 47 f.
Dramas: Greek, I, 189, II, 9; Hebrew, VII, 308; historical, V, 343; religious, VII, 308
Dreams: distinguished from prophetic visions, VIII, 129; interpretation, V, 260, VIII, 46; method of securing visions in, VIII, 28
Drivers' organization, II, 261, 417
Drugs: glossary, VIII, 252; international trade, VIII, 257; names of, VIII, 253; study of, VIII, 245
Drug store, treatise on management, VIII, 257
Druses, and Al-Ḥakim, III, 123
Drusilla, Herodian princess, II, 21
"Dual allegiance," I, 19
Du'ali, al-Aswad ad-, grammarian, VII, 18
Dualism, religious, V, 105 f., VIII, 296, 318; and light and darkness, VIII, 34; in magic arts, VIII, 11; vs. monotheism, VIII, 16; among Paulicians, VIII, 288; Zoroastrian, VI, 302, 305 f.; *see also* Gnosticism; Zoroaster
Dueling, IV, 40
Dukhifat, bird, V, 390
Dulebs, tribal union, III, 333
Du'l Qarnayim, designation of Alexander the Great, V, 329
Dumah, kingdom of, VII, 97
Dunash (Adonim) b. Labraṭ, Jewish settler in Spain, V, 46, VI, 220, 277 f.; accused by Ibn Ezra of blasphemy, VII, 51 f.; criticism of Menaḥem's dictionary, VII, 21 f.; criticisms of Saadiah, VI, 270, VII, 41; linguistic riddles, VII, 219; poems, VII, 22, 236; principle of triliterality, VII, 41 f.; synagogue reader and poet, VII, 146 f.; use of Arabic meter, VII, 22, 195; on verb forms, VII, 36
Dunash ibn Tamim, *see* Ibn Tamim
Dura-Europos, III, 296; church excavated at, II, 393; frescoes, II, 11, 14, 331, 346; inscription, VII, 128; synagogue, I, 14, II, 241, 346
Duran, Profiat, on Ibn Ezra, VI, 280
Duran, Simon b. Ṣemaḥ, V, 283; on mishnaic commentaries, VI, 61; on physician's responsibility, VIII, 238; polemics, V, 85
Duration of the world, computations, II, 16
Dyeing industry, II, 249, 261, IV, 166, 168; Jewish monopoly in Jerusalem, IV, 113
Dyes, durability of, IV, 168; production of, IV, 163

E

Eagle, golden: placed over Temple gate, I, 238, 402

Earth: division of surface, VIII, 214; habitable area, VI, 469, VIII, 215 f.; influence of heavenly bodies on, VIII, 175; measurements, VIII, 168, 213 ff.; rotation, VIII, 163 f.; shape, VIII, 212 f.; size, VI, 46, VIII, 162 f., 215 f., 360

Earthquake: at Antioch, III, 234 f.; churches and synagogues and, III, 232; Ḥananel on, VI, 45 f.; hazard to farming, IV, 153; at Laodicaea, III, 10; Palestinian, VII, 167

Easter: anti-Jewish outbreaks, IV, 55 f.; date, II, 188, 209, 401, VIII, 195, 369; and Passover, III, 11, 248, V, 303, 346, 410; "R. Eliezer" formula for, VIII, 190; *see also* Passover

'Ebedjesu, *see* 'Abd Isho b. Berikha

Eber, descendants of, I, 56

"Ebionite Acts of the Apostles," II, 75

Ebionite sect, II, 74, 348

Ecclesia, term, II, 394

Ecclesiastes, Book of, V, 225 f.; authorship of, VI, 160, 308; commentaries on, V, 231, VI, 270, 469, 477

Eclipse, lunar and solar, IV, 107

Economic conditions: adaptation of talmudic law, II, 262, 264, 291; of Alexandrian Jewry, I, 411; of ancient Israel, I, 67-72, 85 ff., 322-25; changing trends, II, 241-51, 413 f., IV, 150-227, 312-52; competition of burghers and Jews, IV, 60; decrees vs. Jews in Spain, III, 45; effects of Jew-baiting, I, 281; exilic period, I, 108-11, 115, 346-47; inflationary and fiscal pressures, II, 245, 414; Israelites' denunciation of system, I, 88; levies on populace, I, 272 ff., II, 82; and merchants and craftsmen, II, 204; position of women, I, 111, II, 236; procreation and, II, 220, 409; pursuit of goods glorified, II, 256; rabbis' psychological-ethical approach, II, 255, 415; religion and, IV, 221; social outcasts, II, 46 f.; talmudic policies, II, 251-55, 415-18; varied attitudes toward growth of poverty, II, 46; *see also* Agriculture; Banking; Business Transactions; Crafts; Poverty; Taxation; Trade; Wealth; *also under* Political; Social

Economic man, IV, 224-27

Economic theory, IV, 216-24

Ecstasy, prophetic, I, 334; revulsion against, II, 315; as source of knowledge, VIII, 113

Edessa, Christianity in, II, 165; III, 19, 239; elimination of minority groups, III, 57; Jews of, III, 23, IV, 114, V, 203

Edfu, ghetto in, I, 188, 380, 392

Edom and Edomites, I, 55, 56, 156, 162, 224, 307, V, 200; endogamous exclusion, II, 232; enemy of Israel, V, 161 f.; equated with Rome and Byzantium, II, 152, V, 134, VI, 309; expansion into southern Palestine, I, 106, 344; forcibly incorporated into Jewish body politic, I, 189; identified with Jews, V, 126; and Ishmael, VI, 407; list of kings of, VI, 309; messianic war on king of, V, 144 f.; world dominion, V, 143; *see also* Idumaea and Idumaeans

Edrei, Jewish tribesmen from Medina, III, 87

Education, II, 274-79, 421 f.; among Babylonian Jews, VI, 224 f.; communal ordinance, VI, 140 f.; curriculum, VIII, 146; Greek influence, II, 433; Jewish level of, VIII, 220; jurisdiction over, I, 150; for the masses, II, 279; medical, VIII, 236, 255; Muslim, VIII, 222; and "new" Torah, VI, 302; in poetry and language, VII, 150, 191, 223, 292; in preexilic Palestine, I, 323; prestige of learning, II, 201, 235, 276, 279; "reproofs of instruction," VIII, 37; for resisting propaganda, II, 133; responsibility of the academies, V, 18 f.; story of R. Kahana's son, VI, 183 f.; talmudic scheme, VI, 235; and talmudic study, VI, 34 f.; teacher-pupil relationship, II, 422; teacher's compensation, II, 278; universal for men, II, 279; women's, II, 239; *see also* Academies; Scholars and scholarship; Schools; Students; Study

Edward the Confessor, Laws of, IV, 79

Effigy, and sympathetic magic, IV, 92

Eggs, consumption of, V, 249

Egibi, House of, I, 109; pagan names, I, 346

Egica, king of Visigoths, III, 43; decree on converts to Christianity, III, 126; decrees vs. Jewish economic power, III, 45, IV, 156

Egilbert, archbishop of Treves, IV, 99, 290

Egypt and Egyptians: ancient: circumcision, I, 6; conquest by Asarhaddon and Ashurbanipal, I, 96; conscription of free laborers, I, 324; and consumption of sacred animals, I, 309; credit, I, 323; economic conditions, I, 110-11, 346-47; exilic or postexilic period, I, 111, 116, 118, 121, 165; exodus from, I, 308, V, 133, *see also* Exodus; group segregation, I, 117; interaction with Asia, I, 35, 67, 303, 322; Israelites in, I, 35-39, 96, 303-8, V, 167, VI, 303, VII, 181, 290; and Philistines, I, 320; property accumulation by small minority, I, 68; religion, I, 14, 45 f., 52, 199, 207, 311, 373; ritual, I, 40 f., II, 7; Semitic localities, I, 304; treatment of enslaved population, I, 35; *see also* Elephantine

—— Hellenistic and Roman, I, 165, 213, 282, III, 24; antisemitism, I, 188 ff., 381, 383, II, 89, 159; Christianity's slow advance, II, 164, 393; cultural influences, I, 165, 213, 282, 350; economic conditions, I, 251, 260, 266, 382; ethnarch, II, 198; incest, I, 146, II, 229; Jewish group life, I, 247, 281, 283; Jewish population, I, 168, 170, 172, 371, II, 102, 371; Jewish sanctuary, I, 14, 200; Jewish soldiers, II, 93, 94; Jews in semipublic occupations, I, 243; Judeo-Roman war, II, 94 f., 96, 97, 102, 370; language, II, 147; law and judiciary, II, 266, 418 f.; marriage, I, 146, II, 219, 233, 236, 408, 410, 412; nationalism, I, 381; and Palestine, I, 213, II, 94; Samaritans, II, 34, 341; sorcery and magic, II, 16, 21, 22; taxes, II, 105, 106, 373, 399, 413; *see also* Alexandria; Edfu

—— medieval: anti-Jewish riots, VII, 167; Arab penetration, III, 90 ff.; controversies over regional leadership, VI, 214; desertion of land by farmers, III, 168; employment of Jews in public office, III, 155; exilarchic office in, VI, 215; funds for Palestinian poor, V, 37; ideas of size of, VIII, 215; Jewish communities, III, 105 f., IV, 171, VI, 150; Jewish liturgy, VII, 119; Jewish places of worship, III, 296; Jewish refugees from Palestine, IV, 110 f., 113; Karaites in, V, 271 f.; Monophysitism, III, 239, 268; Muslim charges vs. *dhimmis,* V, 95 f.; *negidim,* V, 39 f.; "Palestinian" congregations, V, 49 f.; philological studies, VII, 19; poll tax and passport, III, 166 f.; purchase of church property by Jews, III, 136; rabbinic ordinances, VI, 134 f., 138 f.; ransom of victims of Crusaders by Jewish community, VI, 447; ritual, VII, 276; Samaritan communities, V, 177; scarcity of doctors and drugs, VIII, 257; trade controls, IV, 351 f.

Ehyeh, divine name, VII, 21, VIII, 28, 152 f.

Einlager, IV, 62

Eiovdea Isdraelites, I, 182

'Eis Theos (One God), II, 406

Eklogé, of Leo III, III, 185 f.; recodification of Byzantine law, III, 177

El, Semitic deity, I, 36, 44, 46, 158, 312, III, 93, VI, 409; worship of, I, 37; YW son of, I, 309; *see also* Names, divine

El-Amarna age, I, 55, VIII, 385; decline of commerce after, I, 60; letters, I, 34, 40, 309, 350

El berit, I, 61

Elchasai and the Elkasites, II, 348

Eldad ha-Dani, III, 286, 329, VI, 122; Book of, VIII, 179; genealogy, VI, 433 f.; itinerant storyteller, VI, 220 f.; on the Jewish tribes, III, 116 f., 208; on laws of slaughtering, VIII, 228

Elders, I, 73, 125, 274, II, 201

Elders, Jewish: appointment of, V, 75; authority of, V, 63; communal, V, 50, 54 f., 60, 322; Palestinian, proclamation of leap year, VIII, 194; titles, V, 55, 59

Eleazar, high priest, I, 197

Eleazar, scribe-martyr, quoted, I, 232

Eleazar b. Abina, R., II, 214

Eleazar b. 'Arakh, Tanna, II, 121, 314, VI, 181

Eleazar b. Asher ha-Levi, compilation of Yeraḥmeel's works, VI, 197

Eleazar b. Azariah, Tanna, II, 104, 134, 256, 346, 351, VI, 164; quoted, I, 254

Eleazar b. Pedat, R., I, 180, II, 119, 122, 127, 162, 175, 198, 208, 242, 312, 389, 435, V, 163, VIII, 6; on agriculture, II, 245; historical records left by, II, 113; on Pentateuch, VIII, 20; quoted, II, 153

Eleazar b. Perata, R., I, 265

Eleazar b. Samuel, responsum from Naṭronai, VI, 389

Eleazar b. Shammua', R., II, 126
Eleazar b. Yehudah of Worms, German pietist, VI, 140, VIII, 42; against innovations in prayers, VII, 101; on carrying of weapons, IV, 70; on struggle between God and Satan, VIII, 46; tribute to Abu Aaron, VIII, 43
Eleazar b. Zadok, R., II, 289
Eleazar ha-Qalir, *see* Qalir
Eleazar of Adiabene, I, 183
Eleazar of Bartotha, R., II, 271
Eleazar of Modein, I, 231, 399, II, 16, 98, 122, 271, 317, 435
Elections, to communal boards, II, 201, V, 67 f., 74
Elegies, Zionide, VII, 168 f., 197
Elements: basic cosmic, VIII, 23 f.; created on first day, VIII, 7; Hypocratic doctrine of, VIII, 318; philosophic discussions of, VIII, 222 f.; transmutation of, VIII, 224
Elephantine, Jewish military colony, I, 14, 110, 113, 121, 346, 350, 352; economic conditions, I, 110-11; ghetto life, I, 117; interest rates, I, 323; names, I, 121; papyri, I, 121, 345, 347 f., 351, 352, 360, VI, 66, VIII, 371; prayer and sacrifice, I, 350, 362; relations of Jews and Egyptians, I, 116; support Persian rulers, I, 190; temple, I, 128, 129, 351; women in, I, 113, 114, 340, 348, II, 228
Elephants, I, 77
Elesboas (Kaleb Ella Asbaha), Ethiopian king, III, 68
Eleusian mysteries, I, 181
Elḥanan, legendary Jewish pope, VII, 177
Eli, I, 351
Eliakim, *see* Jehoiakim
"Eliezer, R.," author of *Pirqe:* on Arab treatment of cemeteries, III, 138; formula for Easter, VIII, 190; on Gentiles, VI, 397; *Mishnah* of, VI, 406 f., 412; *see also Pirqe de-R. Eliezer*
Eliezer, R., poet, identified with Eleazar Qalir (*q.v.*), VII, 104, 264
Eliezer, R., son of R. Jose, II, 267; hermeneutic rules formulated by, II, 142, VI, 295
Eliezer b. Hyrcanus, the Great, R., I, 179, 181, 294, II, 9, 37, 104, 114, 116, 117, 121, 139, 148, 222, 227, 228, 237, 239, 296, 377, 408, VIII, 19; alleged pro-Christian leanings, II, 383; alphabet acrostics, VII, 257; controversies with Joshua b. Ḥananiah, II, 276; marital life, II, 221, 230, 409; prayer by, II, 120, 377; quoted, II, 315; a rich landowner, II, 276
Eliezer (b. Jacob?), R., II, 275
Eliezer b. Joel ha-Levi, IV, 36, 70, VI, 118, 138, 371; re *Baraita,* VI, 182; on communal representatives, V, 60
Eliezer b. Nathan, halakhist, III, 219, V, 320, VI, 118, VIII, 262; chronicle, VI, 217 f.; on disposition of land, IV, 158; *Eben ha-'Ezer,* IV, 288; on ordinance against polygamy, VI, 137
Eliezer ha-Qalir, R., *see* Qalir
Eliezer of Touques, VI, 350
Eliezer the Great, R., on the Midrash *Sar Torah,* VIII, 19; *see also* Eliezer b. Hyrcanus
Elijah, prophet, I, 61, 66, 78, 89, 314, II, 68, V, 140; alleged appearances of, III, 153, IV, 107 f., V, 167; Al-'Ukbari's allusion to, V, 195; apocalypse of, III, 16, 19; in folklore, VI, 186 f.; and Joseph b. Yehudah, VIII, 7; in liturgical poems, V, 155; in messianic visions, I, 99, 339, V, 147, 153, 202, 353, 384; and mysticism, VIII, 39; as "one head," V, 159; purism, I, 334; struggle against priests of Baal, I, 87; on Torah, V, 130
Elijah, Palestinian gaon, V, 36, 37
Elijah, unknown author of *Seder Eliyahu,* VI, 160
Elijah b. Abraham, V, 227 f., 388
Elijah Bashyatchi, *see* Bashyatchi, Elijah
Elijah b. Solomon, V, 33
Elijah Gaon, of Vilna, battle against Ḥasidism, VII, 183
Elijah ha-Kohen, V, 35 f.
Elijah-Phineas, eschatological role, V, 153
Elioenai, I, 119
Elisha, prophet, I, 66; and the poor widow, VI, 168; supports Jehu's rebellion, I, 89
Elisha b. Abuyah, II, 155; on injustice, VIII, 102; on Meṭaṭron, VIII, 280
Elisha b. Shinaya, III, 184
Elkasites, II, 51, 348
Ells, Palestinian, V, 27, 303, VII, 63
Eloah, I, 158

Elohim (God), I, 46, 312, II, 162, 311, 335; *see also* El
Elohist, I, 42, 309
Eloi, V, 120
El Shaddai, II, 311
Elvira, Council of, II, 188, 210, III, 35, 50, 196, IV, 42 f.
Elyon, divine name, I, 312
Emanation, doctrine of, V, 226, VIII, 22, 82 f., 91 ff., 101, 113, 318
Emancipation: from state and territory, I, 16-25; Jewish effects of, I, 3; revaluation, I, 21
Emblems: in catacombs and tombs, II, 11; over temple gate, I, 238, 402, II, 13; significance, II, 12 ff.; *see also* Images and symbols
Embroidery, gold, IV, 168
Emesa, revolt in, III, 140
Emicho, count of Mayence, IV, 102 f., 106 f.; defeat at Wieselburg, IV, 106 f.; in German folklore, IV, 140
Emigration: from Germany to England, IV, 80; from Khazaria, III, 206 ff., 215 f.; from Khiva, III, 197; from Nablus, V, 176; from Palestine, III, 48, IV, 113, 221; from Spain, IV, 21; *see also* Migratory movements
Emmanuel, I, 340
Emmaus inscriptions, II, 29
Emmeh, Mar, patriarch, V, 184
Empedocles, VIII, 91; *see also* Pseudo-Empedocles
Emperors, Roman: donations to synagogues, II, 187, 191, 402; imperial worship, I, 244, 404, II, 5, 99, 109; lists of, V, 354, VI, 212; *see also* Rulers
Employment: of Christians by Jews, III, 30, 38, IV, 15, 42, 62, 69, 155, V, 133, 240; of *dhimmis,* III, 140, 150 ff., V, 95 ff.; gainful, rabbinic theory of, IV, 220 f.; of Jews in official capacities, III, 150-61, 302-8, IV, 15, 26, 36-43, 251 ff.; and study, IV, 223 f.; *see also* Occupations
End of days, II, 58, 61, 73, 312 f., 318, 435, V, 160 f., VI, 309; cosmic cataclysm and redemption, II, 59, 60; date, V, 162, 167 f.; envisaged in terms of Temple's destruction, II, 83, 364; portents of, III, 15, 97, 176, V, 142 f., VII, 61; supremacy of Israel, V, 138 ff.
Endogamy, tribal, I, 146, 147, II, 231 f., 411
Endor, Saul at, VIII, 130
Engelbert, archbishop of Cologne, V, 113
England: blood accusation against Jews, IV, 135 ff.; debate on episcopacy, II, 366; effect of Crusades, IV, 148; Jewish architecture, VIII, 159; Jewish communities, IV, 75-86, 276-82; Josephus read, II, 379; landholding and inheritance rights, IV, 156, 163 ff.; massacres of Jews, IV, 124 ff., 302 ff.; population of, III, 100; royal control over Jews, IV, 203 f., V, 63
Enlightenment, era of, VIII, 262 ff.
Enoch, prophet, VI, 437; astrological teachings attributed to, VIII, 176, 178 f.; identification with Idris and Hermes, VIII, 10, 134, 366; Muslim name for, VI, 449; piety, I, 44; roles attributed to, VIII, 282
—— Book of, II, 335, III, 211, VIII, 11, 178, 189; excerpt, II, 39; messianic prophecy, II, 59; speculations on angels, II, 18, 335
Environment: communal adjustment to, V, 3 ff.; effect on aggadic studies, VI, 152 ff.; influence on Jewish philosophy, VIII, 301 f.; Muslim, effect of, V, 371
Epaphroditus, II, 157
Epelytos, I, 375
Ephesus, Third Council of, III, 5
"Ephetics," VIII, 79
Ephraem, Saint, VII, 93, 136; liturgical poems, VII, 84 f., 196; sermons in hymn form, VII, 82
Ephraim, disciple of Alfasi, VI, 87
Ephraim, tribe, I, 65
Ephraim b. Azariah ibn Sahalun, V, 203
Ephraim b. Isaac of Ratisbon, VI, 391
Ephraim b. Jacob, of Bonn, VI, 218; "Book of Remembrance," IV, 119, 124, 307; chronicler of massacres, VII, 179
Epictetus, II, 157
Epicureans, I, 208; defined, II, 278; world outlook, II, 310, 434
"Epicuros," I, 208
Epicurus, VIII, 323
Epicycles, VIII, 164 f.
Epigrams: ascribed to Sirach, VI, 408 f.; on grammar, VII, 242; of Ibn Nagrela, VII, 138; use of, in poetry, VII, 164 ff.
Epigraphy, II, 11-15, 331-34; early Arabic, III, 61; *see also* Inscriptions
Epiphanius, Saint, II, 29, 123, 393

Episcopacy, II, 366
Episcopus, Jewish office, *see* Presbyter
Epistemology, VIII, 78 ff.
Epistle of Barnabas, II, 137
Epistle of Jeremy, I, 197
Epitaphs, *see* Inscriptions
Equality of rights, I, 243; *see also* Emancipation; Rights, legal
Equator, measurement, VIII, 213
Equinox, vernal, VIII, 368
Equity, II, 304
Eratosthenes, VIII, 168
Erech, III, 64
Erfurt, Council of, III, 182
Erfurt, Diet of, IV, 25, 66
Erigena, John Scotus, VI, 273
Erwig, king of Visigoths, III, 43; appeal to Toledan Council, III, 44; and negligent clergy, III, 45
Esau, V, 90; and Edom, V, 129; equation with Christendom, V, 93; Gregory I on, III, 29; Rome's ancestor, VI, 437
Esau, Mount of, I, 344
Eschatology, II, 313; divergent, I, 207-9, 390-91; in German Ḥasidism, VIII, 47; and messianic age, V, 147 ff.; Near Eastern, V, 358; Parsee computations, II, 435 f.; in Pharisaic and Persian philosophies, II, 318; in prophetic writings, I, 99; Samaritan, V, 371; *see also* End of days; Hereafter; Immortality of the soul; Punishments; Resurrection
Eshmunazar, king of Sidon, I, 162, 367
Eshnunna, I, 327
Eshtemo'a, II, 332
Esoteric movements, II, 314, 315, 435
Essenes, VIII, 109; and Cave Men, V, 379 f.; determinism, II, 41; elements that survived, II, 51, 130, 348; heroism, I, 233; ideology and way of life, II, 48-51, 347 f.; influence of 'Anan, V, 391; meat consumption forbidden? I, 407; name, II, 347; oaths, II, 48, 347; pacifism, II, 50; pregnant wife safeguarded, II, 221; sexual abstinence, II, 218; Therapeutae, an analogous order, II, 51, 347; wing of Pharisaic movement, II, 48, 342, 349 f.; writings about, II, 49
Estates: confiscated from Jews, II, 244; increase in number and size, I, 277; *post mortem* distribution of, VI, 85, VIII, 153 f.; settlement of, V, 300 f.
Estates, the, in European feudalism, IV, 87
Estella, IV, 35
Esther, Book of, I, 169, 345, 394, 411, IV, 92, VI, 188; Scroll of, VI, 185, 403, 431; Targum on, VI, 403
Etamps, France, expulsion of Jews, IV, 269
"Eternal" life of the nation, I, 9, 12
Eternity, II, 311; of Israel, II, 153, 389, 396; of Jewish law, II, 161; *see also* Immortality of the soul
Ethical monotheism, I, 10, II, 5
Ethics, I, 10-16, 47, 294-97; contribution of Judaism, I, 294; and human conduct, VIII, 62 ff.; individual and social, VIII, 117 ff.; Jewish, adopted by non-Jews, I, 294; in Jewish medical writings, VIII, 257 f.; in Jewish pietism, VIII, 48 ff.; and law, I, 227, II, 308; in mystic literature, VIII, 21 f.; and reason, VIII, 113 f.; and sex behavior, II, 221, VIII, 53; theme in poetry, VII, 163 ff.; 187 f.; *see also* Moral law
Ethiopia (Abyssinia), I, 169, 372; Falashas in, III, 116; ideas of size of, VIII, 215; Jews in, II, 211 f., 407; native land of Prester John, VI, 434; raids in Arabia, III, 68; slave girls, II, 238
Ethnarch, office of, II, 198, V, 39
Ethnic groups, I, 24, 52; Jewish, in Egypt, I, 117, 283; partition of Palestine among, I, 37, 55; *see also* Ghettos; Segregation
Ethnic unity, I, 39-43, 97, 163, 180, 308-10, 338, 339, 383; conditions in Exile, I, 134; controlling significance, I, 4, 31, 61, 94, 132, II, 227; dual allegiance and, I, 19; exclusivism, I, 155-58, 365-66; marriage as foundation of, II, 217; a positive principle, I, 98, 181; religious vs. territorial principle, II, 290; weakened at times, I, 54, 58, 212
Ethnology, Yosephon's efforts in, VI, 226
Ethnos, I, 168
Etiquette, court, under Faṭimids, III, 171
Etymology: Arabic, VII, 232; in biblical exegesis, VI, 166; Greek, VII, 232
Eucharist, I, 193, II, 71, 75; Saadiah's allusion to, VI, 303
Euclid, teachings preserved by Bar Ḥiyya, VIII, 157
Eudaemonistic progress, I, 21

Eudes, *see* Odo
Eudoxios, II, 12
Eugenics, talmudic, II, 229-37, 411-12
Eugenius III, pope, IV, 7, 59
Eulogy, VII, 98 f.
Eunuchs, II, 219; trade in, IV, 191 f.
Euphrates Valley, II, 261; biblical punctuation in, VI, 238, 241; olive trees, II, 247; settlements, II, 206, 405; *see also* Babylonia
Eupolemus, I, 185, 207, 234, 378
Europe: Continental crusades, IV, 131 f.; influence of Jews, II, 264; travels in, VI, 221 f.
—— Eastern, III, 171-222, 313-40; Crusaders in, IV, 106; effect of clash with West, IV, 91 ff.; importation of labor, IV, 172
—— Southeastern: Jewish settlements in, I, 283
—— Western, III, 24-54, 240-54, IV, 3-88, 235-82; contribution of Jewry to, IV, 86 f.; difficulties of book production, VII, 136 f.; establishment of rabbinate, V, 63; exegetical tradition, VI, 48 ff.; expansion of Oriental trade, IV, 172; feudalism, VII, 176; gravitation of eastern Jewry to, IV, 147 ff.; halakhic miscellanies, VI, 72 ff.; isolation from East, VIII, 43; Italo-Byzantine influences on, VIII, 31 f.; Jewish communal democracies, V, 58-69; Jewish settlement in, IV, 90 f., VI, 437; liturgical compilations, VII, 121 ff.; moneylending, IV, 205 ff.; pioneering agricultural services to, IV, 161; political implication of the Crusades, IV, 124; slavery in, IV, 188 ff., 333; slave trade, IV, 194 ff., 335 f.; written Hebrew in, VII, 47 f., 54
Eusebius of Alexandria, VI, 160
Eusebius of Caesarea, I, 196, 246, 354, II, 27, 94, 131, 144, 161, 372, 379, 389, 401; on language of the Gospels, II, 66, 355
Eustratios, Saint, IV, 192
Euthinos, priestly family, I, 270
Euthymios Zigabenos, V, 338, 348
Eutychius, III, 22
Eve, allegorical meaning of, VIII, 86, 338
Evidence, rules of, IV, 277, 281, VI, 66
Evil, I, 7, VIII, 102
Evil spirits, belief in, VIII, 45 f.; and disease, VIII, 234, 262; magical control of, VIII, 8 ff.; *see also* Demons
Evil-Merodach, king of Babylonia, I, 115
Evreos, Thomas, *silentiarius,* III, 235
Exaltation, mystic, VIII, 279
Excavations, *see* Archaeology
Excommunication: Christian: for employment by Jews, IV, 269; for preferring Jewish witnesses, IV, 16; threat of, to quell riots, IV, 290; for violation of protected rights, IV, 8 f.
—— Jewish, II, 192, IV, 39, V, 17, 65, 207, 220, VI, 134 f.; 'Anan's use of, V, 220; for changes in pattern of prayers, VII, 102; exemption through a hundred men, VI, 136, 138, 394; of Karaites, V, 275 f.; for litigation, V, 5; by a *nasi,* V, 47 f.; for opposing a gaon, V, 53; for recourse to Gentile courts, V, 223; of Samaritans, V, 172; for violation of dietary laws, V, 279; and violation of loyalty oath, V, 36; *see also* Curse
Exegetes and exegesis: biblical, II, 141-47, 385-87, VI, 274-311, 463-86; Benjamin b. Moses and, V, 225; contradictory interpretations, VI, 471 f.; eastern, VI, 281; harmonization, VI, 304 f.; historical, VI, 306-11, 484 ff.; individualistic, VI, 471; Judeo-Christian, VI, 274 f., 304; Karaite, V, 389; legal safeguards of works of, VI, 313; methodology, VI, 286 f.; Muslim, VI, 282 f., VII, 219; Palestino-Babylonian, VI, 305; and philology, VII, 37 f., 43, 52, 219; prolixity, VI, 282; and scientific exploration, VIII, 218; *see also* Bible; Interpretation, biblical; Talmud
Exhortations, VI, 165
Exilarchs and exilarchate, II, 195 ff., 200 f., III, 288; and the academies, II, 291, V, 14, 20 ff., VI, 116; appointment of local judges, V, 50; Arab superstition and, V, 297; authority of, V, 8, 12, 198, VI, 18, 199, 216; Bustanai, V, 141; and the Caliphate, V, 5 ff., 11 f.; establishment in Egypt, V, 36, 38, VI, 215; hereditary principle vs. election, V, 6, 21, 211, 222, 237, VI, 36; installation, VI, 214, VII, 284; Karaites vs., V, 210, 230 ff., 236; omission of, in prayer, VII, 245; religious disputations before caliphs, V, 85; revenues, V, 12 f.,

Exilarchs and exilarchate (*Continued*) 236 f.; rivalry with "dynasty" of patriarchs, II, 198 ff., 205, 403; weaknesses of, V, 8 ff., 179

Exile: Babylonian, I, 18, 22, 106, 345, II, 320, VII, 290, VIII, 125, 205; and assimilation, I, 105, 118; as crucial test, I, 102-33, 341-55; holiness on national scale, I, 154; insecurity, I, 158; leaders' tenacity, I, 160; legislation during, I, 115, 348 f.; as penalty for sins, I, 135, 199, 399; resemblance to age of Moses, I, 143; return to Palestine, I, 158 ff.; social transformations in, I, 112; surplus of men, I, 113; survival in, I, 104, 105, 134

—— Second, III, 195; computations of duration of, V, 153 f., 167 f., 363; connotations of name *galut,* III, 171, 195; effect of, VI, 230 f., VII, 290; as Jewish mission, V, 100 f.; life in, V, 129 f., VI, 438; and messianic ingathering, V, 203; priestly dues in, V, 236; problem of, V, 99 ff., VII, 177, VIII, 126; and repatriation, IV, 62 f.; as retribution, V, 130, VI, 233 f.; in sacred poetry, VII, 181; and sexual transgression, III, 291 f., 300; *see also* Diaspora

Existence, conceptual vs. real, VIII, 88

Exodus: from Egypt, I, 5, 16, 32, 39; Christian charges and, V, 133; creation displaced by, I, 47; date, I, 307; in Hellenistic literature, I, 189; in Jewish chronology, VIII, 205; and later conceptions of God, I, 46; national holiday commemorating, I, 148; non-Israelitic Hebrews among refugees, I, 57; and population under David, I, 320; work of Moses, I, 46-53

—— Book of, commentaries on, VI, 51, 296

Exorcisms and incantations, I, 139, 329, 359, II, 19 ff., 189, 336, 401; by Jesus, II, 67; validity of, II, 316

Expansion of Judaism: natural increase and conversions, I, 171-79, 373-75; *see also* Population

Expectoration, during prayer, VII, 251

Expositio totius mundi et gentium, II, 414

Expropriation, I, 68; of private property, IV, 13, 34, 82, V, 320; right of, II, 252

Expulsion of Jews, IV, 5, 148, 156; from Alexandria, II, 189, 402; as alternative to forced conversion, IV, 6, 57; from Baghdad, III, 100; from Bologna, IV, 27; from England, IV, 76, 84; from France, IV, 61, 80, 156; from Italy, IV, 25 ff., 26; from Khaibar, III, 80; in messianic rationale, V, 162; from parts of Germany, IV, 26, 66, 73, 92, 271; from Sens, IV, 56; *see also* Deportations

Extradition, treaties of, IV, 80

Extramarital relations, II, 225

Eye, diseases of, VIII, 243, 405

Eye doctor, fees, VIII, 254 f.

Ezechielos, I, 189, 197, 381, 385, II, 9

Ezekiel, prophet, I, 103, 342, II, 117; concept of God, I, 134 f., 137 f.; individualism, I, 136, 138, 357; against Israel's claim to special treatment, I, 138; law for the restoration, I, 143; leadership, I, 122, 135; personality, I, 356; recollection of the Temple, I, 122, 350; ritualistic injunctions at variance with the Torah, I, 154; sages mentioned by, I, 307; on segregation of aliens, I, 156; vision of, I, 335, 356, II, 315; wrath provoked by "idols," I, 335

—— Book of, I, 341, II, 436; Pope Gregory's homilies on, III, 29; and proclamation of leap year, VIII, 194; vision of the Chariot, VI, 161, VIII, 5

Ezion Geber, I, 64, 321, 326

Ezra, scribe, I, 106, 114, 116, 125, 142, 160, 162, 180, II, 117; association with Babylonia, II, 206; first scribe, I, 397; historicity, I, 341; no new law, VI, 145; Pentateuch known through, I, 345; racialist extremism, I, 147, 163; on reading the Torah, VI, 256; recension of Torah, VI, 254; restoration under, I, 103; 161; service to mankind, I, 158

—— Books of, II, 60, 351, III, 61; authenticity, I, 104, 343

F

Fables, collections of, VII, 189 f.

Fadl ibn Yaḥya al-, 'Abassid courtier, III, 149

Fadus, Cuspius, I, 239

Fairs, IV, 182 f.; Jewish merchants and, IV, 175; moneylending at, IV, 344; money transfers, IV, 213; and religious holidays, IV, 175, 220

Faith: biblical synonyms, VI, 296; a

democratic possession, I, 154; history and, I, 296; law and, II, 78, 79; and reason, VI, 108 f., VIII, 55-137, 296-346; *see also* Religion
Falasha Jews, I, 169, II, 211, 407, III, 116
Fallowness, Jewish year of, I, 333, 382, II, 263, VI, 307, VIII, 208 f.
Family life, ancient, I, 31, 50 f., 328, 361; in Diaspora, I, 125, 127; halakhic works on, VI, 64; household management, IV, 218; importance in community, I, 361, II, 219, 291, V, 133 f.; and local customs, VI, 122; marriages within family, II, 229 ff., 411; Palestino-Babylonian differences in, V, 29 ff.; position of children, I, 361; position of father, I, 310, II, 309; position of mother, I, 43, 310; procreation, I, 31, II, 210, 218, 219; purity, II, 234; regulation of, I, 145 ff., II, 217 ff., 408 ff., VI, 68, 74; rituals, I, 148, 353; sectarian deviations from law of, V, 190; and sex, VIII, 53; and slaves, IV, 193, 196; taxation, IV, 154; and tribe, I, 317
Famine, in Jerusalem, I, 414; transportation difficulties, II, 245
Fanaticism, religious, in the Crusades, IV, 90, 133 ff.
Farabi, VIII, 65, 122; commentaries on Plato, VIII, 61; influence on Ibn Gabirol, VIII, 325; on theology and politics, VIII, 348
Faraj ibn Salim, *see* Farragut
Far East: early penetration by Jews? II, 212; Jewish trade with, IV, 175; *see also* China; India
Farghani, al-, VIII, 360; comparative sizes of fixed stars, VIII, 162 ff.
Farḥi, Estori, V, 262
Farmers: ancient, I, 71, 277 ff.; compliance with law, II, 242; education of, I, 68, 323; poverty, I, 277, II, 250, 257; public discourses for, II, 275; tithes and heave-offering, I, 277, 279, II, 262
—— medieval: desertion of land, III, 168; and expansion of Islam, IV, 151 f.; land tax, III, 168; and length of synagogue service, VII, 69; migration, III, 168, V, 176 f.; tithes, V, 236; *see also* Agriculture; Fruit culture; Land; Landlords; Landownership
Farm laborers, *see under* Agriculture; Peasants
Farragut (Faraj ibn Salim), Sicilian Jew, VIII, 242
Fars, Persia, mixed population, III, 109
Fast days and fasting, I, 123, 294, II, 134, 140, 143, 182, 380, 385, V, 214, 216, 245, VI, 330 f.; attitude of German rabbis toward, IV, 145; of Heraclius, III, 23; merits of, VIII, 119; Muslims and, VI, 14; Ninth of Ab, IV, 145; Nisan, V, 216, 392; purposes of, IV, 103 f., 109, VI, 16, 86; scriptural readings, VII, 73; self-mortification through, VI, 331; Sivan 20, IV, 138, 145; Yehudah's observance of, VIII, 49
Fatalism, in Muslim theology, VI, 151
Fate, human, astrology on, VIII, 178 f.
Father: creator known as, II, 309; in family relationship, I, 310, II, 309; *see also* Family life
Fatherhood of God, *see* God
"Fathers, merit of the," doctrine, II, 42, 346
Faṭima, daughter of Mohammed, III, 107, 305
Faṭimids, and descent from Faṭima, III, 107, 305; in Egypt, III, 289; emphasis on court etiquette, III, 171; flight of Jews to Byzantium, III, 184; and Jews, III, 105, 154 f., 170, V, 40 f.; Palestinian academies and, V, 33; royal sermons, VI, 153 f.
Fatwa, term, VI, 110
Faustus, the Manichaean, II, 154
Fayyum, I, 266, VII, 19
Fayyumites, V, 197
"Fear of the Lord," I, 11
Feast of Tabernacles, I, 5, 73, 235, 254, V, 217, 279; agricultural labor and, IV, 315; Canaanite origins, I, 72; date of, VIII, 185 f., 188; names referring to, I, 120; poems for, VII, 101, 170
Feast of Unleavened Bread, I, 131, 148; *see also* Passover
Feasts, I, 220; *see also* Festivals
Fees, medical, VIII, 232 ff.
Feet, washing of, VI, 14
Feivish, name, I, 119
Felix, Roman procurator, II, 21
Female deities, *see* Goddesses
Ferdinand III, king of Spain, IV, 28
Fermosa (Raquel), IV, 37
Ferreolus, bishop in Uzès, III, 253

Ferruziel, Solomon: assassination of, IV, 253; journey to Aragon, IV, 252
Fertile Crescent, I, 350; *see also under* Assyria; Babylonia
Fertility cults, I, 361; Canaanite, I, 137, 357; repudiated by prophets, I, 87
Festival of Heracles, I, 229
Festival of the Rejoicing in the Torah, poem for, VII, 282
Festival of Weeks, III, 106, V, 195, 215, 376, 404, VI, 267, VII, 172; *Musaf* services, VII, 276; Saadiah's prayer for, VII, 257
Festivals, I, 5, 58, 125, 220, 395, II, 45; clan and family religious, I, 55; mating, I, 294; *see also* Feast; *also under* respective holidays
Festive seasons, Parsee, II, 317
Feudalism: and agriculture, IV, 153 ff.; Carolingian institutions, IV, 49; vs. centralized controls, III, 185, IV, 65; decline of slave trade and, IV, 187; lack of personal security, IV, 35; and landownership, II, 257, IV, 163 f.; mixture of ecclesiastical and secular jurisdiction, IV, 58 f.; in Persia and Rome, II, 186, 191; separation of the "estates," IV, 87; status of Jews under, IV, 27 f., 41, 53, VII, 175; villein labor and, IV, 155; *see also* Serfdom
Fevers, VIII, 244
Fez, Morocco: academy, VI, 84; center of Jewish culture, III, 108; foundation by Idris II, VII, 225; Ibn Quraish in, VII, 17; Karaite community, VII, 226; Maimonides at, III, 291 f.; massacre of Jews, III, 108; messianic movement, V, 201; religious minorities, III, 124 f., 144 f., V, 79; repercussions of Mohammed's marriage to Ṣafiya, III, 262; use of Onkelos, VII, 5 f.
Fideles, *see* Vassals
Fidelity, oath of, IV, 49, 163
Fig tree, identification with tree of knowledge, I, 253
Figurines, Canaanite: female, I, 43, 310, 318, 329; male, I, 314
Finance, *see* Banking and bankers; Business transactions; Taxation; Trade
Fines: imposition of, VI, 10; for murder, IV, 39, 50, 127 f., 133
Fiqh, Muslim, VI, 24; *see also* Law, Muslim
Firdausi, VI. 271 f., 439
Fire: cosmic principle, VIII, 22; sacred element, I, 353; worshipers of, Zoroastrian, I, 400
Firkovitch, Abraham, III, 197, 202, V, 408, VI, 245
First-aid manual, VIII, 249
First-born, slaying of Egypt's, I, 197
First Cause, VIII, 93, 98
First fruits, I, 279
Firuz Shabur, academy of, III, 99
Fiscus, royal, IV, 41
Fiscus judaicus, I, 411, II, 104, 105 f., 186, 373, 399, III, 191; *see also* Taxation
Fish, consumption of, V, 405
Fishermen, I, 254
Fish-salting industry, I, 255
Flaccus, Avilius, I, 404
Flaccus, Lucius Valerius, I, 188, 380; effort to appropriate temple funds, I, 215
Flag, Jewish, III, 204
Flagellation, *see* Flogging
Flanders, Jewish settlers in, IV, 57
Flavia Neapolis (Nablus), Shechem renamed, II, 123
Flavius Zeuxis, I, 172
Flax, I, 257
Flight, miraculous, in messianic movements, V, 184, 203, 385 f.
Flogging, public, II, 218, IV, 49, V, 224; biblical sanctions for, VI, 91 f.; for cursing, V, 72; for insubordination, VI, 42; rabbis on, IV, 261, V, 16 f.
Florus, French churchman, IV, 54
Florus, L. Annaeus, II, 156
Flour mills, royal, IV, 318
Folklore, II, 4, 316; and apocalyptic visions, V, 152; Arabic prototypes, VI, 187; dating of, VII, 310 f.; on death of Qalir, VII, 270; expanding literature of, VI, 181 ff., 414 ff.; halakhic, VIII, 50 ff.; historical, VI, 188-98, 416-23; literary use of, VII, 76 ff., 187 f.; and messianism, V, 164 ff., 168 f.; Muslim and Jewish, V, 115 f.; and mysticism, VIII, 43; and oral tradition, V, 188; ritual and, V, 249; superstition, V, 258, 348
Folk plays, religious themes, V, 116
Folksongs, VII, 204 f.
Food: Christian and Jewish, III, 50; consumption of, and local customs, VI, 122; decrees governing Jewish con-

verts, III, 42; ritualistic requirements, III, 83 f., IV, 157 f., 188, V, 123, 131; *see also* Dietary laws
Foreigners, attitude of exilic Jewry toward, I, 156
Forgiveness, flogging as means of, V, 17
Form: connected with numbers, VIII, 353; primordial, VIII, 87 f.
"Four ells," V, 303; and private devotions, VII, 63
Four Martyrs, VIII, 19
Fowl: creation of, VIII, 226; prohibitions on, V, 249
France, I, 169, III, 47-54, 250-54, IV, 43-64, 256-70; anti-Maimonidean controversy, V, 47; Arab occupation of, III, 91; blood accusation, IV, 137 f., 307 f.; communal distribution of property, VIII, 156; and Crusades, IV, 128 f., 131 f., 289, VIII, 31 f.; halakhic miscellanies, VI, 74 ff., 362 f.; Jewish mystics in, VIII, 32; Jewish physicians in, VIII, 390; liturgical treatises, VII, 121 f.; moneylending, IV, 205 f.; *produit de Juif,* IV, 62; state organization of Frankish Jewry, V, 62; warned by Maimonides against astrology, VIII, 180; *see also* Gaul
Franconia, Germany, peace proclamation, IV, 71
Frankincense, cost of transporting, I, 250
Franks: Jewish status under, III, 50; *see also* Carolingian Empire; France
Frederick, archbishop of Mayence: compilation of canon law on Jews, IV, 73 f., 241; query on forced conversion and expulsion, IV, 6, 26, 66, 73 f.
Frederick I (Frederick Barbarossa), emperor: on clerical rights over Jews, IV, 59; Crusade led by, IV, 130; intercession for Jews of Münzenberg, IV, 304; policy toward Jews, IV, 68, 71 f., 129, 133, 176
Frederick II, emperor, IV, 22; establishment of government monopolies in Sicily, IV, 168; investigation of blood accusation, IV, 306; privilege of Worms, IV, 68
Freedmen, I, 269, II, 416
Freedom: of movement, IV, 32 f., 63 f., 78, V, 68, 78, VIII, 211 f.; thanksgiving for, VII, 109
Free love, II, 218
Free will, II, 41, V, 196, 228, VII, 22, VIII, 119; foreknowledge of God and, VIII, 128; and influence of stars, VIII, 181; and predestination, VIII, 108 ff., 333 ff.
Freising, Otto von, IV, 120
French language: Rashi's use of, VI, 52, VII, 31; technical terms translated into, VIII, 227
Frescoes, *see* Painting
Friends, Society of, VII, 80
Friendship, poems of, VII, 160 ff.
Frisians, international traders, IV, 327
Friuli, Council of, IV, 26
Frontlets, V, 215, VII, 21
Fruit culture, I, 251, 407
Fueros, IV, 13, 30, 41, 43; *see also* Custumals
Fulbert of Chartres, V, 344
Fulvia, Roman lady, I, 405
Funerals: arts and rituals, II, 287 ff., 424; of rich and poor, II, 287 f.; meals, wine, II, 288; as source of hostility, III, 297; *see also* Burial
Furat b. Shahnata, Jewish physician, VIII, 243
Furqan ibn Asad, *see* Abu'l Faraj Harun
Fusṭaṭ, Egypt: academy, V, 42; "Babylonian" congregation, V, 300 ff.; establishment of exilarchate, V, 36, 38; geonic copies of responsa, VI, 111; Jewish community, III, 105 f., 289; Jewish refugees, III, 294; Maimonides and, VI, 11; persecutions of Christians, III, 123; riots against Jews, III, 122; slave market, IV, 191; synagogues, III, 134 f., V, 28
Future life, *see* Immortality of the soul; Resurrection

G

Gadara, Palestine, II, 65, 174
Gaelic, VII, 222 f.
Gaius, Roman jurist, I, 268, II, 103
Gaius Julius Alexander Berenicianus, II, 4
Galen, Claudius, II, 159, 432, VIII, 250; on cause of death, VIII, 259; on diabetes, VIII, 262; equation with Gamaliel, VIII, 388; on Jewish and Christian doctors, II, 159, VIII, 234 f.; on number of bones, VIII, 230
Galilee, I, 168, II, 105, III, 20, VII, 3; center of Jewish life and learning, II,

Galilee (*Continued*)
123, 164; Christians and churches in, II, 164, 392; cities, I, 224, II, 123; Jesus' teachings in synagogues, II, 67, 69, 355; linen industry, I, 408; under Maccabeans, I, 167-68, 278; population, I, 167, 370, 372, II, 123; social conflicts, I, 224, 278, II, 47, 179
Gallus, jurist, VI, 55
Gallus, ruler, II, 179
Galut, II, 135, 381; *see also* Exile
Gamaliel, ancient sage, equated with Galen, VIII, 388
Gamaliel, Rabban, VIII, 190
Gamaliel I, R., II, 135, 145; astronomer, VIII, 193; quoted, II, 70; teacher of Paul, II, 76
Gamaliel II, R., I, 265, II, 10, 104, 105, 119, 131, 135, 202, 311, 351; address to dispersion, II, 205; apology to R. Eliezer, II, 115; astronomic formula, VIII, 193; burial, II, 273, 288, 290; chairmanship of academy, II, 197, 403; degree of Hellenization, II, 141; descendants, II, 197, 227; lending losses, II, 250; Romans who studied under, II, 300, 430
Gamaliel IV, patriarch, II, 197
Gamaliel V, (Gamaliel b. Hillel), patriarch, II, 188, 193
Games and sports, II, 421
Gans, David, IV, 105
Gaon, title, V, 59; *see also* Geonim and gaonate
Garcia Fernandez, count, IV, 35
Garden of Eden, V, 86, 146, 149, VIII, 273; expulsion from, VIII, 329
Gardens, aesthetic-therapeutic value, VIII, 229
Garmo, priestly family, I, 270
Gates, temple, I, 122, 350
Gaul, I, 169, II, 106; restive tribes in Germany and, II, 106, 373; Visigothic, Jews in, III, 250
Gautier de Chatillon, V, 356
Gaza, I, 225, 255, III, 8; Arab assault on, III, 87; center of learning, III, 102
"Gebalim," king of, III, 210, 331
Geber, *see* Jabir
Gedaliah b. Ahikam, I, 104, 105, 344
Gedaliah ibn Yaḥya, III, 236, IV, 105, 130
Gehenna, V, 149, VIII, 273
Gelasian Sacramentary, II, 169
Gelasius, pope, II, 169, III, 27
Gemara, Babylonian, VI, 57; Ḥananel and, VI, 343; term, VI, 77; *see also* Talmud
Gemaṭrias, V, 86, 89, 157, 167, VI, 166, VII, 290, VIII, 14
Genders: masculine and feminine, VII, 242; monograph on, VII, 48
Genealogical records, I, 125, 272; fifteen generations list, II, 195
Genealogy, in Hebrew Enoch, VIII, 20 f.
Generalissimo, title, II, 196, 403
Generations of Man, The, VI, 197
Generative forces, I, 146
Genesis, Book of, V, 106, 214; commentaries on, VI, 38 f., 282 ff., 467, 479; cosmogony, VI, 228; erotic passages, II, 275; Ḥivi's questions, VI, 301; Muslim controversialists on, V, 89; Rashi on, VI, 51; six seasons, VIII, 201; story of creation, VI, 161; *see also* Creation
Geniba of Babylonia, II, 198
Genizah, Cairo-Fusṭaṭ, II, 297, 428, IV, 173, 175, 177; archives of responsa, VI, 111; method of collection, VII, 139; poetical material, VII, 167
Genizah fragment: on Fusṭaṭ, III, 106; letters from Ḥisdai, III, 156; on 'Umar I's agreement re Jews of Jerusalem, III, 101
Genoa, Italy: Jewish community, IV, 26; merchant-mariners, IV, 332; role of fleet in the Crusades, IV, 332; synagogue, III, 26
Gentiles, II, 187-91, 400-402, V, 100, 187, 265, VIII, 265; 'Anan's attitude toward, V, 218 f.; attracted to synagogues, VII, 128; circumcision of, V, 390; and the commandments, VI, 145, 397, 440; conversion to Christianity, II, 163, 166, 392, 393 f.; discriminations against, II, 124 f., 301, 418, 430, IV, 183; "eighteen laws," I, 180; equality for converts to Judaism, VIII, 125; exclusion from Temple, I, 157, 258; incestuous unions among, II, 230, 231, 411; influence of mystics on Jews, VIII, 15; intergroup relations, I, 6, 141, 155, 157, 159, 179, 193, 319, II, 148, 167, III, 139 ff., 298 ff.; intermarriage with, I, 147, 163, 361, II, 223, 232 f., 401 f., 411 f.; in Jerusalem, III, 101; Jewish prohibition of music of, VII, 205; loans to, IV, 199, V, 128; outlawry of syna-

gogue services, VII, 247; and prophetic gifts, VI, 229, VIII, 133; reference to, in Jewish prayer of thanksgiving, VII, 109; religious disparity, I, 145, 297, II, 170; renting of Jewish houses to, V, 79; sale of slaves to, IV, 193; and study of the Torah, V, 393, VI, 11; trade with, IV, 219 f.; *see also* Antisemitism; Christians and Christianity; Islam; Paganism; *and under* peoples, *e.g.*, Greeks

Geoffroi de Ville-Hardouin, IV, 130 f.

Geography: Hellenistic, VIII, 213; knowledge of, II, 306, 433; VI, 226; study of, VIII, 211 ff.

Geometry, VIII, 153 ff., 354 ff.

Geonim and gaonate: and the academies, V, 14, 48; appeals for funds, V, 23 f.; attitude toward *piyyuṭim,* VII, 103 ff., 132 f.; attitude toward preaching, VI, 155 f.; authority of, V, 16 f., 22 f., 63, 198, VI, 26; chronology, VI, 7, 208, 446; debate on miracles, VIII, 128; and decisions of exilarchic court, V, 16; differences of opinion among, VI, 43; election, V, 24; hereditary succession, V, 14; investiture, V, 24; legal monographs, VI, 65 ff., 362 ff.; liturgical works, VII, 63 ff., 78, 111 ff., 274 ff.; and local customs, VI, 122, 131; ordinances, VI, 131 ff.; Palestino-Babylonian rivalry, V, 37 f., 48, 303; vs. the priestly leaders, V, 36; responsa, V, 52, VI, 29 ff., 339, VIII, 229; and *rishonim,* VI, 334; in Sherira's Epistle, VI, 205; sources for period of, VI, 208; and the Talmud, VI, 21 ff., 77 ff., 242 ff., 363 ff., VII, 14; title, V, 13, 33; transition from Saboraim to, VI, 18 f.; use of vernacular Aramaic, VII, 220; *see also* Scholars and scholarship; *also under* individual geonim, *e.g.*, Saadiah

George, Saint, at battle of Antioch, IV, 96

Georgios, prefect of Phokas, III, 19

Georgius Syncellus, VI, 273

Ger, term, I, 155, 375

Gerard of Cremona, VIII, 158

Gerasa (Jerash), excavators' finds, I, 396, II, 174, 285; renaming of, I, 229, 398

Gerizim, Mount, I, 220, 229, II, 26 ff., 339, III, 9, V, 170, 236

Germany, IV, 64-75, 270-76; aid of Jews to Crusaders, IV, 98; ancient, II, 106, 210, 373, 406; biblical commentary, VI, 278; blood accusation, IV, 138 f.; communal ordinances on polygamy, VI, 385; effect on Jews of Saladin's conquest of Jerusalem, IV, 305; emigration of Jews to England, IV, 80; expeditions against Wends, IV, 131; Fichte on problem of, I, 18; hostility toward Jewish communities, and the clergy, IV, 91 ff.; identification with Ashkenaz, IV, 4; Jewish communities during the Crusades, IV, 98 ff., 116 f., 129 ff., 148, 289 ff., 304 ff.; Jewish folk literature, VI, 187; moneylending, IV, 205 f.; mysticism in, VIII, 32 f.; nationalists appealed to by John's Gospel, II, 359; Nazi historiography, IV, 270; and reforming tendencies among Jews, I, 131; salt mine, IV, 169; sources of Yeraḥmeel's work, VI, 422; upsurge of Jewish learning, VI, 48; *see also* Nazis and Nazism; *also under* individual cities, *e.g.*, Mayence

Gerona, Council of, IV, 43

Gerousiarches, title, II, 404

Gershom b. Yehudah of Mayence, R., IV, 65, 213, V, 62, 64, VI, 27, 48 f., VII, 30; date of death, VI, 345; identification of talmudic terms, VIII, 227; on messianic hopes, VII, 179; mourning for son's apostasy, VII, 177; ordinance vs. polygamy, VI, 135 ff.; penitential poem, IV, 93, VII, 179 f.; on reason for supplying biblical names, VI, 281 f.; recension of Babylonian Talmud, VII, 28; on residence permit, V, 68 f.; responsa, VI, 120, 138; transcript of Yosephon, VI, 191

Gersonides, VIII, 99; on seven pillars of wisdom, VIII, 349

Ger toshab, I, 179, 375

Gervase of Canterbury, IV, 80

Gesta Treverorum, IV, 105 f.

Gezer, city, I, 64, 323

Ghassanids, Christians, III, 66, 68, V, 180

Ghazzali, al-, Muslim mystic, VIII, 15; "anti-rationalism" of, VIII, 320 f.; attitude toward Arabic script, VII, 191; books banned, III, 32, 133; on conversion, III, 131; "Incoherence of the Philosophers," VIII, 84, 113; on jurisprudence, VIII, 70; spokesman for Asha'rite movement, VIII, 248

Ghettos, Graeco-Oriental, I, 188, 380; in

Ghettos (*Continued*)
Elephantine colony, I, 117; Phoenician, I, 176; voluntary, II, 149; *see also* Segregation
Ghosts, belief in, VIII, 45 f.; R. 'Aqiba's encounter with, VII, 245
Gibeon, miracle at, VI, 311
Gibeonites, I, 40
Gigen, *see* Oescus
Gilyonim, term, II, 380
Girard, duke of Lyons, IV, 55
Giudecca, Venice, IV, 25
Glagolitic alphabet, III, 209, 218; characters of Hebraic pattern, III, 330
Glassblowing, IV, 168; in Tyre, IV, 113
Glassware, II, 249, 338, 414
Gleanings left on fields, I, 279
Glebae adscripti, IV, 63
Glory, divine, VIII, 345
Glossary, Mishnaic-Greek, VI, 333
"Glossators," Tosafist, VI, 54 ff.
Glosses: on Prophets, VII, 23, 43; in geonic commentary, VI, 28
Gloucester, England, IV, 136
Gnomon, VIII, 157
Gnosticism, II, 26; VII, 181, VIII, 6 ff., 31; of Bogomils, III, 209; Christian, VIII, 52; criticism of Old Testament, VI, 298; on cyclical changes in history, VI, 438; and dualism, VIII, 34; fountainhead of, II, 335; Jewish ethical, VIII, 118 f.; main traits, II, 315; opposition to, II, 314-18, 434-36; principles of emanation and light, VIII, 22; transition to Neoplatonism, VIII, 39
Goat raising, II, 263
God: ancient Judaism's doctrines of, I, 13, 93, 337, 366, II, 311; and angels, II, 317; attributes, II, 314, 434 f., V, 120 f., VII, 178, VIII, 42, 95-101, 279, 326-29; and Caligula, I, 404; changeability of, VI, 482; commandments concerning, VI, 95, 97, 98 f.; communion with, I, 124, 202, VII, 73 f., 87, 106, 132, 168, 179, VIII, 3 f., 83, 113, 116; covenant with Israel, I, 16, 90, *see also* Covenant; Creator, I, 138, VIII, 91; cult of the "highest," II, 25; and destruction of the Temple, II, 112, 114; direct intervention, II, 141; divine name, appelations and circumlocutions, I, 46, 229, 244, 312, 352, II, 17 f., 162, 311, 314, 335, 357, 361, 394, 434, 435, VIII, 8 ff., *see also under* Names; divine presence, VIII, 27; divine voice, II, 139, 383; "enemies of," IV, 107; eternality and immanence, II, 311; ethical, I, 136, VI, 303, VII, 92, VIII, 290; existence of, VIII, 90 ff., 324; fatherhood, I, 13, 43, 310, 337, 366; foreknowledge, VIII, 110 ff., 128, 259, 334 f.; God formula, "of Abraham, Isaac, and Jacob," II, 23, 337; glorification of, VIII, 23, 345; as God of War, I, 46, 61; Ḥananel on, VI, 45 f.; Ḥivi's questions concerning, VI, 300 f.; holiness, I, 138; identified with local deities, II, 23, 24; incorporeality, I, 13, II, 310, VI, 267 f., 302, VIII, 26 f., 29, 35, 40, 81 f., 97, 100, 284, 286; Israel as "man who sees" Him, I, 182; kingdom of, in prophecy, VIII, 18; likenesses of, prohibited, I, 49, *see also* Imagery; love of, VIII, 114 ff., 337; magic power of name, II, 22 f., 314, 434; Maimonides on essence of, V, 47; martyrdom as "sanctification of the name of," IV, 144; might of, and influence on rain, II, 40, 345; Mosaic, I, 43, 46; Muslim concept of, VI, 6 ff., 151; nature, VIII, 45, 50 f.; observes all laws, II, 135; omnipotence, VII, 182 f., VIII, 18; of patriarchs, I, 46 f.; praised by Jews and angels, VII, 131, 171; quest for knowledge of, VIII, 81 ff., 117, 319 ff.; references to, in *piyyuṭim*, VII, 102; as shepherd, I, 254; sign from, VIII, 361; and sins of Jews, I, 297, II, 112; transcendence, I, 13, 137, 138, 140, 295, II, 42, 311; triune, VII, 264; *see also* Trinity; unity, I, 43, II, 311, III, 93, 292, VII, 85, 95, 172, 179, 182, 250, VIII, 56 ff., 97 f., 152, 290; and the universe, VIII, 87 ff., 112 f., 322 ff.; unknowable, I, 389; will of, VI, 145, 482, VIII, 91 f., 324 f.; *see also* Kingdom of God
Goddesses: mother, I, 43, 318; of fertility and generation, I, 57; *see also* names, *e.g.*, Astarte
Godfrey of Bouillon, IV, 102, 105; on Crusaders' capture of Jerusalem, IV, 295 f.
Gods: belief in deities secondary to God, I, 128; Moon god, I, 44, 45, 311; Phoenician and Punic, I, 374; of primitives, I, 46; rebirth, I, 294; Sumerian-Babylonian, I, 376; worshiped in sec-

ond millennium B.C., I, 308; *see also under* names of gods, *e.g.*, Baal
Goethe: on detached critical analyses, VI, 232 f.; on learning a foreign language, VII, 9
Gog and Magog, II, 60, 83, V, 145, 160, 200, VII, 97
Gold, I, 256; assaying of, VIII, 385; coins, IV, 29, 210 f.; standard, IV, 209 f.; transmutation into, VIII, 224
Golden Age, I, 98, 99, 101, 209; *see also* Messiahs and messianism
Golden Bull, enacted by Andrew II, III, 213
Golden Calf, representations of, III, 140
Golden mean, VIII, 120 f.
Golem, of Yehudah the Pious, VIII, 47
Golgotha, IV, 102
Goliath, I, 332
Gontram, Frankish king, III, 53; welcomed by Orléans, III, 53
Good and evil, balance of, VIII, 119
Good Friday, anti-Jewish outbreaks on, IV, 56
Goose, Mayence woman and, IV, 96
Gordian III, emperor, II, 177
Gorgippia (Anapa), Caucasus, III, 200
Gorni, Isaac, Provençal Jewish troubadour, VII, 151, 204
Goshen, Egypt, I, 37, 40, 304
Gospels, II, 64 ff., 70, 353 ff.; archaeological documentation lacking, II, 63, 74, 353, 361; burning of, II, 132; charge of misquotations in, V, 126; chronological sequence, II, 72, 131, 359, 361, VI, 210; critical problems of texts, sources, etc., II, 360; geographic data, II, 353; Ibn Daud on value of, VI, 207; increasingly anti-Jewish, II, 72; language, translations, II, 65 f., 355, VI, 263, 457; terms for, II, 133; underlying oral formations, II, 66; *see also under* names, *e.g.*, Mark, Saint
Gossip, penalty for, VI, 179
Government, *see* Self-government; State; Theocracy
Governors, provincial, in ancient Israel, I, 75
Gozan, biblical, I, 323, 345
Graeco-Arabic loan words, VI, 422
Graeco-Byzantine world, continuing Jewish contacts with, VIII, 299; *see also* Byzantine Empire
Graeco-Oriental art and music, II, 6-15, 330-34, 402; as distinguished from Greek, II, 334
Graeco-Roman civilization: Arab rule superimposed upon, VII, 30, 32; heritage in science, VIII, 147; hospitals, VIII, 392; interest in Jewish question, I, 183; magic gemmas, VIII, 8; monogamy, II, 227; and Near East, Jews as intermediaries between, VIII, 255 f.; and Phoenician colonies, I, 175; rhetoric, VII, 3, 283; unprepared for monotheism and imageless worship, I, 193; *see also* Hellenism; Roman Empire; *also under* names of respective countries
Graeco-Roman loan words, VII, 141
Graeco-Syrian *Testamentum Domini,* VII, 125
Grain, Palestinian, II, 246
Grain speculators, I, 277
Grammar: Arab, VII, 219, 224; biblical accents, VII, 284; biblical and *payyeṭanic,* VII, 57; development of basic rules, VII, 32-39; as exegetical aid, VII, 40; independent research, VII, 3 ff., 37; parts of speech, VII, 50; rules of, applied to poetry, VI, 40 ff.; *see also* Verbs
Gran, Hungary, III, 207; Council of, III, 212
Granada: Berbers in, III, 156 f., IV, 29; Beza bath, III, 299; destruction of Jewish community, III, 123, 158; influence of scribe, III, 156 f.; Jewish influence, III, 109, IV, 29, V, 45
Grape culture, I, 251, IV, 324
Gratian, *Decretum,* IV, 6, 18 f.
Graves: leveled with ground, III, 140; pilgrimages to, V, 258; *see also* Cemeteries and catacombs
Great Mystery (*Raza rabba*), VIII, 32 f.
"Great Synagogue, Men of the," I, 162, 367, 397
Great War, II, 90-93, 96, 368 f., 372; Essenes in, II, 50; oracle on, I, 210; rebellions following, II, 94 ff.; strength and type of Jewish forces, II, 90 f., 93, 368; sufferings in Antioch community, II, 3; Zealots in, II, 101, 372
Greece: Jewish sources of science and philosophy, VI, 230; Jews transported to Italy by Roger II, IV, 21; philosophy of history, VI, 227; refugees in southern Italy, III, 25; revival of his-

Greece (*Continued*)
torical literature, VI, 199; taxation, III, 192
Greek church, II, 166; *see also* Orthodox Eastern Church
Greek language: Aquila's translation of Scripture, VI, 256; education in, II, 133, 141 f.; Gospels, II, 65, 66, 142 f., 355; Jews' knowledge of, I, 185 ff., 378, II, 133, 141 ff., 147, 385, 387, III, 260; letters and formulas on epitaphs, II, 332; mystics' use of, VIII, 9 f., 16; reading of Scripture in, III, 189; in Sicily, IV, 21; terms used in Talmud, II, 300, 302, VI, 407; "translation Greek," VII, 4; translators of classics, V, 84
Greek law, borrowings from, VI, 5
Greek literature, Arabic translations of, VI, 264
Greeks, achievements in science, VIII, 138 ff., 219; adulation of, I, 228, 399; antisemitism, I, 190, 193, 195, 236, 401, IV, 166; athletics, I, 397; deeds, II, 266; and differences in cultures and creeds, I, 173; early contacts with Jews, I, 184, 283; influence on Christian ceremonies and arts, II, 84; influence on education in Palestine, II, 433; influence of Graeco-Oriental art and music, II, 6-15, 330 ff., 402; Judeo-Greek legal controversy, I, 190, 241; proselytism and, I, 176 ff., 374 f.; wisdom derived from Mosaic antecedents, I, 198; *see also* Hellenism
Greeting ceremony, III, 123, 276, IV, 10, 12, 238, V, 39, 41
Gregentius, bishop of Zafar, V, 111
Gregorios Asbestas, III, 193; treatise on forced conversion, III, 181
Gregory the Great (Gregory I), pope, II, 154, 282, III, 25; aversion to secular songs, VII, 203; distrust of medicine, VIII, 231; exegetical and homiletical works, III, 242 f., VI, 279; reaction to *vox psallentium,* VII, 283; on Jewish question, III, 27 f., 32, 53, IV, 5, 155
Gregory IV, pope, on forced conversion, IV, 6
Gregory VII, pope, IV, 237; warning to Alphonso VI, IV, 37
Gregory IX, pope, Decretals, IV, 240
Gregory X, pope, IV, 12
Gregory of Tathew, Armenian polemist, V, 123
Gregory of Tours, Saint, III, 251; on Cautinus and the Jews, III, 51 f.; debate with Priscus, V, 114; on Gontram's welcome by Orléans, III, 53; veracity of, III, 253
Grimoaldo, duke of Benevento, IV, 20
Grotius, Hugo, VI, 397
Groups, ethnic, *see* Ethnic groups; Ghettos; Segregation
Guadalajara, Jewish community, IV, 251 f.
Guaranties and sureties, VI, 70
Guarnerius, VI, 55
"Guest house," II, 285
Guildford, England, Jewish impost, IV, 81
Guilds: and clan organization, I, 69; discriminatory policies, IV, 170 f.; Jewish, I, 257, 258, 260, II, 249, IV, 199; mercantile, IV, 184 f.; mutual support, II, 260, 417; silk merchants', IV, 183; types, usages, II, 261
Gulgolet, capitation tax, III, 192
Gundissalinus (or Gundisalvus), Dominicus, VIII, 61, 174 f.
Guy of Dampierre, IV, 62
Guzana, interest rates in, in 7th century, I, 323
Gymnasium in Jerusalem, I, 228
Gynarchy, in Egypt, I, 112

H

Habakkuk, Dead Sea Scroll of, II, 53, 349, VI, 158
Ḥabbus, Berber ruler of Granada, III, 157
Habdalah, ceremony, VII, 168; prayer, V, 153, 155
Ḥaberim, I, 375
Ḥabiru (Ḥapiru), I, 34, 40, 44; identified with *'Ibrim,* I, 302, V, 219; non-Israelitic, I, 56
Hadad I, I, 322
Hadassi, Yehudah, V, 191 f., 229, 234, 272; on biblical interpretation, V, 252 f.; *Eshkol ha-kofer,* V, 399; mystical elements in work of, VIII, 30; opponent of astrology, VIII, 180; on rich and poor, V, 239; on study of Hebrew, VIII, 4
Ḥadhramaut, Jewish community, III, 260; prophets of, III, 82; temple of Sin, III, 64, 257

Ḥadith, V, 83, 88; biographical coloring, VI, 24; evolution of, III, 92; Jewish ingredients of, III, 273; on prayer, VI, 15
Hadrian, Roman emperor, II, 97, 108-9; dejudaizing efforts, I, 7, II, 106 ff., 118, 120, 266, 371, 374, VI, 241, VII, 95; places renamed by, II, 107, 380; quoted, II, 22; revolt against, *see* Bar Kocheba
Hadrian I, pope, IV, 18; on relapse of converts, IV, 5
Haduta (or Ḥaduta), priestly poet, VII, 90, 259
Ḥafiz, Persian poet, VIII, 15
Hafṭarah, prophetic lesson, VI, 355, 405
Haga (Haggai), name, I, 120
Haggadah of Passover, I, 189, 197, 381, II, 119, III, 289, V, 392, VI, 15
Haggai, name, I, 120, 121, 349
Haggai, prophet, I, 130, 161, VI, 23; question to the priests of Jerusalem, VI, 483
Hagia Sophia, Constantinople, III, 174, 232, 314, V, 343, VI, 212
Hagiographa, I, 345; 'Anan's attitude toward, V, 212; Aramaic version, VI, 260, 262; number of verses, VIII, 149; as source of Jewish law, VI, 244; textual transmission, VI, 237
Hagiography, V, 116; use of, in sermons, VI, 167 f.
Hai b. David Gaon, VII, 91; on Karaism, V, 276
Hai b. Sherira, Babylonian gaon, V, 48; advice on "things of merit," VII, 137; on appointment of judges, VI, 9; attitude toward Aggadah, VI, 176 ff., 412; attitude toward science, VIII, 68; at Baghdad academy, III, 195; on chronology of *Seder 'Olam,* VIII, 378; commentaries on tractates, VI, 43, 114; vs. corrupt judges, V, 178; death of, VI, 208; defense of Bustanai, VI, 11; on emending Mishnah or Talmud, VI, 347; explanation of King David's harp, VI, 343; and geonic "secret scroll," VI, 23; halakhic monographs, VI, 70 ff., 359 ff.; on letters of authorization, IV, 212; lexicographical work, VII, 26 f.; on local customs, VI, 122 ff.; and messianism, V, 161 f., 200, 206 f.; methodological work on the Talmud, VI, 205 f.; on miracles, VIII, 128; on mystic practices, VIII, 15 f.; on mystic writings, VIII, 27; on observance of New Year's day, VII, 107; poems by, VII, 105, 145 f., 166, 290; on prophet and magician, VIII, 130; at Pumbedita, V, 14, 24; quoted in Nathan's dictionary, VII, 30; on recitation of the *'Abodah,* VII, 90; responsa, VI, 29 ff., 115, 385; on synagogue "messenger," VII, 127; on Talmudim, VI, 17, 176 f.; on Targumim, VI, 260 ff.; volume of correspondence, VI, 113; on words and their context, VII, 68
Haifa, Palestine: defense of, IV, 111; "fortress," III, 102
Hajek, Czech chronicler, III, 216 f.
Ḥakim, al-, Faṭimid caliph, III, 105, 173; on "distinguishing marks," III, 140; persecution of Christians and Jews, III, 111, 184, 289, 298, IV, 57, 271 f.; prohibition of synagogues, III, 135; and the riots in Fusṭaṭ, III, 122
Ha-Kohen, Mordecai b. Hillel, *see* Mordecai b. Hillel ha-Kohen
Ha-kohen ha-levi, Samaritan priests, V, 174
Ha-kohen ha-mashiaḥ, I, 152
Halakhah, II, 293, V, 125; academic differences on principles of, V, 22; Aggadah a handmaid of, II, 298, 429; evolution of, II, 305, 316 f., VI, 36; and local customs, VI, 128; monographs and miscellanies, VI, 62-76, 112, 354-63; Philonic, V, 216; practice, III, 111 f.; and Roman law, II, 299; scholars of, and mysticism, VIII, 37; sectarian deviations from, V, 189; and *shari'ah,* VI, 7, 12 f.; use of Arabic in, VII, 6; written, VIII, 38 f.; *see also* Law
Halakhah ke-batrai, II, 320
Halakhic midrashim, *see* Midrash
Halakhot, VI, 41; "adjudicated," VI, 108
Halakhot gedolot, IV, 195, VI, 23, 81 f., 98, 121, 364 ff.
Halakhot qeṣubot (Adjudicated Laws), VI, 108, 356, 366
Ḥaleb, *see* Aleppo
Halevi, Yehudah b. Samuel, Spanish Jewish poet, I, 5, 20, 295, III, 98, 258, IV, 32, VI, 231, VII, 152, 154; on Adam, VI, 228 f.; anti-Karaism, V, 407; apocryphal poems, VII, 308; on Arabic and Hebrew meters, VII, 200, 202 f., 313; bilingualism, VII, 9; birthplace, IV,

Halevi, Yehudah b. Samuel (*Continued*) 248; on conflict between history and nature, I, 295, VIII, 111 f.; definition of pious individual, VIII, 121; dialogue before the Khazar king, VIII, 3, 22, 62, 67, 84 ff., 125 ff.; on divine origin of Torah, VI, 142; on fast-day, VI, 16; historical rationale of Hebrew, VII, 27; historical theory of prophecy, VIII, 134; on the individual and society, VIII, 120; influenced by Saadiah, VII, 294; on influence of heavenly spheres, VIII, 181 f.; on knowledge and revelation, VIII, 113 ff.; messianic belief, V, 163 f., 365; on movements of the sun, VIII, 166; mystic philosophy, VIII, 39; on natural law, VI, 144 f.; octocentennial anniversary, VII, 295; opinion of Masorah, VI, 247; on origin of all science, VIII, 77; poem on divine government, VII, 174; poems honoring individuals, IV, 251 f., VI, 84, 149, VII, 154; prayers, VIII, 260, 391; on predestination and free will, VIII, 109 f.; on preexistent things, quoted, VIII, 126; problem of the Exile, V, 101; on quest for knowledge, VIII, 84 f.; rationale of Israel's selection and sufferings, IV, 146 f., VIII, 125 f., 127, 133; rationalism of, VIII, 320 f.; on the revelation of Sinai, V, 92; riddle in verse, VII, 162; on role of martyrs and scholars, VI, 439; on sacrifices, VI, 148; on Sadducees, V, 255; on *Sefer Yeṣirah,* VIII, 22; ship as symbol, V, 361; on the soul, VIII, 107; spiritualization of love in poetry, VII, 212 f.; on study of the Torah, VI, 144; on talmudic law codes and natural sciences, VIII, 228; verses in Castilian, VII, 192; on wealth vs. intellectual achievement, IV, 349; wedding poem, VII, 314; Zionide poems, V, 155, VII, 168 f., 197, 300
Ḥalfon b. Nethanel, VII, 295
Halicz, Karaite settlement, V, 285
Ḥalil, Arabic lexicon, VII, 27
Ḥaliṣah, ceremony of, II, 231
Ḥallah, offerings, VI, 10, VII, 274
Hallaj, Ḥussain ibn Manṣur al-, mystic and martyr, III, 133, VIII, 15, 112
Halleluyah, congregational chant, VII, 125
"Hall of reckonings," I, 393
Ḥaluqqah funds, V, 37
Ḥaluṣ, pioneer, III, 212
Haly Rodoam, *see* Ibn Ridhwan
Ham, son of Noah, I, 335, VI, 192; descendants of, VII, 256
Ḥama, R. (Babylonian), II, 290
Ḥama b. Ḥanina, R., I, 254, II, 213, 284
Hamadani, Arab writer, VII, 183
Haman, I, 5, 132, 136; denunciations of Jewish separatism, I, 131; effigy of, IV, 139
Ḥamma b. Tobiah, II, 222, 409
Ḥammanim, I, 352
Hammath: inscriptions, II, 142; synagogue, II, 174
Hammurabi, and Amraphel, I, 301
Hammurabi, Code of, I, 79, 324, 327
Hamnuna, R., II, 221, 283, 289, III, 61, VI, 340; on Mosaic commandments, VI, 9
Ḥanafites, III, 132, VI, 16
Ḥananel b. Ḥushiel, VI, 26, 108, V, 366; commentaries, VI, 45 f., 342, 343; on equality of oral and written laws, VI, 427; influence in southern France, VIII, 292; legal compilations attributed to, VI, 83 f.; quoted in Nathan's dictionary, VII, 30; reply to charges of talmudic anthropomorphism, VIII, 100; transcript of Eldad's *Halakhot,* VI, 221
Ḥananel b. Palṭiel, V, 317
Hanani, I, 322
Hananiah, prophet, I, 116
Ḥananiah, R., II, 46, 125, 206, 225
Ḥananiah, brother of 'Anan b. David, V, 210
Ḥananiah b. 'Aqashia, R., II, 308
Ḥananiah b. Hezekiah, I, 154, II, 436
Hanbalites, III, 132, VI, 16
Handicrafts, *see* Crafts and craftsmen; Industry
Hands, washing of, VI, 14, *see also* Ablution
Hangchow, III, 286
Ḥanina, R., Palestinian Amora, II, 21, 278, 403, VI, 200; on birth under a particular planet, VIII, 178; on days and hours, VIII, 185; objections to polylogy, VIII, 14; riots against ordination of, II, 243, 277
Ḥanina, priest, II, 115, 117, 121
Ḥanina b. Dosa, V, 21
Ḥanina b. Isaac, II, 20

Ḥanina b. Teradyon, martyrdom, II, 100, 371
Ḥaninah Gaon, VII, 259 f.
Ḥaninai, *see* Bustanai
Hannah, martyr, story of, VI, 417
Hannah, Samuel's mother, prayer of, I, 123, 351
Ḥanokh Gaon, VII, 78
Ḥanokh b. Moses, R., V, 45
Hanseatic league, IV, 332
Ḥanukkah, festival of, I, 5, 169, 220, 235, 395, III, 202, V, 284, 407, VI, 167, 269; Karaite rejection of, V, 246, 255; lights, I, 400, VI, 80 f.; Palestinian poem for, VII, 268; Sabbath of week of observance, VI, 162 f.; and Scroll of Antiochus, VI, 189
Hapax legomena, VI, 267, VII, 15, 226
Ḥapiru, *see* Ḥabiru
Hapki'el, angel, VIII, 8 f.
Har, I, 36
Haran, city, I, 33; moon goddess of, I, 44, 311
Haran b. Teraḥ, VI, 437
Harem: as instrument of imperial policy, III, 201; rivalry in, II, 225; for safeguarding women, III, 283; slaves for, I, 324
Hariri, al-, Arab writer, VII, 183, 184 ff.
Harlot's quarters, II, 225
Harmilos, communal titles in, V, 316
Ḥarran: destruction of synagogues and churches, III, 135 f.; religious toleration toward Sabian community, III, 130, VI, 437
Ḥarta de-Argiz, burial place of Hamnuna, VI, 340
Harun ar-Rashid, caliph, III, 160, VI, 107, 220; appeals to Jewish farmers, IV, 151 f.; Charlemagne's embassies to, IV, 45, 174, 257 f., VI, 220; delight in public religious debates, V, 83, 85; destruction of synagogues, III, 135; land tax, III, 168
Harun ibn al-Haik al-Dharir, Arab grammarian, VII, 222
Harun ibn Musa al-Asdi, Arab philologist, VII, 11; critical work on Qur'anic text, VI, 243
Ḥarut, fallen angel, III, 265
Ḥasan b. Mar-Ḥasan, Spanish astronomer, VIII, 376
Ḥasidism, I, 6, 11, 237; ancient, and Pharisaism, II, 342; Franco-German, VI, 46, VII, 183, VIII, 42 ff., 262 f., 293 ff.
Haskalah movement, VIII, 262 f.
Hasmonean Children, Book of, VI, 188 f.
Hasmonean dynasty, V, 256; *see also* Maccabeans
Hasmoneans (or Antiochus), Scroll of, VI, 159, 167, 185, 485; date, VI, 416; use in synagogue services, VI, 167
Ḥatshepsut, queen of Egypt, I, 36, 304
"Havilah," region, Africa, III, 116
Ḥayyuj, Yehudah b. David (Abu Zakariya Yaḥya ibn Daud), Hebrew grammarian, III, 180, VI, 290, VII, 23, 44; Book of Glosses on Prophets, VII, 23, 43; contributions to grammar and philology, VI, 290 f., VII, 60; disciple of Menaḥem b. Saruq, VII, 22, 23 f.; influence of, VII, 44; theory of triliterality, VII, 42 ff.
Ḥazzan, communal official, II, 367, V, 53, 316, VII, 80 ff., 254 f.
Ḥazzan, Israel Moses, R., of Smyrna, VII, 84
Healing: Greek God of, II, 336; by Jesus, II, 67; magic, II, 21, 22, 336, VI, 178, VIII, 21; *see also* Medicine
Heart, and soul, VIII, 107
Heaven, Kingdom of, *see* Kingdom of God
Heavenly bodies, motion of, VIII, 142, 164 ff.
Heavenly family, Zoroastrian concept, II, 317
Heavenly hosts: musical rationale of, VII, 210; participation in prayers, VII, 181 f.; praise, with Israel, to God, VIII, 4, 12 f.; prayers for, VII, 76 ff.
Heavens, seven, guardians of, VIII, 23
Heave-offerings, V, 313 f.
Ḥeber, I, 236, 401
Ḥeber ha-'ir, II, 201, 404
Ḥebrah qadisha, II, 289
Hebraisms, in Arabic, VII, 8 f.
Hebrew, term, as distinguished from Israelite and Jew, V, 126 f.
Hebrew alphabet, III, 209; in Arabic writings, VII, 8, 60, 190 f.; compared to Arabic, VII, 185; and Phoenician alphabet, I, 307; poems on, VII, 91 f., 142, 219; rhymes in order of, VII, 142; and *sefirot,* VIII, 22 f.; and sentence divisions, VI, 239
—— Letters of: classification, VII, 34 ff.;

Hebrew alphabet (*Continued*)
components of verb, VII, 41 f.; double, VII, 38, VIII, 23 f., 25, 150; errors in distinguishing between, VI, 240, 248; final, VIII, 150; and Metatonic cycle, VIII, 192; "mothers," VII, 34; mystic approach to, VIII, 14 f., 284; as numerals, VIII, 150; of the Pentateuch, VIII, 29; permutation of, VII, 21, 38; pronunciation, VI, 250 f.; radical and functional, VII, 32 f., 39, 42, 49 f.; riddles, VIII, 357; role in the Creation, VIII, 282; significance in study of the Torah, VIII, 19 f.; square characters, V, 175, VII, 56 f., VIII, 152; symbolism, VI, 247, VIII, 13, 35 f.

"Hebrewisms," VII, 10

Hebrew language: Abraham's use of, I, 20; antiquity and sanctity of, VII, 14, 27, 55 ff., 60, 158 f., 186, VIII, 77; and Arabic, III, 81, VII, 8, 18, 48, 184 f.; Arabs' lack of knowledge of, V, 89; Babylonian pronunciation, VII, 235; biblical and mishnaic, VII, 5, 56 f.; blend of Aramaic and, II, 142, 147; and Christian scholars, V, 121, VI, 272 f., 462 f.; cultivated by the intelligentsia, VII, 222 f.; development of accents, VI, 237; development of linguistic parallels, VII, 11; dialects, V, 175, VI, 250; diminutive forms, VII, 16 f.; excellence of, VI, 291 f., VII, 158 f., 186, VIII, 217; Gospels, II, 66, 355; Hebrew-Greek interrelations, I, 184, 376; historic evolution, VII, 242; in international trade, IV, 173 f.; Italian pronunciation, VII, 235; Jewish apologias written in, V, 112; literary continuity, VII, 68 f.; medical works in, VIII, 244 ff.; modern Palestinian, VI, 250 f.; neglect of, VII, 45; Palestinian, VII, 235; philosophic tracts in, VIII, 75 ff.; plural forms, VII, 197; prayers (*q.v.*), VII, 68; premasoretic, VII, 233; in religious affairs of Egyptian Jewry, I, 186, 395; religious ingredients, I, 27; in Sicily, IV, 21; stimuli from other languages, VII, 9; study of, II, 145 f., III, 102, VI, 290, VII, 3-61, 219-43; translations from Aramaic into, VI, 56; transliterated into Greek alphabet, I, 187; writing of, in Khazaria, III, 197; *see also* Pronunciation; Roots; Spelling; Verbs

Hebrews: appearance of first, I, 32 ff., 301; Israelitic and non-Israelitic, I, 37 f., 56, 225, 336

Hebron, I, 106, 344; Cave of Machpelah, III, 278; export of grapes, IV, 324

Hecataeus of Abdera, I, 168, 189, 192, 200, 370, 373, 377, 386

Hecataeus of Miletus, I, 184

Ḥedvata, liturgical poet, VI, 248; *see also* Haduta

Ḥefeṣ b. Yaṣliaḥ, VI, 59; reformulation of Jewish laws, VI, 93 ff.

Hefqer, II, 252

Ḥefzibah, in apocalyptic messianism, V, 141, 152

Hegesippus, II, 121, 131, VI, 437; Yosephon's use of, VI, 418 f.

Heifer, red, and purification rites, V, 173

Hejaz, and Mt. Paran, V, 86, 89

Hejira, to Medina, III, 77

Hekhal, I, 332

Hekhalot, VIII, 11 ff.; mystical midrashim, VI, 162, 175, VII, 181; *rabbati,* VIII, 13, 17 ff., 281 ff.; praise of Torah and Talmud, VIII, 17

Ḥelbo, R., II, 148, 238, 388

Helena, empress of Byzantium, III, 156, 183; and the Cross, V, 125

Helena of Adiabene, queen, II, 14

Helgo-Oleg, *see* Igor

Heliopolis, city, I, 304

Helios, zodiacal representation of, VIII, 367

Hell, for evildoers, VIII, 104; *see also* Gehenna

Hellenism: and antisemitism, I, 195; decided in favor of Christianity, II, 251; decline, II, 173-75, 396; hellenization of Jewry, I, 165, 185, 188, 212, 219, II, 142; Jewish heritage of, VIII, 4; and Jewish law, II, 299; Judaism's contribution to, I, 174; and Maccabean revolt, I, 166; paucity of Jewish records, I, 199; Paul as intellectual spokesman, II, 76, 80, 84 f.; Philo as spokesman, I, 201, 388; regional divisions, I, 208, 210, 282; religious propaganda, I, 173, 177, II, 36; Sadducee reaction against, II, 36; Semitic resistance to, I, 370; *see also under* Graeco-; Greek

Hellenistic influences, I, 283; on Christianity, II, 163 ff., 392 ff.; in the Orient,

II, 3, 4, 54; in Palestine, I, 229, II, 299 f., 430; on Persia, I, 131
Hellenistic world: and Christian leadership, II, 83; every fifth inhabitant a Jew, I, 171; growing independence of cities, II, 369; Jews attracted to cities, I, 170; and Palestinian Jewry, II, 89; and sacrilege in a sanctuary, I, 192; self-governing municipalities, I, 167
Hemerobaptists, sect, II, 348, V, 250
Hemorrhoids, treatment of, VIII, 260
"Henotheism," I, 311
Henry I (Henry the Fowler), German emperor, IV, 25; and Diet of Erfurt, IV, 66
Henry II, German emperor, IV, 65 f.; anti-Jewish policy, IV, 92 f.; expulsion of Jews, IV, 66, 271
Henry III, German emperor, IV, 164
Henry IV, German emperor: break with the episcopate, IV, 67, 99; negation of forced conversion, IV, 106; peace treaty, IV, 70; pro-Jewish decrees, IV, 67 f., 71, 102 f., 116 f., 272 ff., V, 62
Henry V, German emperor, IV, 117
Henry VI, German emperor, IV, 134
Henry I, king of England, IV, 78 f.
Henry II, king of England, IV, 80, 124 f.
Henry III, king of England, IV, 311
Heqqesh, V, 213 f., 243, VIII, 240
Heracles, I, 376; festival of, I, 229
Heraclius, Byzantine emperor, II, 179, III, 16, IV, 151, V, 302; attempts to reestablish religious uniformity, III, 24; defeat of Persian armies, III, 18; dream of danger to Christendom, III, 54; "fast" of, III, 23; and Khazars, III, 198; suppression of Judaism, III, 23, 32, 40, 174 f., 220
Herban, debate with Gregentius, V, 111
Herbert of Bosham, VI, 273
Herbs, in magic therapy, VIII, 234
Hereafter, the, V, 166, 228, VIII, 81; animals in, VIII, 230; compensation for suffering, VIII, 126; Maimonides on, V, 164 f.; in messianism, V, 147 ff., 358 ff.; punishment and reward, VIII, 103 ff., 330 f.; *see also* Immortality of the soul; Resurrection
Hereditary principle, in election of officials, II, 202, V, 73 ff.; *see also under* Exilarchs and exilarchate; Geonim and gaonate
Heredity, Mendelian theory, VIII, 242
Ḥerem, see Excommunication; Residence permit
Heretics and heresies: Jewish, III, 233, VIII, 66 ff.; belief in corporeality of God as, VIII, 100; fostered by individualistic exegesis, VI, 471; incorporated in sermons, VI, 171; and liturgical disunity, VII, 64; logic and, VIII, 68; punishment for, III, 9, V, 45 f.; *see also* Apostasy
—— Christian, III, 194, VII, 128, VIII, 32, 46; Manichaean, V, 105 f.; Muslim, V, 375, VI, 235
Hermann, bishop of Prague, IV, 118
Hermann, Premonstratensian monk, V, 112 f., 340 f.
Hermann III, archbishop of Cologne, IV, 99 f.
Hermann of Dalmatia, VIII, 167
Hermeneutics, talmudic, II, 427, 429
Hermes: identified with Enoch (*q.v.*), VIII, 366; invoked in magic formulas, VIII, 9 f.
Hermes Trismegistos, magician, VIII, 10
Hermetic writings, VII, 174
Hermopolis papyri, I, 347, 352
Herod Antipas, tetrarch, I, 238, 401, II, 62, 352; banishment to Lyons, III, 47; palace in Tiberias, II, 15
Herod dynasty, I, 225, II, 90, 91, VI, 192 f.; in Armenia and Chalcis, II, 3 f.; bigamy among, II, 226; despotism of, I, 223; messianism, II, 61, 352; Romanization of, I, 243, 401; social conditions under, I, 217, 281
Herodotus, I, 25, 162, 177, 353, II, 104, 410
Herod's Temple, *see* Temple at Jerusalem, Second
Herod the Great, king of Judaea, I, 220, 223, 225, II, 24; building, I, 236, 237; coins, I, 236; copper mines, I, 256; fiscal reign of terror, I, 262, 280, 410; Greeks attracted to Caesarea by, I, 256; and high priest's office, I, 216; "Idumaean slave," I, 397; and imperial worship, I, 218; Jewish majority in kingdom, I, 167; Jewish soldiers used by, II, 91; and oath of fidelity, II, 36; sale of insolvent Jews, II, 257; Samaria as a "Greek" municipality, II, 27; settlement of Babylonian Jews by, I, 172, 214; Temple rebuilt by, I, 238, 258, 402, II, 9, 213

Heroes, biblical: aggadic works associated with, VI, 159 f.; association of places with, VI, 228; benedictions ascribed to, VII, 66; foreign domination, VI, 192; in historical folklore, VI, 188 ff., 416 ff.; interfaith approach to, VI, 408; role of, in mysticism, VIII, 20 ff.; in storytelling, VI, 168, 186 f.
Heronian formula, VIII, 158
Hero worship, II, 5
Ḥesed Abu Nasr, Jewish banker, III, 158
Hesiod, I, 196
Ḥesna Ebraya, *see* Mosul
Hesperia, and Sefarad, IV, 4
Hexagram of David, II, 11
Hexateuch, I, 330; Samaritan, V, 176
Hezekiah, king of Judah, I, 66, 79, 126
Hezekiah b. David, exilarch, V, 11 f., 40; correspondence, VI, 116
Hezekiah b. Samuel, VI, 27, VII, 13
Hibbat Allah (Nathaniel?) ibn Jumay', *see* Ibn Jumay'
Ḥiddushim (*novellae*), VI, 353 f.
Hierapolis: guilds, II, 261, 417; temple plundered, I, 398
Hierarchy, I, 149-55, 362-65; *see also* Priests and priesthood
Hierocles, II, 159
Hierodules, I, 146
High Holidays, VII, 72; *'Alenu* prayer, IV, 138; length of services, VII, 79 f.; poems for, VII, 93; ritual, VIII, 279
High priest, title, I, 152
Hilai b. Naṭronai, VI, 446
Hilarion, Russian metropolitan, III, 215
Hilary, bishop, III, 52
Hilderic, governor of Nîmes, III, 46
Hillel, I, 180, 221, 265, 269, II, 206, 220, 236, 272, 421, V, 213; authority on law and traditions, II, 37; controversies with Shammai, V, 255; pronunciation, VI, 248; *Prosbol* enacted by, II, 262, 417
—— House of, II, 117, 140, 205; attitude on divorce, II, 228, 410
Hillel II, V, 196; calendar reform, V, 212, VIII, 186, 369
Hillel b. Jacob, IV, 138
Hillukh, Samaritan law, II, 32
Ḥimyara, Jewish community in, III, 65 f., 258 f.; contacts with Tiberian Jewry, V, 180
Hin, pronunciation of, VI, 248 f.
Hipparchus, VIII, 139, 187 f.; list of fixed stars, VIII, 162
Hippocrates, Aphorisms, VIII, 238, 250, 261; on number of bones, VIII, 230
Hippocratic oath, VIII, 238, 242
Hippodrome, Solomon's, VIII, 18 f.
Hippolytus, II, 50, 347
Ḥira, Lakhmid capital, III, 61, 163, VI, 340
Hiram I, I, 64
Ḥisda, R., II, 14, 221, 249, 258, 264, 268; on poverty of cantor, VII, 129 f.
Ḥisdai, Egyptian leader, V, 8
Hisdai b. David, exilarch, VI, 336
Ḥisdai ibn Shapruṭ, Jewish physician, III, 155 f., 183, 198, 201, IV, 29, V, 44, 47, 161, VI, 27; copy of Yosephon, VI, 195; correspondence with king of Khazaria, III, 156, 204 f., 210, 305 f., 324, VI, 219 f., VII, 273; and Ibrahim ibn Ya'qub, III, 217; patron of learning, VII, 20, 22, 146; VIII, 245 f.; translation by, VIII, 65; on use of caves, V, 378
Hisham, caliph, III, 103, VI, 324
Hisham I, Spanish ruler, III, 169 f.
Historical literature, I, 25-26, 100, 340, VI, 198-219, 416-33; Arab, VI, 192, 199, VIII, 77; folkloristic, VI, 188 ff., 217, 232 ff., 416 ff.; Jews' loss of interest in writing, I, 26; medieval, contents, VI, 190; Western, and dominant Jewish historical outlook, VI, 437; *see also under* individual historians, e.g., Ibn Daud; Sherira
History: concepts, I, 8, 47, 293 ff., II, 363, V, 102 f., VI, 218, 232 ff., 404, VIII, 62, 78 ff.; chronology of, VI, 202, VIII, 205 ff., 378 ff.; common, among Israelitic tribes, I, 41; and Hellenistic Jewry, I, 208; historic continuity in new order, I, 135; "lachrymose conception of Jewish history," I, 297, VI, 218, 234, 404; and messianism, II, 99; mystics' outlook on, VIII, 20; nadir of, VI, 230; and nature, I, 5 ff., 12, 18, 101, II, 81, VIII, 111 f.; sources, I, 298-99, 369; significance of biblical, VII, 167 f., 306-11, 484-86, VIII, 86 ff.; supreme religious experience, I, 8, 100 f., 295 f.; synchronization of, with Roman history, VI, 422; theme in poetry, VII, 134, 163, 167 f.; transition

to legend, VI, 233; use in Judeo-Christian controversies, II, 80 f., 136-41, 170, 381-85, V, 119 f., 128 ff.; view of divine guidance, VI, 234; waning interest in totality of, I, 26, 165, 199, 293
Hittite code, I, 327
Hittites: incestuous marriage, I, 146; religious ideas, I, 45
Ḥivi ha-Balkhi, exegetical extremist, III, 134, V, 105, 107, VI, 272, 298-306, 478-84; alleged convert, VI, 302, 303, 482; date of literary activity, VI, 478; new Torah, VI, 302; questions concerning the Bible, VI, 299 ff., VIII, 58; replies to, VI, 303-4, 480 ff.; sources, VI, 299; use of rhymed Arabic prose, VI, 478
Ḥiyya, R., II, 197, 206, 270, 422; mispronunciations of Scripture, VI, 240; "secret scroll," VI, 41
Ḥiyya b. Abba, R., II, 194, 208
Ḥiyya of Sepphoris, R., II, 112, 375
Hodayah Nasi, V, 47
Ḥofshim (coloni), I, 324
Hohenstaufen, in Sicily, IV, 22 f.
Holidays, I, 5, 220, II, 209, III, 50; Christian observance of, IV, 60 f.; computation of dates, V, 279, VI, 203, VIII, 187 ff., 200, 208; disturbance of, IV, 236; double, VIII, 374 f.; Hosha'nah, III, 101; Karaite observances, V, 245 ff.; laws of, VI, 80; observance of, V, 270; prayers for, VII, 124, 180; retelling of biblical narratives, VII, 180 f.; and rise of antisemitism, V, 108 f.; scriptural readings, VII, 72 f.; sectarians and, V, 191 f., 195 f.; *Sefirah* season, V, 283, VII, 67; sermons, VI, 162; trade restrictions on, IV, 219 f.; tunes for prayers, VII, 127; two-day observance, V, 28 f.; *see also* Festivals; High holidays
Holiness, doctrine of, I, 138, 358; of God, VIII, 99; incommunicable nature of, VI, 483
Holophernes, story of, VI, 187
Holy Land, *see* Palestine
Holy Roman Empire: German leadership, IV, 64 ff.; *see also* Germany; *also under* names of emperors
Holy War, Muslim concept of, IV, 90, 291
Holy Week, anti-Jewish assaults, V, 108
Homer, I, 196, VI, 406; papyri, II, 393
Ḥomesh, double tithe, V, 14
Homicide, I, 145
Homilists and homiletics, II, 144, 280, 294, 316, 320, 422, VIII, 30; *see also* Aggadah; Midrash; Sermons
Homonyms, biblical, VII, 12; in Maimonidean system, VIII, 82
Homosexuality, as poetic theme, VII, 158 ff., 308
Honey, I, 252
Ḥoni ha-me'aggel, prayers for rain, II, 349
Honorius, Roman emperor, II, 191, 192
Honorius I, pope, III, 24; on Jewish converts, III, 40
Hora'ah, amoraic age, VI, 17
Hormizd, king of Persia, III, 57
Horn: blowing of, on New Year's day, II, 120, 138, 383, VII, 76, 107; "little horn," V, 87; ram's horn, II, 256, 333, 416; symbol II, 11
Horoscopes, VIII, 178, 183, 366
Horseback riding, ban on, III, 141, 149, 152, 298 f.
Horses, I, 332
Hosea, prophet, I, 89, 91, 99, 336; condemns animal sacrifices, I, 124
—— Book of, V, 163, 239; commentaries on, VI, 165, 289, VII, 38; Karaites on, VI, 473
Hosea, king of Israel, I, 348
Hoshaiah, R., II, 225; mystic speculations, VIII, 6
Hoshaiah II, R., II, 284
Hosha'nah, III, 101
Hospice, communal, VIII, 239 f.
Hospitals: in East and West, VIII, 240; noted, VIII, 236, 389; use of music, VII, 321
Hours: division of, VIII, 373 f.; planetary movements and, VIII, 185
Houses: in Babylonia, I, 109, 346; construction of, VIII, 356; door-post inscriptions, V, 59; figures of devils on doors, III, 140; near mosque, III, 138, 145; ownership and right of preemption, III, 145 f.; renting of, to Gentiles, IV, 158; stone, I, 257, IV, 85, 170, 281 f.
Howden, Richard, on moneylending, IV, 83
Ḥubaysh, Arabic translation of Greek writings, VI, 264

Hud, III, 82
Huesca, Spain, IV, 39
Hugo of Flavigny, IV, 100 f.
Hulaju, conqueror of Baghdad, VI, 11
Ḥuldah, prophetess, II, 286
Ḥullin, tractate, VI, 86
Human and animal figures in art, II, 9, 10, 13, 15, 154, 402
Humanitarianism, I, 22, 155-58, 365-66, II, 3-6, 329, VIII, 124 f.; and belief in "chosenness," II, 170
Humanitas, Graeco-Roman concept, II, 6, 329 f., VIII, 263
Human nature, transformation in, on advent of the Messiah, V, 165, 175
Humility, biblical synonyms for, VI, 296; Jewish ideal of, VIII, 121
Humor, in exegesis, VI, 288
"Humors," physiological, VIII, 260
Huna, exilarch, VI, 17; conflict with R. Ḥanina, VI, 200
Huna, R., Amora, II, 221, 231, 237, 240, 249
Huna, Mar Rab, gaon, VI, 132 f.
Huna b. Joshua, R., VIII, 379
Huna Mari, II, 182, 196
Ḥunayn ibn Isḥaq al-'Ibadi, Syriac Christian translator, III, 80, VI, 264, 271, VIII, 250; on music, VII, 207
Hundred men, in suspending Gershom's excommunication, VI, 136, 138, 394
Hungary, Jews in, II, 210, 406, III, 206 f., 211 ff., 330, 332 f.
Ḥuqqe ha-Torah, VI, 140, 395
Hurrians, I, 36, 313
Ḥusain, grandson of Mohammed, V, 7; wife of, III, 89
Husband: and divorce (*q.v.*), V, 241 f., VI, 394 f.; duties, I, 237; supremacy of, I, 114, 146
Ḥushiel, captive scholar, V, 46; father of Ḥananel, VI, 46, 213; two Ḥushiels?, V, 312 f., VI, 342
Ḥussain ibn Manṣur al-Hallaj, *see* Hallaj
Hydatius, chronicle, VI, 429
Hyderabad, I, 321
Hygiene, ritualistic ablution and, VIII, 262
Hyksos: in Egypt, I, 35 ff., 303; and Exodus, I, 195; feudal cleavages under, I, 54; worship of Seth, I, 304
Hymns: accompanying sacrificial worship, I, 123, 395; alphabetic, VIII, 13; Amun, I, 52; mystic, VIII, 12; numinous, VIII, 23; *see also* Psalms
Hyperetes, communal factotum, II, 367; *see also Ḥazzan*
Hypocrisy, VI, 143
Hypsistos, supreme god, I, 23, III, 62
Hyrcania, I, 131
Hyrcanus II, high priest, I, 218, II, 206
Hyrcanus, John, *see* John Hyrcanus

I

Iamblichus, II, 401
"I am that I am," *see* Ehyeh
Iberia, Armenian, Persian conquest of, III, 22
Iberian Peninsula, center of Jewish intellectual life, VIII, 61; Karaites in, V, 271; medical writings, VIII, 245 f.; *see also* Portugal; Spain; *also under* individual kingdoms and cities
Ibn 'Abbas, 'Abdallah, "the Arab rabbi," VI, 275; on Jewish biblical interpretation, V, 88; warning against "people of the book," V, 88, VI, 444
Ibn 'Abbas, Yehudah b. Samuel, VI, 56, VII, 155
Ibn 'Abd Rabbihi, V, 194
Ibn 'Abdun, of Seville, V, 97; on clothing of *dhimmis,* III, 139 f.; disparagement of *dhimmi* doctors, VIII, 254; on social distinctions between Muslims and non-Muslims, III, 146
Ibn abi ad-Dunya al-Quarashi, VII, 203
Ibn abi al-Bayan, As-Sadid, *see* David b. Solomon
Ibn Abihi, Ziyad, IV, 226
Ibn abi'l Thanna, *see* Yehudah b. Joseph
Ibn Abitur (or Ibn Satanas), Joseph b. Isaac, Spanish scholar, V, 45, VI, 220, VII, 75, 155; Arabic translation of the Talmud, VI, 264; excommunication and exile, VII, 149; liturgical poems, VII, 170 f.; talmudic exegesis, VI, 61
Ibn abi Uṣaibi'a, Arab physician and medical historian, VII, 8, VIII, 236, 240, 247 f., 249; story of physician's fee, VIII, 254
Ibn Abu'l Ḥusain, Abu Sa'id, Samaritan scholiast, V, 89, 175, VI, 271
Ibn 'Adi, al-Haitham, VI, 143
Ibn Adret, Solomon, VI, 136, 390; on animal sacrifice, VII, 79; on communal authority, V, 63

Ibn Aflaḥ, Jabir, *see* Jabir
Ibn al-'Arabi, Muslim mystic, VIII, 15
Ibn al-Ashraf, K'ab, VII, 191
Ibn al-Bazyar, "Book of Conjunctions," VIII, 207
Ibn al-Faqih, III, 205
Ibn al-Furat, vizier, III, 153, 158, V, 10, 11
Ibn al-Hajj al-Abdari, V, 96
Ibn al-Jasus (or al-Gasum), VII, 118, 278 f.
Ibn al-Jauzi, Sibt, IV, 110, VI, 298
Ibn al-Jazzar, Abu Jafar, Muslim medical author, VIII, 236, 396
Ibn al-Kaziruni, Jewish banker of Cairo, III, 160
Ibn al-Latif, scholar of Damascus, VIII, 249 f.
Ibn al-Masarra, Arab mystic, III, 124, VIII, 124, 135
Ibn al-Mu'tazz, Abu'l 'Abbas 'Abdullah, VII, 142
Ibn al-Muthanna, Abu 'Ubaida Ma'mar, Arab philologist, VII, 11
Ibn al-Qalanisi, Muslim historian, IV, 109 f., 295
Ibn al-Qama, IV, 31
Ibn al-Qifṭi, historian of science, VIII, 240
Ibn al-Taras, Sa'id, VI, 206, VII, 228
Ibn al-Waḥshiya, VIII, 217
Ibn al-Wasiti, Muslim sage, III, 128
Ibn 'Allan al-Yahudi, Jewish banker, IV, 202
Ibn an-Nadim, Abu Isḥaq, Arab bibliographer, III, 197, VII, 317, VIII, 167, 224, 240; *Fihrist,* VI, 265, VIII, 148
Ibn an-Naqqash, III, 128, 152; *fatwa,* III, 167 f.
Ibn 'Aqnin, Joseph b. Yehudah, pupil of Maimonides, VIII, 259, 340; alleged Maimonidean letter to, VIII, 3; on denunciations of converts, III, 126; educational program, VIII, 146; identified with Ibn Shime'on, V, 296 (*q.v.*); on Maimonides, VIII, 250; music and mental hygiene, VII, 208 f.; on relapsed converts, III, 127; on useful sciences, VIII, 159; on voluntary exile, III, 291
Ibn ar-Rawandi, Muslim heretic, VI, 298 f.; *Destroyer of the Brain,* VI, 301; *Emerald,* VI, 301
Ibn Aryeh, false messiah, V, 201
Ibn Asad, Abu'l Faraj Furqan, *see* Yeshu'a b. Yehudah
Ibn ash-Shuwaikh, head of Baghdad academy, III, 167
Ibn as-Saffan, Ephraim, court physician, VIII, 248 f.
Ibn Bajja, Abu-Bekr ibn aṣ-Ṣaij (Avempace), VIII, 162
Ibn Bal'am, Yehudah b. Samuel (Abu Zakariya Yaḥya), VI, 95, VI, 277, VII, 201; on Aramaic and Arabic parallels, VII, 230; attack on Ibn Chiquitilla, VI, 311 ff., 485 f.; attack on Saadiah, VI, 277; collection of biblical passages relating to miracles, VII, 201; commentary on Genesis, VI, 282 f.; grammatical monographs, VII, 49; use of methodological innovations, VI, 291
Ibn Baron, Isaac (Abu Ibrahim b. Joseph ibn Benveniste): lexicographic treatise, VII, 27; on verb forms, VII, 49
Ibn Baṭṭuṭa, III, 161
Ibn Buklarish (Beklaresh), Junus (Jonah ibn Isḥaq), medical author, VIII, 248
Ibn Buṭlan, VIII, 388
Ibn Chiquitilla, Isaac: disciple of Menaḥem, VII, 22; ascription of poems by, VII, 302 f.; influenced by Saadiah, VII, 301
Ibn Chiquitilla, Joseph b. Abraham, kabbalist, VIII, 287
Ibn Chiquitilla, Moses, V, 158; biblical critic and poet, VI, 310 ff., 485 f., VII, 155; Hebrew translations, VII, 7, 23, 47; use of methodological innovations, VI, 291 f.
Ibn Danan, Saadiah, of Granada, VII, 225
Ibn Daud, Abraham, III, 203, IV, 214, VIII, 137; on Aḥai's *She'elot,* VI, 339; on aims of philosophy, VIII, 78, 135, 218; on alleged Jewish tampering with biblical text, VI, 254; anti-Christian apologetic purpose, VI, 210; on the attainment of happiness, VIII, 121; biological discussion, VIII, 225 f.; Book or Order of Tradition, III, 156, VI, 30, 131, 206 ff., 233; choice of words, VI, 481; on the commandments, VI, 142 f., VIII, 118; on David b. Zakkai and Saadiah, V, 178, VI, 356; on dreams and prophetic visions, VIII, 133; editions and translations, VI, 209; enumeration of generations of Saboraim,

Ibn Daud, Abraham (*Continued*)
VI, 328; on exilarchs, V, 301; on the existence of God, VIII, 90 f.; on free will, VIII, 110; on Ḥayyuj and Ibn Janaḥ, VII, 44; on Ibn Gabirol, VIII, 75, 84, 92; influence of Aristotle on, VIII, 63; on Karaites, V, 272, VI, 453; on man's love of God, VIII, 115; on matter and form, VIII, 87 f.; organization of material, VI, 208 f.; potential readers, VIII, 71; on preoccupation with science, VIII, 143; sources, VI, 210, 429 f.

Ibn Eleazar (Abenalazar), Jacob, Spanish liturgical poet and translator, VII, 189

Ibn Ezra, Abraham, biblical commentator and poet, IV, 26, V, 152, VII, 155; and astrology, VII, 210 f., VIII, 170 f., 176 ff., 183 f., 365 ff.; astronomic works, VIII, 161, 171 f., 362 f.; attack on Karaites, VI, 290; attitude toward *piyyuṭim,* VII, 104; concerning Balaam, VIII, 133; and Bar Ḥiyya, VIII, 169 f.; on biblical substitute words, VI, 293 f.; birthplace, IV, 248; on the commandments, VI, 396; criticism of verbose commentators, VI, 284 f.; dependence on Rabbanite linguists, VI, 291; on deviations from linguistic rules, VII, 58; dirge over his son's apostasy, VII, 160; on divisions of earth's surface, VIII, 214; on eternality of matter, VIII, 94; on Enoch, VIII, 178 f.; on *Ehyeh,* VIII, 152 f.; *ge'ulahs,* V, 362; grammatical treatises, VII, 50 ff.; on headings for Psalms, VII, 203; Hebrew work on meters, VII, 196, 317; horoscopes, VIII, 178, 366; on Ibn Tamim, VII, 16 f.; on Ibn Yashush, VI, 309 f.; on identification of biblical names and anonyms, VI, 281; on identity of Job, VI, 308; legend on death of, VIII, 368; linguistic riddles, VII, 4; on man's soul, VIII, 106 f.; on Mar Samuel's formula for solar year, VIII, 198 f.; and Masha'allah, VIII, 166; mathematical discussions, VIII, 352; medical writings, VIII, 248; on messianic problem, V, 156; on musicology, VII, 209; observations on human anatomy, VIII, 229 f.; philosophic-ethical treatise, VII, 52; praise of Ibn Chiquitilla, VII, 49; prohibition of lights, V, 403; and proverb on wisdom, VIII, 145; on psalm tunes, VII, 283; puns, VIII, 192; quoted by authorities, VIII, 172; revision of his works, VIII, 171; on Saadiah, VI, 266, 270, VII, 16, 50 f., 141; scientific tracts, VI, 422; on square characters, VII, 56 f.; student's comment on, VI, 467; translations, VII, 7, 23, 47, VIII, 65; on types of poetry, VII, 203 f.; use of *gemaṭrias,* VIII, 152; versatility and prestige, VIII, 160; world-wide influence, VII, 173 f.

—— works, VIII, 62 f.; "Astrolabe," VIII, 177; "Beginning of Wisdom," VIII, 176 f.; "Book of Nativities," VIII, 178 f.; Commentary on Genesis, VI, 175; Commentary on Job, VI, 277, 291; Epistle on the Sabbath, VI, 475 f.; Fundamentals of Astronomic Tables, VIII, 171; "Pisan Tables," VIII, 171

Ibn Ezra, Isaac, son of Abraham, VII, 155, 160

Ibn Ezra, Moses, Jewish poet of Granada, III, 158, IV, 31 f., 159, V, 389; admiration for Arabic poetry, VII, 194; Arabic work on Hebrew poetic arts, VII, 191, 198 f.; attitude toward *piyyuṭim,* VII, 103; on biblical language, VII, 57 f.; bilingualism, VII, 9; career, VII, 153 f., 293 f.; on charges of Jewish anthropomorphism, VIII, 101; on Dunash, VII, 42; on Hermes, VIII, 10; on immortalization through poetry, VII, 147; liturgical poems, V, 362; on "mixture of doubt with certainty" in figure of speech, VII, 315; penitential prayer, VII, 173; poems on the mysteries of existence, VII, 172 f.; survey of Spanish Hebrew poetry, VII, 146 ff., 155; on term for nature, VIII, 112, 335; on worship by men and angels, VII, 210; youthful indiscretions, VII, 291

Ibn Fadhlan, Arab envoy, III, 201, 325

Ibn Fadhlan, Baghdad vizier, VIII, 237

Ibn Fadhlan, Abu 'Ali, Jewish banker of Baghdad, III, 159, 196

Ibn Falaquera, Shem Ṭob b. Joseph, VIII, 137; on effects of liturgical music, VII, 209; epitome of "Fountain of Life," VIII, 74; poem on mental and physical health, VIII, 405; on reading Maimonides' *Guide,* VIII, 312; on Solomon's knowledge of natural sciences, VIII, 387

Ibn Ferrizuel, Joseph (Cidellus): against Karaites, V, 45; Halevi's poem to, IV, 251, VII, 192; service to Alphonso VI, IV, 36
Ibn Ferrizuel, Solomon, IV, 36
Ibn Gabirol, Solomon b. Yehudah (Avicebron or Avicebrol), V, 49, 152 ff., VIII, 61 f., 69, 322; astronomic themes, VIII, 168 f.; bilingualism, VII, 9; career, VII, 152 f., 292 f.; on division of earth's surface, VIII, 214; doctrine of sin, VIII, 119; on the First Cause, VIII, 98; on goal of human soul, VIII, 113 f.; on good and evil, VIII, 119; influences on, VIII, 324 f.; intermediary position of nature, VIII, 335; legend of, VIII, 47; on love of God, VIII, 114 f.; messianic teachings, V, 153 ff., 162 f., 361 f.; poem on a sunset, VII, 163 f.; potential readers, VIII, 73 f.; on purpose of creation, VIII, 106; religious poems, V, 99, VI, 92, VIII, 84, 134; on the senses, VIII, 108; sources, VIII, 324 f.; on sources of knowledge, VIII, 82 ff.; theme of exile, V, 99, VIII, 126; theory of mediation between God and man, VIII, 91 f.; use of allegory, VI, 297, VII, 167 f., VIII, 77 f.; "voluntaristic" doctrine, VIII, 322; wedding poem, VII, 314
—— works, VIII, 302; "Fountain of Life," VIII, 61 f., 74, 92, 112, 135; "Necklace," VII, 49 f., 162; "On the Improvement of Moral Qualities," VIII, 62; "Royal Crown," VII, 151, 153, 171 f., 194, VIII, 62, 92, 106, 168
Ibn Gaon, Shem Ṭob b. Abraham, VIII, 38 f.
Ibn Garcia, III, 98
Ibn Gayyat, Isaac b. Yehudah, jurist and poet, VI, 61, 84, 113, VII, 155; and Alfasi, VI, 87; decision on recitation of *Musaf 'Amidah,* VII, 107; on Ecclesiastes, VI, 270; halakhic works, VI, 73, 354, 360 f.; sacred poetry, VII, 171, 246; support of local customs, VI, 126
Ibn Ḥabib, Moses b. Shem Ṭob, III, 244 f.
Ibn Ḥalfon, Isaac, Hebrew poet, VII, 146
Ibn Ḥamdin, Cordovan *qadi,* III, 124
Ibn Ḥanbal, Aḥmad, VI, 26; *see also* Ḥanbalites
Ibn Ḥasan, Sa'id, of Alexandria, convert to Islam, V, 97 f., 102; on image worship, V, 125; prediction, V, 201
Ibn Ḥawqal, Muslim traveler, VI, 220
Ibn Ḥazm, Muslim theologian, V, 327, VIII, 136; antisemitism, V, 95; biblical criticism, V, 85, 88; on conversion to Islam, V, 102; on the exilarchate, V, 13; on the Karaites, V, 271; religious studies, VIII, 11, 301; and Yosephon, VI, 191
Ibn Ḥisdai, Abraham b. Samuel: attitude toward Arabic script, VII, 191; "Prince and Dervish," VII, 189
Ibn Ḥisdai, Abu Ja'far Yusuf, VIII, 357
Ibn Ḥisdai, Abu'l Fadhl: Jewish convert to Islam, III, 158; adviser of Al-Muqtadir and Al-Mu'tamin, III, 158; musicologist of Saragossa, VII, 206
Ibn Ḥisdai, Joseph b. Aḥmad, VIII, 248
Ibn Hisham, III, 163
Ibn Hud, Muslim mystic, V, 103
Ibn Hudail, Mu'tazilite leader, VIII, 96
Ibn 'Imram, Isḥaq, Muslim physician and teacher, VIII, 236
Ibn Jaḥiz, III, 98
Ibn Janaḥ, Jonah (Abu'l Walid ibn Merwan), Spanish Hebrew grammarian, III, 102, 148, VII, 24 ff., 44 f., 229, 237; accused of plagiarism, VII, 229; on alteration of text by copyists, VII, 150; contributions to grammar and lexicography, VI, 291 f., VII, 7, 24 ff., 44 ff., 229; and David Qimḥi, VIII, 386; medical dictionary, VIII, 248; on neglect of Arabic, VII, 8; on philological debates among Spanish Jews, VII, 3 f.; praise of Masorites, VI, 252; quotations from Yose, VII, 261; Rabbanite scholar, VI, 28, 270; use of multilingual like-sounding words, VII, 223; on word substitutions in biblical text, VI, 293
Ibn Jau, Jacob, Cordovan silk manufacturer, V, 44 f.
Ibn Jumay', Hibbat Allah (Nathaniel?), medical treatises, VIII, 226, 247, 249
Ibn Kafron, Ephraim, disciple of Menaḥem, VII, 22
Ibn Kammuna, Sa'd ibn Manṣur, V, 90, 274; on conversion to Islam, V, 102
Ibn Kaspi, Joseph, VI, 376
Ibn Khaldun, Arab historian, VI, 192, VIII, 122; on the Kahina, III, 91
Ibn Khurdadhbah, VIII, 212; *Book of*

Ibn Khurdadhbah (*Continued*)
Routes, IV, 180 f.; on Byzantine taxation, III, 191, 193
Ibn Kusin, physician in Mosul, VIII, 246
Ibn Lahi'a, exilarch, V, 7
Ibn Megas, Joseph b. Meir ha-Levi, V, 68, 76 f., 168, VI, 58, 61 f., 84, 108, 367; on authority of responsa, VI, 115 f.; on authorship of responsa, VI, 114; *Ḥiddushim,* VI, 353; responsa, VI, 117
Ibn Mubarak, physician and teacher in Cairo, VIII, 236
Ibn Muqlah, vizier, III, 154
Ibn Musa al-Asdi, *see* Harun ibn Musa
Ibn Nagrela, Joseph b. Samuel: Arab revolt against, III, 123, 219; succeeds father as nagid, III, 158
Ibn Nagrela, Samuel b. Joseph, nagid of Granada, III, 156 f., IV, 29, 36, 179, V, 45, 48 f., VI, 113, 215, VII, 26, 30, VIII, 69; acclaimed as patron of learning, VI, 21; aphorisms, VII, 164 f.; controversy with Ibn Janaḥ, VI, 474, VII, 25; correspondence, VII, 165; critique of Qur'an, V, 330; dirge on death of brother, VII, 159 f.; disappearance of writings, VII, 286; epitome of Yosephon, VI, 191; explanation of divine name, VIII, 179 f.; halakhic miscellanies, VI, 72 f., 360 f.; Ibn Ḥazm's attack on, V, 95; *Introduction to the Talmud,* VI, 33, 333 f.; philological work, VII, 45 f., 237 f.; poetic achievement, VII, 151 ff., 296 ff.; on royal patrons, VII, 148 f.; source of rise to power in Granada, VII, 149 f.; sources for geonic period, VI, 208, VII, 45 f.; on Spanish Jewry, V, 58; supply of books to students, VII, 137 f.; on Targumim, VI, 262, VII, 82, 193, 249, 262; use of Arabic, VII, 191; use of Arabic meter, VII, 195 f.; use of personal experiences as themes, VII, 156
Ibn Nuḥ, Joseph, grammatical work, VII, 38 f.
Ibn Paquda, Baḥya, *see* Baḥya
Ibn Parḥon, Solomon, lexicographer, VII, 26, 27 f., 52; on Saadiah, VI, 276; on the use of Hebrew, IV, 173; on veiling of women, III, 142
Ibn Qayyim al-Jauziya, V, 86, 96
Ibn Quraish, Yehudah, of Tahort, Algeria, VI, 264, VII, 17 f.; interest in Berber dialects, VII, 11 f.; on Onkelos, VII, 5, 17; pioneer in comparative linguistics, VII, 11
Ibn Qurra, Ṭabit, Sabean mathematician, VIII, 243; theory of "trepidation" of the stars, VIII, 164
Ibn Qutaiba, poet, III, 148; on interest in history, VI, 198 f.; on the savant, VI, 72
Ibn Raḥamun, Salama (Solomon) ibn Mubarak (Meborakh), Egyptian Jewish physician, VIII, 226
Ibn Ridhwan, 'Ali (Haly Rodoam), of Cairo, VIII, 249, 250; debate with Ibn Buṭlan, VIII, 388
Ibn Riyaḥin, Arab admiral, V, 46 f.
Ibn Sa'd, 'Abdallah, treaty with Nubians, IV, 181
Ibn Ṣaddiq, Joseph, VIII, 67, 69, 137; on knowledge of God, VIII, 118; on man as microcosm, VIII, 62, 103; messianic problem, V, 366; potential readers, VIII, 71
Ibn Sahl, Abraham, of Seville, VII, 191 f.
Ibn Sahula, Isaac b. Solomon, VII, 189 f.
Ibn Sahula, Meir, VIII, 42
Ibn Sa'id, Abu Qasim, Toledan judge: "Categories of Nations," IV, 31, VIII, 264; on Ḥisdai ibn Shapruṭ, V, 47; on Jewish preoccupation with law and biographies of prophets, VIII, 135, 264
Ibn Sa'id, Abu 'Umar Aḥmad, V, 83, VIII, 56
Ibn Salam, Aḥmad ibn 'Abdallah, VI, 265, 275; commentaries on the Qur'an, VI, 282 f.
Ibn Salim, Faraj, *see* Farragut
Ibn Saqawaihi, VIII, 100; Book of Shameful Things, V, 253 f.; identified with Salmon b. Yeruḥim, V, 406
Ibn Sarjado, Aaron, V, 23, 24, 295
Ibn Satanas, *see* Ibn Abitur
Ibn Shahin, Muslim exegete, *tafsir,* VI, 468
Ibn Shahin, Nissim, *see* Nissim b. Jacob
Ibn Shapruṭ, *see* Ḥisdai ibn Shapruṭ
Ibn Shime'on, Joseph b. Yehudah, disciple of Maimonides, VI, 380; identity of, V, 296; *see also* Ibn 'Aqnin
Ibn Sim'an, Isaac, Jewish composer, of Cordova, VII, 206
Ibn Ṣiqbal, Solomon, VII, 188

Ibn Sosan, Yehudah, III, 291
Ibn Suleiman, Yaḥya, *see* Zechariah b. Solomon
Ibn Tamim, Abu Sahl Dunash (Adonim), of Kairuwan, VII, 34, VIII, 24, 59, 236, 246; alleged conversion, VII, 225; lexicographic works, VII, 16 f.
Ibn Tibbon, Moses, VIII, 384
Ibn Tibbon, Samuel, translator, VI, 11, VIII, 64, 306 f.; Maimonides' epistle to, VIII, 72, 232; translation of the *Guide,* VI, 11, VIII, 315
Ibn Tibbon, Yehudah, "father of translators," VI, 270, VIII, 60, 65; apologia for use of Arabic, VII, 6 f.; attitude toward Arabic script, IV, 36 f., VII, 191; censure of Ibn Parḥon, VII, 231; "Ethical Will," VIII, 235, 258; library, VII, 138 f.; translations, VII, 7, 47, 166, VIII, 39
Ibn Tulun, Aḥmad, Egyptian ruler, III, 136, 161; on non-Muslim tombs in Cairo, III, 137
Ibn Tumart, VIII, 98, 326; on the unity of God, III, 292
Ibn 'Ubayya, III, 128; treatise of 1474, III, 135
Ibn Verga, Joseph, IV, 238
Ibn Waqar, Joseph, Spanish kabbalist, VII, 182
Ibn Wallad, Aḥmad, Egyptian philologist, VII, 19
Ibn Yaḥya, Tam b. David, VI, 191
Ibn Yaḥya al-Maghribi, Samau'al, *see* Samau'al ibn Yaḥya
Ibn Ya'qub, Ibrahim, Spanish Jew, III, 214, IV, 169, 174, 194, VI, 434 f.; and Ḥisdai, III, 217, VI, 435; report on journey to central Europe, VI, 221 f., 434 f.; on Slavs, III, 217 f.
Ibn Ya'qub, Solomon b. Joseph, VI, 61
Ibn Yashush, Isaac (Abu Ibrahim): historical biblical criticism, VI, 309 f.; identification of Jobab with Job, VI, 293; monograph on inflections, VII, 49
Ibn Yunus, Egyptian astronomer, VIII, 167; length of solar year, VIII, 198
Ibn Zabara, Joseph b. Meir, poet of Barcelona, VII, 187 f.; Book of Delight, VII, 308 f., VIII, 237
Ibn Zaid al-Ḥasan, III, 115
Ibn Zeraḥ, Menaḥem, VI, 50
Ibrahim, *see* Ibn Ya'qub
Ibrahim (Isaac), son of Neṭira, III, 153
'Ibrim, identity of, with Ḥabiru, I, 302
Iconoclastic movement, III, 178, 193, VIII, 31; alleged Jewish influences on, III, 178; in Near East, VIII, 26
Iconodulism, III, 193 f.
Icons and iconography, V, 125; *see also* Imagery; Images and symbols
Idalius, bishop of Barcelona, III, 250
Ideas, development of, I, 52
Idjma', Muslim principle, V, 169, VI, 145 f., VIII, 324; against individual analogy in linguistics, VII, 58
Idolatry: condemnation of, I, 177, 179, II, 217, V, 347, VIII, 10; Diocletian and, V, 172; at Temple of Jerusalem, I, 335
Idris, identified with Enoch (*q.v.*), VIII, 366
Idris I, forced conversions, III, 281
Idris II, founder of Fez, VII, 225
Idrisi, al-, Muslim geographer, IV, 243, VIII, 214 f.; Book of King Roger, VIII, 212; and Dioscorides' work, VIII, 246; on Tarragona and Lucena Jewries, III, 109, 170
Idumaea and Idumaeans, I, 106, 167, 224, 382, VI, 192 f.; prisoners liberated by, I, 412; protagonists of political principle, II, 48; *see also* Edom and Edomites
"Idumaean slave" (Herod), I, 397
Ifran, Africa, tombstone inscriptions, III, 230
Ifriqiya, province, Africa, III, 107; Spanish immigrants to, VII, 273
Ignatius, Saint, II, 136, 167, III, 243
Ignoramus, reference to, in Jewish prayer of thanksgiving, VII, 109 f.
Igor (Helgo-Oleg), Russian prince, III, 203
Illegitimacy, II, 218, 253; *see also* Bastards
Illiteracy: attitude toward, IV, 167, V, 75, VIII, 295; of witnesses, VI, 255; *see also 'Am ha-areṣ*
Imagery: prohibition of, I, 13, 14, 48, 49, 59, 314, 335, II, 15, 284, 285, 330; departure from prohibition, I, 66; and iconoclasm, III, 178
Images and symbols: in decorative arts, II, 9 ff., 13, 15, 154, 330, 322 f., 402; destruction of statues and, II, 400;

Images and symbols (*Continued*)
emblem over Temple gate, I, 238, 402, II, 13; found in catacombs and tombs, II, 11; in Jerusalem, I, 322; significance, II, 12 ff.; vine symbol, I, 253, II, 13; *see also* Sculptures
Imagination: as "internal" sense, VIII, 79; of prophet, VIII, 131; in storytelling, VI, 168 ff.
Imam, Muslim official, V, 315, VI, 13; descendant of Mohammed, III, 304 f.
Immaculate Conception, VIII, 30
"Immanuel," interpretation of, V, 157
Immanuel of Rome, Hebrew poet, IV, 238, VIII, 48, 176; books copied by, VII, 139; on cantors, VII, 130
Imma Shalom, II, 227
Immigration, *see* Migratory movements
Immolation, self-, *see* Suicide
Immortality, literary, VII, 147 f.
Immortality of the nation, I, 12
Immortality of the soul, I, 9, 12, 137, 207-8, 357, 358, II, 14, 215, 312, 333, V, 166; and funeral rites, II, 289; position of Pharisees and Sadducees, II, 38 f., 344 f.; *see also* Resurrection; Soul
Imperial worship, I, 244, 404, II, 5, 99, 109
Import trade, Jewish role in, IV, 165
"Impostors, three," V, 104, VI, 301
Impurities, physical, I, 81; communicable nature of, VI, 483
'Imram b. Sedaqa, Jewish physician in Damascus, VIII, 236
Imru al-Qais, Lakhmid king, epitaph, III, 61
Inbreeding, I, 146, 360; *see also* Incest; Marriage
Incantations and exorcisms, I, 139, 359, II, 19 ff., 67, 189, 316, 336, 401, VIII, 8 ff., 45 f., 274 ff.; Aramaic texts, VIII, 7 f., 274 f.; divine name in, VIII, 281; eclecticism, VIII, 10; erotic, VIII, 283; magic formulas, VIII, 8 ff., 274 ff.; repetition of, VIII, 284; used during childbirth, I, 329; use of great names in, VIII, 233
Incarnation, doctrine of, I, 13, V, 115, VI, 103, VIII, 30
Incense, I, 127, 129, 352, II, 333
Incest, I, 146, II, 229 ff., 411, V, 221 f., 242 f., 325, VI, 69
Independence, Karaite doctrine of loss of, V, 260
India, VIII, 217; Christians in, III, 285; confused with Ethiopia, VI, 434; impact of science, VIII, 148, 172, 193, 360; influence of Hebrew language, VII, 222; international trade, I, 64, III, 284, IV, 175; and Jewish origins, I, 377; Jews in, II, 212, 407, III, 114 f., 173, 285, IV, 174; numbering, VIII, 150; pariah caste, I, 297; religion, I, 373, *see also* Parsees and Parsiism; religious toleration, III, 130 f.
Indian Ocean, VIII, 214 f.
Indian sages, Jews as descendants of, I, 184
Individual and individualism, I, 8, 136, 138, 357; 'Anan's view of, V, 221; in biblical interpretation, V, 230; communal responsibility for, IV, 40, 134 f., 137 f., V, 4, 100 ff.; and free will, VIII, 109; and Judaism, I, 11, 12, 29, V, 225, VIII, 263; Karaite, V, 234 f., 261; and society, IV, 222 f., V, 4, 100 ff., VIII, 120 ff.; *see also* Responsibility
Indo-European peoples, I, 36; Yosephon re, VI, 226
Indo-Iranian cultures, I, 102
Industry, I, 64, 69, 255-58, 407-8, II, 247 ff.; intensification of, IV, 164-71, 318-22; refined methods of production, IV, 168; reserve labor army, I, 270; sociopolitical strife in Hellenistic centers, I, 271; urban Jews turning to, II, 123
Infants, souls of, VIII, 108
Inferiority, Jewish, Church emphasis on, IV, 10, 12, 16
Infidel, VIII, 66; tax receipt as mark of, III, 168; term, III, 149; *see also Dhimmis*
Inflationary pressures, I, 277, 414, II, 245, 250, 414
Inflection, biblical, principles of, VII, 35
Influence, divine, Muslim concept of, VIII, 134
Informers among Jews, II, 142, 385; funeral of, 287; hatred of, V, 46, 241; punishment of, VI, 134
Inheritance, laws of, III, 158, IV, 16, VI, 4, 67 f.; of converts, III, 10, 158, V, 18, 299; of daughter and son, V, 243; of husband, V, 223, 373; interfaith, III, 301; of land, IV, 162; and mathematics, VIII, 147, 153 f.; moneylenders and, IV, 205; Muslim, III, 143 f., V, 18, VI,

436; under "Ordinances of the Jews," IV, 204; and settlement of estate, V, 300 f.
Injustice, divine, VIII, 103 ff.
Innkeeping, IV, 165
Innocent II, pope: ecumenical council, IV, 11 f.; greeted in Rome by Jewish deputation, IV, 10; struggle with Anacletus II, IV, 10 f.
Innocent III, pope, IV, 227; advice on delinquent Jewish tithe payers, IV, 13; codification of canon law, IV, 19 f.; *Constitutio pro Judaeis,* IV, 8; on employment of Jews, IV, 42; on Jewish slaveholders, IV, 188 f.; protest against disregard of canon law, IV, 16 f.; on usury, IV, 206
Innocent IV, pope, IV, 306
Inscriptions: Afghanistan, III, 282; Africa, III, 230, 335; Arabia, III, 61, 64, 66, 82, 258; Behistun, I, 353; Crimea, VIII, 203; Cyrenaica, III, 108; doorpost, V, 59; Dura-Europos, II, 331, VII, 128; eastern Europe, III, 206 f.; France, III, 48, 251, IV, 260; funerary, I, 378, II, 10 ff., 146, 331 ff.; Fusṭaṭ synagogue, III, 134 f.; grave of Adoniram, III, 244; and Jewish chronology, II, 376; Khazaria, III, 200 f.; Khirbet Mafjar, III, 103; Latin, I, 378; Mesha, I, 336; Monotheistic, III, 66; Nabatean, III, 64; with name of Iao, VIII, 275; on Polish coins, III, 218, 338 f.; preponderance relating to males, III, 252; Samaritan, V, 370; of Shapur I, II, 380, 396 f.; showing spread of Jews, II, 210 f., 406 f.; Sinaitic, I, 35, 314; Spain, III, 34, 244, IV, 33, VII, 313; symbolic, II, 11 ff.; synagogue of Theodotos in Jerusalem, VIII, 239; Ten Commandments, V, 370 f.; Thamudic, III, 258; Venosa, Sicily, IV, 20, VIII, 204
Institute of Research and Study in Medieval Canon Law, IV, 242
Insurance association, II, 261
Intellect, "knowledge of," VIII, 79
Intellectual life, academic, V, 33 f., *see also* Academies; under Byzantine domination, VIII, 30; centers of, IV, 7, 45, 47 f., 112; *see also under* Learning; and disappearance of ancient writings, VI, 438 f.; freedom of, under authority, VII, 211 ff.; of northern European Jewry, VI, 422
Intelligences, intermediary, VIII, 93 ff., 111 ff.; and spheres, VIII, 82, 114, 128, 168 f., 180
Intelligentsia, Spanish, and poetry, VII, 150 ff.
Intention, Judaism's stress upon, II, 307
Intercalation, VIII, 186 ff., 193 ff.; Palestinian-Babylonian dispute, VIII, 194 ff.
Interest, legal restraints, II, 250, 414; rates, I, 69, 261, 323, 409, IV, 198 ff., 214, 342; *see also* Usury
Intermarriage, between Egyptian Jewess and foreign Jew, VI, 138 f.; Karaite and Rabbanite, VI, 135; *see also* Marriage, interfaith
Intermediaries: between God and man, I, 139, 140, II, 42; doctrine of, V, 226, 228, 259, VIII, 91 ff.; protective, II, 17 ff., 42 ff.; *see also* Amulets; Angels; Talismans
International relations, II, 4
Interpretation, biblical: allegorical, II, 320, V, 215, VI, 273, 297, VIII, 77 f., 81, 84, 100, 110, *see also* Allegory; alternative meanings, VI, 287 f., 292 f.; of anthropomorphisms, VI, 258 f.; based on philological evidence, VI, 291 ff.; by common consent, V, 252; disputes over, V, 126; ethical or juristic approaches, VI, 35; geonic rules, VI, 333; Gregory I on, III, 29; hermeneutic elaboration of, VI, 155-63, 294 f., 400-405; hidden vs. ordinary meaning, VI, 166, 175, 275, 286, 290, 294 f., 463 f., VIII, 73; importance of grammar to, VII, 4, 6; independent, V, 221, 235; Innocent II on Jewish, IV, 10; Karaite, V, 213, 278 f.; literal, V, 213 f., 287, VIII, 81 f.; logical, V, 259; masoretic aid to, VI, 252; metaphorical, VI, 279; modes of, VI, 32 f., 166, 177, 412; Mohammed on Jewish, III, 84 f.; Mosaic law extended by, II, 319, 436; Muslim, V, 99 f., VI, 170; sectarian, V, 84 ff., 195 f., VII, 223 f.; talmudic, VI, 35-44, 336-41; traditional, VI, 274 ff.; Trullan synod on, V, 109; *see also* Bible; Exegesis
Interpreters: Jews' linguistic ability as, IV, 173 f., 322; of sermons, II, 280
Intolerance, *see* Antisemitism; Religious liberty
Introduction, letters of, in international trade, IV, 177

Intuition, prophetic, VIII, 131
Iran and Iranian Plateau, *see* Persia
Iraq: Arabic philology, VII, 19; Aramaic proverbs, VII, 220; claims to prophecies, VIII, 134; Muslim conquest of, III, 95; Syriac idiom of Jews in, VI, 453; tax payment and receipt, III, 168; *see also* Babylonia, *also under* cities, *e.g.*, Baghdad
Ireland: Gaelic in, VII, 222 f.; Jewish settlement, IV, 280; Richard Strongbow's expedition, IV, 82
Irenaeus, Saint, II, 145, 168, 408
Irene, Byzantine empress, III, 177
Iron, I, 256, 320
Iron Age, I, 316; relapse into semi-primitive conditions, I, 53; seal cylinders, I, 323
Irrigation, I, 252, 407
'Isa, Jewish physician, VIII, 243
Isaac, patriarch, I, 22, 37, 341, V, 90, 93; age of, VI, 480; and Esau, V, 129; Mohammed on, III, 85; sacrifice of, II, 138, 383, VI, 144, 300
Isaac, Charlemagne's interpreter, IV, 45, 174, 257, 322 f.
Isaac, head of academy of Firuz Shabur, III, 99
Isaac II, Byzantine emperor, III, 188
Isaac al-Lucena, chief reader, VI, 113
Isaac b. Abba Mari of Marseilles, VI, 83, 132, 361 f.; commentary on Alfasi, VI, 88; juridical miscellany, VI, 74
Isaac b. Abraham of Narbonne, VI, 89
Isaac b. Abraham, R., of Sens, IV, 193
Isaac b. Asher ha-Levi, IV, 134
Isaac b. Baruch ibn al-Balia, Spanish astronomer, VI, 61, 354, VIII, 376; and Alfasi, VI, 87
Isaac b. Dorbello, IV, 58
Isaac b. Melchizedek of Siponto, VI, 62
Isaac b. Moses Or Zaru'a, III, 219, IV, 36, 70, VI, 50, 118
Isaac b. Nathan, III, 198
Isaac b. Reuben al-Barceloni, VI, 368
Isaac b. Samuel, Tosafist of Dampierre, IV, 63 f.; on Alfasi, VI, 90
Isaac b. Saul, poet: Ibn Janaḥ's teacher, VII, 44; use of trick word, VII, 150
Isaac b. Sheshet, VI, 55
Isaac b. Solomon ha-Nasi, VII, 238
Isaac b. Solomon Israeli, *see* Israeli
Isaac b. Yehudah, German rabbi, VI, 75, 124
Isaac b. Yehudah ibn Gayyat, *see* Ibn Gayyat
Isaac (Nappaḥa), R., II, 5, 153, 162, 202, 238, 283, 316, VI, 152, 161; on investments, II, 260; on Moses' building of the tabernacle, VI, 163; on pronunciation, VI, 249
'Isa b. Nestorius, Christian vizier, III, 154
Isaiah, prophet, I, 86, 89, 138, 335, II, 173, 397; on animal sacrifices, I, 124; on darkness and light, VIII, 34; death, I, 79; grave, II, 423; prophecy on Aroer, VI, 293; Qumran Scroll, I, 103 f., 342 f., II, 349, VI, 238; religious teaching, I, 99, 339 f.; *Trishagion,* VIII, 13; vision of the watchman, V, 265; warning to rich landowners, I, 68
—— Book of, I, 103 f., 342, II, 349, VI, 238; break in continuity, VI, 310, 311; comment on, VIII, 155; Rashi's interpretation of, V, 157 f.; ratio of vowels to consonants, VII, 314
Isaiah, Second, *see* Deutero-Isaiah
Isaiah b. Mali of Trani, VI, 167
Isaiah ha-Kohen b. Maṣliaḥ ha-Maskil, IV, 110; ransom of scroll of law, IV, 112
'Isawites, V, 182, 193
Isfahan, Persia, II, 204; anti-Jewish riots, III, 55; Jewish community, III, 109; legend of Armilus, V, 359; messianic movement, V, 386; occupations of Jews, IV, 167, 318 f.; Yudghanites in, V, 193
Isfahani, Abu'l Faraj al-, VII, 207; pre-existence of, VIII, 125 f.; redemption, VII, 115; relationship between the Lord and, I, 140, II, 134, 145, 386; reunification of, VII, 113 f., 117, 136; song and chant, VIII, 13; as source of all human wisdom, VIII, 77, 387; tribulations, V, 101 f., 144, 160, 355, VIII, 121
Ishmael, V, 137, 162; designation, V, 126; and Hagar, Arabs as descendants of, V, 93, 99, VI, 309; meaning of name, III, 274; Mohammed on, III, 85 f.; promised "dominion," V, 335; and *Se'ir,* VI, 407
Ishmael, R., II, 133, 230, 232, 237, 238, 251, 270, 282, 289, 430; modes of interpretation, V, 213, 218, VI, 177,

295, 304; as mystic, V, 142, VIII, 6, 179, 279; Rashi on, VI, 51; warning to biblical scribe, VI, 237
Ishmael b. Eleazar, R., II, 286
Ishmael b. Elisha, R., V, 140
Ishmael b. Jose, R., II, 247
Ishobokht, metropolitan, II, 430
Ishoyabh, Nestorian *catholicos,* III, 58, 90, 171
Ishshut, see Marriage
Ishtar, goddess, I, 57, VIII, 10
Ishtar-Sirius festival, I, 294
Isidore of Seville, Saint, III, 37, V, 8, 114; cosmic week, VI, 440; description of psalmody, VII, 283; on enforced conversion, III, 38 f., 247; on Israel and Judah, V, 126; on kingdom of Jews, III, 204 f., V, 130 f.; on laudation, VII, 282
Isidorus, I, 190
Islam: as apocalyptic beast, V, 153 f.; assimilatory trends in, VII, 59; attitude toward Mohammed, VIII, 127 f.; on attributes of God, VIII, 99; and biblical patriarchs, III, 85 f., 266 f., V, 93, VI, 8 f.; and Christendom, Jewish intermediary position, VIII, 255 f.; combination of religion and state, III, 94 f., V, 82; concept of soul's ascent to heaven, VIII, 284; continuity of traditions in Spain, IV, 28; controversies over tradition, V, 209; converts to, V, 105, *see also* Converts; creative syncretism, III, 80-86, 92, 265-68, VII, 11, VIII, 263; *dajjal* myths, III, 109, V, 358, 386; *dar al-Islam* and *dar al-ḥarb,* III, 95, 119, 130; development into world religion, III, 94; effect on Christian countries, III, 46; effect on Jewish farmers, IV, 151 f.; equation with Ishmael, V, 93, *see also* Ishmael; exegesis by Jewish converts, VI, 275; expansion, III, 4, 86-114, 168, 268-84, V, 3 ff., 99; fatalism (*q.v.*), VIII, 109; gold and silver mines, IV, 211 f.; Graeco-Roman and Persian influences on, V, 3 f.; growth of banking, IV, 198 f., 339 f.; *idjma',* principle, V, 169, VI, 145 f., VII, 58, VIII, 324; industrial production, IV, 164 f.; Jewish influence in rise of, II, 211, 433, III, 80 ff., 264 ff., VIII, 255 f., 262 f.; Karaites and, V, 410 f.; methods of acquiring slaves, IV, 332; missionary efforts, III, 94; Muslim traders and, IV, 181; mysticism, VII, 78; nomism, VI, 6 f.; number of daily prayers, III, 266; official creed, VI, 8; oral traditions, III, 273; outlawry of, in Hungary, III, 212 f.; plural marriage, VI, 137; policy of religious toleration, V, 82, 97, 103, 210, 264; preachment of racial equality, III, 98; prohibition of wine drinking, IV, 164 f.; as protector of Judaism, III, 93, VII, 136; religion and state, III, 75, VI, 150 f.; religious orders, VI, 10; Renaissance of, III, 117-21, V, 83, 103, 170, 197, 231, VII, 3 ff., 60 f., 176, VIII, 147, 255 f., 262 f.; on resurrection, VI, 8; rule in Sicily, IV, 20 f.; Samaritans and, V, 368; sectarianism, III, 123, 133, 148 f., V, 136, 169, 183, 189 ff.; segregation of faithful from infidels, III, 97 ff.; standards of education, VIII, 222; term, III, 85, 267, VI, 12 ff., 151; theological conservatism, VIII, 72; theory of prophecy, VIII, 134
Isma'ili, sect, VIII, 325; controversies over great imams, VIII, 134
Isolationism, *see* Segregation
Isonomia, see Rights, legal
Isopoliteia, see Rights, legal
'Isqa, contract, IV, 201
Israel (people): Chosen People, II, 383, V, 125 ff., 137, 285; eternity of, II, 39 f., 396, III, 17, V, 101 f., VI, 146; focal position in world history, I, 47, VI, 227 ff., 438 ff.; and influence of the stars, VIII, 175 f.; ingathering of, VIII, 217; and Judah, V, 126, 264, 285; mission of, VIII, 134 f.; political impotence, VII, 177 f., VIII, 19; precedence over angels, VIII, 279
Israel (state): ancient: corporate responsibility, II, 42; and Damascus, I, 322; divided kingdoms, I, 93 f.; education, II, 274; governmental diffusion, I, 63, 73-77, 325-27; international position, I, 63, 67; interplay with history of many nations, I, 16; kings' reverence for the men of God, I, 78; on Merneptah stele, I, 307; name, I, 41, 182, 309; origins, I, 32-62, 298-319; sepulchres of kings, II, 286, 423; towns, I, 72; *see also* Judah
—— Northern: aliens in, I, 107; divi-

Israel (*Continued*)
sion into new districts, I, 77, 326; fiscal structure, I, 326; government, I, 73 ff.; relations with Judah, I, 29, 325, II, 61; Samaritans as survival of, II, 28; *see also* Samaria
Israel, republic, I, 3, 18, 29, II, 296
Israel al-Naqawa, VII, 149
Israel b. Samuel ha-Ma'arabi, V, 261
Israel b. Simḥah of Baṣra, acquisition of biblical manuscript, VI, 447 f.; gift to Karaite synagogue, VI, 246 f.
Israeli, Isaac b. Solomon, Jewish physician and philosopher, III, 157; "Book of Elements," VIII, 222 f., 298 f.; commentary on Genesis, VI, 226 f., 282; definitions of memory, VIII, 80; eschatological doctrine, VIII, 105; "Guide for the Physician," VIII, 258; Ibn Tamim on, VII, 16; "internal" senses, VIII, 79 f.; on matter and space, VIII, 88; medical training, VIII, 236; medical works in Latin translation, VIII, 394 f.; on nature as healer, VIII, 260; on philosophic interpretation, VIII, 73; quoted, VIII, 234; works, VIII, 59, 65, 137, 243 f., 298 f., 394 f.
Israeli, Isaac, the Second, VIII, 371, 376
Israelites, ancient: absolute obligation of righteous living, I, 83; in Babylonia, I, 106, 275, *see also* Exile, Babylonian; brotherhood of all Jews, I, 41, 63, 94, 274, 330; clan structure, I, 54; creative artists, I, 14; in Egypt, I, 35-39, 305; Falasha descent from, II, 212; rabbinic adage, VIII, 66; relations with other Hebrews, I, 38; settlement abroad, I, 39, 94; tribal divisions, I, 55
Issachar, tribe, III, 208; children of, VI, 269, VIII, 199; division of hours, VIII, 373
Isserles, Moses, VI, 26
Istanbul, *see* Constantinople
Italy: ancient: agriculture, I, 251; anti-Jewish feeling, I, 246, 248, II, 103; Christianity in Northern, II, 165; fatherland of all races, II, 151; Jewish captives of Titus, VI, 216; proselytes and descendants in, I, 283
—— medieval: awakening of scientific interests, VIII, 171, 245; Byzantine influence in, III, 25; capital punishment, V, 316; dating of records, VIII, 204; dependence on sharecroppers, III, 244; development of religious philosophy, VIII, 60; folk tales, VIII, 43; foreign domination, VII, 304; foreign trade, IV, 4 f., 186; homiletical learning, VIII, 30 f.; influence of Abu Aaron, VIII, 44; influence of Palestinian customs, VI, 47; inquiries to scholars, VI, 119; introduction of dyeing and silk industry, IV, 168 f.; Jewish communities, III, 24-33, 109, 180, 189, 240-44, IV, 20-27, 242-45, VI, 217; Jewish martyrs in the Crusades, IV, 106; Jewish ownership of Christian slaves, III, 243; Jewish population, IV, 24 f.; Judeo-Christian relations, IV, 20-27, 242-45; mishnaic commentaries, VI, 62; opposition to science, VIII, 171; origin of Yosephon, VI, 195; Renaissance, VIII, 147; spread of Jewish communal development from, V, 60 f.; suicide of Jew in Saracen raid, VI, 194; synagogue tunes, VII, 130; talmudic lexicon for Jews of, VII, 29 f.; *see also under* individual cities, e.g. Rome
Ittobaal, king, I, 322
Itureans, I, 224, 396
Ius gentium, II, 300, 303
Izates, king, I, 168

J

Jabariya, school of Islamic philosophy, VIII, 109
Jabir (Geber or Jebir) ibn Aflaḥ, VIII, 162, 163 f., 201; alchemistic treatises, VIII, 225
Jaca, Spain, IV, 318; voluntary segregation, IV, 35
Jacob, patriarch, I, 22, 37, 41, V, 90, 93 f.; blessing of Reuben, VI, 259; Gregory I on, III, 29; image of, VIII, 13; ladder, VI, 297, VIII, 84; and proclamation of leap year, VIII, 194
Jacob, R., in Palmyra, III, 63
Jacob, (French?) traveler, III, 104
Jacob b. Ahron, I, 340
Jacob b. Amram, Kairuwan leader, V, 40
Jacob b. Asher, VII, 206; on Psalm 91, VII, 283
Jacob b. Ephraim the Syrian, VII, 223 f.

Jacob b. Ḥayyim, *Biblia Rabbinica,* VI, 255
Jacob b. Mordecai Gaon, VI, 31
Jacob b. Moses ibn Abbasi, VI, 353
Jacob b. Nathaniel al-Fayyumi, V, 204
Jacob b. Nathaniel ha-Kohen, traveler, VI, 225
Jacob b. Nissim, of Kairuwan, V, 52; inquiry to Sherira, VI, 204, 329
Jacob b. Reuben, V, 230
Jacob b. R. Naṭronai, R., V, 74
Jacob b. Tanumas (Tanḥuma), III, 21, 237, V, 116
Jacob b. Yagar, R., VI, 52
Jacob b. Yequtiel, IV, 17, 77, 92, V, 59; appeal for papal intervention, IV, 57, 66, 97, VI, 219; on titles of Jewish leaders, III, 233
Jacob ibn Eleazar, *see* Ibn Eleazar
Jacobite Church, V, 9
Jacob of Orléans, IV, 205
Jaffa, I, 255, II, 91; congregation in, II, 199; forcibly Judaized, I, 256; inscriptions, I, 378; necropolis, II, 14, 174, 286
Jaffe, Mordecai, R., VII, 125; on Rashi's commentaries, VI, 50
Jafia b. David of Monzon, IV, 37
Jahmiya, Muslim theologians, VIII, 343
Jalutiyites, sect, V, 197
James, Saint, apostle, II, 70, 74, 75, 82, 131, 361; liturgy, VII, 65
James II, king of England, III, 94
James of Edessa, Syriac scholar, VI, 241
Jamnia, *see* Yabneh
Januarius, bishop of Sardinia, III, 242
Jao, god, I, 382, II, 22
Jaoel, angel, II, 22; *see also* Yehoel
Japheth, descendants of, VI, 192, VII, 256
Jason, high priest, I, 185, 229, 398
Jason of Cyrene, I, 198, 207, 217, 232
Jativa Spain, paper manufacture, IV, 169
Jaubari, Zain ad-Din al-, V, 96
Jauhar, Faṭimid general, III, 154
Jebir, *see* Jabir
Jebusites, I, 72; Jerusalem taken from, I, 65
Jeconiah, Jewish king, III, 90
Jehoiachin, king of Judah, I, 119, 343, II, 195, 206, 435; in Babylonian captivity, I, 115, 116, 348; cycle of, V, 247
Jehoiakim (Eliakim), king of Judah, I, 78, 115, 327
Jehoshaphat, king of Judah, I, 141; VI, 309 f.; reforms, I, 75, 328
Jehovah: name of God, I, 13, V, 120, VI, 449; *see also* God; Tetragrammaton
Jehu, king of Israel, I, 73, 89, 325, 335
Jenghiz Khan, III, 206
Jephet b. 'Ali, Karaite exegete, V, 159, 196, 237, 389, VI, 78, 308 f., VIII, 60; on chronology of Creation, VIII, 203; comment on books by Gentiles, VIII, 247; grammar as exegetical aid, VII, 38; influence of Saadiah on, VI, 473; messianic interpretations, V, 260; on prophecies addressed to Hosea, VI, 289; on social justice, V, 238 f.; translation of Old Testament, VI, 270 f.
Jephet b. Sa'id, V, 256
Jerash, *see* Gerasa
Jeraua, North African tribe, III, 91
Jeremiah, prophet, I, 86, 89, 104, 112, 117, 136, 153, 331, II, 20, III, 61, VI, 174; categories of sciences, VIII, 142; condemns soothsayers, I, 87; employs scribe, I, 334; on individual conscience, I, 84; injunction to build and plant, I, 109; messianic prediction, IV, 96; on Sabbath, I, 360; and Scythian invasions, I, 96, 338; on supremacy of worship in the heart, I, 83; on universalism and peace, I, 122; uses term Torah, I, 331
Jeremiah, R., amora, II, 20; expectation of resurrection, II, 312; on foolish Babylonians, II, 208
Jerez de la Frontera, VIII, 240
Jericho, I, 354; conquest of, I, 307; fertility of region, I, 252; Khaibar Jews in, III, 87; ritualistic customs, II, 7, VII, 66; traditional tomb of Moses, III, 308
Jeroboam I, king of Northern Israel, I, 327, V, 254; images erected by, I, 66; followers of, VIII, 311; revolt, I, 75; schism of, VI, 207
Jeroboam II, king of Israel, I, 67, 95
Jerome, Saint, II, 108, 144, 168, 189, 192, 240, 256, 373, 377, III, 196 f., V, 114, VI, 248, 272; on fall of Rome, III, 14, 234; *Hebraica,* VI, 273; quoted, II, 210, 269
Jerusalem: Israelitic: altars prohibited,

Jerusalem (*Continued*)
I, 128, 140; animal sacrifices, V, 123; David's conquest of, I, 65, 312; fall of, and Jubilee years, VIII, 210; governed by Viceroy, I, 75; as heart of country, I, 72; high ecclesiastical officers, I, 81; Judean public life centered in, I, 83; king of Salem, I, 45; population, I, 168; preexistence of, VIII, 126
—— postexilic and after: archives, II, 99; Christians in, II, 82, 164; Cicero on conquest of, I, 192; a city state, I, 160, 221; collections for the poor, II, 82; emigration from, I, 345; fall of, II, 131, 341, 374, 377, III, 238, V, 199, 354; "Foundation Stone," III, 269; as "God's sanctuary" V, 49; graves and tombstones, II, 286, 333, 423; Greek structures in, I, 228, 401; Hellenistic party and the Jews, I, 193, 398; Jewish congregations, II, 199; "metropolis" of scattered Jewish settlements, I, 66, 218 f., 250, 284, 348, II, 55; metropolitan economy, I, 276; name, I, 229, 321, 398, II, 107; Persian imperialism, I, 129-32, 353-55; pilgrimages to, I, 213 f., 258, 392, II, 108, 118, 374; priestly schools, VIII, 228; rivalry with Gerizim, II, 27; synagogue of Theodotos, VIII, 239 f.; tanners exempted from pilgrimages to, IV, 166; under the Seleucids, I, 216, 229, 369, 393; walls, I, 130, II, 369; *see also* Temple at Jerusalem
—— Roman and medieval, III, 22; Arab conquest, III, 87 f., 101 f.; Arabic and Hebrew names of, III, 87 f., 269; "Babylonian" congregation, V, 37, VII, 65; captured by Crusaders, III, 102, IV, 109 f., 295 f.; Christian patriarchate, III, 20; chronology based on, V, 119, 130; Church of the Holy Sepulcher, III, 103, 279, IV, 57, 58, 257; expansion of Jewish community, III, 101, 277 f.; "Jewish market," IV, 180; Judeo-Christian relations, III, 38, 101, 160, 316 f.; Karaites in, IV, 112, 296 f., V, 222 f., 233 f., 237, VI, 246 f., VII, 226; Latin kingdom of, IV, 106-16, 294-99; mass conversion of Jews, III, 182; Mongolian siege, V, 368; Mosque of the Rock, III, 101, 134, 269, 272; "Mourners for Zion," (*q.v.*), V, 185; Muslim cemetery, III, 297; Muslim discrimination against Jews, III, 147; Muslim respect for holiness of, III, 269; "on high," V, 142, 146, 148; orientation toward, VI, 14, VIII, 211; Palmyrenes and destruction of Temple, III, 62; period after second fall, VI, 230; period of Jewish control, III, 73; Persian capture of, III, 21 f.; pilgrimages to, IV, 94 f., 166; prohibition of Jewish residence in, IV, 296 f.; Rabbanite academy, III, 104, IV, 24 ff., 302 ff., V, 233 f., 237, VI, 215, 245; removal of crosses from, III, 102; Seljuk rule, III, 104, IV, 94, 115 f.; Talmud of, VI, 331, *see also* Talmud, Palestinian; 'Umar's treaty with Christians of, III, 97, 269; under Hadrian, II, 97, 107 f., 123; Wailing Wall, III, 278, V, 236

Jesse, stock of, V, 157

Jesuits, Spanish, *scientia media* of God, VIII, 128

Jesus Barabbas (Bar Abba-the Father's Son), II, 72

Jesus Christ, II, 148, 357, 387, VIII, 134; alleged statement on vengeance, IV, 102; called disciple of Joshua b. Perahiah, II, 148, 387 f., V, 119; called impostor, V, 104; Chalcedonian formula re nature of, III, 5; contemporary treatment of, II, 63, 353; date of birth, II, 353, VI, 207, VIII, 206; dates of crucifixion and resurrection, VIII, 187; debates on, V, 118 ff., 343 ff.; descent, II, 65, 136, 140; disciples and their beliefs, II, 70, 71, 73, 74 f., 83; early references to, II, 131; expectations before coming of, II, 31, 58-62; foretold destruction of Temple, II, 74, 83; Gregory on reversion to the Jews, III, 243; and the high priesthood, V, 343; historicity of, and sources about, II, 63 ff., 353 ff.; homage of Moses, V, 138; Jewish repudiation of, II, 130 ff., 379 ff., V, 118 ff., 343 ff., VII, 177 f., VIII, 133; Josephus on, II, 131, 379, VI, 418; and Judaism, I, 180, II, 63, 65, 67, 70, 356; Karaites on, V, 263 f., 344; "kingdom of God" gospel, II, 68 ff., 73, 77, 357; language, II, 65 f.; last words, II, 358, V, 120; link with John the Baptist, II, 62, 65, 68; as Messiah, II, 64, 65, 67-75, 357, III, 15,

249 f., IV, 91 f., V, 117 ff., 343 ff., VI, 171, VIII, 127; Mohammed and, III, 81; and money-changers, I, 258; mystic body of, VIII, 277; name in Thamudic inscription, III, 258; recognized as prophet, V, 186, 192, 219; Roman opposition, II, 70, 134, 358; "sonship" and timelessness of, II, 81, 364; teachings, II, 67 ff., 77, 358; trial and execution, II, 70, 71 f., 358; visions of, II, 71, III, 229; *see also* Christians and Christianity; Cross; Crucifixion of Jesus; Messiah
Jethro-Hobeb, I, 38; legend, V, 129
"Jew," as derogatory term, III, 5, 147, IV, 9, 307, V, 126, 136
Jew-baiting, *see* Antisemitism
Jewelers, IV, 170, 214 f.
"Jewry Wall," Leicester, England, IV, 281
Jezebel, queen, I, 78, 322, 334
Jibal, Spain, III, 109
Jindibu, Arabian king, III, 61
Jinns, VIII, 10; *see also* Demonology
Jizya (poll tax), III, 163 f., 170; *see also* Taxation
Joash, king of Israel, I, 73, 91
Job, I, 136, 307, II, 227, V, 167; cited as authority for scientific studies, VIII, 219; identity of, VI, 293, 308; Tobiah b. Eliezer on, VI, 174
—— Book of, I, 151, 364, VIII, 344; commentaries on, VI, 460, VII, 186; priestly influence, I, 150; Saadiah's version of, VI, 266, 270, 460
Jobab, king of Edom, identification with Job, VI, 293
Joce de Brakelond, IV, 84
Joel, prophet: date of, VI, 310; ideal of, I, 154 f.
—— Book of, V, 201
Joel b. Isaac ha-Levi of Bonn, VI, 391
Joel b. Pethuel, III, 63
Johanan b. Matya, R., II, 257
Johanan (b. Nappaḥa), R., II, 13, 110, 133, 146, 148, 175, 194, 197, 203, 207, 221, 234, 235, 249, 264, 286, 305, 307, 315, 317, 392, 400, 409, VI, 11, 167, 336, VII, 62; on astronomical computations, VIII, 161; compunctions about informer, II, 142, 385; condemnation of pleonasms, VIII, 14; on the divine Chariot, VIII, 6; on fast days, II, 134, 380; on Men of the Great Synagogue, VII, 65 f.; on Mishnah, II, 294; on prayers, VI, 44, VII, 66; quoted, II, 245, 246, 256, 268, VIII, 19; removed barrier between groups, II, 242; sentiments toward Rome, II, 152 f., 414; on synagogue attendance, II, 283; on Torah and the poor, II, 277; views disputed by R. Simon, II, 161; on "younger teachers," II, 262, 417
Johanan b. Nuri, R., II, 205
Johanan b. Toreta, R., II, 87
Johanan b. Zakkai, R., I, 262, 279, II, 101, 121, 128, 132, 197, 205, 220, 314, 396; on charities, II, 270; demand upon Vespasian II, 120, 377; leadership, II, 111, 117, 197, 403; on Nebukadrezzar, VIII, 26; rebuilder of national life, II, 277; teachings, II, 113-19 *passim,* 375, 376
Johanna, countess of Flanders, IV, 344
Johannes, Norman proselyte, *see* Obadiah (Johannes)
Johannes Hispalensis (or Hispanus), *see* Avendeath
Johannes Scholasticus, III, 187
John, Saint, II, 75, 82
—— Gospel of, II, 64, 66, 71, 72, 75, 83, 359, 361, 364
John bishop of Spires, IV, 74; protection of Jews, IV, 98 f., 101 f., 142
John I, Monophysite patriarch, VI, 263
John I (John Tsimiskes), Byzantine emperor, III, 193, 317, V, 162
John I, king of England, IV, 77, 204; appointment of first Jewish presbyter, V, 63; privilege to Jews, IV, 164, 170
John Cinnamus, Byzantine historian, III, 212
John Hyrcanus, Jewish ruler, I, 189, 223, 225, 235, 236, 276, 369, 400, 410, II, 27, 29, 339; appeal for restoration of Joppa, I, 255; conquests, I, 167, 224; slur on genealogical purity of, I, 227, V, 9
John of Capua, translations by, VII, 189
John of Damascus, V, 109; Christian writer, VII, 142; polemics vs. Islam, V, 84
John of Ephesus, III, 231
John of Gischala, II, 347
John of Nikiu, II, 402, III, 18, 235
John of Saxony, VIII, 175
John Rufus, bishop of Mayuma, III, 229

John Rylands Library, Manchester, V, 372
John the Baptist, Saint, I, 402, II, 62, 352; association with Jesus, II, 62, 65, 68; and Damascus sect, II, 52, 348; sacraments connected with, II, 75, 361
John the Essene, II, 51
Jonadab, son of Rechab, I, 89
Jonah, prophet, II, 20, 336
—— Book of, I, 158
Jonah, R., Amora, VIII, 213
Jonah (b. Abraham Gerondi) the Pious, R., VI, 61
"Jonathan," Targum, VI, 258 ff., 455 ff., VIII, 203
Jonathan b. David ha-Kohen of Lunel, VI, 88, 106, 119, 369 f.; correspondence, VI, 119, 380
Jonathan b. 'Uzziel, II, 386; *see also* "Jonathan," Targum
Jordan, river, I, 55
Josce of Gloucester, IV, 82
Jose b. 'Aqabiah, R., II, 145
Jose b. Ḥalafta, R., I, 251, II, 112 f., 125, 273, 310, 311, 319, 434; burial place, V, 37; chronology compiled, II, 141, 376, 384, VI, 200, 231, VIII, 208; on the *Hallel,* VII, 69; quoted, II, 250
Jose b. Netanel, II, 117
Jose b. Qisma, R., II, 100
Jose of Ma'on, II, 193
Joseph, patriarch, I, 37, 40, 304; marriage, I, 39; Messiah of house of, I, 99; as prophet, VIII, 132; and the wolf, VI, 170
Joseph, Khazar king, III, 196, 201; correspondence with Ḥisdai, III, 156, 210, 305 f., 324, VI, 219 f., VII, 273; Halevi's dialogue, VIII, 3, 22, 62, 84 ff., 125 ff.; importation of Jewish scholars, III, 203
Joseph, R., Amora, II, 74, 308; against Aramaic, VII, 6; defined "Epicurean," II, 278; on division of biblical verses, VI, 238; expert in viticulture, II, 414
Joseph, son of Tobiah, II, 349
Joseph (b. Jacob?), R., of Sura, chronological computations, VIII, 202
Joseph b. Abraham al-Baṣir, V, 233, 242 f., VII, 220, VIII, 60
Joseph b. Asher, of Chartres, IV, 124
Joseph b. Gershom, Jewish judge in Alexandria, V, 47 f.
Joseph b. Gurion, *see* Yosephon
Joseph b. Ḥanina, R., II, 115, 312, 376
Joseph b. Ḥiyya, gaon, V, 15
Joseph b. Isaac, poet, VII, 294
Joseph b. Isaac of Orléans, Tosafist, VI, 388
Joseph b. Isaac Sambari, *see* Sambari
Joseph b. Jacob b. 'Ali, booklist, VI, 360 f.
Joseph b. Jacob bar Satia, *see* Bar Satia
Joseph b. Meir ha-Levi, *see* Ibn Megas
Joseph b. Meir ibn Zabara, *see* Ibn Zabara
Joseph b. Moses the Elder, R., VI, 120
Joseph b. Nuḥ, V, 233; translation of Old Testament, VI, 270
Joseph b. Phineas, Jewish banker of Baghdad, III, 152 f., V, 10
Joseph b. Samuel, editor of *Sefer ha-Yashar,* VI, 198
Joseph b. Shemariah, V, 35 f.
Joseph b. Yehudah of Babylonia: benediction before *Shema',* VI, 131; mystic experience, VIII, 7
Joseph b. Zedekiah, V, 311
Joseph Bonfils, *see* Tob 'Elem
Joseph ha-Arukh (il Lungo), VIII, 285
Joseph (b. Joshua) ha-Kohen, Jewish chronicler, III, 39, 92, IV, 130
Joseph ha-Ma'arabi, VI, 380
Joseph ibn Abitur, *see* Ibn Abitur
Joseph ibn Abulmana, sheikh, III, 115
"Joseph's Prayer," I, 182
Josephus, Flavius, I, 35, 168, 174, 177, 184, 185, 190, 231, 255, 257, II, 9, 15, 20, 75, 83, 104, 120, 157, 195, 205, 280, 314, 349, 409, 423, III, 61, 62, 211, VIII, 253; on antisemitism, I, 177, 194, 382, 383; documents in, I, 242, 377; and era of Creation, VIII, 208; on Essenes, I, 233, II, 48, 49, 50, 347; genealogy, I, 272; Greek influence upon, I, 186, II, 38; on Herod, I, 236; on Jewish law, II, 117, 279; on Jewish magician, II, 21; on Jewish marriage, II, 223, 234; on Jewish race, I, 198; on messianic impostors, II, 61; and Pharisaism, II, 38, 342, 343, 344; on pilgrimages, I, 214; quoted, I, 223, 402, II, 47, 147; on rise of Christianity, II, 131, 379, VI, 418; on Roman wars, II, 90, 92, 93, 94, 99, 102, 368, 372; on Sadducee individualism, II, 41; on Samaritans, II, 26, 29, 30, 36, 37, 339, 341, 342; Slavonic version, II, 379, VI,

191 f., 417 f.; speech before fall of Jerusalem, VI, 192 f.; on suicide, VI, 193; term "theocracy" coined by, I, 152, 223, 271; wealth in Temple treasury, I, 215; widely read, II, 379; and Yosephon, VI, 190; on Zealots, II, 47
Jose the Galilean, R., II, 133, 142, 230; computations of, VIII, 6; son of, II, 267
Joshua b. Gamala, II, 421
Joshua b. Ḥananiah, R., I, 179, 221, 265, 294, II, 8, 21, 116 f., 119, 125, 139, 218, 275, VI, 35, 107; alphabet acrostics, VII, 257; on loss of the Temple, II, 112, 375; on rich and poor, II, 270; rise to leadership, II, 276; student of Greek, II, 142
Joshua b. 'Ilan, Rabbanite, on era of Creation, VIII, 204
Joshua b. Levi, R., I, 376, II, 122, 276, 295; on books of Aggadah, VI, 157; on confession, VII, 79 f.; mystic sayings, VIII, 6; quoted, II, 422
Joshua b. Nun, biblical leader, I, 53, 307, 308, 325, 354; miracle at Gibeon, VI, 311
Joshua, Book of, II, 30, 340
Joshua b. Peraḥiah R., II, 20, 148, 262, 336, 388, 421, V, 119, VI, 207
Joshua b. Qarḥa, R., II, 267
Josiah, king of Judah, I, 73, 91, 126, 183, 345; destruction of Bethel, I, 346; effort to revive militia, I, 84; reformation under, I, 79, 83 ff., 330, 331, 332, *see also* Reformation, Deuteronomic; tragic end of, I, 339
Josiah (Ḥasan) b. Zakkai, counter-exilarch, V, 11 f.
Jotapata, siege of, VI, 193 f.
Jotham, parable of, I, 93
Jubilees, Book of, II, 344, 383, V, 167, VIII, 191, 208, 368; on coming of the Kingdom, II, 59; excerpt, II, 43; on intermarriage, II, 232; on the Law, II, 73
Jubilee year, I, 85, 332, V, 199 f., 404; effect on land ownership, IV, 160; first, VIII, 209
Judaea and Judaeans, VII, 3; agriculture, I, 251; aristocracy's contempt for masses, I, 224; education, II, 274; Jewishness of the people, II, 123, 277; and Jews of Galilee and Arbatta, I, 167; name changed, II, 123, 132, 380; political downfall, I, 247, II, 92, 132, 151; relations with Rome, I, 218, II, 90; variety of balsam, VIII, 253; wool industry, I, 408; *see also* Judah; Palestine
Judaei, term, IV, 271, V, 126
Judah, kingdom, I, 57, 73, 224; boundaries, I, 94, 345; depopulation in sixth century, I, 105; diffusion of government, I, 72-77, 325-27; exiles in Babylonia, I, 106, *see also* Exile, Babylonian; and prophetic literature, II, 28; scepter of, V, 118, 130, 313, VI, 193; Sennacherib's campaign against, II, 95; towns, I, 72; unity with Israel, I, 29, 94, II, 61, V, 126, 264, 285; in western Asiatic affairs, I, 67; *see also* Israel; Judaea and Judaeans; Palestine
Judah, son of Jacob, I, 61; descent from, II, 351, VI, 200; marriage, I, 39
Judah, Jewish doctor in Salerno, VIII, 245
Judah, R., Hindu, II, 212
Judah, R., son of R. Shalom, on Aramaic prayers, VII, 66; on the Mishnah, VI, 257 f.
Judah I, R., II, 20, 135, 146, 187, 193, 197, 205, 227, 248, 272, 280, 316, 400, 403, 408, 436, V, 167, 256, 359, VI, 17, 24, 181; against Aramaic, VII, 6; Amoraim in academy of, VIII, 6; authority of opinions of, VI, 31; editorship of Mishnah, II, 206 f., 294, 295, 426, VI, 99, 201, 205; on Ḥiyya's speech habits, VI, 240; Maimonides' study of, VI, 102; proclamation of defective months, VIII, 187; Saadiah's biography of, VI, 203; shipowner, II, 249; on destruction of the Temple, VI, 167
Judah II, II, 193, 194, 197, 276, 281
Judah al-Barceloni, *see* Yehudah b. Barzillai al-Barceloni
Judah-Aristobulus, I, 224
Judah b. Baba, R., II, 120, 126
Judah b. Batira, II, 36, 227, 262; adherence to Pharisaism, II, 56
Judah b. Ezekiel, II, 146, 208, VII, 129
Judah b. 'Ila'i, R., II, 153, 176, 224, 248, 250, 251, 257, 283, 376, 378, VI, 31; epigram on physicians, VIII, 233
Judah b. Naḥmani, R., VI, 178
Judah b. Ṭabbai, V, 255
Judah b. Tema, II, 421

Judah Maccabee, I, 185, 231, 369
"Judah's rod," V, 8
Judaica perditio, III, 29
Judaica perfidia, III, 31
Judaicus, title, II, 92
Judaism: and Aristotelianism, VIII, 63 ff., 305 ff.; Christians' lack of knowledge of, V, 114; continuity of, VI, 3; contributions to Christianity, III, 208 f., 221, 243, V, 136, VI, 8, VIII, 51, *see also under* Christians and Christianity; Judeo-Christian relations; contributions to magical lore, VIII, 10 f.; controversies within and without, VIII, 66-75, 310-15; evolution of aggadic lore, VI, 36; heterodoxy vs. Oral Law, V, 104 f., VI, 22, VIII, 51 ff.; history as prime element in, I, 4-16, 294-97, VI, 204 ff., 227 ff., 438 ff., VIII, 86 ff., 125 ff.; *see also* History; importance of synagogue, VII, 62; influence on Islam, III, 80 ff., 265 ff., VI, 7 ff.; and medical studies, VIII, 265; messianic hope in, V, 206 f., 366; Mohammed on, III, 83 f.; natural and social factors in expansion of, III, 110 f.; number of sects, V, 183, 197, *see also* Sectarianism; outlawry of, III, 177, 220, *see also under* Outlawry; papal charge of inferiority of, III, 31 f.; religio-juridical evolution, VI, 3-151, 321-98; religious conflict between masses and philosophers, VIII, 57 ff.; restoration of Sanhedrin (*q.v.*) for calendar reform, VIII, 191; and self-realization, VII, 59 f.; and study of Hebrew, VII, 4; synthesis with Hellenism, VIII, 32, 76; unity within diversity, V, 205 ff.; universalism and particularism, VIII, 123 ff., 345; *see also* Converts and conversion; Proselytes and proselytism
Judaizanti, Russian sect, III, 216
Judan, R., on Gentiles and synagogue sermons, VII, 128; homily on Canticles 1:1, VI, 155
Judas Iscariot, II, 71, 359
Judas of Galilee, I, 263, II, 47, 101; leadership in family of, II, 48
Judeo-Arabic language, IV, 197, V, 227, VII, 60, 221; linguistic peculiarities, VII, 8
Judeo-Christian relations, II, 188 f., 427; affected by local conditions, IV, 14; and Anacletus II, IV, 10 ff., 237; *Basilika* and, III, 187; in biblical studies, VI, 240 f., 272; blood accusations (*q.v.*), IV, 80; canon law on, III, 194, 212, IV, 9 ff., 18 f., 241 f.; charge of Jewish disloyalty, IV, 37 f., 55 f.; complicated by burghers, IV, 65, *see also* Burghers; controversy over Messiah (*q.v.*), VII, 178 f.; cooperation among physicians, VIII, 236, 265; during the Crusades, IV, 89 ff., 116 ff.; Cyril's controversial tract, III, 210; denunciations of Jews, V, 131 ff.; effect of Almohade regime on, IV, 31; effect of, on Rashi and Tobiah, VI, 173; fiscal pressures, IV, 12 ff., *see also* Taxation; in France, III, 50 f.; fraternization, IV, 21 f., 52; growing animosity, IV, 132-39, 306-8, VI, 230; and inheritance rights, V, 299; intellectual contacts, VI, 272 ff., 279, VII, 173 f., VIII, 364 ff.; in Italy, III, 26 f., 241; Karaite attitudes, V, 263 f.; lack of unity in common cause vs. Muslims, III, 57, 137, 159; in Latin Kingdom of Jerusalem, IV, 113 ff.; legal debates, VI, 141 f.; linguistic reciprocity, VII, 10; litigation, III, 190, IV, 15 f., 41 f., 49, 69, 78; and local customs, VI, 128; monastic quarrels and, IV, 84; moneylending and, IV, 202 f.; and Mosaic law, VI, 4; outlawry of sex relationships, IV, 9, V, 133 f., *see also* Intermarriage; pietism and, VIII, 48 ff.; in Portugal, III, 160; precedent set by Sisebut, III, 38; pro-Jewish intervention, IV, 142 f.; protection against alleged Jewish attacks, IV, 9 ff.; public disputations in Cairo, III, 160; rabbinic law on, V, 100; religious debates, V, 108 ff., VII, 84, *see also* Controversies; religious holidays and trade, IV, 219 f.; and religious observances, V, 122 ff.; resentment over royal favoritism, IV, 40, 50 f., 77, 80 f.; role of religion in, VII, 176 ff.; sectarian controversies, III, 57, *see also* Sectarianism; and sexual morality, III, 300; socioeconomic factors, IV, 60, 65, 121 ff., 141 f., V, 126 f.; in Spain, III, 160, IV, 158 f.; violence in, III, 38, 241, IV, 89 ff., 139 ff.; and voluntary segregation, III, 144 f.; in western Europe, III, 173 f.
Judeo-Christians, *see* Christians and Christianity

Judeo-Greek language, I, 186
Judeo-Muslim relations, III, 102, 145, 166, 171 ff., 302, IV, 30 f., 225 ff., V, 108, 134; and biblical interpretation, VI, 274 f.; and communal control, V, 47 ff.; and consumption of wine, IV, 164 f.; controversies, V, 83 ff., 326 ff.; *see also* Controversies; and the Crusades, IV, 91; Faṭimid persecution, IV, 58; and language, VII, 9; legal evolution and, VI, 7 ff.; sectarianism and, V, 169; socioeconomic issues, V, 96 ff., 334 ff.
Judeo-Roman wars, I, 212, II, 89-102, 106, 121, 368-71; *see also* Bar Kocheba; Great War; Hadrian; Roman Empire; Trajan
Judeo-Samaritan relations, V, 172 f., 177
Judeo-Slav relations, III, 213 ff.
Judges and the judiciary, I, 68, 75, 80, 328, II, 137, 265-69, 418 ff., IV, 215, V, 395; appointment of, V, 20, 50, 71, 75, VI, 9, 122; compensation, II, 278; corruption of, V, 178; eminence of, VI, 325; exilarchic, V, 14 f.; influence on evolution of law, VI, 13; ordination, titles, II, 419; personal responsibility for errors, II, 268; preexilic, I, 80, 328; preservation of the law, IV, 222; proceedings at city gate, I, 80; Rabbanite, and illiterates, IV, 167; rules governing decisions by, V, 237 f., VI, 30 f., 46; status in Islam and Judaism, VI, 9; *see also* Jurists
Judges, Book of, I, 340; period, I, 32, 39
"Judges in the gate," VII, 245
Judgment, day of, I, 5, 144, V, 149
Judgment and retribution after death, II, 31, 38, 40, 41; *see also* Punishments
Judith, Book of, VI, 186 f.
Judith, queen of Poland, III, 219
Julian, Samaritan king, V, 170
Julian of Toledo, Saint, IV, 47, V, 114, 130 f.; *Liber Responsionum,* III, 45; on messianic character of Jesus, III, 249 f.; relations with Jews, III, 250
Julian the Apostate, Roman emperor, I, 282, II, 151, 154, 179, 186, 187, 194, 274, 374, 376, 391, 392, 398, 399, 403; adversary of Christian rule, II, 159 ff., 391; Jewish reaction to advances by, II, 160, 392; legendary visit of Tiberian rabbis, V, 350; request to Jews for prayers, VII, 265; and the Temple of Jerusalem, II, 155, 160, V, 144
Julianus, revolutionary, II, 96, 370
Julianus, Marcus Antonius, II, 93, 369, 372
Julia Severa, II, 24, 338
Julius Africanus, III, 15, VIII, 189, 206
Julius Capitolinus, II, 400
Jumièges, monastery of, IV, 59
Jundeshapur, medical academy, VIII, 236, 241
Juno, goddess, I, 374
Jupiter, god, I, 374
Jupiter Capitolinus, Temple of, II, 13, 106, 373
Jurisdiction: capital, V, 45; civil, IV, 101, V, 57 f.; communal, V, 64, 317; of local rulers, IV, 72 f.
—— ecclesiastical, IV, 73 f.; difficulties of, IV, 98 ff.; in England, IV, 77 f.; in France, IV, 53-64; and Jewish quarter, IV, 266; over monarchs and princes, IV, 54; secular resistance to, IV, 13; transfer of control over Jews to, IV, 65 f., 274
—— royal: of Carolingians, IV, 48 ff.; and the clergy, IV, 59, 68; decentralization, IV, 72 ff.; expansion, IV, 72; of Frederick Barbarossa, IV, 71; local resistance to, IV, 22 f.; and moneylending, IV, 82 f.; weakness of, IV, 95
Jurisprudence: English, IV, 78 f.; economic theory, IV, 200 f., 216-24
—— Jewish, II, 298-309, 429-33, VI, 3-151, 321-98; based on equity, II, 304; Byzantine, halakhic works, VIII, 31; and Christianity, II, 134; commercial law, II, 302, 304, 431, IV, 179, 186; ethics and, II, 308; enforcement of, II, 265, 291; independent from Roman and Sassanian, II, 299; influence on Jewish economy, II, 251 ff., 264, 415 ff.; Judeo-Christian concepts, II, 303, 432; judiciary, I, 80, II, 137, 265-69, 418 ff., *see also* Judges and judiciary; legal fiction, II, 304, 432; legal principles, I, 327; legal status of Jews in Rome and Persia, II, 104, 180-87 *passim,* 398 f.; "natural law" in, II, 432; and non-Jews, II, 265, 301, 430; Philo's work on legal practice, II, 418; tenacity of customs, II, 302
Jurists, IV, 215; leadership of, VI, 149;

Jurists (*Continued*)
Muslim, and literary style, VI, 94; need for biological data, VIII, 227; poets among, VII, 151; Spanish-Provençal, VI, 56
Jus divinum, V, 78
Jus gentium, II, 300, 303, VI, 5
Just, the, preexistence of, VIII, 125 f.
Just, Book of the, V, 353, VI, 233, VIII, 43; biblical story, VI, 197
Justice: appeal to public conscience for, V, 66 f.; attribute of God, VIII, 42; ideal of, I, 25, 45 f.; and mercy, II, 433; and necessity, VIII, 109 f.; public administration of, VI, 122; social, Karaite and Rabbanite, V, 238 f.; *see also* Judges and Judiciary
Justice, Book of, VIII, 265
Justin I, Byzantine emperor, III, 68
Justin II, Byzantine emperor, III, 17
Justinian I, Byzantine emperor, II, 178, 181, 243, 267, 304, 401, 409, 413; age of, III, 4-15, 229-35; Code of, II, 178, 303, 375, 397, 425, 432, III, 185, 191, 231, 233 f., VI, 322, VI, 54; interest rates set by, IV, 198; on Nestorians and Jews, III, 229; *Novella* 131, III, 8 f.; *Novella* 146, III, 11, 85, 189, 233, V, 26, 55, 209, VII, 94 f.; ordinance on Scripture reading, III, 12, 189; outlawry of study of Oral Law, III, 12, V, 26, VI, 153, 261, VII, 83, 94; peace with Kavadh I, III, 17; reprisals against Jewish ecclesiastical sanctions, V, 56; and Samaritans, II, 33, V, 170 f.; support of Western vs. Eastern Church, III, 7
Justinian II, Byzantine emperor, III, 198
Justin Martyr, Saint, II, 132, 138, 139, 145, 151, 223, 380, 382; V, 115, VIII, 133; quoted, II, 163, 167; on Simon Magus, II, 32, 341
Justus, Samaritan king, V, 170
Juvenal, bishop of Jerusalem, III, 20
Juvenal, poet, I, 179, 194

K

Ka'aba stone, III, 86, V, 86
Ka'b al-Aḥbar (Al-Ḥabr), III, 92, 272, VI, 275
Ka'b ibn al-Ashraf, Medinese poet, III, 72, 76
Kabbalah, VI, 297, VII, 182, 306, VIII, 8, 55, 277; classification of souls, VIII, 338; doctrine of creation, VIII, 94; doctrine of emanation, VIII, 22; transition to Neoplatonism, VIII, 39; *see also* Mystics and mysticism; rise of, VIII, 11-53, 277-95; in Spain, VIII, 14; and the Torah, VIII, 282
Kadesh, I, 42
Kahana, R.: on destruction of Tadmor, III, 62; story of, VI, 183 f.
Kairuwan: academies, V, 40, VI, 9, 213 f.; center of Jewish medical learning, VIII, 396; Copts and Jews from Egypt, III, 90; exegetical works, VI, 45; group from, in Fez, III, 145; Ḥushiel (*q.v.*) in, VI, 342; inquiry re Eldad, VI, 241; interest in history of Judaism, VI, 204; Jacob b. Nissim (*q.v.*) in, VI, 426; Jewish community, III, 107, V, 39 f., 306; legality of local customs, VI, 122; letters of authorization, IV, 212 f.; liturgical compilations, VII, 116 f.; moneylending in, IV, 339; mosque, III, 280; *negidim,* V, 51, 312, VI, 213 f.; proponents of written transmission of tradition, VI, 427; scholars, VI, 28, *see also under* individual scholars, *e.g.,* Ḥananel; transcripts of geonic responsa, VI, 113
Kalam and Mutakallimun, V, 121, VIII, 61, 89, 129, 136, 311; Arabic definition of, VIII, 136; arguments re creation, VIII, 89; doctrine of divine attributes, VIII, 97, 326; on predetermined life span and medical treatment, VIII, 259
Kalat al-Hammad, Algeria, VI, 84, 367
Kaleb Ella Asbaha, *see* Elesboas
Kallah assemblies, II, 245, 247, 276, 277, V, 20, VII, 13; months of, II, 422
Kallah, tractate, VI, 183
Kalonymide family, IV, 46, VI, 117, VIII, 50; and Otto II, IV, 273; transplanted from Lucca, V, 60 f.
Kalonymos b. Meshullam, defender of Mayence, IV, 103
Kalonymos b. Shabbetai, of Rome, IV, 105
Kalonymos b. Ṭodros, Jewish leader in Narbonne, IV, 47
Kalonymos b. Yehudah, of Mayence, IV, 145; lamentations, VII, 181
Kankah (or Mankah), Indian mathematician, VIII, 148

Kapparot ceremony, V, 249, VI, 125
"Karaimic tongue," V, 247
Karaites and Karaism, I, 30, II, 130, III, 161, 189, 221, IV, 38, V, 181 ff., 209-85, 388-416; analogistic method, VII, 236; and 'Ananites, V, 222-26, 395 f.; on anthropomorphic passages in the Aggadah, VI, 268; appeals to history, V, 251; Arabic works translated into Hebrew, VII, 7; attitude toward magic practices, VIII, 28; attitude toward synagogue, VII, 274; biblical research and interpretation, V, 159, 278 f., VI, 244 f., 275 f., 278 f., 287 ff., 305 ff., 445, 471 ff., VII, 36 f., 51; in Byzantium, IV, 294, V, 56, 272, 399, VI, 173, 366; and calendar controversies, VIII, 184, 194 f., 203; conversion to Islam, III, 112; designation, V, 232; determined minority, V, 257-67, 408-11; and divine attributes, VIII, 100; doctrine concerning loss of independence, V, 260; in Egypt, V, 257 f., 268, 272, VI, 134 f.; exilarchs, VI, 200 f.; Ibn Daud on, VI, 206; on Jesus, V, 344; and Khazar Judaism, III, 202 f.; laws and regulations, V, 240-51, VI, 108; on levirate, V, 332; linguistic superiority, VI, 290, VII, 6, 36 f., 51; linguistic use of rabbinic literature, VII, 56; liturgy, VII, 43, 64, 70, 110 ff., 244, 248; Muslim conversions to, V, 412; in northwest Africa, VII, 226; opposition to secular learning, VIII, 246 ff.; on oral tradition, VI, 427, VII, 78, 223, VIII, 58 ff.; origin of, V, 187, 405, 407 f.; in Palestine, IV, 111 f., VI, 118, 245 f.; proselytizing, V, 267-75, 412-14; pseudo-messiah, V, 202; reaction to Saadiah's translation, VI, 270 f.; recitation from vocalized scrolls, VI, 244; reestablishment of patriarchate, V, 32; religious philosophy, VIII, 60 ff.; reverence for the law, VIII, 312; Saadiah on, V, 94; Samau'al on, V, 335 f.; in Spain, VII, 228; studies of Arabic science and grammar, VII, 38; on substitute words, VI, 294; survivors of conquest of Jerusalem, IV, 111 f.; on true and false prophets, VIII, 130; view of David's injunction to Solomon, VII, 174 f.
Karbala, battle, V, 7
Karet, premature death, V, 241
Karkara, battle, III, 61
Karo, Joseph, VIII, 292 f.; on animal sacrifice, VII, 79; law code, VI, 26, 115; on medical fees, VIII, 233
Kartir, statesman, II, 317, 435
Kaspi, Joseph, of Provence: charges against local rabbis, VIII, 68; "Ethical Will," VIII, 361
Kavadh I, king of Persia, II, 183, 213, III, 68 f.; and the Mazdakite movement, III, 56; peace with Justinian, III, 17; prohibition of burying the dead, III, 22; and the Samaritans, III, 56
Kavvanah (intention), II, 307
Kemosh, god, I, 90
Keneset Israel, II, 285
Kenites, tribe, I, 46, 57, 60, 313
Kenizzites, I, 57
Kephaleiton, capitation tax, III, 191 f.
Keret legend, I, 301, 401
Kertsh (Panticapaeum; Samkartsh), III, 205
Kessan, city, I, 304
Ketubah, see Marriage contracts
Keturah, Abraham's wife, I, 39
Khabaroi, III, 212
Khaibar, Arabia, III, 163; derivation of names, III, 64; expulsion of Jews, III, 80, 86; Jews vs. Mohammed, III, 79; Mohammed's treaty with, III, 96, 262, 264, 274; refugees from, V, 179 f.; 'Umar and, III, 262
Khalid ibn Yazid, 'Umayyad prince, VIII, 224
Khalisioi, III, 212, 332
Khanfu, China, III, 115
Khaqani, Al-, vizier, III, 152
Kharaj, land tax, III, 162 f., 274 f., IV, 214
Kharijites, Muslim sect, V, 180, 186 f.
Khazars and Khazaria, III, 173, 196-206, 323-30, V, 130 f.; and Ashkenaz, IV, 235; Christians and Muslims, III, 199; conversion, III, 196-99, 323 ff.; and the gaonate, V, 23; Ḥisdai ibn Shapruṭ on, V, 161; influence of Jews of, III, 221; instruction in Judaism, VIII, 273; invasion of Adharbaijan, III, 199; and Karaites, III, 202 f.; migrants from, III, 206 ff., 215 f.; migrants to, III, 177, 183, 196 f.; military campaigns, III, 199; and neighboring Slavs, III, 203, 208; religious syncretism, III,

Khazars and Khazaria (*Continued*) 200-206, 327-30; rice cultivation, IV, 161; role in Jewish history, III, 110; trade, IV, 181; Ugro-Finnic stock, III, 204
Kherson, Cyril's journey to, III, 209
Khirbet Kerak ware, I, 323
Khirbet Mafjar, inscription, III, 103
Khiva (Khwarizm), III, 212, 326; emigration from, III, 197
Khorasan, Persia, III, 109; Karaites, V, 229; messianic movement, V, 200; wedding custom, VI, 122, 395
Khosroe I, king of Persia, II, 178, 183 f., III, 18, VIII, 241; fiscal reform, III, 162; treatment of Jews, III, 56
Khosroe II, king of Persia, II, 185, 399; letter to Emperor Maurice, III, 235; reign of, III, 58; uprising vs., III, 17
Khozran, mosque destroyed by Khazars, III, 203
Khwalisi, III, 212, 332
Khwarizm, *see* Khiva
Khwarizmi, Muhammed b. Musa al-, II, 307, VIII, 153, 158, 355 f.
Kidenas, II, 16
Kiev (city and state), Ukraine, III, 217; archaeological investigations, III, 213; Jewish quarter, III, 217, 222, 337 f.; Petcherskii (Cave) Monastery, III, 215 f.; trade center, IV, 176
Kilayim, I, 253
Kilwa, Africa, III, 116
Kindi, al-, V, 124, 347
Kingdom of God, I, 337, II, 68, 318, 357; coming of, on earth, II, 58 ff., 73 f., 351, 361 (*see also* End of days); teachings of Jesus, II, 68, 69, 73, 77, 357
"Kingdom of wickedness" (Rome), II, 153
Kings, ancient, I, 63-101, 320-40; Anilaeus, I, 168, III, 63; Asinaeus, I, 168, II, 213, III, 63; divine qualities, I, 336; effort to remedy social wrongs, I, 84; graves, II, 286, 423; and the Great Sanhedrin, V, 75; Herodian, I, 225, *see also* Herod, dynasty; Herod the Great; Jeconiah, III, 90; obligations of, I, 92; ritualistic functions, I, 271, 337; status "under the law," II, 200, VI, 10 f.; and study of Scripture, VI, 143; weakening of power, I, 75, 91, 328; *see also* Adiabene; Monarchy; Ruler
—— medieval: Arab, III, 61; Bulan, III, 198, 199, 326; Dhu Nuwas, III, 66 ff.; divine right of, IV, 53 f.; Jewish V, 130 f.; parable of slaves and, VIII, 36; Samaritan, V, 170 f., 367 f.; Nehardea, III, 62 f.; *see also* Caliphs; Emperors; Monarchy; *also under* names of individual rulers
"Kings," seven, vowels as, VII, 53, 241
King Solomon's Throne and Hippodromes, mystical midrash, VIII, 18 f.
Kirmanshah, Persia, V, 10
Kislev, month, V, 31, 227
Kitchen, public, II, 273
Knights Templars: employment of Jewish officials, IV, 37; land grants to Jews, IV, 159
Knowledge: and action, VIII, 345; basis of, VIII, 79; and love of God, VIII, 114 ff., 337; and revelation, VIII, 113 ff.; *see also* Gnosticism
Kofer, term, V, 375
Kohelet, see Ecclesiastes
Kohen and *Kohanim,* I, 149, 272, 274, 413; *see also* Priests
Kohen Zedek, on ablution, V, 30
Koiné, I, 187, VI, 240
Kol Nidre, prayer, V, 248 f., VI, 125, 389, VII, 78, 131
Kozari, Poland, III, 218
Kozarzów, Poland, III, 218
Koziba, *see* Bar Kocheba
Kresimir II, king of Croatia, III, 210
Kronos, I, 374
Krum, czar, III, 209
Kufa, Babylonia: Jewish community, III, 89 f.; mosque, III, 148; Najran Jews transplanted to, III, 271; school of Arabic philology, VII, 15, 19, 58, 222; synagogue, III, 134
Kurdistań: Jews in, II, 210; Kurds excluded from Judaism, II, 222; messianic movement, V, 202
Kuta, I, 107
Kyrios, divine name, II, 18, 335
Kyrios Christos, cult of, II, 62

L

Labi, Solomon, VIII, 34
Lachish, garrison, I, 327; ostraca, I, 334
Ladino, language, I, 186, VII, 9; literature, VI, 187
Ladislas Herrmann, king of Poland, III, 219

Labor: free (hired), I, 70, 71, 267-71, 325, 412, IV, 170; breaches of contracts, II, 304; *corvée,* I, 65, III, 192, 236, IV, 56; cost of, and book production, VII, 137; Jewish attitudes toward, I, 9 f., 412, II, 256-60, 416, V, 74; Karaite attitude toward, V, 239 f.; laws, IV, 155, 170; names of workers, I, 408, 409; prestige of skilled workers, IV, 167 f.; ratio between slaves and, I, 325, IV, 154 f.; shortage, II, 263; social status, I, 88; wages, I, 270, 276, 325, II, 257, IV, 170, 321; *see also* Landlords; Proletariat; Slaves

Lag be-'omer, IV, 145

Lakhmids, dynasty, V, 180; and Ḥimyarites vs. Christians, III, 68; Jewish communities, III, 61

Lamentations, Book of, I, 134, 343, V, 357; commentaries on, VI, 174, 472, VII, 22, 37; midrash on, VI, 164, VII, 82; use of compilations on, VI, 167; use in rituals for Ninth of Ab, VII, 168

Lanciano, Italy, IV, 27

Land: claim of individual Jew to Palestine soil, V, 27, 303; Jewish alienation from, IV, 151-58, 168, 312-14; measurement, III, 163, VIII, 155; Palestinian, conferred by God upon Israelites, I, 88; Persian control, II, 184; purchase of, VI, 147; reclamation, IV, 161 f.; redistribution of, I, 333, II, 104 f., 373; taxation, II, 118, 242, 245, IV, 152, *see also* Land tax; tenure, IV, 163 f.; *see also* Agriculture

Landlords: absentee, I, 72, 277, II, 246; Isaiah's warning, I, 68; and landless groups, I, 280, II, 343; and tenants, I, 280, II, 105, 247, 257 f., 416; under Vespasian, I, 265

"Land of Israel," II, 261; *see also* Palestine

"Land of Onias," I, 394

Landownership: accumulation, III, 182; continuity, III, 31; division into ever-smaller parcels, I, 280; expansion, IV, 13; expropriation, I, 68 ff., 85, 265, II, 343; Gregory's attitude toward, III, 244; by individual or clan, I, 74; law of *siqariqon,* II, 104, 372; real estate mortgages, I, 109; responsibilities of, IV, 222; sales and leases to non-Jews, II, 124 f., 261; as source of political power, IV, 163 f.; of Spanish Jewry, IV, 159 f.

Landscapes, VIII, 229

Landsmannschaften, I, 125

Land tax, III, 162 f.; burdensome effect of, III, 168; imposed by Muslims, III, 96

Land tenure, I, 277; *see also* Landlords

Langobards, III, 243 f.; and Jewish law, III, 244; persecution of Jews, III, 32

Language: approaches to study of, VII, 34; in international trade, IV, 173 f.; basic laws of, VII, 40; Bible translations, II, 142 ff., 386 f., *see also* Bible; classification of, VI, 226; historical grammar of biblical, VII, 242; Jews' use of various, I, 4, 19, II, 141 ff., 145 ff., 385; legal, in Talmud, II, 300, 302; Neo-Punic and Hebrew, I, 374; of Samaritans, II, 340; "seventy languages," VIII, 217; tablets inscribed in six different, I, 52; talmudic, VII, 28-32, 231 f.; *see also* Philology; *also under* respective languages, *e.g.,* Hebrew

Laodicaea, VIII, 241; Council of, II, 188, VII, 128; earthquake, III, 10

Laographia, I, 190

La Palloza, Spain, inscriptions, IV, 33

Last Supper, II, 71, 359

Lateran Council: First, IV, 7, 235 f., 238

—— Second, IV, 7, 238

—— Third, IV, 8, 10, 236, 240; on employment of Christian servants, IV, 15; and Philip II Augustus, IV, 62; on testimony of Christians and Jews, IV, 16

—— Fourth, IV, 13; on practice of physicians, VIII, 231; imposition of tithes, IV, 154

Latin Kingdom of Jerusalem, IV, 106-16, 294-99, VI, 434; armed pilgrims, IV, 131; dissolution of, V, 203; new institutional forms, IV, 114 ff.; status of Jews, IV, 114 ff.

Latin language: Bible, VI, 272, 292; in Eastern provinces, II, 300; in scientific literature, VIII, 171, 243 f., 364, 403; in Sicily, IV, 21

Law: Ancient: Byzantine, III, 11, 177, 185-90, 318 f.

—— Egyptian: codified, II, 300

—— Graeco-Roman: and Jewish legal adjustments, II, 415; sanctions im-

Law (*Continued*)
posed on temple robbery, I, 215, 393
—— Hellenistic: codified, II, 300; influence upon Roman law, II, 303; Jewish indebtedness to, II, 302, 431
—— Jewish, I, 82; binding force of every detail, II, 138; bridging irreconcilable contradictions, I, 181; Canaanite origin of the "casuistic," I, 80; ceremonial or ritualistic, I, 81, 142, 196 f., 227, 359, II, 307-9, 433; Christian attack on, II, 134; commandment to "ransom captives," I, 259; controversy under John Hyrcanus, I, 227; Diaspora Jewry governed by Palestinian, I, 201, 221, 245, II, 320; divine origin, I, 7, II, 319; and egalitarian trends, I, 48, 83, 313; eternity of, II, 161; exilic ideals, I, 163; forgotten and restored, II, 37, 206; formulated partly outside Palestine, I, 162; Halakhah, II, 293, 298, 299, 305, 316, 429; idealistic slant of biblical, I, 76; impact of the, I, 10, 140-48, 359-62; influence on Roman codes, III, 231 f.; invalidated in messianic age? II, 73, 161, 298, 360, 365, V, 124, 347, 358; "is not in heaven," II, 139; Jesus came to fulfill, II, 67, 69; Jesus' disciples' adherence to, II, 74, 78, 361; on just prices, II, 255; Karaite expansion of, V, 224; moral, I, 80, 81, 227, II, 307-9, 328, 433; needed in exile, I, 140, 143; of Pharisees, II, 37 f., 45; Philo's restatement, II, 253, 415; preexistence of, VI, 8; pre-Mosaic, II, 136, 382; proselytism, I, 181; protection of basic prayers, VII, 101; recodification, VI, 76-84; recognized no special privileges, I, 75; reinterpretation of, V, 54, 61; religion and, I, 77-84, 327-32, II, 78 f.; of Sadducees, II, 36, 37; Samaritan *ḥillukh,* II, 32; sanctified daily pursuits, I, 9; study of, imperative, II, 120, 121, 251, 269, 275, 279; talmudic religion and, II, 215-321, 408-36; teaching to Gentiles forbidden, II, 430; term Torah in Jeremiah, I, 331; universality, I, 204; *see also* Moses; Pentateuch; Religion
—— Roman: VI, 4, III, 35, 49, 174, 231, *see also* Justinian; Hellenistic and Jewish influence, II, 303; Jewish independence of, II, 299, 429 f.; on usury, IV, 199 f.
—— Sassanian, II, 181, 299, 301, 303, 429 f.
—— Medieval: civil, V, 57 f., 224 f., VIII, 144; feudal, in Spain, IV, 41; Frankish and Langobard, influenced by Jewish, III, 244, 252; local, settlement of disputes by ordeal, IV, 40 f.; on segregation, V, 79 f.
—— Jewish: and agriculture, IV, 156 ff.; applied by pietists, VIII, 52; on attending houses of worship, III, 302; attitude of mystics toward, VIII, 17 ff.; business, IV, 185, VI, 71, *see also* Trade; on castration, IV, 192; Christian repudiation of, V, 122 ff.; codes, V, 212, 261, VI, 25 f., *see also* Codes, legal; compendia of, as source of responsa, VI, 118; conflict for control over, V, 211 ff.; consolidation of traditions, VI, 16-27, 327-32; on corporal punishment, IV, 261; on disposition of land, IV, 158; on divorce (*q.v.*), IV, 20; early Western books, VI, 48 ff., 66, 72 ff., 84 ff., 113 ff.; equation of Oral and Scriptural, V, 181; on family, VI, 321; formulation of, V, 212; geonim and, V, 52, *see also* Geonim and gaonate; immutability of, VI, 144 f., 371; international uniformity of, IV, 174, 176; Karaites and, V, 230 ff., 240-51; of the kingdom (state), IV, 270, V, 77 f., 332; on land ownership, IV, 160 f.; and Langobard law, III, 244; Maimonides on study of, V, 76; on marriage to captive woman, III, 89, V, 8; and mathematics, VIII, 149, 153 ff.; and medicine, VIII, 238 f., 253; method of analogy, VII, 236; and occult practices, VIII, 55; philosophy of, VI, 141-51, VIII, 70 ff., 123 ff.; and *piyyuṭim,* VII, 103; preoccupation with, VIII, 143 f.; and prophecy, VIII, 132; rational, V, 325, VI, 142 ff., VIII, 117; reign of, VI, 3-151, 321-98; respect of German pietists for, VIII, 49 f.; and ritual, VII, 122; Samau'al on, V, 100; and scientific fact, VIII, 139 f.; sectarian deviations from, V, 189 ff.; and segregation, V, 79; sources of, VI, 244; support of, in the Aggadah, VI, 178 f.; unbroken con-

tinuity of, V, 3, *see also* Tradition; uniformity, VI, 108, 117 ff., 148 ff.; *see also* Judges; Jurisprudence; Jurists; Oral Law; Rabbis and Rabbinate; Talmud
—— Muslim, V, 18, 210, 213, VI, 63 ff., 78, 94; analogy in, VII, 236; biographical material, VI, 24; on business transactions, IV, 185 f., 351; civil and religious equality of minorities, III, 132, IV, 225; codification, VI, 107, 363; concubinage and, IV, 195; on *dar as-sulḥ,* III, 130; effect of Church and Roman law on, III, 174; foreign elements in, VI, 324; on interfaith partnerships, IV, 331; interpretation of, VI, 6-16; and Jewish *heqqesh,* V, 213; on public office, IV, 226; reign of, VI, 149 ff.; and religious persecution, III, 124; schools of, VI, 16 ff.; on slaves, IV, 195; on synagogues, III, 135; system of responsa, VI, 110; on usury, IV, 197
—— Ostrogothic, III, 25 f.
—— Syro-Christian, II, 303 f., 432, VI, 4 ff., 322 ff.
—— Visigothic, III, 36, 245 f.; on Christian servants of Jews, IV, 314 f.; *see also Leges Visigothorum; Lex Romana Visigothorum*
"Law of the kingdom," V, 77 f.
Laws, adjudicated, *see Halakhot qeṣubot*
Lawyers, *see* Jurists
Laziness, charge of, against Jews, V, 132 f.
Leadership: centered in Palestine, I, 247; Jewish, of Semitic world, I, 210; revolutionary, I, 86
—— communal, V, 3-81, 293-325; attitude toward magic practices, VIII, 54; conservatism of, VIII, 67; dilemma of philosophers among, VIII, 68 ff.; Karaite, V, 237 f., 261; poetic laudation of, VII, 147; scholars, II, 120, 197, 204-8 *passim,* 291, 403, V, 179, VIII, 263 f.; *see also* Elders; Geonim and gaonate; Rabbanites; Rabbis and rabbinate; Scholars and scholarship
Leah, and Rachel, VII, 188
Leander, archbishop, III, 36
Leap year, V, 246; cycles, VIII, 204 f.; proclamation of, VIII, 187, 193 f., 200
Learning: centers of, III, 102, 104, VII, 30; lack of, and sectarianism, V, 373; professionalization of, IV, 221, V, 76; rabbinic, IV, 215 f.; specialization of, VI, 72; transmission of aggadic, VI, 173; upsurge of, VI, 48; *see also* Academies; Education; Scholars and scholarship
Lease, Hebrew-Arabic, IV, 320
Leeds fragment, II, 29, 339
Legal problems: meaning of words involving, VII, 13; sermons instigated by, VI, 169
Legal status of Jews, *see* Rights, legal
Leges Visigothorum (*Liber judicum*), III, 36; lack of clarity, III, 44; regulations re Jews, III, 42
Leicester, England, "Jewry Wall," IV, 281
Leningrad fragment of Palestinian Talmud, II, 13, 333
Leo I, pope, III, 5
Leo IV, pope, IV, 90
Leo VII, pope, IV, 6
Leo, Roman emperor, II, 304
Leo III (the Isaurian), Byzantine emperor, III, 175 f.; *Basilika,* III, 186; *Eklogé,* III, 177, 185 f.; suppression of Judaism, III, 220
Leo VI (the Wise), Byzantine emperor, VI, 154; *Basilika,* III, 181; "Book of the Prefect," IV, 170, 183, 321 f.; *Epanagogé,* III, 186, 318; *Novella* 55, III, 180 f., 186, 318; ordinance re Scripture reading, III, 189
Leo Mung, patriarch of Ochrida, III, 210
Leon, Spain, IV, 28; false Messiah, V, 199
Leonardo Fibonacci of Pisa, VIII, 156, 158, 352
Leontopolis, Egypt: district, II, 12; temple, I, 14, 219, 220, 350, 394, V, 123
Leo of Naples, VI, 418
Leopold V, duke of Austria, IV, 72
Lepers and leprosy, I, 275, II, 249, V, 133, 250; Maimonides on, VI, 179
Lerida Spain, IV, 37, 247
Lèse majesté, I, 92, 336
Letter of Aristeas, I, 172, 185, 196, 251, 261, 384
Letters, Lachish, I, 334; *see also* El-Amarna; Responsa

Levi, house or tribe of, I, 274, 318, V, 202; genealogies, I, 329; redeemer from, II, 351
Levi, R., II, 138, 254, 312
Leviathan, V, 148, VIII, 10
Levi b. Ḥamma, R., VI, 407
Levi b. Ḥayta, R., II, 424
Levi b. Jephet, V, 233, 241 f., VI, 248
Levi b. Sissai, R., II, 268, 281, VI, 36
Levirate marriage, I, 79, II, 231, 411, V, 93, 216, 224, 332, VI, 65, 81, 138
Levites: ancient, I, 413, VI, 10, VII, 259; adherents to Mosaic religion, I, 59, 414; modern, I, 414; numbers of, in Palestine, I, 272 f., 413; in Pharisaic leadership, II, 117; relations with priests, I, 329, 362; tithe for, I, 280; *see also* Priests and priesthood
Leviticus, Book of: explanation, VII, 22; fragment, I, 331; as text for priests, II, 275
Lexicography, VII, 12-32, 223-33; Arabic, VII, 26; biblical, VII, 229 f.; *see also* Dictionaries
Lex Romana Burgundionum, III, 49
Lex Romana Visigothorum (*Breviarium Alarici*), III, 35, 49
Libanius, II, 188, 414
Liberalism: departure from traditional Judaism, I, 27; and nationalism, I, 28, 361
Liber judicum, see Leges Visigothorum
Libraries: Canaanite, I, 306, *see also* Ras Shamra; Christian and Muslim, compared, IV, 28; mosque, VII, 138, VIII, 246; school and congregational, VII, 138
Licentiousness, fought by rabbis, II, 217
Life: attachment to, I, 12; divine attribute, VIII, 96 ff.; Jewish way of, I, 174, II, 216, 217; and kindling of fire, V, 283
Life after death, *see* Immortality of the soul; Resurrection
Life span, II, 220, 408, VIII, 259, 336; Maimonidean responsum on, VI, 112
Light: creation of, VIII, 94 f.; and darkness, V, 106 f., VI, 305 f., VIII, 34 f.; divine Glory, VIII, 129; kindling and burning, V, 216 f., 223, 244, 283; prayer, VI, 126; principle of, VIII, 22; Sabbath, V, 269, VI, 16, 389, VII, 72; on Zion, VII, 115 f.
Lilith, II, 19, VIII, 10
Limoges, France: burning of ruler's effigy, IV, 92; sufferings of Jewish community, VI, 219
Lincoln, England, "Jews' court," IV, 281
Linen industry, I, 257, 408, II, 248
Linguistics, *see* Philology
"Linon," false Messiah of, V, 199
Lipit-Ishtar, code, I, 327
Lisbon, Portugal, IV, 132, 305
Literature: Jewish, I, 178; Al-Ḥarizi's literary criticism, VII, 186; apologetical, I, 195-99; historical, I, 25-26, 100, 340, VI, 29 f., 188-219, 416-33; Musiv style, VII, 202; poetry and belles-lettres, VII, 135-213, 286-321; popularization of, I, 141; proverbial, I, 141; in Renaissance of Islam, VII, 60 f.; sayings of Jesus traced in, II, 67; scientific, VI, 169; talmudic, II, 294-98, 425-29; translation of major works, I, 52, 187; *see also* Midrash; Old Testament; Talmud; *also under* respective branches, *e.g.,* Poetry
—— Muslim: *isra'iliyat,* VI, 168; *Kalilah ve-Dimnah,* VII, 189; works on poetic art, VII, 316 f.
Litigation: business, settlement by compromise, IV, 176 f.; Byzantine laws on, III, 190; excommunication for, V, 5; exilarchic judges, V, 14 f.; Jewish, formula for, III, 195; Judeo-Christian, III, 190, IV, 15 f., 41 f., 49, 69, 78; oath in, IV, 41 f., 253, 255; rights of Jews in Barcelona IV, 41 f.; rules of evidence, IV, 277, 281; and state courts, V, 5; *see also* Courts; Judges; Oaths; Witnesses
"Little Lord," VIII, 16
Liturgy: Christian, VII, 68, 84 f.; antisemitism in, V, 352; Jewish influences on, VII, 84 f.; political overtones, VII, 266; written transmission, VII, 258
—— Hebrew, II, 282, VI, 244; accuracy of halakhic contents, VII, 274; adjustments, II, 182; blame for changes in, VI, 42; compilation and crystallization of, VII, 63 ff., 245 ff.; disparities in ancient sources, VII, 109; dynamic approach to, VII, 131 ff.; efforts at unification, VII, 68 ff., 87, 279; incorporation of improvised prayers, VII, 86; Judeo-Christian interrelations, II, 134, VII, 84 f., 252; juristic-liturgical treatises, VII, 105-24, 271-81; Karaite,

V, 247 f., 392, 404 f.; linguistic difficulties, VII, 66 ff.; Maimonides' codification of, V, 28, VII, 118-21, 279 f.; memorizers, VII, 85 ff.; messianic theme in, V, 150 ff.; music, II, 8, 155, 330, VII, 125-31, 281-85; and mystical literature, VIII, 12; Ninth of Ab, V, 152; opponents of standardization, VII, 106 ff.; Samaritan modifications, II, 340; talmudic latitude on, VII, 108 f.; traditional, preservation of, VII, 106 ff.; *see also Piyyuṭim;* Poetry, liturgical; Prayers; Psalms; Ritual

Lives of the Prophets, II, 20

Loans, I, 109; contracts, I, 261; foreclosure and bondage, I, 161; *see also* Moneylending; Usury

Loan words, Greek, VI, 355, VII, 141, VIII, 229; Latin, VI, 355, VII, 141; Persian, VII, 141, VIII, 229; *see also under* the respective languages

Logic: and faith, VIII, 83 f.; and religious philosophy, VIII, 67 f.

Logos: doctrine of, I, 202, 392, V, 121, VIII, 101, 129; mediation through, VIII, 91; Philonic, V, 380; "shadow" equated with, VIII, 273; "son," VIII, 96

"Logos Christology" of Paul, II, 81, 364

Lombards, derogatory term, IV, 207

London, riot involving Jews, IV, 124

Longchamp, William, bishop of Ely, IV, 127 f.

Lord of Hosts, I, 61, 128; old concept of, I, 137

Lord's Prayer, II, 84, 138; and prayer for mourners, VII, 67; *see also Qaddish*

Lost tribes, *see* Ten Tribes

Lot, patriarch, VI, 39; names of wife and daughter, VI, 170; story of, V, 90

Lothar II, emperor, IV, 11

Lotharingia, VI, 48

Louis I (the Pious), emperor, IV, 18, 44; and Church leaders, IV, 51; controversy over succession, IV, 52; and Jewish slave trade, IV, 193 f.; privileges to Jews, IV, 48-53, 260 ff., V, 62; trade charters, IV, 48 f.

Louis II, emperor, IV, 25 f., 61

Louis VI, king of France, IV, 59

Louis VII, king of France, IV, 61; outlawry of relapse to Judaism, IV, 61

Louis the Child, emperor, IV, 65 f.

Love, Canaanite goddess of, I, 363

Love poems, VII, 157 ff., 212 f.

Loving-kindness, religious duty, I, 175

Loyalty: aspersions on Jewish, II, 398, IV, 37 f., 55, 265, V, 131 f.; to the community, V, 4, 162, VIII, 263; division of, V, 162; oath of, IV, 49, 163, V, 35 f.; political, V, 293 f.

Lucca, Italy, IV, 26

Lucena, Spain, III, 34, V, 298; academy, V, 49, VI, 84; Book of Deeds, IV, 316; the hundred benedictions, VII, 110; Jewish community, III, 109, 124, 170; scholars, VI, 84 f., 149

Lucian of Samosata, II, 21

Lucifer, V, 132

Lucretia, VI, 232

Luke, Saint, I, 170, II, 23, 362

—— Gospel of, II, 66, 72, 73, 86, 355, 357

Lukuas-Andreas, Cyrenian king, II, 95, 370

Lulab ritual, II, 119

Lull, Raymond, V, 89

Lunar calendar, II, 125, 206; accepted by Jews, I, 44; *see also* Calendar; Moon

Lunel: academy, VI, 87 ff., 106, VII, 54; Jewish population, IV, 48

Lusius Quietus, II, 96, 371

Lute, VII, 210

Luther, Martin, I, 9, VIII, 83

Luxury items: of gold and silver, IV, 212; growing demand for, IV, 172; trade in, IV, 214

Lydia, I, 102, 216

Lynching, II, 85, V, 57; legalized, I, 239, 402; as punishment for sexual transgression, I, 402, II, 365, III, 143, 300

Lyons, France: charter for merchants of, IV, 48, 50; under Duke Girard, IV, 55; fairs, IV, 175; false Messiah, V, 199

Lysias, I, 217, 394

Lysimachus of Jerusalem, I, 185

M

Maacah, I, 66

Ma'arri, Abu'l Ala al-, Arab poet and

Ma'arri, Abu'l Ala al- (*Continued*) skeptic, V, 103 f., VIII, 124; on unity of mankind, VIII, 263
Ma'arufiah, term, IV, 185, 331
Ma'aseh ha-geonim, IV, 183, VI, 65
Ma'aser, biblical tithe, IV, 13
Macarius Magnus, II, 391
"Maccabean" martyrs, I, 230, 232, VI, 167
Maccabee, name, I, 369
Maccabees, house of: archaizing efforts, I, 225; coins, I, 225, 235, 369, 401, II, 36; conquests, I, 224, 250; corruption, I, 284; despotism, I, 223; drive for access to Mediterranean, I, 255; funerary monuments, II, 14; Hasmonean letter, I, 395; internal conflicts, I, 217, 237, 397, 401; Jewish vitality enhanced by, I, 166; Karaite condemnation of, V, 256; and lamp for Ḥanukkah, I, 235; priestly family, I, 271; priestly messiah, V, 356; in rabbinic literature, II, 139; significance in sociopolitical controversies, I, 399; zealots, I, 165
—— revolt by, I, 201, 216 f., 229 ff.; chronology, I, 394; first "war of religion," I, 233, II, 38, IV, 95 f.; and Hellenism, I, 166, 167; Jewish soldiers, II, 42, 94, 98; manumissions resulting from, I, 259; miracle tales, V, 407; objectives, II, 38; and possession of Bibles, VII, 86
—— Books of, I, 197, 232, 377; Book of the Hasmonean Children, VI, 188 f., 416 f., 484 f.
Macedon, I, 190, 234
Macedonia, III, 186, IV, 107
Macedonius, patriarch of Constantinople, III, 6
Mâcon, First Council of, IV, 188
Madaïn (Ctesiphon), III, 136
Madda', term, VI, 378
Magdalos, Egypt, I, 111
Magdeburg, Germany: merchants' guild, IV, 184 f.; monastic privilege over Jews, IV, 65
Maghariya, V, 192
Maghribi, Samuel b. Moses al-, V, 234; on duties of priests and judges, V, 237 f.; laws of incest, V, 243; liturgical poems, V, 249; on profanation of women, V, 240
Magi, I, 141, II, 181, 183, 190, 317, 347, VI, 302, VIII, 46
Magic arts, VI, 103; charges re, V, 96, 132; Christians' belief in Jewish powers, II, 189, 401; connection with alchemy, VIII, 224; distinguished from miracles, VIII, 130; and medicine, V, 334, VIII, 233 ff.; and mysticism, VIII, 27 ff., 46; opposition to, I, 82, 87, 139, II, 17, VIII, 234; popular beliefs and practices, I, 329, II, 15-23, 336 f., 390; protection from supernatural forces, VIII, 4; and science, VIII, 274; square, VIII, 354; sympathetic, IV, 92; texts, I, 139, 358, II, 156, 390, VIII, 233, 394; and women, I, 347, II, 21; *see also* Incantations and exorcisms
Magister judaeorum, official, IV, 49, V, 63
Magna Graecia, II, 392
Magna Mater, cult of, II, 168
Magyars: "black Ugrians," III, 204; Jewish settlements among, III, 206 ff.; and Khazars, III, 211 f.; *see also* Hungary
Mahbub, *see* Agapius
Mahdi, Muslim concept, V, 163, 185
Maḥoza, Babylonian city, II, 199, 205, 242, III, 58 f.; upper classes, II, 277
Maimon b. Joseph, father of Maimonides, III, 291 f., VI, 58; interpretation of Psalm 90, VIII, 126
Maimonides, *see* Abraham Maimonides; Moses b. Maimon
Maimuni, Abraham b. Moses, *see* Abraham Maimonides
Maimuni, Moses, *see* Moses b. Maimon
Majus, taxation of, III, 191
Makhir, Babylonian scholar, IV, 45, 47
Makhir b. Abba Mari, *Yalqut ha-Makhiri,* VI, 404
Makhir b. Yehudah: law collection, VI, 74 f.; lexicographical work, VI, 362, VII, 30
Makkot, tractate, VI, 53
Malabar spices, I, 321
Malachi, Book of, I, 114, 127, 151, 154, 158, 367; rejection of divorce, I, 114
Malalas, Byzantine chronicler: legend of Solomon and Tadmor, III, 62; on Samaritan delegation to king of Persia,

III, 17; on uprising of Antioch Jewry, III, 6
Malchiah, I, 352
Malchus Kleodemus, II, 31
Maledictions: in liturgical poetry, VII, 179; *see also* Curses
Males, preponderance over females in Jewish settlements, III, 252
Malik ar-Ramli, V, 182, 196
Malikians, *see* Ramlites
Malik ibn Ajlan, III, 65
Malik ibn 'Anas, jurist, VI, 94; on intermarriage, III, 142, on vocalized Qur'an texts, VI, 244
Malix ibn Dinar, Muslim mystic, VIII, 112
Malikites, III, 123, VI, 11, 16
Malka, R., V, 15
Malko of Palmyra, II, 407
Malvern, England, VIII, 174
Mameluks, III, 172
Ma'mun, al-, *see* Al-Ma'mun
Ma'mun al-Amiri, Egyptian vizier, VIII, 248
Mamzer: exclusion of, I, 147; term, II, 409
Man: dignity of, as created in God's image, I, 49; influence of stars on, VIII, 175 ff.; love of God, VIII, 115 ff.; microcosm, VIII, 103; relation to God and the universe, VIII, 108 ff.; *see also* Individuals and Individualism; Mankind
Manasseh, king of Judah, I, 78, 79, VI, 122, 143
Mancosi, term, IV, 212
Mandaeans and Mandaism, II, 26, 51, 348, 433, III, 160, VIII, 276
Manethon priest, I, 36, 195, 304, III, 149
Mani, prophet, II, 178; Ibn Daud re, VI, 208
Manichaeans and Manichaeism, II, 26, 178, III, 82, 177, 186, 242, V, 344, VIII, 31, 296; as "heresy," V, 107 f., VI, 171; strictures on the Old Testament, VI, 298, 303; survivals of dualism, V, 105 f., VIII, 46
Mankah, *see* Kankah
Mankind: early history of, VI, 192; emergence of concept of, VIII, 263; history in terms of spiritual evolution, VI, 228; liturgical poems on nature of, VII, 180; poets' concern with problems of, VII, 176
Manna, miracle of, VI, 269, 300
"Man of War," God as, I, 46, 61
Manṣur b. Sahlan, VIII, 246
Manuel I (Comnenus), Byzantine emperor, III, 184, VI, 434; *Novella* 55, III, 195
Manufactures and trades, II, 248 ff.; *see also* Industry
Manuscripts: illuminated, VIII, 246; mutilation of, VII, 137; Samaritan, V, 372
Ma'onite synagogue in Tiberias, II, 199, 404
Maqna, Mohammed's treaty with the Jews of, III, 79
Maqqari, al-, III, 148
Maqrizi, VI, 243, VIII, 161; on 'Anan, V, 219; on conversion of Copts to Islam, III, 123; on Muslim libraries, VII, 138; on synagogues, III, 106, 135
Mar Abba, *see* Abba, Mar
"Mar" b. Rabina, VII, 75
Marcella, wife of Porphyry, II, 159
Marcian, Roman emperor of the East: Monophysites' petition to, III, 5; rescript of 452, III, 234
Marciana, Saint, III, 8
Marcion, heresiarch, II, 73, 167, 394, V, 107
Marcionites and Marcionism, II, 408, III, 209, VI, 298, VIII, 16, 31, 42; *see also* Gnosticism
Marcus Rutilius Lupus, II, 95
Marcus Tittius, II, 202
Mardan Farukh, Pehlevi author, V, 105 f., 121, VI, 271; biblical criticism, VI, 303 ff.; *The Decisive Solution of Doubts,* VI, 301 ff.
Marduk, god, I, 93, 105, 327, 349
Marḥeshvan, month, V, 31, 227
Mari, palace of, I, 77, 300
Mari ha-Levi, gaon, VI, 446
Marinus, Jewish thinker at Athenian academy, VIII, 241
Marisa, Palestine, I, 224
Marissa, Sidonian colony of, I, 374
Mark, Saint, II, 68; identification with Syriac Marcus, VI, 458
—— Gospel of, II, 64, 66, 70, 71, 72, 73, 357, 359, 364

Marqa, Samaritan poet, II, 340 f., VII, 64; quoted, II, 31
Mar Rab Huna, *see* Huna, Mar Rab
Mar Rab Raba, *see* Rab Raba, Mar
Marrakesh, Morocco, III, 108
Marranos and Marranism, III, 44, IV, 6, 293
Marriage: abstention from, II, 209; 'Anan's rules, V, 217 f., 221 f.; bridal sheet, V, 242; of converts, III, 112, IV, 255 f.; customs, II, 218, VI, 122 f., 130, 391; of divorcées, V, 18; during mourning, VI, 120; early, I, 265, II, 219, 238, 408; economic considerations, II, 220, 409; good luck sign, VIII, 184; incest, I, 146, II, 229 ff., 411; Karaite and Rabbanite, V, 265 f., 413; levirate, I, 79, II, 231, 411, V, 93, 216, 224, 332; Maimonides on, VI, 179; matriarchal forms, I, 310; monogamy or polygamy, I, 112, 347, II, 223-29, 409 f., VI, 135 f., 393 f.; morality demanded, II, 221 ff., 228; presentation of ring, V, 283; priestly, I, 376, II, 235, V, 240; prohibited degrees in, I, 146, 275, V, 92 f.; promotion of, II, 127; with proselytes and with heathens, I, 376, II, 232; rabbinic law, V, 134, 190, VI, 81 f., 134 ff., 393 f.; scholar's eligibility, II, 235; sectarianism and laws of, II, 408, V, 190; settlement, II, 220, 303; with a slave, III, 89; substitute, II, 231; in Talmud, I, 275, II, 217-23, 408 f.; within tribe, I, 146, 147, 360; *see also* Bride; Bridegroom; Divorce; Levirate marriage; Wedding
—— interfaith, I, 114, 147, 163, 189, 361, 376, II, 223, 232 f., 401 f., 411 f., III, 10, IV, 9, 52, 114, 241, V, 100; Byzantine law on, III, 189; in France, III, 50; Jewish attitude toward, III, 143; legislation on, III, 36 f., 42, 143, 189; Muslim attitude toward, III, 299 f.; and preponderance of males, III, 252; religious laws vs., III, 142
—— contracts (*ketubot*), I, 113, II, 236, IV, 195 f., V, 265 f., VI, 85, 128; and biblical law, VI, 24 f.; and loans, VI, 132; pledge against polygamy, VII, 138
Mar Samuel, *see* Samuel, Mar
Marseilles, France, VI, 60
Martel, Charles, III, 199
Martha, daughter of Boethos, I, 262
Marthad-ilan Ahsan, *see* Dhu Nuwas
Martial, II, 156
Martini, Raymond, II, 296, 427, VI, 196, VIII, 33; compilation of aggadic sayings, VI, 171 f.; *Pugio fidei,* V, 357
Martyrologies, I, 190, II, 100; in folk plays, V, 116; of Jewish people, VIII, 345; use of, in sermons, VI, 167 f.
Martyrs and martyrdom: Christian, I, 230, 399, 400, II, 167, 383, 394; "heathen," I, 190, 248, 381, II, 108
—— Jewish, I, 230-33, 399-400, II, 100, 139, 215, III, 39, 57, 125, VI, 193 f.; child martyrs, IV, 135 f.; in Crusades, IV, 95 f., 103 f., 133, 138, 144-47, 218, 309-11; first urge to, I, 48; four martyrs, VIII, 19; glorification of, VIII, 127; Isaac prototype of, II, 383; Pharisees, II, 100, 371; records of, VI, 234; seven Maccabean, I, 230, 232; the Ten, I, 231, II, 370, IV, 285, VIII, 283; *see also* Massacres of Jews; Persecutions; Pogroms
Mar 'Uqba, *see* 'Uqba, Mar
Marut, fallen angel, III, 265
Marwan II, caliph, III, 288
Mar Zuṭra, *see* Zuṭra, Mar
Masada, I, 252, II, 370, VI, 193
Masarjawaih, Jewish medical writer, VIII, 236, 256; medical works, VIII, 242 f., 393
Masawaih, Christian doctor, VIII, 234
Masbotheans, sect, II, 348
Masgeda (mosque), VI, 13
Masha'allah, Jewish mathematician, III, 99 f., 152, VIII, 148; astronomic works, VIII, 166 f.; building plans for Baghdad, IV, 170, VIII, 59
Mashal le-mah ha-dabar domeh, parable, VI, 167
Mashiaḥ, biblical term, V, 157; *see also* Messiah and messianism
Mashqin, tractate, VI, 62
Maslama al-Majriti, VIII, 355, 363
Maṣliaḥ b. Elijah ibn al-Bazaq, R., of Sicily, VII, 30
Masons, IV, 170, 321, VIII, 159
Masorah, II, 145, 386, III, 72, V, 176, 195 f., VI, 20, VII, 28; details of, VI, 247; final formulation, VI, 251; spelling and pronunciation (*ketib* and *qeri*), VI, 293, 443; Syriac, VI, 443; and systematic rules of grammar, VII, 32

Masorites, I, 336; contribution to Jewish life, VI, 253; detailed monographs, VI, 252; early generations, VI, 424; linguistic decisions and meaning of words, VII, 13; Palestinian, VI, 245 f.; principles of Creation, VIII, 15; refinement of biblical text, VI, 249-55, 449-53; on the seven "kings," VII, 53; symbols for cantillation, VII, 126 f.; Tiberian school, V, 305, VI, 253, 262
Massacres of Jews: commemoration of, IV, 89 ff., 144 ff.; in England, IV, 124 ff.; in Germany, IV, 104 f.; memorial services, VII, 99; reaction to, IV, 139 ff.; theme of liturgical poets, VII, 179; *see also 'Aqedot;* Pogroms
Masses, the: adherence to the commandments, VIII, 81; Aramic speech replaced by Arabic, VII, 67, 223; attitude toward, V, 238 f.; exploitation of, I, 84; illiterate, V, 394, *see also 'Am ha-areṣ;* inequalities and suffering, I, 276, V, 238 ff.; obstacle to professionalized medicine, VIII, 232; and religious philosophy, VIII, 67 ff., 137; suspicion of merchants, IV, 184
Mass hysteria: in age of Crusades, IV, 100 ff.; and mass suicide, IV, 104; and messianism, V, 167
Mas'udi, Arab geographer, V, 84; on chess, VIII, 356; on Khazar tribunal, III, 200; "Meadows of Gold," III, 182, VIII, 215; popular saying on the *mawali,* III, 149
Materialism, VIII, 78 ff.
Mater synagogae, II, 240, 413
Mathematics: Jewish students of, II, 306 f., 433, VIII, 146-60, 349-57; and astronomy, VIII, 167; definition, VIII, 144 f.; Kaspi's program of education, VIII, 361; in *Mishnat ha-Middot,* II, 307, 433; and music, VII, 209; orthodox objectors to, VIII, 142
Matilde, queen of England, IV, 81
Mating, festival of, I, 294
Matrand, Saracen "king," IV, 46
Matriarchal society, I, 43, 310; surviving vestige of, VIII, 275
Mattathias of Modein, I, 229, 231
Matter, VIII, 101; eternality of, II, 311, VIII, 94; and form, VIII, 114, 325; primordial, VIII, 87 ff., 93 f., 322 ff.
Matthew, Saint, II, 66
—— Gospel of, II, 68, 72, 73, 74, 359, V, 348
Matthew of Edessa, Armenian chronicler, III, 184
Mattiah b. Heresh, II, 56
Maulana Jalalu'ddin Rumi, Muslim opponent of rationalism, VIII, 83
Mauretania, I, 169; *see also* Morocco
Maurice, Byzantine emperor, II, 399, III, 17; persecution of Jews, III, 19, 236
Mausolea, *see* Tombs
Mawali, Arabic term, III, 148 f.
Maximinus, Roman emperor, II, 400
Maximus, Valerius, II, 24
Maximus Confessor, VI, 304
Mayence, Germany: academy, IV, 7, VI, 74 f.; *'aqedot,* IV, 103 ff., 144 f., 292, 309 f., VI, 193; attempts to protect Jews of, IV, 99; burghers and Jews, IV, 100; congregation of ghosts, IV, 103 f., 292, VIII, 46; Diet of, IV, 130; expulsion of Jews, IV, 26, 73; Jewish community, IV, 66, 103 f., VI, 48; martyrdom of a Jewess, IV, 96; pun on name, IV, 67; residence permits, V, 69; return of Jewish refugees, IV, 116; "sages of," VII, 30
Mayence Anonymus, IV, 102, 287 f., 290, VI, 218
"May he rest in peace," formula, II, 333
Mazdaism, *see* Parsees and Parsiism
Mazdak and Mazdakites, II, 182, 222, 231, 251, 409, III, 55, 69, 255
Meal-offering, I, 129
Meals, blessings associated with, VII, 115
Me'am zar, term, II, 409
Meat, I, 254; and milk, VI, 258 f.; prohibitions on, III, 42, 51, 84, IV, 61, V, 92 f., 218, 249; tax, VIII, 386
Meaux, Abbey of, IV, 204; Council of, IV, 18
Meborakh, *nagid,* V, 41 f.
Mecca, V, 86; flood, and letter from Caliph, VII, 4; Jewish community, III, 263; Ka'aba stone, III, 86, V, 86; Mohammed's relations with Christians and Jews in, III, 76 f.; pilgrims to, III, 88, 302, VIII, 211; turning toward, during prayer, III, 296
Mechanics, VIII, 159 f.; Muslim knowledge of, VIII, 356
Media, I, 102, V, 178, 183, 223; association with Babylonia, II, 205; "remnant" in, I, 106

Mediators, *see* Intermediaries
Medicine: ancient, II, 306, 307, VIII, 251
—— medieval, VIII, 221-66, 384-405; 'Anan on practice of, V, 259, 282; Arab historians and biographers, VIII, 254; book ascribed to Ibn Ezra, VIII, 361; discrimination in practice of, III, 146 f.; Jewish reliance on non-Jewish authors, VIII, 253 ff., 265; and theology, VIII, 259; toleration of study of, VIII, 265; tradition vs. experience, VIII, 234 ff.; *see also* Physicians; *also under* individual doctors, *e.g.*, Asaph; Moses b. Maimon
Medievalism: incipient, II, 172-214, 396-407; Babylonian supremacy, II, 204-9, 405; Christianity's authority after Constantine, II, 172; decline of Hellenism, II, 173-75, 396; intergroup relations, II, 187-91, 400-402, 427; Jews' new legal status, II, 176-87, 396 ff.; local autonomy, II, 198-204, 403 f.; in Roman and Sassanian empires, II, 172 ff., 396 ff.; segregation and self-government, II, 191-98, 402 ff.; shrinkage in Jewish population, II, 209; widening of geographic basis, II, 210-14, 406 f.
Medina (Yathrib), III, 63; Jewish tribes in, III, 76, 78, V, 109; pilgrims to, III, 88; refugees from, III, 87, V, 179 f.
Medinah, term, V, 298
Mediterranean Sea: islands of eastern, I, 169; Maccabean drive for access to, I, 255; Phoenician ships sailing, I, 64; trade routes, IV, 172 f.
Mediterranean world: Assyrian shadow over, I, 67; Jewish expansion throughout, I, 167 ff., 210, VII, 13, 107; Palestine's political position, I, 215 ff.; Phoenicia's contact with, I, 39; proselytes and their descendants in, I, 283; *see also under* names of countries and cities
Megiddo, I, 183; archaeological excavations, I, 122, 317, 320, 350; stables, I, 326
Megillat (or *Sefer*) *bene Ḥashmona'i,* VI, 188 f., 269, 416 f.
Megillat Ta'anit (Scroll of Fasts), II, 140, 384
Meḥasiah, academy, and annual fast, VI, 330
Meir, R., I, 255, II, 9, 119, 133, 145, 148, 224, 230, 316, VI, 31, 155; aggadic notes, VI, 158; as author of unnamed mishnah, VI, 204; and Beruriah, legend of, VI, 408; on the hundred benedictions, VII, 110; moves against waste, II, 273; quoted, II, 124; sermon, II, 280; "Story of R. Meir," VI, 168 f., 185, 408; wife, II, 239, 408
Meir b. Baruch: on Rashi's ordinances, V, 64; on taxation, V, 78
Meir b. Isaac, R., cantor of Worms, V, 376, VII, 144, 193; liturgical poems, VII, 246
Meir b. Isaac Katzenellenbogen, I, 302
Meir b. Simon, Narbonnese scholar, V, 115; on the Book of the Bright Light, VIII, 37; on interest, V, 128; on usury, IV, 224
Me'iri, Menaḥem, VI, 37
Meisterlein, Sigmund, IV, 117
Melakhah, I, 9
Melcart, god, I, 322
Melchizedek, king of Salem, I, 45, 312; David's claim to succession of, I, 322
Meleager of Gadara, I, 194
Melitene, Armenia, III, 18, 58
Melito of Sardis, V, 126
Mellitus, abbot, II, 154
Melody, *see* Tunes
Melons, tale of Elijah and, VI, 415
Memor books, IV, 287, 310, VI, 213, 217
Memory: and knowledge, VIII, 79 f.; masoretic aids to, VI, 251; *see also* Mnemotechnical devices
Memphis, Egypt, I, 111
Memra, I, 389
Men: preponderance over women, I, 113 f.; supremacy in family, I, 146; *see also* Man
Menahem, king of Israel, I, 77
Menahem, Zealot leader, II, 58
Menaḥem (b. Hezekiah), name of Messiah, V, 357
Menaḥem b. 'Ammiel, messiah, V, 157
Menaḥem b. Ḥelbo, VI, 294
Menaḥem b. Jacob b. Saruq, VI, 278; controversy with Dunash, VII, 21 ff., 147, 195, 237 f.; dictionary written in Hebrew, VII, 7, 20 f., 48; Hebrew style, VII, 237; letter to Ḥisdai, VII, 228; on power of the pen, VII, 149; rhymed prose, VII, 201 f.
Menaḥem b. Jacob of Worms, IV, 124
Menaḥem b. Michael, V, 260

Menaḥem b. Simon of Posquières, VI, 468
Menaḥem b. Solomon, Italian homilist, VII, 244, 277; encyclopedic philological-exegetical work, VII, 48
Menahem b. Solomon Al-Roḥi, *see* Alroy, David
Menaḥem ibn Zeraḥ, *see* Ibn Zeraḥ
Menasseh, tribe, III, 208
Menasseh b. Ibrahim al-Qzaz, Jewish governor of Syria, III, 154
Mendelssohn, Moses, VI, 337
Mendicancy, II, 272
Menelaus, high priest, I, 229
"Men of the Great Synagogue," I, 162, 367, 397
Menstruation, V, 250; alleged Tannaitic work on, VI, 181 f.; laws of, VI, 73 f., 86
Mental hygiene, VIII, 229, 258, 260 f.
Merab, name, VI, 293
Mercenaries, I, 326; Israelitic, employed by Assyrians, I, 346
Merchants, I, 60, 256, II, 250; bankers, as, IV, 201; communal ordinance re, VI, 139, 395; custom duties paid by, IV, 65 f.; death of, and *'agunot,* IV, 184; discrimination against, IV, 183; divorce of, IV, 184; knowledge of writing, III, 82; multilingual, IV, 181; new route opened to, I, 64; non-Jewish, IV, 50, 179 f., 327; in Poland, III, 218; privileges to, IV, 48, 50, 62, 179, 182, 327; proportion of population, IV, 171; as religious propagandists, I, 173; suspicion of, among the masses, IV, 184; Syrian, IV, 173, 323; taxation of, III, 169; and competitors, I, 260, II, 431; transfer of holdings, VIII, 224; treaty of racial equality, IV, 63; widespread business deals, IV, 174; *see also* Peddlers
Mercy: attribute of God, VIII, 42; and justice, *see* Justice
"Merit of the Fathers" doctrine, I, 135, II, 42, 346
Merkabah (Ezekiel's vision), II, 315
Merkabah mysticism, VIII, 11-29, 55, 58, 277-87, 355; ascent of the soul to heaven, VIII, 105; German pietists and, VII, 44; Maimonides and, VIII, 73; *see also* Chariot
Merneptah, pharaoh, I, 307, 308; stele, I, 41
Meroe, built by Moses, VIII, 382
Merovingians: attitude toward Jews, III, 47-54, 250-54, VIII, 43; decree of 614, III, 250
Merseburg, Germany, provision for Jews, IV, 65 f.
Merv, Persia, III, 166
Mesene, district, II, 208, 405, V, 179
Mesha, king of Moab, I, 90; inscription, I, 336
Mesharsheya Gaon, VI, 446
Meshekh, Khazaria, III, 202
Meshullam b. Kalonymus of Lucca, VI, 117 f.
Meshullam b. Moses of Béziers, VI, 89
Meshullam b. Nathan of Melun, VI, 118 f.
Mesopotamia, I, 57, II, 96; democracy, I, 325; deportations to Asia Minor, I, 373; "remnant" in, I, 106; *see also* Assyria; Babylonia
Messenger: and the Messiah, V, 185, 191; *see also* Mohammed
"Messenger of the people," *see* Cantor
"Messenger to Zion," VI, 110
Messiah and messianism, I, 7, 10, 12, 17, 18, 21, 31, 99, 118, 164, 180, 208, 215, II, 58-62, 351 f.; III, 97, 176, IV, 57 f., 294, V, 118 ff., 138-208, 353-87, VII, 201, VIII, 123; apocalyptic-aggadic, V, 139-50, 185, 353-60, VI, 170 f.; Arius and doctrine of, V, 379; astrological computations, VI, 231 f., 439 f., VIII, 183; "breath" of, V, 145; and belief in second coming of Christ, III, 15; and contemporary events, V, 162; and the Crusades, IV, 302; date of advent, V, 119 f., 153, 161, 164, 167 ff., 199, 225, 363, VI, 230 f., 232, 309, 439 f., VII, 61, 178, VIII, 183, 186, 206 f., 361, 372; differing outlooks, II, 31, 58 ff.; and "end of days," II, 61, 73, 122, 139, 312 f., 351, V, 147 ff., 359, 371; expectations and downfall of Rome, I, 210, II, 397; false messiahs, III, 16, V, 168, 182-205, 366 f., 374-87; as goal of creation, VIII, 322; Graeco-Roman, II, 5, 329; and idealization of past, I, 99; Innocent II re, IV, 10; interfaith, V, 168 f.; Karaite speculations, V, 260 f., 409; Khazars and, III, 204; "lowly" (*'ani*), I, 152, 364; and magic arts, VIII, 47; and Mohammed, III, 77 f.; Moses and, I, 99, V, 174 f., 371; and

Messiah and messianism (*Continued*) nationalism, V, 155 f., 184-91, 344 ff., name of Messiah, VIII, 273; oriental view, I, 97; and Persian conquest of Palestine, III, 21; poetic and exegetical derivations, V, 150-59, 360-63; portents, V, 142 ff., 201, VI, 402; preexistence, V, 120 f., 141, 146 f., VIII, 126; prophets and prophecies, I, 98, 157, 159, 180, 339, II, 61 f., 68, 72, VI, 309; in Psalms, I, 339; rationales, V, 159-66, 363-66; as realization of Jewish political aspirations, V, 160; and reestablishment of Jewish state, V, 184 ff.; and religious martyrdom, IV, 96 f.; and revolutionary action, II, 95, 101, 121, 372, III, 263, V, 144 ff., 191 ff., 353 f., VII, 97 f.; in Salonica, IV, 107 f.; and sanctification of the Temple and Jerusalem, VIII, 41; and sectarianism, V, 166-70, 182-97, 366 f., 374-82; superhuman nature of Messiah, V, 141 f., 146 f.; timelessness, II, 81; Torah "abrogated," II, 161, V, 122, 124, 347; two messiahs, V, 144 f., 160, 185, 191, 356, *see also* Messiah b. Joseph; "watches" at the Temple, VII, 90; Yinnon, V, 153; *see also under* individual messiahs, *e.g.*, Bar Kocheba; Jesus

—— beliefs: of Abraham ibn Ezra, V, 156 ff., 363; of Abraham bar Ḥiyya, V, 162 f., 364; of Hai Gaon, V, 161 f., 364; of Ibn Gabirol, V, 152 ff., 361 f., 364; of Maimonides, V, 164 ff., 364 ff.; of Philo, I, 208, II, 5 f., 329; of Saadiah, V, 160 ff., 363 ff., VI, 481; of Samaritans, II, 31, 341, V, 170 f., 174 f., 367 ff.; of Virgil, II, 329

Messiah b. David, V, 160, 168; and Elijah, V, 144 f.

Messiah b. Joseph (or b. Ephraim), II, 351, V, 143 f., 160; and Armilus, V, 364

Messina, Sicily, IV, 23

Metals: evasion of duty on, IV, 329; in Palestine, I, 256, VII, 48

Metal workers: Alexandrian, I, 260; Kenite, I, 60

Metaphor, in Hebrew poetry, VII, 198

Metaphysics, Greek: adapted by Jewish philosophers, VIII, 138; *see also* Philosophy

Meṭaṭron, angel, I, 335, V, 142; derivation of name, VIII, 281; identified with Enoch, VIII, 282; mystic school of, VIII, 16

Metempsychosis, *see* Transmigration of the soul

Meter: Arabic, VII, 193 ff.

—— Hebrew, VII, 194 ff., 313 f.; biblical, VII, 194 f.; forms of, VII, 196; and music, VII, 202 f.

Methodius, apostle, brother of Cyril, III, 187, 209 f.; in Moravia, V, 339; possible fate of Moravian followers, IV, 194

Methodology, talmudic, VI, 27-35, 63 f., 332-36; concern with chronology, VI, 201 f.

Metibot, authorship of, VI, 373 f.

"Metonic cycle," VIII, 189, 195

Metronymic, use of, VIII, 275

Metropolis, Jewish, I, 212-15, 392-93

Metuens, *see* Semiproselytes

Metz, Germany, IV, 91

Mezuzot, door-post inscriptions, V, 59

Mhebodh, Persian general, III, 58

Mibtaḥiah, I, 113, 114

Micah, prophet, I, 87, 99, 352

Michael, archangel, II, 18, 19, V, 142

Michael, Monophysite patriarch, III, 136

Michael II, Byzantine emperor, III, 178, 193

Michael III (the Drunkard), Byzantine emperor, III, 179

Michael Basilius, Christian monk, VII, 183

Michael the Syrian, VI, 263

Michaes, Treves convert, IV, 293, 310

Middot, hermeneutic rules, V, 213; *see also Mishnat ha-Middot*

Midianites, I, 46, 57, 313, V, 353

Midrash: aggadic, II, 294, 296, 316, 320, III, 16, 235, 240, VI, 6, VIII, 277 f.; anthropomorphic legends, V, 259; apocalyptic, III, 93, 235, 237, 239, VI, 170 f.; attributed to Elijah, VI, 160; on books of the Bible, VI, 161 f.; halakhic, II, 294, 301, VI, 38; hermeneutics, II, 144, 427, 429; heyday of, VI, 154 f.; and martyrdom, IV, 96; measurements of the earth, VIII, 214; messianic, V, 146; on number of stars, VIII, 163; origin of, VI, 407; problem of dating, VI, 407; supernaturally oriented, VIII, 278; tannaitic, theory of, VI, 409; transition from, to historical literature, VI, 233

Midrashim: *Abba Gorion,* VI, 188; *Agur,*

VI, 160; *Bereshit rabbati,* V, 146; *Ekhah rabbati* and *Ekhah zuṭa,* VI, 167; *ha-Gadol,* V, 72; *Hashkem,* VI, 40, 339 f.; *Konen,* VIII, 214; *Leqaḥ ṭob,* III, 210; *rabbah,* V, 91, VI, 406; *Sod ha-'ibbur,* VIII, 193; *Tanḥuma,* V, 217, VI, 40, 409; *Va-Yosha',* VI, 188; *Yelamdenu,* VI, 170
Mieszko II, king of Poland, III, 217, 218
Mieszko III, king of Poland, III, 218
Migdol, Egypt, I, 111
Migratory movements, I, 172, 373; among subject races, I, 106 f.; and biblical narratives, I, 37; from Palestine, I, 393, II, 173, 204, 208, 210, 405 ff.; measures to stem, II, 123, 377; of Nestorians to Persia, II, 164
Milan, III, 30
Mile, and parasang, VIII, 213 f.
Milestones, Roman, I, 378
Miletus, inscription, II, 9, 330
Milḥemet miṣvah, II, 100, 372
Military colonies, I, 348, 394; *see also* Elephantine
Military movements: messianic, V, 192 ff., 203 f.; sectarian, V, 191 ff.
Military service: ancient, I, 14, 84, 121, 313, 350, 352, II, 90 f., 93, 179, 368; Deuteronomic laws, I, 332; in Egypt, I, 110, 346; soldier-farmers, II, 266; subjects sold to serve, I, 95; titles of commanders, II, 403; *see also* War
—— medieval: of Jews, III, 7, 236; and Byzantine Empire, II, 179, 398, III, 7 f., 18 ff., 236 f.; Jews excluded by Roman law, II, 179, 186; in Faṭimid campaigns, III, 107; freedom from, and taxation, III, 310; at Gaza, III, 87; in Germany, IV, 70; Khaibar, III, 79; in Khwarizm, III, 326; in Palmyra, III, 104; in Persian campaigns, II, 179, 398, III, 18 f., 57, 73; in Spain, III, 92 f., IV, 36; at Tyre, III, 19 f.
Millenary movement: Christian, as antecedent to Crusades, IV, 91 f.; Jewish, V, 354; *see also* Messiah and messianism
Millennium, "day of the Lord," VIII, 191
Minerals, I, 257; names of, VIII, 253; study of, VIII, 225
Mines and mining, IV, 169 f.; gold and silver, IV, 211 f.; salt, IV, 169
Minet el-Beida, I, 49, 306
Minim, I, 376; *see also* Heresies and heretics
Minorca, Spain, I, 370, III, 245
Minorities, religious: in Latin kingdom, IV, 114 f.; legislation on religious rights, III, 128 f.; V, 97; polemics and apologias, V, 83-94, 326-33; primacy of society over, VIII, 120 f.; protected, III, 57, 120-72, 288-312, IV, 42, 86, 185, V, 4, 82; *see also Dhimmis;* in Sicily, IV, 115
Mintmasters, IV, 29, 210 f.; in royal employ, III, 218, IV, 72; transfer of holdings, VIII, 224
Minucius Felix, II, 382
Miracles, VI, 300; biblical tradition of, VII, 201, VIII, 28 ff.; commentary on, VI, 310 f.; intervention, VIII, 179; of Jesus, II, 67; legends of, IV, 136, VIII, 47; in messianic tales, V, 192, 199; performed by Mohammed and Moses, V, 91 f.; performed only through men, I, 98; as proof of veracity, V, 205; rationales of, VI, 177, VIII, 128 ff., 342 f.
Miriam, prophetess, I, 365; false accusation of Moses, VI, 179
Miriam, daughter of Naqdimon b. Gurion, II, 113
Mishael, biblical hero, I, 116
Mishael b. 'Uzziah, VI, 248
Mishawayh (or Mesvi) al-'Ukbari, V, 182, VI, 254; approach to Jewish calendar, V, 382; syncretism, V, 196 f.
Mishawayhites, V, 182, 195 f.
Mishnah, I, 114, 270, III, 3, V, 256, VIII, 278; availability of, VI, 201; Babylonian, VI, 456; codification, II, 206 f., 294, 301, V, 254, VI, 258; commentaries on, VI, 28, 61, 76, *see also* Moses b. Maimon; concordance to, VII, 29; description of Temple service, VII, 90; dictionary of, VII, 15; divisions omitted from comment in Gemara, II, 305; ethical or juristic interpretation, VI, 35; on intermarriage, II, 232; Justinian's ban on reading of, III, 12, 233; language of, VII, 11, 15, 56 ff., 223, 242 f.; laws governing economic relations, IV, 217; legal code of Pharisaism, II, 44, 344; merits of decisions, VI, 30 f.; oral vs. written transmission, II, 425, VI, 205, 258, 426; and proselytes, I, 376; Saadiah Gaon on, V, 26;

Mishnah (*Continued*)
on sacrifices and Onias priests, I, 219; sequence of tractates, VI, 204; spelling and interpretation, VII, 12 f.; study of, VI, 267, VII, 71; unraveling various strains in, II, 295 ff.; warning against philosophic speculation, VIII, 5 f.; writing and chronology of, VI, 203 ff.
Mishnah of R. Eliezer, see under Eliezer, R., author
Mishnaic-Greek glossary, VI, 333
Mishnat ha-Middot, II, 307, 433, VIII, 154, 354
Mishnat Massekhet Kallah, VI, 182 f.
Misrepresentation, "law" of, II, 255, 303
Missionary efforts, *see* Conversions; Proselytes and Proselytism
Mithraism, II, 151; VIII, 31; initiation, I, 181; spread of, II, 164
Mithridates I, king of Parthia, II, 229
Mitridates Potions, VIII, 257
Mizraim, Noah's grandson, I, 335; *see also* Egypt
Mnaseas, I, 382
Mnemotechnical devices, VII, 3, 42, 234, 251; Hebrew cyclic formulas, VIII, 190, 370 f.; in oral transmission, VII, 88, 149; rules, VII, 32
Moab and Moabites: biblical, I, 55, 56, 57, 307, VI, 303; ancestry, V, 90; copper, I, 60; displaced by Nabataean Arabs, I, 190, VI, 308; endogamous exclusion of, I, 158, II, 232; Israel's animosity toward, I, 156; Israelites' dominion over, I, 345
Mobeds, see Magi
Mob violence, and the Crusades, IV, 90
Modestinus, Herennius, II, 375
Mohammed, VIII, 134; alleged will, III, 262; ascension, V, 94, VIII, 284 f.; blasphemies against, III, 137, V, 94; called an impostor, V, 104; circulation of sayings attributed to, VI, 201; declaration of belief, III, 86; importance of Abraham to, III, 81, 85 f., 266, VI, 8; imputed biblical allusions to, V, 89 f., VI, 307; on individualistic interpretation of the Qur'an, VI, 471; Islam as political movement, III, 94; and Jewish sectarians, V, 171, 192, 264; Judeo-Christian influences on, III, 81 ff., 263, 265 ff., V, 168; legend of assassination of, III, 262; linking of with biblical prophecy, V, 86 ff., 89 f., 117 ff., 157, 186, 219, VIII, 133; on lunar year, VIII, 370; the "madman," V, 94, 264; in Medina, VII, 191; miracles, V, 91, 92; and Moses, I, 41, II, 27, III, 81, 85; numerical value of name, V, 100; origin of enmity toward Jews, III, 76; professed illiteracy, III, 263; on religious toleration, III, 124, 131; and tombs of the prophets, III, 136; traditions and Muslim law, VI, 24; treaties with Christians, III, 86 ff., 163; treaties with Jews, III, 79 f., 86 ff., 262, 264, 274; and unification of Arabian Peninsula, III, 75; victory of, as a miracle, V, 99 f.
Mohammed ibn Musa al-Khwarizmi, *see* Khwarizmi
Mohar, II, 220, 236; *see also* Marriage, contracts
Moisevich, Ephrem, Kievan Jew, III, 216
Monarchy, I, 91; opposition to, I, 93 f.; power and drawbacks, I, 64-66, 320-22; rise of, I, 61; Saadiah on, V, 72; and prerogatives of patriarch and exilarch, II, 200; *see also* Kings; Rulers
Monasticism: Damascus sect, II, 52; Essenes, II, 49
Monastic orders and monasteries, II, 269; Cistercian, IV, 84; privilege to, IV, 65; and transfer of land, IV, 13
Monenergism, III, 21, 24, 248
Money: embezzlement of sacred, I, 245; exchange of, VIII, 385; Maimonides on accumulation of, IV, 220 f.; in precapitalistic system, I, 69, 318; Saadiah on the power of, IV, 217; and social differentiation, I, 60; trade in, I, 132, 214, II, 250, 414, IV, 197-215, 338-49; transfer of, IV, 209 ff., 212 f.; *see also* Banking; Capitalism; Coins and coinage; Currency; Poverty; Wealth
Moneylenders and moneylending, I, 20, 109, 261, 265, 346, II, 250, III, 217, IV, 75, 197-207, 338-44, V, 128; attitude of pietists toward, VIII, 48 f.; Byzantine legend, V, 348; Christian, IV, 121; and coreligionists, IV, 199, 203, 205; in France, IV, 62, VI, 128 f.; Karaite, V, 258; pledges, IV, 202 f., 341 f.; and political rivalries, IV, 82; religious laws, IV, 198 ff., 338 ff.; royal protection, IV, 78, 82 f.; and state officials,

IV, 201 f.; *see also* Banking; Interest; Usury
Mongols: in Baghdad, III, 123; conquest of Khazaria, III, 206
Monogamy, I, 347, II, 223-29, 409 f.; and R. Gershom's ordinance, V, 135 f., 393 f.; in Roman society, II, 226; sects practicing, II, 408; *see also* Polygamy
Monophysites, II, 168, III, 259, V, 7, VI, 263; in Arabia, III, 268; and Council of Chalcedon, III, 240; in Egypt, III, 239, 268; massacre of, in Edessa, III, 19, 239; on the nature of Christ, III, 5
Monopolies, royal, IV, 113
Monotheism, V, 105, VI, 229, 234, VIII, 16; antecedents, I, 43-48, 83, 310-13; in ancient Gentile world, I, 313; conflict between faith and reason, VIII, 80 ff., 87 ff., 319 ff.; and emancipation from nature, I, 31; ethical, I, 10, II, 5; Hellenization of Semitic, I, 196; historical, I, 4-10, 13, 31, 61, 294, II, 5; and pagan spouses, II, 232, 411; influence on Zoroaster, I, 341; Judeo-Christian-Muslim, III, 82, 93, 221, VIII, 56; Mosaic, I, 43, 51, 314, 315, 316; of Philo, I, 208, II, 5; primitive I, 44, 311; treaties of religious toleration, III, 130; and Trinitarianism, VIII, 95 f.
Monotheletism, III, 21
Mons Judaeorum, IV, 29
Monsters, eschatological, V, 148, VIII, 10
Montanists, III, 176, 186; martyrdom, III, 177
Montesquieu, Charles Louis, baron de, III, 43
Monteverde catacomb, II, 331
Months: Jewish, VIII, 188; Babylonian names adopted, I, 118; and creation, VIII, 368; intercalation, II, 125; length of, V, 224 ff., VIII, 187 ff., 196 f., 369 ff.; lunar, V, 218; solilunar harmonization, VIII, 184 ff., 368 ff.; two New Moon days, VIII, 374; *see also under* names of months, *e.g.,* Nisan
Montpellier medical school, VIII, 298
Moon: association of Sabbath with, I, 359; calendar based on, I, 44, II, 125, 206; creation of, VIII, 203; linked with sun, I, 45; and rise and fall of prices, VIII, 361; size, VIII, 162 f.; worship, I, 44, 45, 311
—— new: controversy over basis of proclamation, VIII, 194 f.; and dating of religious holidays, V, 28 f., 217, 227, 248; nativity, VIII, 196 f.; observation of, V, 94, 211, 246, VIII, 205; proclamation of, VI, 216, 253, VIII, 186, 200; sanctification of VIII, 193 f., 228; services, VII, 73
Moon god, I, 44, 45, 311
Moors: Jewish aid to, in Sicily, IV, 244; Spanish, IV, 30, 335; *see also Mozarabs*
Morality, *see* Ethics; Marriage; Sex
Moral law: authority of priest, I, 81; equality of ritual and, II, 307-9, 433; source of all law, I, 227; *see also* Ethics
Moravia, IV, 72
Mordecai, I, 119, 136; reply to Esther, I, 116
Mordecai b. Hillel ha-Kohen, V, 60, 118; quotations from Gershom, VI, 385
Mordecai's Dream, VI, 167, VIII, 278
Moriscos, *see* Moors
Morning Ablutionists, II, 51
Morocco: Abu'l Kamal Tamim's rebellion, III, 122; Arab-Jewish relations, III, 90 f.; charges of Jewish conspiracy, III, 46; communal elders, V, 51; Jewish communities, II, 108, 281, VI, 24; and Mohammed's decrees of religious toleration, III, 124; Mozarab churches, III, 126
Mörs, Germany, IV, 104 f.
Mortality rate, II, 220
Mortara, Edgar, V, 113
Mortgages, I, 109, II, 303, 304; laws on, VI, 83
Mosaic law, *see under* Moses; *also* Old Testament; Pentateuch
Mosaics, II, 10, 285, 330, 402
Moses, prophet, I, 16, 22, 43, 142, VIII, 134; and Meroe, VIII, 382; apotheosis, II, 27; Arab legends of, III, 63, 161, 280; Assumption of, II, 47, 59, 346; Blessing of, II, 31; called an impostor, V, 104; center of religious controversy, VI, 479; "curses," I, 85; descendants of, V, 192; desire to view divine Glory, VIII, 129; distinguished Israel from other Hebrews, I, 56; divine name revealed to, I, 13, 309, VIII, 132; elevation of, VIII, 127 f.; enduring work, I, 40, 59, 62, 143, 205, 295, 315; and ethnic society, I, 43; historicity, I, 341; humility of, VIII, 121; identified with Hermes Trismegistos, VIII, 10; in-

Moses (*Continued*)
voked deeds of the Fathers, II, 42; law of, I, 79, 150, 178, 204, II, 159, 319, IV, 49; legend on homage to Jesus, V, 138; levitical ancestry questioned, I, 318; list of Edomite kings, VI, 309; Maimonides on, VI, 229; midrashic apocrypha on, VIII, 278; miracles, V, 91; and Mohammed, I, 41, II, 27, III, 81, 85; mosques associated with, III, 161, 280; name, I, 315; names in family, I, 38, 305; "prayer of," VIII, 126; priests' claim to descent from, I, 330; reception by heavenly hosts, VII, 182; religion, I, 4, 41, 44, 46-53, 58, 59, 65, 313-16; religious league organized by, I, 51; reputed knowledge of alchemy, VIII, 223; return as Messiah looked for, I, 99, V, 174 f.; role of, in mysticism, VIII, 20; and Samaritans, II, 31, 32, V, 174 f.; saved Israel, I, 90; Sinaitic revelation, II, 161, V, 93, VI, 8, 91, 100, 228, 232, 269, 300, 356, VIII, 6, 41, 294; snake symbol, I, 66; source of calendar computations, VIII, 205; status as prophet, VIII, 132, 229; synagogue of Damwah and, III, 106; tradition of astronomic calculations, VIII, 196; traditions of burial place, III, 161, 308; wife, II, 38, 39; woman's position in family improved by, I, 58; *see also* Exodus; Law; Pentateuch

Moses, Chronicle of, VIII, 179

Moses, Jewish scholar of Cyprus, III, 184

Moses, R., Kievan scholar, III, 217; Commentary on the Mishnah, VI, 61

Moses b. Asher, *see* Ben Asher, Moses

Moses b. Elijah Bashyatchi, *see* Bashyatchi, Moses

Moses b. Ḥanokh, captive scholar, V, 46 f., 53 f., VI, 332

Moses b. Jacob of Cordova, VI, 361

Moses b. Joseph ha-Kohen of Mayence, IV, 128 f.; use of magic, VIII, 7

Moses b. Joseph of Narbonne, VI, 354; and the written Halakhah, VIII, 38 f.

Moses b. Joshua Narboni, VIII, 115

Moses b. Kalonymus, R., of Lucca, VII, 181, VIII, 44

Moses b. Maimon, I, 408, II, 221, 255, 381, 408, 424, III, 106, 119, 222, IV, 114, V, 49; and Aaron Ben Asher's biblical manuscript, VI, 247; on ablutions, VI, 14; on Abu 'Isa, V, 380; on age of talmudic scrolls, VI, 21; on the Aggadah, VI, 177 ff., 412 f.; anatomical observations, VI, 103, 379, VIII, 230, 387; animosity toward Zuṭṭa, VI, 432; on Arab historical writing, VI, 199; Arabic stylist, VII, 8, 221; on Aristotle, VIII, 82, 93; on astrology, VIII, 111, 180 ff., 335, 366 f.; astronomic writings, VI, 103, 379, VIII, 162, 164 f., 199 f., 357; authority over Fusṭaṭ community, VI, 11, 432; autographs, VI, 351, 388, VII, 8, 280; basic doctrines of Judaism, I, 408, V, 229, VI, 101 ff., VII, 175; on biblical synonyms and homonyms, VI, 297; on capital crimes, V, 17, 45, 280 f.; castration of slaves, IV, 191; on cause of death, VIII, 259; on charges of biblical falsification, V, 92; on Christians, III, 161, V, 57 f., 118 f., 365, VI, 11; codification of liturgical observances, V, 28, VII, 81, 108, 118 ff., 276; commentaries, I, 376, VI, 297, 352; on concluding lines of Torah scroll, VI, 253 f.; concordance between faith and reason, VIII, 81 f., 321; controversy over, VI, 104 ff., VII, 175, VIII, 40, 68; on Daniel's prophecies, V, 87; debt to Saadiah, VII, 119; vs. deviations from talmudic law, V, 52; on diabetes, VIII, 262; disagreements with predecessors, VI, 26, 133, 378; on disposition of private property, V, 320; on divorce and marriage, III, 112; doctrine of God, VIII, 87 ff., 322 ff.; on domestic employment, IV, 196, V, 240; on economic status and religion, IV, 217; on enforced conversion to Islam, III, 125; on commandments, VI, 143, VIII, 115, 118; esteem for exilarch, V, 12; on ethics of Judaism, VIII, 117 f., 122 f.; exegetical methods, VI, 297; family, III, 115, 126, false messiahs, V, 198 ff., 382 ff.; on figures of speech, VII, 317; on individual rights and public welfare, IV, 222; influence of, V, 49, VI, 106, VIII, 137; influence of Ḥefeṣ on, VI, 96; and Jewries of western Europe, III, 173; on the Karaites, V, 266, 280; on length of seasons, VIII, 201; life as physician, VIII, 232 ff., 249 ff., 388 f., 398 ff.; on linguistic techniques, VI, 294; on lowly trades,

IV, 167; on magic, VIII, 29; on man's freedom, VIII, 110; on man's love of God, VIII, 115 f.; marriage ordinance, VI, 134 f., 138 f.; on music, VII, 205 f., 208; Muslim denunciation of, VIII, 250; Muslim physician's tribute to, III, 147 f., VIII, 249 f.; *negidim* descendants, V, 48; octocentennial, VIII, 398 f.; opinion of his own work, VI, 99, 106, 120 f., 380, VIII, 71; on Palestinian land ownership, IV, 160 f., 316; "perpetual" ordinance, VI, 136; physicians' oath ascribed to, VIII, 239; on physician's qualifications, VIII, 260; poems, VII, 105, 271; on political power, V, 72; on preaching, VI, 156; prohibition of teaching Torah to Gentiles, VI, 275; on prophecy, V, 87, VIII, 131 f.; propositions requiring no proof, VIII, 80; on psychological factors in healing, VIII, 261, 404; on purposes of Jewish law, VI, 142; on qualifications of a messenger, VII, 129; quoted, II, 252, VIII, 82, 101 f., 115, 120, 124, 164 f.; on ransoming captives, IV, 177; rationale of suffering, V, 101 f.; on rational law, V, 78, VI, 144, VIII, 338; reaction to *piyyuṭim,* VII, 102, 133; reconstruction of transmission of oral law, VIII, 210 f.; rejection of Arab arguments on creation, VIII, 89 f.; reproduction of his writings in Hebrew, VII, 7; restrictions on Jewish trade, IV, 220; on sale of Jewish house to Gentile, III, 146; and Samaritans, V, 172, 177; on scholars, V, 76; semioracular style, VI, 104; on a translator, VIII, 65 f.; on sexual transgressions, III, 143; on site of Temple, VI, 228; on slaves, IV, 190 ff.; on the soul, VIII, 108; sources of decisions, VI, 104 f., 380; Spanish collections of essays on, VI, 378; on state and local authority, V, 71 f.; and Sultan Al-Afdhal, VIII, 260 f.; support of local customs, VI, 127; on testing drugs, VIII, 257; theory of "negative attributes" of God, VIII, 98 f., 327 f.; theory of sacrifices, VI, 147 f.; thirteen principles, V, 229, VII, 175; on the Universe, VI, 146, VIII, 161 ff., 357 ff.; use of allegory, VIII, 86; use of alternate talmudic readings, VI, 413; on use of knowledge of the sages, VIII, 142; use of the sciences, VIII, 135; on verbal charms, VIII, 234; warning to Torah scribes, VI, 254

—— works, VIII, 250 ff., 308 f., 398 ff.; editions by American Academy for Jewish Research, VIII, 307 ff.; Antidotarium, VIII, 257; *Book of Commandments,* VI, 26, 59, 97 ff., 178 f., 375 ff.; *Code,* III, 143, IV, 218, 223, 316, V, 164 f., 261, VI, 31 f., 99-107, 376 ff., VII, 280, VIII, 71; commentary on the Bible, VI, 297; *Commentary on the Mishnah,* III, 143, V, 166, VI, 57-61, VII, 185, VIII, 116; correspondence, VI, 119 ff., 388, VII, 54; "Epistle on Conversion," VIII, 126; *Epistle to Yemen,* III, 291, V, 78, 198, VIII, 64; "Glossary of Drug Names," VIII, 252; *Guide for the Perplexed,* IV, 218, VII, 220, VIII, 64, 70-73, 306 f.; "Medical Aphorisms," VIII, 238 f., 250, 261 f., 388; "Regimen Sanitatis," VIII, 260 f.; supplement to Alfasi's work, VI, 88 f.; "Treatise of Logical Terms," VIII, 144 f.; treatise on fits, IV, 318

Moses b. Naḥman, R., of Barcelona, V, 114, VIII, 24; kabbalist exegete, VI, 26, VII, 306; defense of Alfasi, VI, 88; on month of Tishre, VIII, 184; and recitation of *Musaf 'Amidah,* VII, 107 f.; refutation of Maimonides, VI, 98; and Tosafists, VI, 56

Moses b. Napthali, *see* Ben Naphtali

Moses b. Samuel, Karaite, V, 411

Moses b. Solomon of Salerno, VIII, 315

Moses b. Yehudah, VI, 89

Moses b. Yequtiel the Elder, IV, 142

Moses ha-Sefardi, former name of Petrus Alphonsi (*q.v.*), VIII, 174

Moses Khalfo, R., of Sicily, VII, 30

Moses of Castoria, Jewish scholar, III, 210

Moses of Crete, false messiah, III, 16, V, 168, 366 f.

Moses of Khorene, Armenian historian, I, 169, II, 204; on origin of Armenian Jews, III, 110

Moses of Pavia, Jewish martyr, IV, 105

Moses the Preacher (ha-Darshan), of Narbonne, V, 146, VI, 171 f., 196, 405, 410, VII, 30, VIII, 32, 38; Book of the Bright Light and, VIII, 33; influence on Qimḥi, VI, 280

Mosque, I, 15; associated with Moses,

Mosque (*Continued*)
III, 161, 280; center of secular life, VI, 154; churches and synagogues converted into, III, 123, 136, 140, 148, 297; derivation of term, VI, 13; and height of neighboring buildings, III, 138, 145; imitation of synagogue, III, 297; interruption of service, V, 67; libraries, VII, 138, VIII, 246; magnificence of structures, III, 134
Mosque of the Footprints, Damascus, III, 161
Mosque of the Rock, Jerusalem, III, 101, 134, 269, 272
Mosul (Ḥesna Ebraya or Ashhur), III, 99; cantor-preacher of, VII, 81; Jewish provincial administration, V, 43; Jews' greeting to 'Ali, III, 276
Mother: supremacy of, I, 43, 310; *see also* Family
"Mother Church," designation, II, 168
"Mother earth," I, 57, 318
Mother-goddess, I, 318
Motion, eternality of, VIII, 90
Mountain, holy, *see* Gerizim, Mount
"Mourners for Zion," V, 32, 185, 257, 258, 271, 376, VI, 10
Mourning: days of, I, 294; over destruction of the Temple, II, 111 ff., 375 f., V, 27; external signs of, V, 27; laws on, VI, 63, VII, 267; marriage during, VI, 120; Naṭronai on, VI, 382; *qaddish* prayer, V, 59, VII, 67; for a scholar, VI, 83
Movement, freedom of, IV, 32 f., 63 f., 78, 85, V, 68, 78, VIII, 211 f.
Movements, planetary, effect on earth, VIII, 185
"Moyses Hall," Bury St. Edmunds, IV, 282
Mozarabs (Christian Moors), III, 155; Bodo and, IV, 52; employed by Al-Manṣur, III, 126; in Spain, IV, 27; and Jews, IV, 31; Visigothic code and, III, 127
Mu'awiya: founder of 'Umayyad dynasty, III, 88; concentration of landholdings, III, 163; destruction of Colossus of Rhodes, III, 235; and Jews in Tripolis, III, 104
Mubarrad, Baṣran philologist, VII, 234
Mubashshir ha-Levi, Rabbanite scholar, VI, 270, VII, 15 f.
Muḥammad 'Ali, VI, 13
Muhammad b. Zakariva ar-Razi, *see* Razi, Muhammad
Muḥibb b. 'Atiqa, VIII, 233
Mu'izz, al-, Faṭimid caliph, VIII, 246
Muktafi II, al-, caliph, charter to Nestorian *catholicos,* V, 6; offer of alliance from Berta di Toscana, IV, 245
Mula Ismael, Moroccan sultan, III, 94
Mulla Yaḥya, Arab author, VIII, 244
Mundhir, Lakhmid king, III, 68
Municipalities, *see* Cities
Münster, Sebastian, VI, 191
Muntafil, Arab poet, III, 157
Münzenberg, castle, IV, 304
Muqaddasi, VI, 192; on Christian and Jewish occupations, IV, 166, VIII, 236; on minorities in Jerusalem, III, 102; on mixed population of Persian towns, III, 109; on paper manufacture, IV, 169; on sects in Arabia, III, 72
Muqtadir, al-, *see* Al-Muqtadir
Murabba'at, cave, V, 188
Murals, *see* Painting
Murashshu Sons, I, 109; records, I, 110, 118, 120, 349
Murder: Crusaders' attitude toward, IV, 101; indemnities for, IV, 39 f.; of infidels as righteous act, IV, 133, 140 f.; penalty for, III, 132, IV, 35, 39, 48 f., 50, 69, 128; of a priest, IV, 281; punishment for, VI, 134
Murviedro, Spain: alleged inscription on tombstone of Adoniram, III, 34, 244, VII, 313
Musa al-Uswari, Iraqi orator, VII, 10
Musa ibn al-Azar (b. Eleazar), Jewish court physician, VIII, 246
Musa ibn Nuṣair, governor of Morocco, III, 91
Musar, term, VIII, 348
Mushkhanites, V, 192 ff.
Music, I, 123 f.; Arabian, VII, 204 f., 207; Hebrew origin of Christian, VII, 84, 130; hymns and psalms, I, 52, 123, 150, 395; natural and artificial, VII, 210; of Jews, Greeks, Christians, II, 8 f., 155, 330, 389; secular, VII, 128, 129 f., 206; therapeutic value, VII, 206, 208 f.; at Temple, I, 123; trends and theories, VII, 125-31, 202-11, 281-85; 318-21; *see also Ḥazzan;* Israel Moses; Cantors; Singers; Singing
Musiv style, VII, 202
Muslim-Christian relations: commerce

and, IV, 172; conflicts, V, 199; era of Crusades, VIII, 256; hostility in, IV, 186; Nestorians and, V, 6; political and economic issues, V, 95 ff.; religious disputations, V, 326; in Spain, IV, 37 f., 93 f.
Muslim-Jewish relations, *see* Arab-Jewish relations; Judeo-Muslim relations
Muslims: academy leadership and hereditary principle, V, 297; Arab-Berber rivalries, III, 155 f.; and Arabic speech, VII, 18; arguments re Bible and Qur'an, V, 86 ff., 327 ff., VI, 298; on castration, IV, 191 f.; charges against Jews and Christians, III, 145, IV, 243, V, 95 ff.; and the Crusaders, IV, 102, 107 ff., 295; demagogic religious appeals to, III, 123; on descent from house of David, V, 38; economic theories, IV, 218 f.; emphasis on ceremonial laws, VIII, 17; employment of Christians, IV, 15; ethnic strains, III, 103; and faith of "infidels," V, 82 f.; and foreign languages, VII, 9 f.; inheritance rights, and infidels, V, 18; Jewish charge of licentiousness, V, 134; and Karaites, V, 263 f.; mechanical knowledge, VIII, 356; messianic belief, V, 200 f.; need to feel superior, III, 4, 96, 138, IV, 28, V, 99; Norman campaigns vs., IV, 23; and Nubians, IV, 181; and Palestine and Jerusalem, III, 269 f.; possibility of rise in social status, III, 149; and prayer, VI, 13 f.; prestige-mindedness, III, 170 f.; rejection of anthropomorphism, VIII, 100; relations with Samaritans, V, 171 f., 176 f.; resentment of non-Muslim officeholders, III, 154 f.; and Saturday, V, 91 f.; and "slaves," III, 302, IV, 42, 333; Spanish, massacre of, IV, 132; status in foreign lands, III, 129; taxation of, IV, 114; *see also* Arabs; Islam; Law, Muslim
Mustanṣir, Faṭimid caliph, III, 158
Mutakallimun, *see* Kalam and Mutakallimun
Mutawakkil: decree re behavior of "protected peoples," III, 139 f.; destruction of synagogues, III, 135; use of church as mosque, III, 148
Mu'tazilites, Arab rationalists, V, 198, VI, 187, VIII, 60 ff., 66 ff., 72, 103, 298; on attributes of God, VIII, 96, 328; on the Hereafter, VIII, 104; on predestination and free will, VIII, 109
Mutilation, as punishment, III, 186 f.; of slaves, IV, 191
Mysteries: of existence, VIII, 7 ff.; religious, VIII, 80 f.; of the universe, VII, 172
Mystery religions, ancient, I, 387, VIII, 31; pagan cults, I, 388
Mystic communion with God, I, 202
Mystics and mysticism, I, 201, VIII, 3-54, 58, 273-95; and alchemy, VIII, 225; astrological, VIII, 179 ff.; and biblical interpretation, VI, 297 f.; ecstasy, VIII, 82 f., 116; in Hebrew liturgy, VII, 78 f., 131; interfaith borrowings, VIII, 112 f.; literature, VIII, 11 ff., 25, 27 ff., 277 ff.; magic square, VIII, 354; on meanings of numbers and letters, VIII, 151, 191; Muslim, V, 103, VIII, 15 f.; nomistic, VIII, 52; poetry of, VII, 181 ff., 272 f.; reception by leaders and public, II, 314, VIII, 24 ff.; *She'ur qomah*, VI, 177 f., VIII, 25 f., 286; use of Arabic, VII, 193; *yorede merkabah*, V, 146; *see also* Chariot; Gnosticism; Kabbalah; *Merkabah* mysticism
Mythology: Babylonian, I, 294, VIII, 10; Greek, II, 4

N

Nabataeans, I, 57, 167, 254; inscriptions, III, 64; spread of, III, 60
Nablus, Samaritan center, V, 171 ff.; Crusaders and, V, 172; emigration from, V, 176
Nabonidus, king of Babylonia, I, 119, 132, 349, 355, III, 64 f.
Naboth, I, 68, 93
Nag-Hammadi, II, 435
Nahawend, Persia, III, 110, V, 223; sects in, V, 183
Nahawendi, Benjamin b. Moses, *see* Benjamin b. Moses
Naḥman (b. Jacob), R., Babylonian Amora, II, 198, 240, 259, III, 62; temporary marriages, II, 226, 410; wife, II, 239
Naḥman b. Isaac, R., II, 222
Naḥmani, Rabbah b., II, 243, 413

Naḥmanides, *see* Moses b. Naḥman
Nahor, I, 33
Nahrawani, Nissi al-, liturgical poet, VII, 144, VIII, 13
Naḥshon b. Zadok Gaon, of Sura, V, 14, VI, 425; "circle" of 247 years, VIII, 192; commentaries, VI, 42; denunciation of *piyyuṭ,* VII, 101; on local customs, VI, 124 f.; mystic writing attributed to, VIII, 25; on sale of slaves to Gentiles, IV, 193; on scholars of Kairuwan, V, 22, 77 f.
Nahum, prophet, I, 338, VI, 309
Nahum of Gimzo, VI, 186
Nahum of Media, I, 221, II, 205
Nahum the Libellarius, II, 37
Najara Israel, mystical poet, VII, 204
Najran, Arabia, III, 163; attacks on Christians of, III, 66; Christian community and Mohammed, III, 78, 80; evacuation of Jews to Kufa, III, 271
Names: of angels and demons, VIII, 8 f., 21, 275; Arabic and Jewish mixture, III, 148; Aramaic, I, 120, 121, 349; compounded with Baal and Yahweh, I, 59, 318; in Elephantine, I, 121; forms used for Jesus, II, 357; identification of biblical, VII, 16, 18, 25, 29; as key to history, I, 121, 350; means of protection, II, 20, VIII, 8 f., 21, 275; in Palmyrene inscriptions, II, 211, 407; personal and place names, I, 33 f.; Semitic, among Hyksos rulers, I, 304; substitutions, VI, 293 f.; talmudic, VII, 14; theophorous, I, 129, 352; transliteration of, under Islam, III, 303; *see also* Place names
—— adoptive, I, 349; Babylonian, I, 118 ff., 349; double, I, 310; Hellenistic, I, 373, II, 174; Hebrew and Roman, III, 207; Persian, VIII, 277
—— divine: appellations and circumlocutions, I, 46, 229, 244, 312, 352, II, 17 f., 162, 311 f., 314, 335, 357, 361, 394, 434, 435, V, 120, VI, 130, 249, 409, 449 f., VII, 12, 21, VIII, 26; components of, VIII, 152; derivatives of attributes of God, II, 314, 434 f.; in Elephantine papyri, I, 352; Greek equivalent, I, 229; improper use of, VIII, 29; in incantations, VIII, 8, 27 ff., 284; in liturgical selections, VII, 247 f.; magic power, II, 22 f., 314, 434, VIII, 9; in mystic schools, VIII, 16; precentor's omission of, VIII, 294; reverence for, VII, 139; sanctification of, VI, 83, VII, 65; used in Samaritan oaths, II, 434
—— Hebrew, I, 6, 119, 120, 302, 349; adopted by Khazars, III, 202
—— Jewish, I, 119, 120, 392, II, 211, 407; paucity of in Edfu ghetto, I, 392
Naples, IV, 24; Jewish defense of, III, 7, 25; population, IV, 243
Naqdimon b. Gurion, II, 114, 221
Narbonne: Council of, II, 423, III, 253, IV, 154, 157; Jewish community, IV, 45-48, 58, 258-60, VIII, 38 f.; Jewish "king" of, IV, 46 f., 259, VI, 421; Moses the preacher, VI, 171 f., 410, VIII, 32; Naṭronai and, IV, 258 f.; scarcity of books, VII, 139; surrender to the Franks, IV, 45 f.; taxation, IV, 154; tombstone inscription, III, 48
Narsai, Nestorian, VIII, 275
Narses, exarch of Italy, II, 178, 398
Narses, Syriac poet, VII, 199
Nash papyrus, I, 186, 379, VI, 238
Nasi, title, V, 48, 59, VIII, 69, 370; *see also* Patriarchate
Nasiruddin at-Tusi, on astronomy, VIII, 145
Nasr b. Sayyar, III, 166
Nathan, prophet, I, 65
Nathan, R., II, 14, 381, VI, 17
Nathanael of Yemen, VII, 47
Nathan b. Abraham, V, 34, 274, 295; commentary on the Mishnah, VI, 57 f.
Nathan b. Abraham, Gaon, VI, 57
Nathan b. Isaac, the Babylonian, VI, 36; on the appointment of local chiefs, V, 50; description of exilarchic installation, V, 7 f., VI, 36, VII, 284; "Report," VI, 213, 430 f.
Nathan b. Yeḥiel, of Rome, Hebrew lexicographer, II, 411, VI, 28, VIII, 227; Arabic and Greek etymologies, VII, 232; dates of birth and death, VII, 231; lexicon for Babylonian Talmud, IV, 308, VI, 340, VII, 29, 231 f.; quotations from Naṭronai, VI, 383; synagogue in Rome, V, 59; Tanḥum's supplementary work, VII, 31; on use of Ṣemaḥ's work, VII, 224
Nathan of Ṣoṣita, VI, 186
Nation, Jewish: importance of, I, 8, 12 f.
Nationalism: ancient: definition, I, 27, II, 372; emancipation from state, I,

25, 31, 93-96, 237, 338; failure to secularize Jewish life, I, 28; Jesus' aloofness, II, 69, 73; Jewish conception accepted by world at large, I, 28; national-religious ideology, I, 5, 28, 96, 163, 225, 228; Pharisees representatives of, II, 344; reality of, II, 214; safeguard against national extinction, I, 163; and territory, I, 16-25 *passim,* 53-61; and universalism (*q.v.*), I, 31, 158
—— medieval, VII, 168, 211 f., VIII, 125 ff.; in Jewish philosophy, VIII, 86 ff.; Karaite, V, 219, 258, 268, 282; in poetry, VII, 163; upsurge of, V, 184-205, 375-87, VII, 211 f.; and voluntary segregation, III, 144
—— modern: in Russia and Poland, I, 29
Nations, family of, Yosephon on, VI, 226
"Nations, seventy," VIII, 216
Naṭroi (Naṭronai) b. Emunah Gaon, VI, 37
Naṭrona (or Neṭirata), name, II, 178, 397
Naṭronai b. Ḥabibai (Ḥakhinai), exilarch, IV, 47, 258 f., V, 15, 47, VII, 21
Naṭronai I b. Nehemiah, gaon, on followers of Severus, V, 190, 193 f., 207
Natronai II b. Hilai, gaon, V, 14, 227, 382, VI, 31, VII, 65; correspondence with Spain, VI, 41; on debts collectible from property, VI, 132; on the hundred benedictions, VII, 110 f.; on intercourse with a slave, IV, 195; on Lucena, III, 109; mystic writing attributed to, VIII, 25; on neglect of biblical studies, VI, 236 f., 313; on prayer, VI, 15, VII, 76; reaction to Karaite schism, V, 276; on recitation of the Aramaic Targum, VI, 264; on suppression of *hafṭarah,* VI, 42; on study of the Talmud, VI, 34 f.; on vineyards, IV, 163; on vocalized Torah scrolls, VI, 244
Natural causes, and actions of man, VIII, 111 ff.
Natural law: doctrine of, II, 136, VI, 5, 144 ff.; Greek vs. Judeo-Christian background, VI, 397; increasing role in legal philosophy, II, 432; Saadiah's discussion of, VIII, 335; unchanging, VIII, 90
Natural sciences, VIII, 142, 222-30, 384-87
Nature: antinomy between spirit and, I, 296; control of forces of, VIII, 4; defiance of, I, 163-64, II, 321; emancipation from, I, 8, VIII, 46, 111 f.; healing powers, VIII, 260; and history, I, 5 ff., 12, 18, 101, 296; Paul's use of word, II, 81; in poetry, VII, 163 f.
Naubakht, an-, Persian astronomer, III, 99, 100, 152
Naubakhti, translator, V, 84
Naukratis, I, 190
Navicularii, guild, II, 249
Nazirites, sect, I, 42, 78, II, 51, 348
Nazis and Nazism, I, 18, 296, 324, II, 427, IV, 270 f., VIII, 386; impact upon Jews, I, 347, II, 356 f.
Nea Moné, monastery, III, 192
Neapolis, formerly Schechem, II, 28; *see also* Nablus
Near East, I, 394; circulation of Mohammed's sayings, VI, 201; concepts of nature of ruler, VIII, 18; corruption of nations of, I, 284; cultural synthesis, VII, 59; eschatology, V, 358; ethics, III, 283; ethnic movements, I, 36, 305; feudalism and landholding, IV, 152, 318; folklore, VI, 183, 415 f.; Greek emporia, I, 184; Hebrew deeds, IV, 320 f.; Jewish craftsmen, IV, 167 f.; popular philosophies, VIII, 5, 151; power of the word in, VII, 87, VIII, 14; rigidity of court etiquette, III, 171; role of Jews in cultural exchange, VIII, 255 f.; sectarianism and biblical interpretation, VI, 276 f., VII, 223; socioeconomic changes, IV, 26, 186, 337, V, 96 f., 126 ff.; synagogue readers, VII, 58 f.; *see also under* countries and cities
Nebiim, I, 59, 78
Nebukadrezzar, I, 115, 130, 344, V, 119, 132, VIII, 26; Jephet b. 'Ali's comment on, VI, 308; Jewish refugees from wars of, III, 64; places chosen for settlement by Jews, I, 107; and Tadmor, III, 62
Necho, pharaoh, I, 183, 327
Neck, tax receipt stamped upon, III, 168
Necropoles, *see* Cemeteries and catacombs
Nedarim, commentary on, VI, 53

Negev, ancient, I, 252, II, 368
Negidim, provincial leaders of Jewry, in Egypt, V, 39 ff., 56, 308 f.; Kairuwan, V, 51; term, V, 39 f.
Nehardea, Babylonia, I, 168, II, 206, 207, 247, 317, 405, 435; academy, VI, 455; adherence to Galilean custom, VI, 124 ff.; Jewish principality, III, 62 f.; and Pumbedita, VI, 24; work on biblical text, VI, 239
Nehemiah, R., II, 127, 307, 378; *Mishnat ha-middot,* VIII, 147
Nehemiah b. Hacaliah, I, 73, 85, 114, 116, 118, 144, 151, 160, 180, 353; concludes covenant, I, 161; historicity, I, 341; racialist extremism, I, 147, 163, 361; on reading the law "distinctly," VI, 258; restoration under, I, 103; service to mankind, I, 158
—— Book of, I, 104, 343, III, 61
Neḥemiah b. Ḥushiel, messiah, V, 143, 157
Nehemiah b. Kohen Zedek, V, 23 f.
Nehorai, R., physician-shopkeeper, II, 121, IV, 179
Neḥuniah b. ha-Qanah, R., VIII, 33 f.
Nehushtan, I, 66
Neighbors, legal protection, II, 252
Neo-Babylonian Empire, I, 102; *see also* Babylonia
Neoplatonism, V, 381 f., VIII, 61, 76; and Christianity, II, 159; influence on Ibn Gabirol, VIII, 325; rise of, VI, 258
Neo-Phythagoreans, I, 208
Nero, Roman emperor, II, 57, 96, 100, 103; persecution of Christians, I, 191
Nerva, Roman emperor, II, 83, 106
Nesi'im, Karaite, V, 263
Nestor, III, 215
Nestorians, II, 164, 188, 191, III, 259 f.; *catholicos,* III, 88 f., V, 6; charge of John Rufus vs., III, 229; equation with Jews, III, 8, 243; religion and law, VI, 4; in Sassanian Empire, VI, 271; school of Jundeshapur, VIII, 236; Trinitarian doctrine, VIII, 96, 326
Nestorius, III, 5
Neṭira, house of, Jewish bankers of Baghdad, III, 152 f., 167, V, 10 f., VI, 214
Neumes, VII, 282
Neuss, Germany, IV, 134
Neutrality: of Jewry, on Islam and Christendom, IV, 91; political, of Jews, III, 235
Neva, Transjordan, VI, 381 f.
New Antioch, III, 6 f., 58, 255
"New Christians" (forced converts), III, 177; *see also under* Christians and christianity; Converts and conversion
New Covenanters, V, 188, 215, 219, 380, VI, 78; *see also* Damascus sect
New Moon, holiday, I, 6, 44, 286
New Testament: anti-Jewish polemists and, V, 108; Arabic versions, VI, 265; Jewish attitude toward, V, 85; language of, I, 186; late interpolations and canonization, II, 73, 131; Muslim charges of Christian falsification of, V, 88; scholarship divided, II, 358; social aspects, II, 356; "translation Greek," VII, 4, 7; *see also* Bible; Gospels; *also under* names of books and versions
New Year's Day, I, 5, 144, 294, VIII, 188; animal sacrifice, VII, 78 f.; dating of, V, 31, VIII, 195; customs, VI, 125; fasting on, VI, 330; *Musaf 'Amidah,* VII, 107 f., 127, 172; observance, V, 248, VII, 107; prayers, VII, 76; *Tashlikh* ceremony, III, 241; two-day celebration, V, 29
Nibridius, archbishop of Narbonne, IV, 52
Nicaea, First Council of, II, 188, 401; decision on date of Easter, III, 248, VIII, 369
—— Second Council of, III, 177-78, IV, 5 f., 189
Nicanor of Alexandria, I, 262
Nicephoros I, Byzantine emperor: and banking, IV, 198; on calling Arabs Saracens, III, 302
Nicephoros II (Nicephoros Phokas), Byzantine emperor, III, 193; conquest of Crete, IV, 190
Nicetas, son of Jason, II, 24
Nicetas Choniates, Byzantine historian, IV, 166, VI, 212; on Constantinople fire, IV, 130 f.
Nicholas, Byzantine monk, VIII, 246
Nicholas I, pope, III, 209
Nicolaus of Damascus, I, 218, 242, 272, 401, II, 342; on descent of Antipater, VI, 193
Nichomachus of Gadara, VIII, 151
Nicon Metanoites, Saint, III, 184, 318

Nies Babylonian Collection, Yale University, I, 332
Nihavend, Persia, V, 223; *see also* Nahawend
Nihilism, V, 103
Nile, river, III, 116; canal, III, 155
Nilus, abbot of Rossano, VIII, 245
Nineveh: fall of, I, 96, 338; Petaḥiah's visit to, VI, 435; repentance in, II, 384
Ninos, *see* Nineveh
Ninth of Ab, IV, 145, VI, 167; liturgy, V, 152, VIII, 82 f., 257; mourning for Temple on, II, 112, 193, VII, 82 f.; poems for, VII, 143; replaced by 'Anan, V, 214; yearly gathering, II, 108, 118, 374; Zionide poem in ritual for, VII, 168 f.
Nippur, city, I, 107; banking and commerce, I, 108, 109, 346; exilic community around, I, 134; incantations, VIII, 21; magicians of, VIII, 10
Nisan, month, I, 294, V, 217, 224
Nishmat, prayer, II, 75
Nisibis, VI, 245; academy, VIII, 58, 392; center of biblical studies, VI, 240 f.; Ezra synagogue, VI, 436; history of, VI, 443; school of, VI, 256 f.
Nissi b. Nuḥ, Karaite, V, 229, 253; "Commentary on the Ten Commandments," VII, 220
Nissim b. Jacob ibn Shahin of Kairuwan, III, 298, V, 48, 312, VI, 205; folkloristic collection, VI, 184-88, 414-16, 420, VII, 183, 311, VIII, 50; introduction of *shabbata de-rigla,* V, 40; Secret Scroll, VI, 33, 335 f.; on *The Scroll of Antiochus,* VI, 416 f.; works on the Talmud, VI, 33, 45, 335 f., VIII, 97
Nissim b. Moses, V, 8
Nissim of Qaṭiyah, III, 138
Niẓam al-Mulk, vizier, III, 151 f.
Noah, patriarch, I, 44, 307, II, 223, V, 87, VI, 39, VIII, 134; astrology and, VIII, 176
—— Book of, II, 336
Noahide commandments, I, 375, VI, 5, 145
Nomadic ideals, I, 89, 335, 336
Nomads: and agriculture, I, 55, 301; and religion, I, 47; seminomadic tribes, I, 33, 41, 315, 333; *see also* Tribes
Nomenclature, theophorous, I, 129
Nomism, VI, 141, VIII, 32
Nomocanon, III, 187, 191, 319
Noph, Egypt, I, 111
Normandy: Church of, IV, 269; Jews in, IV, 77
Normans: policy in Palestine, IV, 113 f.; rule in Sicily, IV, 21 ff.; taxation of, III, 191, 193
North Africa, *see* Africa, North
Northampton, England: Council of, IV, 277; *donum,* IV, 303
Norwich, England, IV, 135, 306 f.
Notation, musical: Byzantine, VII, 282; ekphonetic, VII, 282
Novel, VI, 187 f.; *see also* Historical literature
Novellae, VI, 62, 353 f.; *see also* Justinian; Leo VI
Novgorod, excavations, III, 334
Nubia, IV, 181
Nu'man III, Lakhmid king, III, 70
Numbers, Book of, V, 219; and first-born males, VIII, 149; scholion on, V, 175
Numenius, I, 199; attitude to Judaism, II, 157
Numerals, VIII, 146-60, 349-57; Hindu, VIII, 150, 360; letters as, VIII, 150 f.; symbolism, VI, 157 f.; systems of, VIII, 150 f.
Numerical principle, in cosmic structure, VIII, 284
Numerical values: of Arabic and Syriac letters, VIII, 150; of biblical words and phrases, V, 86 ff.; of divine name, VIII, 281; and the gates of Understanding, VIII, 294; of Hebrew letters, V, 167, VI, 164, 166, 242, VII, 250, VIII, 14 f., 147, 150, 290; of Messiah's name, V, 357; of Mohammed's name, V, 100; of opening line of poem, VII, 289; in riddles, VIII, 357; of words, V, 167; *see also Gemaṭrias*
Nuns: expulsion from Sens, IV, 56; Sister Catherine, Jewish convert, V, 113
Nuremberg, Germany, IV, 117
Nurses, Christian, of Jews, IV, 269
Nuzi tablets, I, 302, 327

O

Oaths: in criminal vs. civil litigation, IV, 253, 255; of Damascus sect, II, 52,

Oaths (*Continued*)
54; of Essenes, II, 48, 347; of fidelity, II, 36; IV, 49, 163; Hai's monograph on, VI, 71, 359 f.; in interfaith partnerships, IV, 331; in Judeo-Christian litigation, IV, 41 f.; *more judaico,* III, 149, 194 f., 322, IV, 20, 49, 61; of office, II, 110, 375; physicians', VIII, 238 f., 242, 391; and readmission of Karaites, V, 274; relating to end of days, II, 312; Samaritans' use of divine name in, II, 434; taken by Saadiah Gaon, V, 20; three imposed on man by God, II, 115; *see also* Blasphemy; Curse
Obadiah, prophet, VI, 229; Book of, V, 158 f.
Obadiah, Khazar king, III, 201
Obadiah (Johannes), Norman proselyte, III, 141, 169, 190, 320, IV, 294, V, 202, 260
Obadiah, *see* Abu 'Isa al-Isfahani
Obedience: to divine law, VI, 142; to will of God, VI, 218
Obscurantism, and conservatism, VIII, 68
Observation, astronomic, VIII, 173; and calendar computations, VIII, 194, 369; difficulties of, VIII, 161 ff.
Observatories, astronomic, VIII, 161
Occult sciences: and astrology, II, 15 f., 44, 334; and German pietism, VIII, 50 ff.
Occupations, industrial, IV, 165 f.; ratio of Jews employed in, IV, 171, VIII, 236; *see also under* individual occupations, *e.g.,* Crafts and craftsmen; Trade
Oceans, geographic knowledge of, VIII, 214 f.
Oculist, Jewish, VIII, 237
Odenath of Palmyra, II, 177
Odo (Eudes), French king, IV, 43
Odo, scholastic, VI, 273, 463
Odors, V, 327; industrial, II, 248
Oescus (Gigen), III, 207
Office, public, *see* Public office
Officials, Jewish: in royal service, III, 150-61, 303-8, IV, 15 ff., 29 ff., 36-39, 45, 251-53
—— communal: appointment, V, 71; election, V, 67 f.; hereditary principles and, V, 73 f.; number, V, 60; specialized, V, 51
Oikonomia, term, IV, 218
Oikumene, V, 117 f.
Oinomaos of Gadara, II, 281
'Olah, I, 353
'Olam, term, II, 389
'Olam ha-ba, term, V, 148
Oldenburg, *see* Sopron
"Oldest Collection of Bible Difficulties by a Jew," VI, 305 ff.
Old Testament, IV, 51; Arabic translation, VI, 264; canonization, II, 144 f., V, 262; Christians' use of, II, 144, 145, 170, VI, 241, 257, VIII, 77, 95 f.; critique of Mardan Farukh, V, 106; controversy over interpretation, V, 85 ff., 129, 135, 136, *see also* Interpretation, biblical; deviations from law of, V, 93; doctrine of Chosen People (*q.v.*), V, 125 ff.; "Hebrewisms" in translations of, VII, 10; Latin and other late translations, II, 144, 385, VI, 272 ff., 462 f.; messianic allusions, V, 157, *see also* Messiah and messianism; on moneylending and usury, IV, 199; Muslim arguments based on, V, 86 ff.; Paulicians and, VIII, 288; poetic rhythm, VII, 313 f.; prophecies, V, 174, *see also* Prophets and prophecy; reevaluation of postexilic period demanded, I, 103, 341; references to divine attributes, V, 120 f.; stabilization of text, VI, 292, 442; strictures on, II, 167 f., 394, V, 88, 106, 330 f., VI, 298, 303, VIII, 128; subjects in liturgical poems, VII, 85; taboos, V, 250; tendency to give greater credence to records, I, 32; *see also* Bible; *also under* names of books, *e.g.,* Esther; *and under* versions, *e.g.,* Septuagint; *see also Masorah;* Masorites
Olive oil: quality, II, 246; uses, I, 253, II, 247
Olive press, use in forced conversion, III, 180, 315
Olivet, Mount: Rabbanite pronouncements from, V, 279; site of worship by Jews, III, 101
Olive tree, Jews likened to, II, 173
Olympic games, I, 236
Omar, Covenant of, *see under* 'Umar I; 'Umar II
Omnipotence, of God, VIII, 96 f.
Omniscience, of God, VIII, 96 f.; *see also* Attributes, divine; God

Omri, king of Israel, I, 73, 322; dynasty of, rebellion against, I, 89
Ona'ah, term, II, 255
One, number, VIII, 151 f.
Onias, military commander, II, 94
Onias IV, high priest, I, 14, 200, 386; temple of, I, 219, 394, II, 12, 93, 126; temple priests, I, 219
Onias the Just, identified with Righteous Teacher, II, 349 f.
Onkelos, Targum, II, 146, 346, 386, VI, 256; Aramaic counterpart to Aquila ('Aqilas), VI, 256, 260 f.; concordance to, VII, 29; decline of use in Fez, VII, 5 f.; masoretic recension, VI, 258 f., 312; Rabbanite reverence for, VII, 227; and Targum Jonathan, VI, 456
Onkelos the Proselyte, VI, 260
Onomatological studies, I, 350; *see also* Names
Ontology, and the existence of God, VIII, 324
Ophir, I, 321; identification of, III, 116, VII, 18
Ophthalmology, VIII, 405
Opportunity, equality of, II, 279
Optics, VIII, 159
Oracles, I, 154, 210, 391; attributed to Balaam, I, 313; fallen into desuetude, I, 82, 152
Oracular lots, I, 49, 314
Oral Law (Deuterosis), II, 65, 207, 294, 314, III, 189, V, 188 f., 209, 374, VI, 22 f.; Byzantine suppression of, III, 12 f., 233, V, 26, VI, 261, VII, 83, 94 f., 256; esoteric, II, 314, VIII, 52; influence, II, 294; Karaite repudiation of, V, 213, 218, 246, 251 ff., 272, 274, VI, 275; Maimonides on transmission of, VI, 100, VIII, 210 f., 380; memorizers of, VI, 37; Pharisaic defense of, VI, 438; Rabbanites and, V, 218, 282; sectarians and transmission of, VI, 201; *see also* Law; Talmud
Oral study, II, 275, 281, 421
Oral transmission, *see* Transmission, oral
Oran, battle of, III, 127
Orations: device used by Yosephon, VI, 193; Graeco-Roman, VI, 163 ff.
Orators, Greek, employment of *tachygraphoi,* VI, 157
Orchards, IV, 162
Ordeal: trial by, I, 329, IV, 40, V, 205; by combat, IV, 40, 92; exemption from, IV, 49, 69, 77 f.; water, IV, 137 f.
Ordinances (*taqqanot*): communal, V, 64, VI, 46, 131-41, 392-95; termination of, VI, 136; *see also* Decrees
Ordination: ancient, II, 201, 419; of judges, VI, 9; restoration of, VIII, 191
Ordoño III, of Leon, III, 155 f.
Orestes, prefect, II, 402
Oria, Italy: capital punishment in, V, 57; Jewish community, III, 180
Orient, mass migrations to, II, 210
Oriental art, *see* Graeco-Oriental art and music
Oriental factor in decline of Hellenism, II, 173 ff.
Oriental renaissance led by Jews, I, 210, 212
Origen, II, 23, 81, 131, 151, 391; VI, 157; Christian doctrine and theories, II, 161; Egyptian citizenship, II, 412; estimates of converts, II, 163; *Hexapla,* VI, 248; written transmission of works, VII, 258
Original sin, doctrine of, II, 433
Orléans, France: fairs, IV, 325; Jewish community, IV, 57; synagogue, III, 53
—— Second and Third Councils of, III, 50, 51, 252, IV, 156 f.
Orosius, Paulus, VI, 429
Orphans, V, 321; economic and social status, I, 275, II, 271; legal protection, II, 253; writ of appointment for guardians, VI, 67
Orthodox Eastern Church, V, 109, VII, 65, 84; attitude toward Jews, III, 185; commemoration of Najran martyrs, III, 67; formula on nature of Christ, III, 5; linguistic freedom, VII, 68; vs. Monophysites, III, 259; Romanos I and, III, 182; Russian conversion, III, 221; Russian sectarianism, III, 216; theological controversies in Palestine, III, 21
Orthodoxy, Jewish, I, 31; departure from, as apostasy, II, 292
Oshaiah *or* Oshaya, R., II, 21, 247
Osiris, I, 335
Ossuaries, II, 63, 287
Ostraca, I, 78, 213, 252, 318, 334
Othniel, son of Kenaz, II, 37
Otot ha-Mashiaḥ, V, 143
Otranto, Italy, IV, 24, VI, 119
Otto I (Otto the Great), emperor, III,

Otto I (*Continued*)
155, IV, 65, VI, 222; ambassadors in Cordova, VI, 435; coronation, VI, 420
Otto II, emperor, IV, 47, 65; and Kalonymide family, IV, 273
Otto III, emperor, IV, 238
Otto of Freising, chronicler, VI, 434
Ouargela, *see* Warjalan
Outhouses, Persian, VI, 344
Outlawry: of Christianity, III, 132; of forced conversion, IV, 236; of Islam, III, 212 f.; of relapse to Judaism, IV, 61; of violence, IV, 70
—— of Judaism, III, 24, 174, 186, 193; *under* the Almohades, III, 111 f., 124 ff., 290 ff.; by Dagobert, III, 47; by Heraclius, III, 32, 174 f., 220; by Leo III, III, 313; by Phokas, III, 237; by Trajan in Cyprus, III, 19 f.
Ovid, I, 382, II, 241
Oviedo (Coyanza), Council of, IV, 43
Ownership, *see* Landownership; Property
Oxford, England, IV, 81
Oxyrhynchus papyri, I, 395, II, 244

P

Pacific Ocean, VIII, 214 f.
Pactum, term, III, 249
Paganism, II, 310; and Christian Church, II, 140, 151 ff., 154 f., 163, 169 ff.; deities identified with the God of Jews, II, 24; intellectual counterattacks, II, 156 ff., 390 ff.; "pagan revival," II, 160
Pagan temples: adornment and worship in, II, 6, 7; contributions by Jews, II, 24
Paganus, term, II, 166, 393
Painting: frescoes in Dura-Europos, II, 11, 14, 331; in synagogues, II, 11 ff., 154, 331, 402
Palaestina, new name for Judaea, II, 123, 380; *see also* Palestine
Palaestina Tertia, III, 61
Palermo, Sicily: Muslim capital, IV, 20 f.; synagogue, III, 30; transfer of Jews to clergy, IV, 22
Palestine: Ancient, Israelitic: agriculture, I, 55 ff.; celebration of Jubilee years, VIII, 210; copper-producing areas, I, 60; early ties with Arabia, III, 61; education in, I, 323; Egypt's relations with, I, 35, 67, 316, 322; ethnological make-up, I, 34, 57, 104, 307, 320; geography, I, 33, 53 f.; handicrafts, I, 69, 323; influence, I, 53-61, 316-19; Israel's birthplace, I, 32 ff., 42, 53 ff., 101, 161, 302, 308, 316; invasions of, I, 63, 344; myth re emigration of Canaanites, I, 374, III, 214 f., 271, 335; Phoenicia's relations with, I, 306, 374, III, 214 f.; population, I, 64, 320; sacrificial and nonsacrificial worship, I, 123; trade and industry, I, 77, 327; urbanization, I, 71, 85
—— postexilic and talmudic: agriculture, I, 250-55, 406-7, II, 104 f., 245, 246, 373, 406 f.; Alexander's conquest of, I, 184, 228, 338, VIII, 205; ancient Hebrew dialects, VII, 40; and Babylonia, I, 282, II, 205, 207 f.; burial in sacred soil of, II, 289; calendar and festivals, I, 220; cattle raising, I, 301; cemeteries of Jews, I, 378; center of Jewish life, I, 116, 165, 212-49, 277, 392-405, II, 82, 204, 206 f., 321; centers of learning: students, II, 207 f.; charter granted to Jews, I, 216, 369, 393; Christianity (*q.v.*), II, 62, 82, 164, 204; churches, II, 392; controls over, II, 125 f.; economic conditions, I, 108, 258, 262-71, II, 102, 246; emigration from, I, 172, II, 123, 204, 208, 210, 377, 405 ff.; effect of antisemitic movements in other lands, I, 219, *see also* Antisemitism; freedmen within Jewish communities, I, 269; Greek funerary inscriptions, I, 378; harlots' quarters, II, 225; and Hellenism, I, 228 f., 398; Herod's fiscal reign of terror, I, 262, 410; historic importance, I, 392; internal animosities, I, 162, 281, 284, 367, II, 116; Jewish bourgeoisie, I, 280; Jewish state, I, 250; "Judaea," a confusing term, I, 397; Judaism, formulation of, I, 133; land measures, II, 104, 372, 373, *see also* Land; law formulated again outside the country, I, 162; marriage laws and customs, II, 221, 226, 227; patriarchate (*q.v.*), II, 126, 192-206 *passim,* 209, 403; and Persian Empire, I, 160, 162; population, I, 168, 371, 372, II, 27; Restoration, I, 105, 112, 114, 157-63, 366-68; resurrection from the dead in, II, 40; and Rome, I, 237 ff., 247 ff., 263, 402-5, II, 89, 96 ff., 102 f., 104 ff., 368-73

passim; Sadduceeism, II, 36; sculptures, II, 9; sectarian divisions, II, 3 ff.; self-determination of coastal Greek cities, I, 225; slaves and free workers, I, 267-71, 412, IV, 190; social stratification, I, 262-67, 271-76, 413-14, II, 279, 343; social turmoil, I, 249-85, 349, 406-15; Syriac-Aramaic dialect, VII, 84; taxation, I, 411, II, 185 f., *see also* Taxation; theocratic regime, I, 163, 165, 221-27, 395-97; trade and industry, I, 255-58, 407-8, II, 248 f.; value of residence in, VI, 230 f.; weaknesses undermining, I, 212; woman's social status, I, 114; *see also* Judaea and Judaeans

—— High medieval: academic independence, V, 24-32, 302-5; Arab conquest, II, 179, III, 62, 102 f., V, 99, VII, 97; attachment of Jews to, IV, 94, V, 26 ff., 198, VI, 230 f.; Babylonian Jews in, V, 303; banking, IV, 198; Book of Precedents, VI, 64 f., 355 f.; Charlemagne's alleged protectorate over, IV, 257 f.; under the Crusaders, IV, 109 ff., 295 ff.; desertion of land by farmers, III, 168; earthquakes, IV, 153; emigration from, III, 48, 113, IV, 221; evolution of Jewish law, VI, 5 ff.; exilarchate, VI, 199 f.; four ells of land, VI, 134, V, 27, 303, VII, 63; as geographic lodestar, VIII, 211; God's gift to Israel, VI, 51; Jewish expansion, III, 100 f.; Judeo-Christian relations (*q.v.*), III, 77; Karaites in, V, 222 f., 271, 395, VI, 288 ff., 472 f.; VII, 18, 37 ff.; Khazar hope of military conquest, III, 204; as land of Israel, VIII, 125; landownership, IV, 151 ff., 312 f.; law codes, VI, 82 f.; loss of direct contact with, V, 58; merchants, IV, 327 f.; messianic hope of return to, V, 27, 155, 185, 202, 221, 282, 358, VII, 168 f., 178; messianic movement, V, 202, 384 f.; Muslim respect for holiness of, III, 269; mutual hostility of Christian sects, III, 161; Persian-Jewish collaboration in, III, 20; pilgrimages to, IV, 131, V, 31 f., VI, 225 f.; plant life cycles, V, 246; poll tax, III, 191 f.; population, III, 103, 237; proclamation of new moon, VIII, 186, *see also under* Moon; ritualistic autonomy, VII, 24 ff., 65, 94 f., 246, 302 ff.; sectarian strife, III, 102; self-assertion of Jewish communities, V, 24-32, 302-5; Seljuk rule, III, 104, IV, 94, 285; spread of Arabic, VI, 256; spread of Hebrew liturgy from, VII, 101; Tobiah's letter for pilgrim to, VI, 174 f.; Tulunide rulers, V, 222; variations in local customs, V, 26 f., 302 f., VI, 122 ff., 389; *see also* Academies; Exilarchs and exilarchate; Latin Kingdom of Jerusalem; Rabbis and rabbinate; *also* place names

Pallughta (Pumbedita?), messianic movement in, V, 184

Palm-trees, I, 253; grove of Frederick II, IV, 160; plantations limited, I, 262; as symbol, II, 11, III, 70

Palmyra and Palmyrenes: caravan trade, II, 417, III, 62, VIII, 168; communal leaders, V, 50; conversions and religious syncretism, II, 159; exclusion from Judaism, II, 222, 232; god Hypsistos, III, 62; inscriptions, II, 211, 407; Jews in, II, 210, III, 104; legend on descent of Palmyrenes, II, 222, 232, III, 62; repulse of Shapur I, II, 177, III, 62

Palṭiel b. Shefaṭiah, Jewish leader, III, 154, V, 40 f.

Palṭoi Gaon, VI, 27, 108

Pamphlet literature, I, 87, 334, VI, 214 f.

Panaetius, II, 4

Pannonia, Hungary, II, 210, III, 206

Pantheism, Babylonian, I, 314

Panticapaeum, *see* Kertsh

Papa, R., II, 248, 249, 251, 288

Papacy: attempts at supremacy, II, 198, 401, IV, 95; attitude toward Jews, III, 27 ff., IV, 14, 47; *Constitutio pro Judaeis,* IV, 7 f.; Jewish appeals to, for redress, IV, 17, 97 f.; and Jewish community of Rome, IV, 4 ff.; protection for Church holdings, IV, 59; revenue, IV, 12 ff., 239 f.; sociopolitical relations with Jewish communities, IV, 7 ff.; *see also* Christian Church; *also under* names of popes

Papal States, III, 243; ecclesiastical tithe, IV, 13, 239

Paper: introduction of, IV, 169, VI, 184; and production of books, VII, 136

Papias, Christian teacher, II, 66, 75, 361

Papias, R., VIII, 36

Papiscus, II, 133

Pappus b. Judah, II, 239

Pappus, revolutionary, II, 96, 370
Papyri, Aramaic, I, 347, 360, *see also under* Elephantine; Greek, I, 213, 255, 266, 378, 392, *see also under* special collections, *e.g.*, Oxyrhynchus papyri; preserved in Egypt, I, 213
Papyrus, I, 252; cost of, and book production, VII, 136; trade monopoly, I, 261 f.
Parables, in sermons, VI, 166 f.
Paradise, preexistence of, VIII, 125 f.
Paran, Mount, identification of, V, 86, 89
Parasang, unit of length, VIII, 213 f.
Parasitic class, I, 275
Parchment, I, 252; production of, IV, 319; requirements in use of, VII, 286
Parents, *see* Family life
Pariah status of Jews, I, 23, 24, 297
Paris: Benjamin of Tudela on, IV, 60; conversionist pressure on Jews in, III, 52; Fifth Council of, III, 51
Parlor games: poetic improvisations, VII, 150 f., 162; riddles, VII, 4
Paroikia, term, II, 381
Parousia, II, 73
Parsees and Parsiism, II, 180, 183, 184, 190, V, 375; and burial, II, 290; eschatological computations, II, 318, 342, 435; expansion, I, 102, II, 251; incest encouraged, II, 229; interrelations with Judaism, I, 159, 366, II, 317 f., 436; law a basic constituent, I, 227; marriage, II, 219, 229, 231; rejection of sacrifices, I, 127; religious exclusiveness, I, 117, 159, 348, II, 150, 257; *see also* Persia; Zoroaster; Zoroastrianism
Parthia, II, 95 f., 97; and Hellenism, II, 174; marriage and incest, II, 229; and Sassanian empire, II, 174
Particularism, religious, I, 96-99, 339; *see also* Nationalism
Partnerships: interfaith, IV, 177, 185 f., 338; lenders and borrowers as, IV, 200 f.; Muslim law on, IV, 331; among shopkeepers, IV, 327
Pascal, Blaise, V, 101
Paschal II, pope, IV, 114
Passover (*Pesaḥ*), I, 5, 148, 214, 254, 361, 381, III, 202, V, 227, 236, 246; agricultural labor and, IV, 315; association with blood accusation, IV, 135 ff., 306 f.; coincidence with Easter, II, 188, 209, 401, III, 11, 248, V, 303, 346, 410; date of, VIII, 185 f., 187 ff., 195; Haggadah, I, 189, 197, 381, II, 119, III, 289, V, 392; laws relating to, V, 122 f.; lambs, I, 148, 221, 372, V, 173, 217, 223, 236; prayer for dew, VII, 98; ritual, II, 119; sectarians and, V, 196, 217; theme in sacred poetry, V, 153, VII, 181; wine drinking, VII, 116
Passport (*aman*), dependent on poll tax, III, 166
Past, idealization of, I, 99-100, 340; *see also* History
Pateressa synagogae, II, 413
Patriarchal society, I, 43, 310
Patriarchate: Christian: Cyril elevated to, II, 190; Juvenal, III, 20
—— Palestinian: control of calendar proclamation, II, 206, 209, VIII, 186 ff., 368 ff.; disaffection and resentment toward, II, 269; office, its functions and decline, II, 126, 192 ff., 195, 197, 200 f., 209, 268, V, 179; rabbis' cooperation with, II, 291; reestablished by Karaites, V, 32; rivalry between "dynasty" of exilarchs and, II, 198, 205, 403
Patriarchs, biblical, I, 32 ff., 301; divine pledge to, I, 335, V, 99; dualist attack on, V, 106; God of the, I, 43; influenced by earthly trigon, VIII, 180
Patrons, literary, VII, 147 ff., 186
Paul, Saint, I, 170, 209, 221, 294, II, 70, 74, 80, 151, 164, 265, 381, 383; Athenian disputes, II, 79 f., 362, 363, 389; attitude toward nature, II, 81; burned magic books, II, 23; and Catholic Church, II, 86, 366; and the Chosen People, V, 126; controversialists on, V, 119; cooperation with Jerusalem community, II, 82; disciples, II, 365; epistles, II, 78, 81, 84, 85 f., 362, 365, VII, 109; failure in Rome, II, 165; father of, II, 36, 56; and Hellenistic Jewry, II, 76, 80, 84, 85, 366; history as means of propaganda, II, 80; leadership, II, 76-87, 361-67; missionary efforts, II, 76, 78, 79 f., 82, 83, 86, 165, 362, 365; reputed knowledge of alchemy, VIII, 224; on Savior's sonship and timelessness, II, 81, 364; use of Hebrew and Greek, I, 185, 187
Paul, patriarch of Antioch, III, 5 f.
Paulicians, III, 179, 183, IV, 107, VIII, 31

Paul of Samosata, II, 407
Paulus, Roman jurist, III, 35
Paulus Aemilius of Verona, III, 250
Paulus Alvarus, IV, 53; and convert Bodo, V, 126
Pauperes, IV, 106
Pavia, Italy: Council of, III, 32; disputation, IV, 26
Pax Romana, I, 250, II, 6, 57, 58, 249
Peace: concessions made, I, 23, II, 188, 400; efforts to establish international and domestic, II, 115 f., 376; formulas used for the dead, II, 424; prayers for, II, 115, VII, 265; proclamations, royal, IV, 70 ff.; treaties with church and state, IV, 89 f.
Peasants: in ancient Palestinian towns, I, 71; equation with *paganus,* II, 166, 393; exploitation of "free," I, 85, 260; freeholders under Vespasian, I, 265; as tenants, II, 105; taxation and flight, II, 245, 414; *see also under* Agriculture; Farmers
Pedagogy, *see* Education
Pedaiah (Shenazzar), I, 349
Peddlers, IV, 180, 184; of "elixir of life," VI, 154
Pedro II, king of Aragon and Sicily, IV, 132; decree on tax exemptions, IV, 39; privilege to Huesca, IV, 39
Pedro Alfonso, *see* Petrus Alphonsi
Pehlevi records, I, 341
Pekah, I, 155
Pelagonia, *see* Macedonia
Pella, I, 225; Christians' removal to, II, 82, 99, 132
Penalties, *see* Punishments
Penance, German system of, VIII, 52
Penitence: in Judaism and Christianity, IV, 95 f.; period of national mourning, IV, 145; *see also* Poetry, liturgical
"Penitential tariff," VIII, 52
Pentagram of Solomon, II, 11
Pentateuch (Torah), I, 140 ff., 359, II, 30, 135, IV, 47; 'Ananites on, V, 212 f., 393; on angels, II, 18; canonical material, I, 317; children's lessons in, II, 275; commentaries on, V, 212, VI, 51, 479, VII, 114; copies for study and recitation, VI, 244; division of commandments, II, 421; Eleazar b. Pedat on, V, 163 f.; ethical sanctions, I, 357; excommunication before scrolls of, V, 17; and Ezekiel's law, I, 154; as first written book, VIII, 77; fragments, I, 331; *Hekhalot rabbati* on, VIII, 17; Ibn Ḥazm's study of, V, 85, 88; known through Ezra, I, 345; Masoretic, V, 197; modes of interpretation, V, 254, *see also* Interpretation, biblical; Mosaic authorship, I, 330; number of letters and verses, VI, 237 f., 442, VIII, 15, 149, 238; on observation of the Sabbath, V, 92, *see also* Sabbath; official readers, II, 283; "Onkelos" (*q.v.*) to, VI, 258; Persian manuscript of, V, 183; Philo on, I, 199; preservation of, and precision of speech, VII, 3; punishment for burning scroll of, I, 239; reading cycle, V, 28, 405; reading of, in Hebrew and Aramaic, VI, 256; references to the Messiah, V, 118; Samaritan Pentateuch, II, 30, 32, 340, VI, 442; Samaritan Triglot, VI, 271; segregationist prohibitions, V, 100, 335 f.; sorcery denounced, II, 17; summary of rational and divine law, VI, 142 f.; translation inadequate, II, 143; weekly readings, in synagogues, II, 280, 281, 422, VII, 72; on women, I, 111; *see also* Bible: Law; Old Testament; Torah; *and under* names of books, *e.g.,* Exodus
Pentecost, I, 5
Peons, Persian, II, 257; *see also* Agriculture; Peasants
"People of the book," III, 81, 164, V, 82, 236, 400, VI, 19; warning against, VI, 444
Pepin the Short, Frankish king, IV, 259
Pepper, as medium of payment, IV, 182, 347
Perctarit, Langobard king, III, 32, IV, 25
Peregrini, II, 226
Perfet, nephew of Saltel, IV, 159
Perfet (Profet), Sheshet b. Solomon, IV, 36 f.
Peroz Shapur, Persian emperor, III, 55, 109
Persecutions: of Christians by pagans, I, 400, IV, 57, VII, 256; by Almohades, III, 122 ff.
—— of Jews, II, 215 f., IV, 89 ff., 105, V, 108 f., VI, 427, VII, 177; Byzantine, III, 199; under Caliphate, III, 122 ff., 289 ff., *see also* names of caliphs; history of Jews as series of, I, 400;

Persecutions (*Continued*)
inescapability of, II, 215; "lachrymose conception of Jewish history," VI, 234, VII, 247; and liturgical creativity, VII, 83 f.; local or individual, VI, 218 f.; pogroms, I, 191, 266, II, 189; for possession of Bible, VII, 86; *see also* Antisemitism; Atrocities; Martyrs and martyrdom; Massacres of Jews, Murder

Persia: Achaemenid and Parthian, I, 102 f., 106 f., 169, II, 26, 206, III, 18, V, 119 f.; Aramaic used in, I, 159; assimilation of racial and religious groups, I, 111, 131, 181; and Egypt, I, 190; family distinction valued, I, 125; imperial policy, I, 129-32, 142, 162, 184, 353-55; and Judaism, I, 228, 341, II, 317; Phoenician ghettos, I, 176; policy toward Jews, I, 103, 116, 129 ff., 163, 348, 354 f., 372; Samaria as a district capital, II, 27; self-determination under, I, 166; semicapitalist economy, I, 109; *see also* Achaemenids; Parsees and Parsiism; Parthia

—— Sassanian, V, 230, VI, 54, VII, 255; admixture of names in, VIII, 275; Arab penetration of, III, 88 f.; attitude to burial, II, 290; caste system, II, 176, 181, 279, 403; changing attitudes, II, 213; Christians in, II, 164, 181, 399, III, 89, VI, 271; dates borrowed from eschatology of, II, 318; destruction of Antioch, III, 6 f.; exilarchate, II, 195 ff., 200 f., 205, 291, 403, VI, 200; expedition to India, II, 212, 407; family distinction valued, I, 125; fiscal reforms, III, 56; immigration of Nestorians into, VI, 271; influence after decline of Hellenism, I, 283, II, 174; intergroup relations, II, 190, III, 128 f.; invasion of Armenia, III, 18; and Jewish refugees, III, 8, V, 180, VIII, 241; Jewish revolt, II, 182 f., 399, VI, 199 ff.; 423 f.; Jewish schools, VI, 54; Jews in, II, 172-214 *passim*, 317 f., 396-407, III, 8; "king of kings," VIII, 18; and Lakhmids, III, 61, 63; last king of, III, 19; legal system, II, 299, 302 f., 429 f., 431; legislation against *Shema'*, VII, 95; Magi, II, 181, 183, 190, 317, 347; medical literature, VIII, 235 f.; polygamy and incest, II, 226, 229; rank and titles of officials, II, 196, 403; religious beliefs and policy, II, 173, 213, VI, 3; religious controversies, V, 106; Rome and, II, 176 ff., 213, 396 ff.; rule by religious fanatics, II, 213; Samaritan refugees in, III, 255; status of minority groups, III, 54 ff., 120, 254 ff.; tax system, II, 180, 184 ff.; *see also* Babylonia; Exilarchs and exilarchate; Lakhmids; Parsees and Parsiism; Parthia; Sassanians; Zoroaster; Zoroastrianism

—— under Islam: autonomy of local usages, VI, 126; and the *catholicos,* III, 89; dualism in, V, 104; expansion of Jewry in, III, 109; inquiries to geonim, VI, 113; Jewish traders in, IV, 174; Karaites, V, 397 f.; messianic movement, III, 204, V, 203 f.; poetry and music, VII, 318; reading of *haf-ṭarah,* VI, 42; reversal of policy toward Jews, III, 239; sectarianism, III, 57, V, 183 ff.; taxation system, III, 162, 255; traveler's report of population, VI, 224; *see also under* cities, *e.g.,* Isfahan

Persian language, II, 146, 147; classical forms vs. dialects, VII, 5; talmudic loan words, II, 206, 405, VII, 141; translation of Bible into, VI, 271

Perso-Byzantine wars, III, 17, 18 ff., 74 f.; and the Caliphate, III, 86 ff.; Jewish participation, III, 18-24, 57, 236-40, VIII, 235; Samaritans and, III, 17 f., 235 f., V, 170 f.

Personality, inner conflicts, I, 21

"Personality principle," II, 265

Perushim, the, II, 342, 343; *see also* Pharisees and Pharisaism

Pesaḥ, I, 5; *see also* Passover

Pesaḥ, Khazar commander, III, 203

Pesaḥim, tractate, VI, 86, 382

Pescennius Niger, I, 263, II, 400

Pesher, commentary, VI, 158

Peshiṭṭa: canonical Syriac, VII, 4; origin of, II, 386 f., VI, 257, 454 f.; textual exactitude, VI, 241; *see also* Aramaic language; Syriac language

Pesiqta de-R. Kahana, VI, 162

Pesiqta rabbati, midrash, VI, 165, VII, 130, 182

Pesiqta zuṭrata, VI, 175

Petaḥiah b. Jacob of Ratisbon, Jewish traveler, VII, 129; chronological framework of journey, VI, 437; on Jewish communities in Byzantium, III, 195;

Jewish population, III, 104, 113; on Khazaria, III, 201 f.; messianic computation, VIII, 47 f.; travels, VI, 222-26, 435-37
Petcherskii Monastery, III, 215
Peter, Saint, II, 70, 71, 82; crucifixion and burial, II, 74, 361; Epistles, II, 74, 362; espouses nomistic Judeo-Christianity, II, 74 f., 361; Hebrew prayers ascribed to, II, 74 f., VII, 92; identification with Cephas and others, II, 74 f., 361
Peter the Hermit, IV, 98; bridge over the Danube, IV, 107
Peter the Venerable of Cluny, V, 116, 341; on "Alphabet of Ben Sira," VI, 169; antisemitism, IV, 122, 301 f.; on Jews and farm labor, IV, 155
Petra, III, 61
Petronius, and Caligula's statue, I, 219, 231
Petrus II (Candiano), doge: antisemitism, IV, 25
Petrus Alphonsi (Pedro Alfonsi; formerly Moses Sefardi), Christian convert and scientist, V, 115 f., VIII, 173 f.; on the attributes of God, V, 345; on Jesus' word on the cross, V, 120
Phanagoria (Sennaja), III, 202
Pharaohs: and the *Apiru* (Hebrew), I, 38, 56; *see also under* individual names, *e.g.*, Akhenaton
Pharisees and Pharisaism, I, 142, 166, 226, 234-38, II, 35-54, 342-50, V, 250, 255; Christians and, II, 70 f., 75, 343; contemporary sects, II, 46-54, 346-50; democratic trends, I, 175; doctrines elaborated, I, 221, 226, 237, II, 38, 308 f., 310-14, 320, 344 f., 434; educational system, II, 46, 274; and enslavement of Jews, I, 267; and era of Creation, VIII, 208; Essenes, II, 48-51, 342; expansive and popular force, II, 36, 344; and government, I, 216, 223, 237, 401, II, 56, 117; influence on Islam, VI, 8; Jesus' denunciation of, I, 173, II, 67, 336, 356; Mishnah a legal code of, II, 44, *see also* Mishnah; Talmud; name, II, 35, 342; number, II, 36, 342; priestly revenues, I, 272, 280; and proselytism, I, 181; and rebellions against Rome, II, 90, 100 f.; ritualistic implements displayed, II, 336; strengths and weaknesses, II, 56; struggle with Sadducees, I, 180, 234, 402, II, 35, 36, 38-46, 343 f.; subjection to law, I, 11; Zealotic faction, II, 47 f.
Phatir, III, 52
Philanthropia, Graeco-Roman, VIII, 263
Philanthropy, *see* Charity; Humanitarianism
Philip II (Philip Augustus), king of France, IV, 128 f.; expulsion of Jews, IV, 61, 80, 156, V, 78; "extradition" treaty with Count Thibaut, IV, 204; moneylending charter, IV, 204-6, 393; treaties re Jews, IV, 62 f., 204, 269 f.
Philipp, archbishop of Cologne, IV, 275
Philipp, eunuch, fraternization with Jews, IV, 21 f.
Philipp, landgrave, IV, 341
Philippopolis, Transjordan, II, 174, 175
Philip "the Arab," emperor, II, 174, 177
Philistines, I, 39, 53, 55; disarming of Israel, I, 60 f.; infiltration of Palestine, I, 63, 320; use of iron, I, 320
Philo Judaeus of Alexandria, I, 66, 177, 181, 199-207, 386-90, II, 8, 9, 55, 137, 198, 315, 391, 409, VIII, 85; apologetic interests, I, 391; on authenticity of biblical text, VI, 236 f.; definition of name "Israel," I, 182; delegate to Caligula, I, 241; description of Jewish congregations, VII, 125; doctrine of creation of time, VI, 469, VIII, 91; doctrine of intermediaries, V, 226; on Essenes, II, 49, 51, 347; exegesis, I, 202, 387, VI, 35; extra-Jewish sources of, I, 388; on Golden Age, I, 209; on imagery, II, 15; on immortality, I, 207, 390; on incest and intermarriage, II, 233; on Jewish expansion, I, 171; on law, I, 204, 387, II, 253, 280 f., 415, 418; on *logos,* II, 202, 389, V, 121; on marriage, II, 229; meaning of "father," II, 309; meaning of *philanthropia* transformed, II, 269; and Midrash, II, 320; monotheism and messianism, I, 208, 232 f., II, 5 f., 329; on Moses, I, 199; and natural law, VI, 144; on *nouveaux riches,* I, 266; on Palestine's historic importance, I, 392; Paul's indebtedness to, II, 85; and Pharisaism, I, 206, II, 36, 56, VII, 80; on pilgrimages, I, 214; quoted, I, 200, 203, 205, II, 152; on sabbatical year,

Philo Judaeus of Alexandria (*Continued*) II, 271; static philosophy, I, 205 f., VIII, 76; on status of Jews in Alexandria, I, 403; survival of doctrines and concepts, II, 206 f., V, 188, VI, 410, VIII, 4; symbolism, II, 13; use of Greek, I, 186; views on prophecy, VIII, 344; on women, II, 241, 413; writings, I, 201, 387, V, 216, 380

Philology: Arabic, VII, 9 f., 15, 19, 234; analogistic and anomalistic approaches, VII, 34, 52, 58, 224 f.

—— Hebrew: acceptance of discoveries in, VII, 46 ff., 238 ff.; classifications, VII, 36; comparative linguistics, VII, 11 ff., 60; debates over, VII, 23, 46, 165; historical shortcomings, VII, 55 ff.; independent research, VII, 49; neglected in Babylonia, VII, 19; and poetry, VII, 211; schools of, VII, 21; Spanish, VII, 19-28, 41-46, 227-31, 236-38; talmudic, VI, 28

"Philomena," and Narbonne, IV, 46

Philosophy: Arab, VIII, 89 f.; German, I, 296

—— Greek: influence on Jewish thinkers, VIII, 55 ff.; letter symbolism, VIII 284; and Moses, I, 174; and reinterpretation of Jewish tradition, VIII, 76 f.; *see also under* individual philosophers, *e.g.*, Aristotle; Farabi

—— Jewish, VIII, 55-137, 296-346; commentaries on, VIII, 65 f.; dilemma of translators of, VII, 220; diverse elements in, VIII, 3 ff.; Ibn Daud's references to, IV, 218 f., VI, 209; and medieval thought, I, 206; messianic ideology, V, 159-66, 363-66; and music, VII, 207 f.; neglect of works of, VIII, 137; pietistic and nationalistic, VIII, 39; poets and, VII, 151, 171 f.; and prophecy, VIII, 127-35, 342-45; rationalistic, I, 201; and science, VIII, 222 ff.; speculation vs. revelation, VIII, 85; subservience to religion, VIII, 81; written in Arabic, VII, 8; *see also under* individual philosophers, *e.g.*, Moses b. Maimon; Philo Judaeus; Saadiah Gaon

Philo the Elder, I, 198, 386, II, 31, 341; epic on biblical themes, VII, 167

Phineas, I, 38; longevity, VIII, 211

Phineas, head of Rabbanite academy of Jerusalem, VI, 245

Phinehas b. Meshullam of Alexandria, VI, 380; and Maimonides, VI, 98

Phocylides, I, 184

Phoenicia and Phoenicians, I, 55; and Canaanites, III, 91; circumcision, I, 6; colonies, I, 39, 175; conversion to Judaism, I, 176, 374; expeditions in Far East and Africa, III, 116; relations with Palestine, I, 61, 306; religion, I, 374

Phokas, Byzantine emperor, III, 16; outlawry of Judaism, III, 19, 237

Phonetics, Hebrew, VI, 242; masoretic development of, VI, 249 ff.

Photius, patriarch, III, 181; commendation of Cyril, III, 210

Phrygia, I, 216

Phylacteries, II, 189, 335 f., V, 59, 122, 215, 218; manual of laws on, VI, 65, 93, 475, VII, 21; Qumran, VII, 244

Physical education, II, 421

Physicians, I, 275; *dhimmis,* Muslim attitude toward, III, 152, V, 96 f., VIII, 254; Muslim, status of, VIII, 237, 398

—— Jewish, II, 185; access to medical literature, VIII, 235 f.; all-round knowledge of patient, VIII, 260; canon law on treatment by, III, 175, 194; charity practice, VIII, 258; to Christian lord, IV, 113 f.; court, IV, 37, 253, VIII, 232 ff., 246, 248 f., 255; ethics of, VIII, 234, 238; fees, VIII, 254 f.; Hippocratic oath, VIII, 238, 242; humility of, VIII, 391; interfaith cooperation in medical studies, VIII, 265; musical therapy, VII, 208 f.; number of, VIII, 255, 389 f.; professionalization of, VIII, 232 ff.; training, VIII, 221 f., 255; *see also* Surgeons and surgery; *also under* individual physicians, *e.g.*, Asaph Judaeus; Moses b. Maimon

Physics: definition, VIII, 145; interest of philosophers, VIII, 222 f.; as a science, VIII, 142

Piast dynasty, Poland, III, 217

Pierleoni, Peter, *see* Anacletus II

Pierre de Lubières, archbishop, IV, 58

Pietism: Jewish compared with Christian, VIII, 48 ff., 295; heterogeneous elements in, VIII, 45 f.; Italo-German, VII, 175-83, 205, 303-7, VIII, 14, 32 f., 42-50, 293-95; on medical interference with God's will, VIII, 231 ff.; *see also* Ḥasidism

Pigeon-fanciers, I, 254; disapproval of, I, 275
Pig symbol, II, 152; "in Zion," VII, 97
Pilgrimages: and geographic knowledge, VIII, 211; leap year and, VIII, 376; to Mecca, III, 88, 302, VIII, 211; to Medina, III, 88; to Palestine, I, 213 f., 258, 392, II, 108, 118, 374, IV, 94 f., 131, 283, 284 f.
Pinḥas, Palestinian poet, VII, 268
Pinḥas b. Yair, R., VI, 410
Pioneers: Jews as, III, 222, IV, 161, V, 62, 319, VIII, 159; in Khazaria, III, 197
"Pious, Book of the," VI, 404; on care of the sick poor, VIII, 258, 265; on medical fees, VIII, 233; on preventive medicine, VIII, 261; *see also* Pietism
Pi-Ra'amses (House of Raamses), I, 38
Pirates, I, 256, 407; capture of slaves by, IV, 192; raids on shipping, IV, 184; ransom from, IV, 177 f.; scholars captured by, V, 46 f.
Pirqe de-R. Eliezer, II, 296, III, 163, VI, 168, 170, VII, 66, VIII, 147; on calendar proclamations, VIII, 194; on chronological problems, VI, 307; cycle of 84 years, VIII, 191
Pirqoi b. Baboi, V, 181, 282 f., VI, 22, 65, 81, 253; on liturgical deviations, VII, 65; on Palestinian scrolls, VII, 286; on *piyyuṭim,* VII, 103, 125; on Yehudai, VI, 79; on religious restrictions of Jews, VII, 84, 95
Pisa, Italy, IV, 26
Pishon, river, III, 116, VI, 266, 281
Piyyuṭim, V, 151, 249, VII, 63 ff., 89-105, 259-71; acceptance of, VII, 100 ff., 132 f.; in Aramaic, VII, 192 f.; on attributes of God, VII, 178; debt of Spanish poets to, VII, 270; German mysticism in, VIII, 44; imitations, VII, 104; improvisations, VII, 82 f., 86, 143, 255; language of, VII, 103 f.; melodies for, VII, 125 f.; opposition to, VII, 100 ff., 149; popularity of, VII, 269; posttalmudic, VII, 57; refrains, VII, 127 f.; *see also* Liturgy; Poetry
Place names: biblical, VI, 211; Hebrew transliteration of, VI, 223; identification of, VI, 266, 281; Jewish, in France and Poland, III, 218, 251, 338; talmudic, VII, 14
Placitum, term, III, 42, 249
Plagiarism, VII, 299, 308; by translators, VII, 312
Planets: comparative sizes, VIII, 162 ff., 360; conjunctions of, VIII, 180 f.; distances from earth, VIII, 184; position of, VIII, 164
Plantations, I, 252
Plants: identification of biblical, VI, 474; life cycles of, V, 246; names of, VIII, 253; poisonous, VIII, 258
Plato, I, 174, 199, II, 4, 6, 157, VIII, 57, 61; *Laws,* VIII, 61; legendary meeting with Jeremiah, VIII, 320; on negative attributes of God, VIII, 98; neoplatonism (*q.v.*), V, 381 f.; *Republic,* VIII, 61; Semitic pronunciation of name, VI, 449; social ideal, I, 295; superiority of Torah, VI, 142
Plato of Tivoli, VIII, 148; collaboration with Bar Ḥiyya, VIII, 266; translation by, VIII, 155
Pledges, laws of, VI, 68 f.
Pleonasms, in mystic writings, VIII, 14
Pliny the Elder, I, 210, 250, 251, 252, II, 5; *Natural History,* VIII, 253; quoted, II, 49, 151
Plotinus: method employed by, II, 320; theory of emanations, VIII, 91 ff.
Plural forms, interpretation of biblical, V, 120
Plutarch, I, 251, II, 24; ignorance of Jewish customs, II, 390
Pneumatikoi (spiritualists), II, 85, 365
Pococke, Edward, VI, 60
Poetry: Egyptian, VIII, 325; Greek, VII, 314; non-Hebraic by Jews, VII, 190 ff.; Syriac, VII, 203
—— Arabic: biblical reflection of, VII, 201 f.; homosexuality as theme, VII, 158 ff.; influence of, VIII, 325; quest for innovation, VII, 142; written by Jews, VII, 191 ff.
—— Jewish, IV, 38, 216, VII, 89-105, 140-83, 259-71, 288-307; acrostics, VII, 14; "adornments," VII, 197 f., 201 f.; antipathy of jurists to, VII, 149; in Arabia, III, 72, VII, 191 f.; art of, VII, 193-202, 313-18; astronomic themes, VIII, 168 f.; biblical influences, III, 261, VI, 292, VII, 201 f., 316; chain verse, VII, 179 f., 306, 316; chastity of, VII, 212; decline in the East, VII, 47; development in Spain, VI, 188, 255, VII, 146-75, 291-303; didactic, VII, 192;

Poetry (*Continued*)
distinction between sacred and secular, VII, 98 f.; figures of speech, VII, 198; lines reading backward and forward, VII, 151, 185, 197 f.; linguistic devices, VII, 34, 57 ff., 199 ff.; and martyrs, VI, 218; meter in, VII, 22, 41, 194 ff., 313 ff.; names of Palestinian poets, VII, 259; praise of great leaders, VII, 147 f.; priestly poets, VII, 90 f.; rhymed, VII, 88 ff., 261; in Rome, IV, 238; Saadiah's book of grammatical rules, VII, 15; secular themes, VII, 155-69, 296-300; of self-praise, VII, 153, 292; theme of national history, VII, 166 ff., 211, 300; use of, for teaching grammar, VII, 49 f.; of vengeance, IV, 143 f.; vocalized, VI, 260; Zionide elegies, V, 260, VII, 168 f., 298 f.

—— liturgical, III, 233, V, 362, 376 f., VI, 44, 92, 263, 372, 424, VII, 89-105, 169-83, 260-71, 300-307; Arabic meter, VII, 195; Aramaic versions, VI, 263; *Ashirah ve-azamrah,* VII, 182; background, VIII, 30; biblical themes, VII, 134, 167 f.; Christian, VII, 84; composed by synagogue readers, VII, 58; distinguished from secular, VII, 143; effect of music, VII, 209; Franco-German, IV, 309, VII, 144 f.; imitators, VII, 268; improvisations, VII, 82 ff.; individualistic, VII, 132 f.; innovations in terms and forms, VII, 40; as link among communities, VII, 144 f.; on martyred English Jews, IV, 124; and messianism, V, 150 ff.; mystical, VII, 252, VIII, 12 ff.; penitential, IV, 93, 106, 138, 145, 286 f., VII, 145, 170, 173, 179 f.; *qerobot,* VII, 66 f., 318; *Sefer Qerobah,* VII, 202, 318; *seliḥot,* VII, 99; *see also Piyyuṭim*

Pogroms: Alexandrian, I, 191, II, 189; catastrophic results, I, 266; *see also* Massacres of Jews

Poitiers, battles of, III, 91

Poland: Jewish communities, III, 206, 217 ff., 338, VII, 178; leader of Slavonic tribes, III, 217; secular Jewish nationalism in, I, 29

Polemics: anti-Jewish in Christian liturgy, VII, 85; religious, V, 83 ff.; *see also* Controversies, socioreligious

Political conditions: moneylending and, IV, 82; and Palestino-Babylonian struggle for communal control, V, 47 ff.

Political power, I, 116, 164, 192; emancipation of nationality and religion from, I, 22, 237; Israelites' weakness vs. democracy, I, 325; lack of, rationalized, I, 23; prophets' deprecation of, I, 96; *see also* Civil rights; Self-government

Political reverses following Judeo-Roman conflicts, II, 102-8, 110

Political rights, IV, 7 ff., 69

Political science, VIII, 144; Arab contributions, VIII, 122

"Political Zionism," I, 28

Politics: Jewish influence on, under the Caliphate, III, 154; and literary talent, VII, 147, 149; liturgical allusions to, VII, 97; participation in by Kievan Jews, III, 216

Polybius, I, 229, 248

Polycarp, Saint, II, 167, 394

Poll tax (*gulgolet, jizya, kephaleiton*), I, 240, 242, II, 373, 375, 399, III, 96, 163 f., 170, 191 f., IV, 151 f., V, 18; in Arabia, III, 80; *aurum coronarium,* III, 191; collection of, V, 5; and estimates of Jewish population, III, 113; exemption from, III, 113, V, 76; in Fez, III, 263; humiliation, III, 167; in Muslim Babylonia, III, 99, 191; and residence permits, V, 69; in Sicily, IV, 23; *see also* Taxation

Polygamy, I, 112, 347, II, 223, 410; Christian Rome's opposition, II, 226; 231; legal theory, II, 227; outlawed, VI, 135 ff., 393 f.; *see also* Monogamy

Polytheism, I, 45, 202, 352; assailed, I, 177, VI, 298; monarchical, I, 44, 312

Pomegranate, I, 253

Pompeii, II, 332

Pompey, Roman general, I, 167, II, 13, 103; occupation of Palestine, I, 223, 237, II, 27

Pontius Pilate, I, 238, 368; cruelty to Samaritans, II, 33; Jesus' trial before, II, 70, 72

Poor, the: charity and social welfare, II, 269 ff., 420, V, 37, 414; communal responsibility, V, 178, VIII, 295; funerals of, II, 287; landless, I, 68; medical care, VIII, 258, 391; Rabbanites and, V, 178, 238; standard of living, V, 239; terms for, II, 269; tithe for, V, 235; a

title of distinction, I, 152; troubled by need to disregard laws, II, 77; *see also* Charity; Poverty; Slaves and slavery
Pope, *see* Papacy
Population: ancient: biological balance, I, 156, 171-79, 373-75, II, 219, 238, 408; Christian and Jewish ratios, II, 163, 165 f., 393; decrease in Jewish, II, 210, 243; Israelitic, I, 64, 320; numerical and geographical expansion, I, 167-71, 369-72; of Roman Empire, II, 183, 209, III, 283 f.; urban and rural, I, 276
—— medieval: of Byzantine Empire, III, 195, 322 f.; under the Caliphate, III, 99 ff., 113 f., 293; in England, IV, 277; increase in, IV, 70 f.; Persia, III, 110; reports of travelers, VI, 224; of Rome, IV, 240; *see also* specific countries and cities
Pork, consumption of, III, 43, V, 131, VI, 14
Porphyry, Bible critic, II, 158 f., 391, 401
Portugal: Crusaders in, IV, 132; Jews of, IV, 35; Judeo-Christian relations, III, 160
Poseidonius, I, 194, II, 5, 188, 400
Post mortem examination, VIII, 230
Pothos, son of Straton of Gorgippia, III, 200
Potiphar, and his daughter Asenath, VI, 170
Pottery, I, 320, 326
Poverty, I, 262 ff.; Babylonia's wealth and, II, 247; extremes leveled, II, 242; and learning, II, 256; varied attitudes toward, II, 46; *see also* Poor, the
Power: attitude toward, I, 22, V, 101; Jewry's lack of, V, 176, 194; political, effect of, V, 72 ff.
Praeparatio evangelica, III, 221; *see also* Eusebius of Caesarea
Prague, III, 217, 218; admission of Jews to, IV, 274 f.; forced conversion of Jews, IV, 100; transferral of holdings by Jews of, IV, 118; visited by Jewish traders, VI, 222
Prayer books, V, 26, 28, VII, 63 ff., 105-18, 271-78; attributed to Rashi, VI, 75; Karaite, V, 248, 408; nucleus in Naṭronai's responsum on benedictions, VII, 110; oral transmission, VII, 85 ff.; printed, VII, 81; Saadiah's, V, 31, VI, 15, 69, 92; scarcity and high cost of, VII, 123 f.; Ṣemaḥ, V, 248; Sephardim, VI, 15; *see also* Amram; Saadiah Gaon
Prayers, I, 186, 379, II, 146; against heretics, II, 135, 381; antiquity of, VII, 65; Arabic, VII, 101; Aramaic, VI, 453 f., VII, 192, 244 f.; avoidance of controversial subjects, V, 151; basic, VII, 79, 105 f., 112, 131 f.; composed by synagogue readers, VII, 58; concentration on meaning, VII, 74, 128, VIII, 14; daily, VII, 245; deviations from talmudic practices, V, 59; for economic betterment, II, 256; enumeration of commandments, VI, 92; forbidden, V, 26, 302 f.; freedom to recite in any language, VII, 66; geonim on, VI, 43 f.; *Habdalah,* V, 153, 155; *Hallel,* VII, 69; improvisation, VII, 82 f., 86, 143, 255; influence on heavenly intermediaries, VII, 76 f.; interruption of, II, 286, 423, V, 66 f., 321; Karaites and, V, 248; *Kol Nidre,* VI, 389; of laudation, VII, 131; loud-voiced, VII, 74 f.; memorization of, VII, 85 ff., 124, 257 f.; Mishawayh's injunctions on, V, 196; music and, VII, 125-31, 207, 281-85; in Muslim practice, III, 266, VI, 13 f.; for Ninth of Ab, II, 112, 375; order of, VII, 106; orientation toward Jerusalem, I, 213, 392, III, 81, VII, 78, VIII, 211; penitential, VII, 178; of petition, VII, 70, 74, 86 f., 114, 120, 140 f.; posture, I, 351, VII, 74 ff., 141, VIII, 3; private, VII, 72, 108; *pro perfidis Judaeis,* II, 169, 395, V, 351 f.; proselytes', I, 182; prostration in, VII, 74 f.; from the Psalms, VII, 44; public recitation, II, 7, 134, 281; *qaddish,* II, 84, 146, V, 59; for rain, II, 40, 345, 349; regulations concerning, I, 376, II, 119 f., 138, 282, VI, 69, VII, 84, 133; for ruler, I, 130, 245, 404, V, 293; and sacrifices, I, 123 f., 350; for "the scholars of Babylonia," V, 25; "secret lore" in, VII, 64; silent, VII, 248; of Simon b. Yoḥai, III, 274, IV, 296, V, 353; standardization, II, 119, 377; and study, VII, 143; of thanksgiving, VII, 109; tunes for, VII, 127; variations in local customs, VI, 122, 125 f.; *Yigdal,* VII, 175; *Yismaḥ Mosheh,* VI, 327; *see also* Liturgy; *Piyyuṭim;* Poetry;

Prayers (*Continued*)
Ritual; *and under* individual prayers, *e.g., 'Alenu; Azharot*
Preachers: invention of detail, VI, 170 f.; itinerant, VI, 156; rabbis as, VI, 155 ff.; *see also* Homilists and homiletics; Sermons
Precentor, *see* Cantor
Precious stones, medicinal value of, VIII, 225
Predestination, II, 41, VIII, 108 ff., 333 ff.; and life span, VIII, 259; *see also* Free will
Predicables, list of, VIII, 329
Predictions, astrological, VIII, 179 f.; according to astronomic doctrines, VIII, 181 f.; *see also* Prophets and prophecy
Preemption, houseowner's right of, III, 145 f.
Preexistent things, VIII, 125 f.; talmudic enumeration of, V, 147
"Prefect, Book of the," IV, 170, 183, 321 f.
Pregnancy, intercourse prohibited during, II, 221
Premonstratensians, V, 112 f.
Přemysl Ottokar II, king of Bohemia, IV, 137
Presbyter or episcopus: office of English Jewry, V, 63; women as, II, 240
Prester John, III, 205, VI, 434
Preventive medicine, VIII, 261
Prices: and calendar cycles, VIII, 209, 361; gyrations of, II, 247, 414; just, II, 254 f., 416, IV, 222 f.; regulation of, I, 85, II, 261, 417
Priest cities, I, 146, 360
Priestesses, Vestal, I, 146
Priestly Code, I, 111, 142, 150, 156, 359, II, 308; *see also* Leviticus, Book of
Priestly dynasty, founder of, in Jerusalem, I, 330
Priests and priesthood: Egyptian, I, 149, II, 107; Muslim, VI, 9 f.; Persian, II, 317; *see also* Magi
—— Jewish: anointment of, I, 152, 364, 414; aristocracy, I, 149, 272, 274; authority of, I, 74, 76, 81, 140, 149 ff., 153, 271, 281, II, 117; chain of ordination, V, 36; cleavage, I, 273; coinage right in Jerusalem, I, 130, 166, 353; continuity of, after the fall of Jerusalem, VII, 259; and continuity of law, I, 82; culture and character, I, 154; custodians of Scripture, VI, 236; gifts to, VI, 69; high-priestly office, I, 216, 271, 273, 393, 414; and house of David, VI, 215; Karaite, V, 235 f.; *ha-kohen ha-levi,* V, 174; learning and educational opportunities, II, 117, 120 f.; in Leontopolis, I, 219 f.; marriage, II, 234, V, 18, 240; as masons and carpenters, I, 258; and Mosaic religion, I, 59; nation of, I, 163, VII, 80, 125; numbers of, in Palestine, I, 272, 413; Pharisees, I, 237, II, 45 f., 52, 117; poets among, VII, 90 f.; priestly blessing and other rituals, II, 119; and prophets, I, 149 ff., 365; relations with levites, I, 329, 362, 413; resisted conversion to other creeds, I, 414; ritualistic segregation, I, 149, II, 282; Samaritan, V, 173 f.; as state officers, I, 229; tax exemption, II, 413; tithes and dues paid to, I, 130, 272, 280, 413, II, 105, 118, *see also* Tithes; titles conferred at ordination, II, 120; vestments, I, 239, II, 284, VII, 145; the Wicked Priest, II, 53 f., 349; *see also Kohen and Kohanim;* Levites; Rabbis and rabbinate
—— *see also* Clergy
Prime Cause, VIII, 110
Primum mobile, VIII, 164 f.
Princes, and Jewish property, IV, 15 f.
Princes of captivity, *see* Exilarchs and exilarchate
Printing presses, Hebrew, VI, 279
Priscus, court jeweler, III, 52; debate with Gregory of Tours, V, 114
Prison, Jewish, V, 43
Prisoners of war, I, 95, 259, 325; as slaves, II, 258; treatment of, III, 150
Private ownership, *see under* Property
Privileges: to cities, IV, 23, 35 f., 38, 42, 67 f., 71 f.; to Jews, I, 240 ff., IV, 78 f., 164, 170, 205, V, 62, 324; to merchants, IV, 48, 179, 182; monastic, IV, 65; payment for, IV, 142 f.
Prochownik, Abraham, alleged Polish king, III, 217
Proclus, VIII, 57, 61
Procopius, II, 142, 179, 393, III, 7; on Iberians, III, 22; and portentous disasters, III, 16; on the Samaritans, V, 367 f.
Procreation: duty of, I, 31, II, 210, 218, 219, V, 134

Procurators, *see* Roman Empire
Produce: agricultural, and taxes, IV, 151 f.; and tithes, IV, 314
Produit de Juifs, department in French Treasury, IV, 62
Professions, IV, 197 ff., 215 f.; specialization, VIII, 160
Profiat Duran, *see* Duran, Profiat
Profits, II, 255, 416
Pro (perfidis) Judaeis, prayer, II, 169, 395, V, 351 f.
Proletariat: free, I, 324; landless, I, 76; urban Jewish, I, 281
"Promised land," I, 42, 46
Promotus, Jewish convert to Christianity, V, 126
Pronunciation, Hebrew: changes in, VI, 240; difference between Karaites and Rabbanites, VI, 247 f.; double, VI, 450 f.; and meaning, VI, 443; regional variations, VI, 239, VII, 28; "Sephardic," VIII, 233; and spelling, VI, 243 f., 293; system, VI, 259 f.; of transliterations, VI, 248
Propaganda, anti-Jewish: I, 188, 192, IV, 133 ff.; *see also* Antisemitism
—— Christian, VIII, 48, 177 f.; *see also* Converts and conversion
—— Jewish religious, I, 172 ff., 272, 274, 372, 375; and attitude toward converts, II, 147 ff.; economic and social forces, I, 174; Christian fears of, IV, 9; Gentile reaction, I, 209, 246; *see also* Proselytes and proselytism
—— political: court poets and, VII, 147
Propedeutics, VIII, 142
Property: accumulation by small minority, I, 68; acquisition by Jews, IV, 42, 116 f.; attitude of princes toward Jewish, IV, 15 f., 50; Church, IV, 204 f.; communal, V, 18; confiscation of, III, 45 f., 169, 193, IV, 13, 34, 82, 156; damage or destruction prohibited, II, 254; debts collectible from, VI, 132; of *dhimmis,* III, 143 f., 146; disposal of, IV, 79, 203 f., V, 320; interfaith, III, 301 f.; legal protection for women's, II, 236, 412; mortgages, II, 303, VI, 83; private ownership vs. communal control, I, 89, II, 252, 415, IV, 221 f., 351; registration of, IV, 83; sales and leases to Gentiles, II, 124 f., 261; seizure of debtor's, II, 303; tax, IV, 81; and the tithe, IV, 13; transfer of, IV, 22, 59f., VI, 358; 'Umar I re captured lands, III, 95 f.; urban, IV, 161; *see also* Houses; Land
"Property of iron sheep," II, 236, 412
Prophets and prophecy, I, 22, 84-91, 104, 153, 197, 199, 339; activities, I, 87 ff.; addressed to Gentile nations, VI, 280 f.; 'Anan's attitude toward, V, 212; applied to contemporary events, VI, 308 ff.; attempts to punish, I, 78; bands of, I, 153; biblical, V, 86 ff., 140, VI, 228 ff., 310; cessation of, I, 152, 364, II, 139, VI, 230; on "day-star," V, 132; degrees in, VIII, 132, 344; on deliverance from Egypt, I, 16; enumeration of, VI, 197; false or true, I, 87, 333; gift of prophecy, VI, 228 f., VIII, 125; grasped meaning of abnormal situation, I, 98; individual aspirations, V, 198; interfaith recognition, V, 186; interpretation, V, 150 ff., 175; and kings, I, 63-101, 320-40; and laws, I, 82, II, 319, 436; and massacres by Crusaders, IV, 110; messages of, and historic tact, VI, 234; messianic, I, 98, 339, II, 68, V, 117 ff., 165 f., 200; and miracles, VIII, 28; Mohammed and, V, 90; Muslim doctrine of transmission, V, 21; opposition to imagery, I, 335; philosophic argument for, VIII, 127-35, 342-45; qualifications of, VIII, 131 f.; radical concepts of survival, I, 90; rank of, VIII, 132; return of prophetic gift to Israel, V, 384; revelation through, VIII, 85; role in theological debates, V, 86 ff., VIII, 28; and sages, chronology of, VI, 202; sectarian recognition of, V, 192; silenced, I, 79; social ideals, I, 84-91, 295, 332-36; supernatural death of, I, 339; tombs, II, 286, 423, III, 136; transmission of gift, VIII, 134
—— books of: I, 345; in Aramaic, VI, 260; Cairo and Leningrad manuscripts, VI, 245, 253, 446; *haftarot,* VI, 41, 244; philological notes on, VII, 23, 43; number of verses, VIII, 149; as source of Jewish law, VI, 244; textual transmission, VI, 237
Prosbol, II, 262, 302, 304, 417, IV, 200, VIII, 209
Prose, rhymed, VII, 201 f.
Proselytes and proselytism, I, 172 ff., 179 ff., 283, 373, 375, 376, 382, II, 147-

Proselytes and proselytism (*Continued*) 50, 387 f., III, 46, 110 f., 118 f., 178, 215, IV, 9, V, 112, 135 f.; Christian, III, 52, 65 f., IV, 54 ff., V, 111, 112 f.; descendants of, I, 274; differing attitudes toward, I, 180; Egyptian, I, 190; effect upon Jewish thought, II, 150; female, II, 233; Jewish-Gentile relations affected, II, 148; Karaite, V, 267-75, 411-14; legal fiction about, II, 231; Muslim, III, 94, V, 89; place in social scale, II, 234; and public office, I, 243; semiproselytes, I, 415, II, 149; treatment, I, 181, 203, II, 282 f.; tests of genuine conversion, II, 149, 388; *see also* Converts and Conversions; Propaganda
Proselytos, I, 155, 177, 375
Prostitute: children of, II, 218; definition of, V, 240
Prostitution, religious, I, 405
Protection, royal, IV, 35 f., 40 f., 60, 66, 70 ff., 79, 80 f.; Carolingian charters, IV, 48 f.; of cities, IV, 60 f.; ecclesiastical vs., IV, 73 f., 98 ff.; of merchants, IV, 185; of minorities (*q.v.*), III, 120-72, IV, 42, 86, 185; *see also* Privileges; Rights, legal
Protective intermediaries, *see* Intermediaries
Proto-Sinaitic inscriptions, I, 35
Provence, V, 61, VI, 280; anti-Maimonidean controversy, VIII, 68; bridge between east and west, VIII, 229; court poets, VII, 146, 151; dialects, VII, 20, VIII, 229, 386; reception of Bar Ḥiyya's works, VIII, 361; scholars, VI, 468, VIII, 55, *see also under* individual scholars, *e.g.*, Abraham b. David; schools of Gershom (*q.v.*) and Rashi (*q.v.*), VI, 87 f.; sectarianism in, IV, 132, VIII, 32
Proverbs, Aramaic, in northern Iraq, VII, 220
Proverbs, Book of, VII, 163, 164 f.; authorship, VI, 160, 308; commentaries on, VI, 285, 289 f.; individualistic tinge, I, 357; priestly influence, I, 150; reconciliation of nationalism and universalism, I, 158; Saadiah's Arabic translation, VI, 268; use in sermons, VI, 167; *see also* Wisdom
Przemyśl, Poland, III, 219
Psalmody, *see* Singing
Psalms, biblical, I, 123, 340, 362; attribution of authorship, I, 322, VI, 307 f., 310; in Canaanite ritual, I, 350; commentaries on, VI, 288, 310, VII, 38; effect of mispronunciation on meaning, VI, 443; individualistic tinge, I, 357; king's, I, 130; Leningrad manuscripts, VI, 288, 472; liturgical use, I, 363, VII, 41, 69 ff., 247 f.; messianic, I, 339; number of verses, VI, 238; pre-exilic, I, 340; Psalm 2, V, 157, 239 f.; Psalm 90, VIII, 126; Psalm 91, VII, 282 f.; Psalm 139, VIII, 78; recited to music, I, 150; VII, 129, 203, 320; symbols for cantillation of, VII, 126; texts of, III, 265; translations, VI, 273; Zionist aspirations, VII, 247; *see also* Wisdom
Psammetichus I or II, I, 110, 346
Pseudepigrapha, I, 385, II, 145; contribution to mysticism, VIII, 5; messianic speculation, V, 139; preserved in Slavonic translations, III, 211; *see also* Apocrypha
Pseudo-Baḥya: eschatological punishments, VIII, 105; "Investigation of the Soul," VI, 478 f., VIII, 303; reference to Ḥivi, VI, 302
Pseudo-Clement, II, 166, 393
Pseudo-Dionysius of Tell-Maḥre, III, 237; tale about Severus, V, 193
Pseudo-Empedocles, VIII, 324
Pseudo-Eupolemus, II, 16, 31, 334
Pseudo-Ezekiel, *see* Ezekiel
"Pseudo-Isidorian Decretals," IV, 241
Pseudo-Jonathan, II, 346; as commentary, VI, 457; *see also* Targum Jonathan
Pseudo-Philo, VI, 196 f., 421 f.
Pseudo-Saadiah: Commentary on Canticles, VI, 157, 362; Commentary on *Yeṣirah,* VIII, 45, 95, 326
Pseudo-Scylax, I, 367
Psyche, Greek term, II, 14
Ptolemais (Acre), I, 190, 225
Ptolemies, dynasty, I, 224; Jewish supporters, I, 190; religious exemption granted to Jews, I, 244
Ptolemy I (Ptolemy Soter), king of Egypt, I, 172, II, 34
Ptolemy III (Ptolemy Euergetes), king of Egypt, II, 331
Ptolemy IV (Ptolemy Philopator), king of Egypt, I, 244

Ptolemy VI (Ptolemy Philometor), king of Egypt, I, 196, 220, II, 34
Ptolemy VIII (Ptolemy Lathyrus), king of Egypt, I, 215
Ptolemy (Claudius Ptolemaeus), VIII, 139, 187 f.; *Almagest,* VIII, 172; astronomical tables, VIII, 170; fractions of hour, VIII, 373; on humility, VIII, 340; system, VIII, 164 f.; *Tetrabiblos,* VIII, 178, 376
Publicans, I, 275, 279; status among Jews, II, 185
Public office: II, 186; Al-Muqtadir's decree re, VIII, 236; and art of literary composition, III, 156 f.; classes excluded from Jewish, V, 73 f.; and converts, III, 179 f., V, 74; corruption, V, 5, 178; effect of quest for, V, 72 ff.; honors and responsibilities, II, 201 ff.; Jews' participation, I, 243, II, 110, 180, 181, 375, III, 120, 150-61, 187 f., 213, 303-8, 319, V, 95 ff., 333 f., IV, 9 f., 19, 226 f.; judges and other court officials, II, 268 f., 419; local, V, 50; oath of fidelity and, II, 110, 375, IV, 49
Public opinion, appeals to in services, VI, 139
Public welfare, individual rights and, IV, 222
Public works, Jewish corvée labor on, IV, 56
Puento del Castro, Spain, IV, 33
Pufendorf, Johann, V, 229, 272
Pumbedita, academy, II, 207, III, 59, V, 13 ff., 24, 276; archives, VI, 112 f.; and Babylonian Talmud, VI, 17 f.; controversy with exilarchs, V, 10 ff., 15; and fasts, VI, 330; preeminence and decline, V, 18 f., 23 f.; Rab at, VI, 428; *see also* Pallughta
Punctuation: antiquity of, VII, 60; Babylonian system, VI, 241, 259; old Palestinian, VI, 249, 446; and pronunciation, VI, 239; system of Syriac Christians, VI, 241; Tiberian system, VI, 245, 253; *see also Masorah*
Punishments: after death, VIII, 47; geonic methods, V, 16 ff., 298 f.; inflicted on family of criminal, I, 136; mutilation, III, 186 f.; prayer for remission of, VII, 92; or rewards after death, I, 137, II, 31, 38, 40, 41; as seen by prophets, I, 90; sin and, I, 136; to uphold authority of courts, II, 267, 419; *see also* Capital punishment; Excommunication; Fines; Flogging
Purification rites, V, 173
Purim, I, 5, 169, 220, IV, 139, V, 214; charitable dues, VI, 139
Purity, in family life, I, 147, 149, 159; Karaite, V, 250; laws of, I, 147, VI, 60, 69; *see also* Ethnic unity
Puteoli (Dicaearchia), I, 261, 409
Pyrrhos, patriarch, III, 174
Pythagoras, I, 233; doctrine of numbers, VIII, 151; geometric theorem, VIII, 354 f.
Pythagoreans, and numerical principle, VIII, 284

Q

Qaddish, prayer, II, 84, 146, V, 59
Qadhi, VI, 9; *see also* Judges and judiciary
Qadosh, I, 358; *see also* Holiness
Qalir, Eleazar (Eliezer), R., liturgical poet, V, 151 f., VII, 40, 58, 82, 96-100, 263-66, VIII, 60; charged with linguistic errors, VII, 58, 104; cycle of jubilee years, VIII, 191 f.; derivation of name, VII, 96; on duration of world, VIII, 372; identity confused, VII, 104, 264 f.; improvisations for benedictions, VII, 86; influenced by mysticism, VII, 97, VIII, 12; legendary account of death of, VII, 270; liturgical poems, VII, 96 ff., 133, 263 ff.; *see also Piyyuṭim*
Qalon, term, V, 94
Qamḥi, *see* Qimḥi, David
Qara, Joseph, VI, 262; on the Aggadah, VI, 294
Qara, Simon, *Yalquṭ Shime'oni,* VI, 161 f., 404, VIII, 43 f., 50 f.
Qarafi, Aḥmad as-Sinhaji al-, Muslim controversialist, V, 119; list of scriptural passages, V, 329 f.; use of Christian Jew-baiting, V, 108 f., 346
Qarmatians, V, 103 f.; and messianic expectations, VI, 485; revolt, III, 88; and the "three imposters," VI, 301
Qaṭiyah, Sinai, III, 138
Qayyara, Simon, VI, 26, 174; *Halakhot gedolot,* VI, 77 f., 81 f., 91 f., 333, 339, 364 f., 372 f., VII, 278; Ḥefes' criticism of, VI, 374 f.; on intercourse with a slave girl, IV, 195; on liturgical problems, VII, 68, 110; and the Pales-

Qayyara, Simon (*Continued*)
tinian Talmud, VI, 22; reformulation of Jewish law, VI, 91 ff., 372 f.; on the *sefirah,* V, 283; six hundred and thirteen commandments, VII, 172
Qedushah, prayer, VII, 78
Qeṭina, R., VI, 45
Qiʿas, analogy, V, 213 f.
Qiddushin, tractate, VI, 98
Qimḥi (Qamḥi), David b. Joseph, V, 132, 159, VI, 280 f., 467 f.; on authorship of Psalms, VI, 307 f.; commentaries on Jeremiah and Isaiah, VI, 468 f.; commentary on Exodus, VI, 296; commentary on Hosea, VI, 289 f.; grammatical works, VII, 53 f., 241; lexicon, VII, 26; rationalist approach, VI, 467; translations into Romance dialects, VIII, 386
Qimḥi, Joseph b. Isaac, V, 128, 130; collaboration with his sons, VII, 53 f.; on family life, V, 134, VIII, 53; Ibn Ezra's influence on, VII, 52; on Jacob Tam, VII, 53; rating of the sciences, VIII, 143; *Sefer ha-Berit,* V, 111, 339; on the Torah, V, 349
Qimḥi, Moses, doctrine of paradigms of Hebrew verb, VII, 53, 241
Qirqisani, Abu Yusuf Yaʿqub, V, 232, VI, 244, VIII, 26; on ʿAnan and Karaism, V, 229 f., 254, 259 f., 387 f., 395 ff.; on anthropomorphism, VIII, 100; "Book of Lights," V, 398, VIII, 60, 130, 247; on Christianity, V, 118 f., 263; on circumcision, V, 215; debate with Jacob b. Ephraim, VII, 223 f.; defense of Judaism, V, 84; description of sects, V, 172 f., 182 f., 191, 206, 261 f., 380; exegetical propositions, VI, 36 f., 287; Ibn Daud vs., VI, 207; influenced by Saadiah, VI, 211, 460; on Jewish translators into Arabic, VI, 265; liturgical use of Psalms, VII, 70; on magic and divination, VIII, 28 f.; on Palestinian Hebrews, VII, 235; on prophets and miracles, VIII, 130; reference to mystical writings, VIII, 12; on Sabbath regulations, V, 244; on suicide, VI, 194; writings, V, 398
Quackery, medical, VIII, 233 ff., 237 f.
Quadratic equations, VIII, 158
Quakers, *see* Friends, Society of
Queen of Heaven, goddess, I, 104, 112, 311, 347; *see also* Astarte
Quietism, political, VIII, 109
Quinisext of 692, III, 175; *see also* Councils, Church
Quintillian, II, 368
Quirinius, census, I, 263, 410
Qumisi, Daniel b. Moses al-, Karaite Bible commentator, V, 185 f., 223, 228 f., 233, VII, 274, VIII, 26; on ʿAnan, V, 256 f.; condemnation of mystic writings, VIII, 12, 32, 283; exegetical works, VI, 276, 283 f.; on inheritance rights, V, 243; on mathematical calendar computations, VIII, 194 f.
Qumm, battle of, V, 193
Qumran sectarians, VI, 409, 442; *see also* Dead Sea Scrolls
Quraiẓa, tribe, III, 261
Qur'an, III, 263 ff., 268; alleged absence of contradictions, V, 87; attitude toward anthropomorphism, VIII, 114; on attributes of God, VIII, 96, 99; ban on retelling stories from, VII, 167, 180; and biblical predictions re Mohammed, V, 90; copy "written" by Abu'l Munajja, III, 155; "createdness" vs. preexistence of, VI, 307, VIII, 341; debates over, V, 83, 85 ff., 327 ff., VI, 236; 254; decrees on religious toleration, III, 124, 167, 169; exegesis of, VI, 165, 275, 282, 292, 471 f.; on the Greeks in Arabia, III, 75; *hamza* sign, VI, 250; Hebrew script, V, 329; on the Hereafter, V, 148, VIII, 105; and Isthmus of Suez, IV, 173; Judeo-Christian influences on, III, 80 ff., 265 ff., 269; language of, III, 81, VI, 460, VII, 4, 10, 220; as law, VI, 7 ff.; Mohammed and, VI, 8 f.; moneylending on copy of, IV, 340 f.; Muslim praise of, V, 87; praise of David, V, 7; *qalon* and *qolon,* V, 94, 410; relation to Bible, V, 83, 90; source of Jewish folk tales, VI, 187; standard text, VI, 242 f.; translations of, III, 263, VI, 11
Qurra, Theodore abu, V, 122
Qurra b. Sharik, Egyptian governor, III, 165 f.

R

Raamses II, king of Egypt, I, 37
Rab, title, II, 201
Rab (Abba Arikha), I, 175, 176, II, 21, 133, 190, 205, 315, 316, 417, 422, 424,

VI, 124, VII, 62; animosity to Persians, II, 176, 396; business advice, II, 260; on correct spelling, VII, 12; feats of piety, VII, 285; founder of Sura academy and synagogue, II, 207, VI, 24, 239, 428, VII, 108; grave of, VI, 436; improvised prayers, VII, 89; market supervisor, II, 254; marriage regulated by, II, 218; own marriages, II, 226, 239, 410; Palestinian teachings in Babylonia, VIII, 6 f.; on precision of speech and preservation of Torah, VII, 3; on purchase and revision of scriptural texts, VI, 441; quotation from the "secret scroll," VI, 41; quoted, II, 239, 273; on secular music, VII, 129; the wealthy anathemized, II, 242, 274, 277

Raba, II, 133, 208, 264, 272, 277, 278, 283, 308, 406, 417; advocate of proselytism, II, 149; on conduct of women, III, 112; on correct spelling, VII, 12; and measurements of the earth, VIII, 213; poem improvised for, VII, 89; quoted, II, 209, 254

Raba (R. Abba), disciple of Yehudah Gaon, VI, 65, VIII, 187; juridical tract, VI, 40, 80 f.

Raban Maur, IV, 44, 256

Rabbah bar bar Ḥana, II, 176, 306, 396, 433

Rabbah b. Aboah, II, 149

Rabbah b. Naḥmani, II, 243, 316

Rabbah b. R. Huna, II, 268

Rabban, title, II, 120

Rabbana, title, II, 198

Rabbanites, III, 203, IV, 253; adherence to Aramaic, VII, 6; al-Baqillani on, V, 84; attitude toward magic, VIII, 12, 29, 283; on attributes of God, VIII, 100; biblical exegesis (*q.v.*), VI, 235 f., 244, 277 ff., 288 ff.; "Book of Stars," VIII, 364; chronology of Creation, VIII, 203; and circumcision, V, 215; in Constantinople, IV, 294; and the Crucifixion, V, 118; Egyptian, VII, 120, 137; Ibn Daud on, VI, 207; intercalation based on computations, VIII, 194; in Jerusalem, IV, 111; legal codes, VI, 78, *see also* Law; lexicographic interpretation, VII, 51; liturgy (*q.v.*), VII, 70, 73 f., 110 f.; medical law, VIII, 247; neglect of the poor, V, 178, 238; on oral tradition and reading of Scripture, VI, 243; on prophets and miracles, VIII, 130; reconstruction of history of Jewish tradition, VI, 203; religious observances, V, 191, 244 f.; return to Palestine, V, 186; and Saadiah's translation of the Pentateuch; VI, 269 f.; sectarian opposition, V, 375; Spanish, advances in grammar and lexicography, VI, 290 f.

—— and Karaites (*q.v.*), VI, 173; borrowings from, V, 281 f., 413, VI, 461; controversies, V, 56, 211, 228 ff., 275-85, 414-16; intermarriage, V, 265 ff.; joint worship, VII, 280; on origins, V, 255; separation and readmission, V, 9, 273 ff., 413 f.

Rabbi, title, II, 120, 201, V, 60, 283

Rabbis and rabbinate: aggadic works ascribed to, VI, 159; allegations of biblical falsification, V, 92; and *'ame ha-areṣ* (*q.v.*), I, 278; and Arabic language, VII, 6 f., 46, VIII, 263; and Aramaic written translations, VI, 257; astronomic teachings, VIII, 193; on biblical laws, V, 122 ff.; on biblical prophecy, V, 87; on choice between conversion and death, IV, 146; commandments enacted by, VI, 98; condemnation of corrupt provinces, V, 178 f.; on corporal punishment, IV, 261; and dairy products, IV, 315; on deposits with bankers, IV, 208 f.; dialect of, as independent language, VII, 56 f.; education, II, 117, 306; emigration to Persian Babylonia, II, 405; essentials of Judaism, VI, 91; establishment of, in Western Europe, V, 63; ethical ideals, VIII, 120 ff.; expansion of learning, VI, 25; farmers, II, 414; foreign influences, II, 319; Franco-German, V, 60 f., VI, 50, 55 f., 94, 117 f., 205, 295, 336, 371, 387, 427, 441; and God as king, VIII, 18; on interfaith partnerships, IV, 331; and Julian the Apostate, V, 350; and labor, I, 258; leadership, II, 129-71 *passim*, 197, 204, 242, 261, 276, 279, 291, V, 56, VI, 3; on levitical tithes and heave-offerings, IV, 313 f.; on liberal professions, IV, 215 f.; and local judges, V, 20; on love of God, VIII, 116 f.; and magic (*q.v.*), II, 317, VIII, 233 f.; Maimonidean chronology of, VI, 202; manumission of slaves discouraged, II,

Rabbis and rabbinate (*Continued*) 269; on marriage and procreation, V, 134; martyrs, (*q.v.*), IV, 96; and medical practice, VIII, 238; on Messiah (*q.v.*), V, 119 f., 357; on moneylending (*q.v.*), IV, 197 ff., 338 ff.; on money transfers, IV, 212 f.; music banned by, VII, 319 f.; and mysticism (*q.v.*), VIII, 283; as national heroes, VI, 168; a new sort of theocracy, II, 279; ordinances, VI, 134 ff., 392 ff.; ordination, II, 120, 201, 419; and personal slaves, IV, 193; polygamy among, II, 227; and physicians, VIII, 231 ff.; and *piyyuṭim*, VII, 101 ff.; on loyalty to the state, IV, 270; poverty and wealth, II, 265 f., 277, 278; on prayers in Hebrew, VII, 68; preachers (*q.v.*) among, VI, 155 ff.; on price structure, IV, 222 f.; as professional class, VIII, 232 f.; proselytism (*q.v.*) discouraged, I, 175; religious observances, IV, 310; and religious speculation, VIII, 69; responsa (*q.v.*), VI, 109 ff., 116 ff., 381 ff.; rules of interpretation, VI, 287, 297; on sacramental wine, IV, 165; and the Samaritans, V, 172; and shepherds, I, 254; on slave trade, IV, 188 ff., 193; social control, IV, 222; on span of evildoers in Hell, VIII, 104; on speech clarity and precision, VII, 3; on supernatural world, VIII, 27; talmudic commentary of Italian, VI, 353; on tanners, IV, 166 f.; as tax collectors, V, 65 f.; tax exemption, II, 243, 244, 277, 413; theory of state and local government, V, 71 ff., 77 ff.; tombs glorified, II, 279; views of the earth, VIII, 212; on viticulture, IV, 162 f.; *see also* Amoraim; Elders; Geonim; Priests; Rabbanites; Scholars; Talmud; Tannaim

Rabbula, bishop of Edessa, III, 57; and the Peshiṭta, VI, 454

Rabina, II, 251, 276; on recitation of psalm, VII, 69; redactor of Babylonian Talmud, II, 296, 426

Rabina the Younger, VI, 17 f.

Rab Raba, Mar, VI, 132 f.

Races, human, VI, 192, 226

Rachel's tomb, II, 14

Racial equality, Islamic theory of, III, 98

Racial mixtures, I, 39

Radegund, princess, III, 22

"Radhanites," IV, 328

Radicalism, ancient, I, 228

Radulph, Cistercian monk, leader of Second Crusade, IV, 120 f.

Raffelstetten, Germany, IV, 65 f., 301

Raḥem, prayer, II, 375

Raḥmi'el, angel, VIII, 8 f.

Rain: as messianic portent, V, 201; and moon, VIII, 175; prayers for, II, 40, 345, 349, 385, III, 260, V, 27, 303, VIII, 202

Rainer papyrus, I, 378

Ra'is, Arabic title, V, 48

Ralph de Diceto, IV, 124

Ralph of Coggeshall, IV, 85

Ramadan, V, 246

Ramah, "guest house" in, II, 285

Ramleh, Palestine: commercial center, IV, 180; evacuation of, IV, 109; Karaites in, VI, 246; Muslim administrative capital, III, 102 f.; Samaritans in, V, 171 f.; Solomon b. Yehudah vs. Nathan b. Abraham, V, 34; synagogues, V, 28

Ramlites (or Malikians), V, 182

Ramon Berenger III, count of Barcelona, IV, 37

Ramon Berenger IV, count of Barcelona, IV, 30 f., 37, 42, 207; writ of indebtedness, IV, 252

Ram's horn, II, 256, 333, 383, 416

Ransom of captives, IV, 109, 110 f., 177 f.

Raqqa, Mesopotamia, VIII, 139; birthplace of Al-Muqammiṣ, VIII, 393; center of learning, VIII, 243; Jewish "philosophers" of, VIII, 67

Rashbam, *see* Samuel b. Meir

Rashi (or Yiṣḥaqi), Solomon b. Isaac, R., II, 289, 424, IV, 144, 157, 162; agadic interpretations, V, 157 f.; on ban of settlement, V, 68 f.; date of birth, VI, 245; on days of the Messiah, V, 148 f.; exegetical work, VI, 49-53, 61, 180, 278 ff., 344-49, 465 f., 475; French translation of technical terms, VIII, 227; on local customs, VI, 128 f.; methodological approaches, VI, 348; ordinances, V, 64, 319 f.; on peculiar formation of verbs, VII, 47; prayer book attributed to, VI, 75, 362 f.; responsa by, VI, 118, 385 f.; school of, VI, 34, 53 ff., 75 f., 202, 278, 362 f., 386, 467; student days, VI, 345; talmudic-geonic learning, VI, 173 f.; on Targum

of Hagiographa, VI, 262; use of Hebrew dictionaries, VII, 20, 31
Rashid, ar-, *see* Harun ar-Rashid
Rashid ad-Din, execution of, V, 97
Ras Shamra (Ugarit), I, 45, 52 f., 302, 306, 309, 312, 401; bread and wine offerings, I, 316; *Keret* legend, I, 301, 401; marriage, II, 229; school for scribes, I, 315; Ugaritic alphabet, I, 307; Ugaritic poems, I, 48, 63, 306, 311, 312, 334, 350; worship of Athtar and Astarte, I, 318
Ratherius, bishop of Verona, IV, 25; *De qualitatis conjectura,* IV, 26
Rationalism: Arab, VIII, 66, 129; Muslim opponents of, VIII, 83 f.
—— Jewish, VIII, 55-137, 296-346; in biblical exegesis, V, 259, VI, 259, 267, 274-81, 298-306, 463-68, 478-84; denial of astrological predictions, VIII, 176; and messianic expectations, V, 159-66, 363-66; and moral values, VIII, 113 ff.; opposition to mysticism, VIII, 37 ff.; and prophecy, VIII, 132; in religious poetry, VII, 175; *see also* Philosophy; Reason
Rational power, VIII, 107
Ratisbon, Germany: mass baptism of Jewish community, IV, 100; privilege, IV, 67, 71 f.; trading center, IV, 175 f.
Ravenna, Italy: exarchate, III, 24; Judeo-Christian relations, III, 241
Raw materials, production of, IV, 163
Rawandi, ar-, Muslim agnostic, V, 103, 337, VI, 298, 477, VIII, 129
Raymond, archbishop of Toledo, IV, 32 f.
Raymond, count of Sens, V, 114
Raymond de Bollène, archbishop of Arles, IV, 59
Razi, Aḥmad ar-, IV, 159
Razi, ar- (Rhazes), Muhammad b. Zakariya ar-, VI, 301, VIII, 225, 242, 390
Reader, *see* Cantor
Real estate, *see* Land; Property
Reason: and faith, VI, 108 f., VIII, 55-137, 296-346; and nature, VI, 285 f.; reliability of findings of, VIII, 78 ff.; *see also* Rationalism
Rebirth, *see* Immortality of the soul
Reccared, king of Spain, III, 32, 36, 245 f.
Recceswinth, king of the Visigoths, III, 41
Rechabites, I, 42, 78, 89, II, 48
Rectangle, formula for measuring, VIII, 157
Redeemer: personal, in Jewish theology, I, 118, V, 163; *see also* Messiah and messianism
Redemption: atonement and, V, 217; communal, I, 259; computation of date of, V, 149 f.; as cosmic cataclysm, II, 59; individual and collective, VII, 132 ff.; of Israel from Egypt, VII, 115, *see also* Exodus; messianic, V, 141 ff., VIII, 127; poems of, V, 153, VII, 181; via penitence and martyrdom, IV, 95
Red Sea: crossing of, VI, 300; Song of the, VII, 279
Reform, Catholic, IV, 10, 28
Reformation, Israelitic, *see* Deuteronomic reformation; Protestant, VI, 306
Reformers, III, 110, VII, 64
Reform Judaism, I, 26, 228, II, 344; and nationalism, I, 28, 361
Refuge, cities of, I, 360; *see also* Asylum
Regimentation, II, 260-65, 417 f.
Rehoboam, king of Israel, I, 74
Reḥomai, R., VIII, 37
Reims, Council of, III, 252
Rekhub-el, god, I, 357
Relics, Christian, pilgrimages in quest of, IV, 283
Religion: comparative study, I, 102-3, 103-4, V, 84, VII, 11; disputations, II, 133, 136 ff.; "eternal" elements, I, 16; Persian, I, 129, *see also* Parsees and Parsiism; and political power, I, 22, 237; and science, VIII, 219; Semitic settlers' influence on, I, 175
—— Jewish: Antiochus IV and apostasy, I, 217, 229; autonomy under Christian emperors, II, 191; civic duty, I, 234; conflicts, I, 61 f., 228; crucial test in Exile, I, 102-33, 341-55; cultural influences affecting, I, 46, 58; in declining Second Commonwealth, II, 54; fertility cults, I, 318; genius of Israel's, I, 41; hegemony of Jerusalem, I, 219; and history, I, 4 ff., 99 ff., 295 ff., 340; imageless worship, I, 322; Israel's "popular," I, 4, 59, 62, 83, 98, 104 f., 128, 161, 219; Jews relieved of imperial worship, I, 244; and law, I, 77-84, 142, 227, 327-32, II, 293 ff., 307, 425 ff., VI, 3 ff.; monotheism (*q.v.*), I, 4-10, 43-46, 294; Mosaic, I, 4, 41, 44, 46-53, 58, 59,

Religion (*Continued*)
65, 313-16, *see also* Moses; and music, VII, 207 f.; and nature, I, 4 ff.; optimism of, I, 8; Palestinian controls over world Jewry, II, 125 f.; a *religio licita,* I, 117; sacrificial worship condemned, I, 123-29 *passim, see also* Sacrifices; Samaritan (*q.v.*) a relapse into the preprophetic, II, 28; and society, I, 3-31, 59, 123 ff., 132, 258, 293-97; sources of, I, 161, 298-99; syncretism (*q.v.*) and sectarianism (*q.v.*), II, 3 ff., 23 ff., 26 ff., 330-50; synthesis of a national and universal religion, I, 28, 31; and territory, I, 17, 99-100; theocratic state founded in Palestine, I, 165; unifying bond in Egypt, I, 36; and woman's position in family, I, 58; and worship, VII, 62
—— *see also* Christians and Christianity; Converts and conversion; Gnosticism; God; Judaism; Law; Parsees and Parsiism; Priests and priesthood; Proselytes and proselytism; Rabbis and rabbinate; *also under* names of sects, *e.g.,* Sadducees
Religious holidays, *see* Holidays
Religious liberty, II, 191; in ancient empires, I, 117; relative immunity of synagogue, II, 284; *see also* Rights, legal; Self-government; Toleration, religious
Religious objects, ransom of, VI, 447
Religious observances, IV, 60 f., 310; in Babylonia, V, 246; Byzantine laws on, III, 190; charge of Jewish laxity in, V, 124 f., 135 f.; of Christian servants employed by Jews, IV, 314 f.; controversy over, V, 122-25, 346 f.; differences between Babylonia and Palestine, V, 28 ff., 246, 255; farm workers and, IV, 156 f.; followers of Severus, V, 193 f.; Karaite, V, 214 ff., 282 ff.; in Khazaria, III, 202 f.; local variations in, V, 59, VI, 121 ff., 389 ff.; ritualistic, and blood accusation, IV, 135; Samaritan, V, 173 f.; Scriptural recitations, V, 151; sectarian, V, 190 ff., 195 f.; *shabbata de-rigla,* V, 40; and trade, IV, 219 f.; *see also* Law; Liturgy; Ritual; Sabbath; Synagogue
Religious toleration, *see* Toleration, religious
Religious unity in times of crisis, I, 61
Religious universalism and particularism, I, 96-99, 339
Remigius of Auxerre, IV, 257
"Remnant," doctrine of the, I, 30, 97, 106
Renaissance: Hebrew, reconsideration of liturgical formulas, VII, 67; of Islam, III, 117-21, V, 83, 103, 170, 197, 231, VII, 3 ff., 60 f., 176, VIII, 147, 255 f., 262 f.; Italian, VIII, 147; twelfth century, IV, 311
Repatriation, forced, of Jewish exiles, IV, 62 f.
Repentance, I, 294, II, 308 f., 384, 433; doctrine of, VIII, 105; fasting and, VI, 16; preexistence of, VIII, 273; and redemption, V, 160; Ten Days of, VIII, 74
Repetition, ritualistic import of, VIII, 284
Rephidim, battle, I, 317
Research Institute for Hebrew Poetry, Jerusalem, VII, 261, 271
Res gestae divi Saporis, II, 238, 380, 397
Reshep, I, 49
Resh kallah, title, V, 59
Reshut ha-rabbim, II, 252
Residence permit (*ḥerem ha-yishub*), IV, 71, 185, V, 68 f.; and excommunication, V, 17; Gershom b. Yehudah and, IV, 65, 213
Responsa: in Arabic, VII, 6; authority of, VI, 115; authorship, VI, 114 f., 384 f.; compilations of, V, 115, VI, 29 ff., 113; geonic, V, 32, VI, 29 ff., 109-16, 339, 381-85, VIII, 229, *see also under* names of geonim; and origin of talmudic commentaries, VI, 41; preservation of, VI, 383 f.; rabbinic, VI, 116-21, 386-88, *see also under* names of rabbis; to series of related questions, VI, 382; in support of local customs, VI, 122 ff.; talmudic, VI, 110, 381 f.
Responsibility, communal, for common welfare, II, 251, 269, 270, 271, 273, 291, *see also* Communities, Jewish; individual, II, 41, 44; mutual, I, 10, 135 f., 146, 356, II, 217
Restoration to Palestine in antiquity, I, 157, 158-63, 366-68
Resurrection, doctrine of, I, 9, 12, 207, 208, 390, II, 14, 111, 312, 318, V, 175, 228, 260, VIII, 104; Maimonides on,

V, 22, VI, 119, 413; messianism and, V, 166; in Muslim creed, VI, 8; Pharisaism's conception, II, 38, 344 f.; poems on, VII, 267; and return of Jesus, II, 71, 73, 359; Saadiah's interpretation, VI, 286; sectarian opinions of, II, 31, 39, 345, V, 196; stressed above immortality (*q.v.*), I, 208
Retaliation, law of, I, 79
Retribution, I, 136-37; *see also* Punishments
Reuben, Jacob's blessing of, VI, 259
Revelation: Bible as, VI, 294, 307 ff., VIII, 127; Judeo-Christian reliance on, II, 159, VIII, 85, 113; media of, VIII, 342; and reason, VIII, 82; relationship to history, I, 296; Sinaitic, II, 161
Revenues: clerical, IV, 58, 65 f., 74, 153 f.; exilarchic, V, 12; farming of public, I, 262; imperial, from Jews, V, 5; papal, IV, 14; priestly, I, 272; state, IV, 87, 89 f., 201, 203 f., 213, 225 f.; in Temple treasury, II, 44; under the Caliphate, III, 150; *see also* Taxation
Revivalists, Crusading fanaticism engendered by, IV, 102, 120
Revolts: in Northern Israel, I, 95; against Romans, I, 212, 265, 266, II, 90-102, 368-72, *see also* Judeo-Roman wars; *also under* names of wars, *e.g.*, Great War
Rewards, I, 137; after death, I, 137, II, 31, 38, 40, 41; *see also* Punishments
Reziel, Book of, VIII, 11 ff., 27
Rezin of Aram, I, 155
Rhazes, *see* Razi, ar-, Muhammad
Rhetoric, Greek, influence on Jewish homilies, VI, 163 f.
Rhodes, I, 236; Colossus of, III, 16, 235
Rhyme: in alphabetic order, VII, 142, 294; forms of, VII, 200; in Hebrew poetry, VII, 197 ff., 314 f.; as mnemotechnic aid, VII, 88
Rhythm, *see* Meter
Rice, cultivation of, IV, 161
Rich, the, *see* Wealth
Richard I (Richard Lion-Heart), king of England: appointment of first Jewish presbyter, V, 63; on Crusaders in England and Normandy, IV, 127 f.; debt to Aaron of Lincoln, IV, 303; policy toward Jews, IV, 78 f., 163 f., 304; riot at coronation of, IV, 124 ff., 140
Richard, son of Nigel, *Dialogus de Scaccario,* IV, 80 f., 205
Richard of Devises, IV, 125, 136, 140
Richard Strongbow, *see* Strongbow
Richulf, archbishop of Mayence, IV, 45
Riddles: linguistic, VII, 4; poetic, VII, 162; use of numerical value of letters, VIII, 357
Righteous Teacher, II, 53, 349, 350
Rights, legal of Jews, III, 13, 24 ff., 294, IV, 22 f., 49; in ancient Babylonia, I, 115-17, 348 f.; Barcelona custumal, IV, 41 f.; in Byzantium, III, 13, 153, 173-90, 313-20; in Carolingian Empire, IV, 43-53, 256-64; in early Roman Empire, I, 239 ff., II, 398; in England, IV, 75-86, 276-82; in France, III, 47-54, 250-54, IV, 53-64, 264-70; inequality of, IV, 35, 39 f.; in Germany, IV, 64-75, 270-76; in Hungary, III, 211-13, 332 f.; in Italy, III, 24-33, 240-44, IV, 5-27, 235-45; royal alliance and, IV, 50 ff.; in Spain, III, 33-46, 244-50, IV, 27-43, 245-56; under the Caliphate, III, 120-72, 288-312; of women, I, 111, II, 303, 304, 306; *see also* Charters; Inheritance; Privileges; Property; Toleration, religious
Ring, use of at weddings, V, 283
Rites, Sacred Congregation of, V, 351
Ritual: Christian, II, 71, 84, 154, 155, 365
—— Jewish: appeal of ceremonial, II, 149, 189, 191; of blood, I, 51; and chronological cycles, VIII, 209; deviations from, I, 200, 351, II, 7, 182, 399; equality of moral law and, II, 307-9, 433; food requirements, I, 189, II, 217, 306, *see also* Sacrifices; funerary, II, 340; Graeco-Oriental contrasts and influences, II, 6 ff.; Jeroboam's innovations, V, 254; link between synagogue and Temple, II, 119, 376; local customs, VI, 59, 123 f.; origin of, VI, 392; Palestinian vs. Babylonian, V, 28 ff., VIII, 228; prayers for rulers, VII, 265; reinterpretation of ancient, I, 315; segregation of priests, I, 149; *see also* Liturgy; Prayers
Ritual murder, *see* Blood accusation
Robbery, II, 46; distinguished from theft, VI, 147
Robert, count of Normandy, IV, 289
Robert I, king of France, IV, 92

Robert II (Robert the Pious), king of France, V, 114
Robert of Gloucester, IV, 140
Rodoam, Haly, *see* Ibn Ridhwan
Roger I, king of Sicily, IV, 22, VIII, 215; attack on Thebes, IV, 168 f.
Roger II, king of Sicily, IV, 11, 21; privilege to Messina, IV, 23; silk robe, IV, 168
Roger de Moulins, IV, 114
Roman-Byzantine emperors, anonymous list of, III, 317 f., V, 354, VI, 211 f., 430
Roman Catholic church, *see* Church, Christian
Romance languages: Jewish influence, II, 406; translations of Bible and prayer book, II, 144; *see also under* individual languages, *e.g.*, French
Romances, fictional, VII, 183 ff.
Roman Empire: agricultural supply sources, II, 246; anarchical conditions in society, II, 225, 234; anti-Jewish sentiment, I, 190, 246, II, 103; burial customs, I, 382, II, 423; caste system, II, 176, 242; Catholicism the heir of, II, 85 ff.; Christianity, II, 63, 83, 85, 86, 150, 152, 165, 366, 393; circumcision outlawed, II, 97, 107, 109; class differences, II, 242; continuity of traditions, IV, 4; controversies with Palestine, I, 238, 248, 250, 263, II, 104; decline of, II, 213, III, 4; dictatorial regime, II, 57, 420; economically most advanced region of, I, 258; Edom identified with, II, 152; family degrees and marriage laws, II, 230; fiscal system, I, 262 ff., II, 100, 105 f., 183 ff., 399, *see also* Taxation; Hellenism and, II, 173 ff., 396; and Jesus, II, 70; Jewish attachment to emperors, I, 190; Jewish communal freedoms, V, 58 f., VIII, 193; and Jewish law, II, 300, 430; Jewish population, I, 171, III, 283 f.; and Jewish religious customs, I, 179, 238, 382, II, 284; Jewish settlements, III, 49; Jews in, I, 166, 170, 371, II, 210; "kingdom of wickedness," II, 153; law courts, II, 266, 419; legal and political status of Jews, I, 240, 403, II, 108 ff., 320; marriage, I, 226-34 *passim;* morals, I, 191; Persia and, II, 176-86, 213, 396-98; pessimism, II, 57 f., 89; Phoenician ghettos, I, 176; policies toward Jews, I, 195, 209, 248, II, 89, 97, 100, 106 ff., 118, 120, 187 ff., 213; political-military world mission, II, 329; polygamy opposed, II, 226, 231, VI, 137; population, I, 371, II, 183, 209; proselytism, I, 176, II, 150; provincial administration, II, 103 f., 373; religious inspiration of imperialism, II, 152, 388; revolts against, I, 212, 219, 265, 266, II, 90-108, 368-72, *see also* Judeo-Roman wars; robbery and piracy preserved as source of slave supply, II, 46; Samaritans in, II, 33, 342; self-control of officials, I, 239; seven day week, I, 6, VIII, 185, 368; slave-holding by Jews, II, 259, 416; syncretistic tradition, II, 11 ff., VIII, 32; treaty of alliance with Judaea, I, 218; unfolding and fusion of religions, II, 86; in vision of Daniel, II, 59, V, 140 ff.; Yosephon on, VI, 192; Zealotic faction's resistance to oppression of, II, 47; *see also* Byzantine Empire; Holy Roman Empire; *and under* names of emperors, *e.g.*, Hadrian; Trajan
Romanos, Christian *melodos,* VII, 82, 127, 142
Romanos I (Lekapenos), Byzantine emperor, III, 179; attempts to suppress Judaism, III, 179, 182, 203, 317 f., IV, 25
Romanos II, Byzantine emperor, VIII, 65
Romanos III, Byzantine emperor, VIII, 246
Roman roads, I, 172
Rome, city: alien groups in, I, 248; Christians in, III, 31; Church Councils of, IV, 9; council of Jewish elders, V, 55; Eleazar's observations in, II, 113; equated with Edom, V, 145, VI, 407; equated with a pig, V, 131; evil power of, VIII, 19; Jewish community, I, 284, II, 199, 332, IV, 4 ff., 11, 13 f., 240, V, 55, 59 f., VI, 216, VII, 29 f.; Jewish exile, VII, 290; Jews expelled and readmitted I, 246; Judeo-Christian relations (*q.v.*), III, 27; Menaḥem b. Saruq's work, VII, 48; messianic predictions, V, 143 ff., 354; public schools, II, 279; success of Jewish religious propaganda, I, 191; "synagogue of Severus," VI, 401
Rom family, publishers, VI, 348 f.
Romizanes Shahrabaz, III, 22

Romualdus, IV, 21
Romulus, equated with Armilus, V, 145, VI, 481
Roots, Hebrew, VII, 41; alphabetical listing by last letters of, VII, 27; biliterality or triliterality of, VII, 39, 42, 46 f.; "Book of," by Ibn Janaḥ, VII, 24 f., 45, 229, 237
Rosh ha-Shanah, tractate, VI, 352
Rossi, Azariah de', V, 365, VI, 210, 422, VIII, 183
Rossi, Giovanni Bernardo de, VI, 255
Rostov, Russia, archaeological investigations, III, 213
Rothschild, Edmond, baron de, III, 232
Routes, trade, IV, 172 f., 180 f., VIII, 212
"Routes, Books of," VIII, 212; *see also* Ibn Khurdadhbah
Royal alliance, IV, 28 ff., 87; and disposition of Jewish property, IV, 59 f., 203 f.; and economic enterprise, IV, 36-43, 45, 225 f.; and legal status, IV, 50 ff.; protection through, IV, 45, 141
Royal grants, of Jewish persons and property, IV, 59 f.
Royal power, *see* Kings; Monarchy
Rüdiger-Huozmann, bishop of Spires, IV, 74, 98 f., V, 79; privilege to Jews, IV, 74, 205, 275
Rudolf Brugensis, VIII, 363
Rufinus, Christian exegete, VI, 292
Rulers: ancient worship of, I, 244, 404, II, 5, 99, 109; concepts of nature of, VIII, 18; jurisdiction of local, IV, 72; oath of allegiance to, II, 36; patrons of poets, VII, 148 f.; the perfect, I, 199; prayers for, VII, 265; *see also* Emperors; Kings; Monarchy
Russia: archaeological findings, III, 333 f.; conversion to Greek orthodoxy, III, 221; Jewish settlements, III, 213-17, 336 f.; meat tax, VIII, 386; name for Khazars, III, 204; origins of first Slavic state, III, 334; pig symbol, II, 152; secular Jewish nationalism in, I, 29; Slavonic Josephus, II, 379; *see also* Josephus
Ruth, V, 90
—— Book of: commentary on, V, 400, VI, 472; date, I, 366
Ruthard, archbishop of Mayence, IV, 99, 116 f.
Rutilius Namatianus, Claudius, II, 188, 400

S

Saadiah Gaon, III, 119, 197, 221 f.; acrostic of name, VII, 141, 144; on Agur, VI, 402; "analogistic" approach, VII, 34; appointment to Sura, V, 21, VI, 356; on atomistic theory, VIII, 88; attitude toward Arabic meter, VII, 194; on attributes of God, VIII, 96 f.; on authorship of mystical literature, VIII, 25; on authorship of Psalms, VI, 307; on biblical chronology, V, 120; calendar regulation, V, 30 f., VIII, 196; on character of the universe, VIII, 78 f., 165 f., 213 f.; chronology of the Mishnah, VI, 203 f.; the community and Jewish law, V, 4 f.; computation of date of Messiah, V, 164; concentration on meaning of prayer, VII, 74; controversy with Ben Meir, V, 181, 196, 212, VI, 126, 430, VII, 115, VIII, 195, 196 ff.; controversy with David b. Zakkai, V, 10, 21 ff., 74, VII, 277; on creation *ex nihilo,* VIII, 89; on darkness and light, VIII, 34; debates on lexicographic contributions of, VII, 15 ff.; and decisions of the exilarchic court, V, 200 f., 297 f., 300 f.; defense of Judaism, V, 84, 126, VIII, 100; on deviations from biblical law, V, 93; doctrine of the "second air," VIII, 342; vs. dualists and Christians, V, 107, 126; exegetical principles and methods, VI, 296; on faculties of human soul, VIII, 117; formula for confession, VII, 253 f.; geographic observations, VIII, 217; Ibn Ezra's epigram on, VI, 279; on immutability of Torah, VI, 145; influence of, VI, 271, 276 f., VIII, 45; on interpretation of *ketib* and *qeri* in the Masorah, VI, 292 f.; on Israel as a nation, VI, 231; on Jewish skeptics, V, 104 f.; on Jewish sufferings, VI, 439; and Karaites, V, 277 f., 295, 397, VI, 276, 471; lack of historical criticism, VI, 269; on laws of nature, VIII, 335; literary use of personal experiences, VII, 289; on magic practices, VIII, 29; on man's love of God, VIII, 115; medical observations, VIII, 244; messianic rationale, V, 159 ff., 363 f.; on miracles, VIII, 128 f.; motivations for behavior, VIII, 120; on *Musaf,*

Saadiah Gaon (*Continued*)
VII, 91; nature of the Hereafter, VIII, 104; on neglect of ritual tradition, VII, 106; on number of commandments, VI, 92 f.; on perfect government, V, 71 f.; on physiological reactions to music, VII, 208; on the power of money, IV, 217; on prohibition of murder, VIII, 113; quest for innovation, VII, 142; quest for office, V, 72 f.; on recital of Scripture, VII, 69; rejection of transmigration of souls, VIII, 36; religious disputation, V, 121; reply to Ḥivi, VI, 302 ff., 478 f., VII, 143, VIII, 58; request of aid from Jewish banking families, III, 154; vs. ritualistic divergences, VI, 125 f.; on the soul, VIII, 107; on sources of knowledge, VIII, 79 ff.; style, VII, 142; theories of creation and eternity of the world, VIII, 78 f.; theory of exile, V, 100 f.; theory of prophecy, V, 21; use of Aramaic, VII, 67

—— works: Arabic translation of Hebrew Bible, VI, 265 ff., 312 f., 458 f.; *Beliefs and Opinions,* VI, 195, VIII, 59 ff., 313; Book of Chronology, VI, 211; Book of Commandments, VI, 95; commentaries on Mishnah and Talmud, VI, 28, 42; Commentary on Book of Creation, VI, 242, VIII, 24 (alleged), 59, 151; Commentary on the Thirteen Hermeneutic Modes, VI, 32, 304 f., 335; correspondence, V, 16, VI, 208; Dictionary of the Mishnah, VII, 15; exegetical works on the Bible, VI, 114, 284 ff.; halakhic monographs, IV, 209, VI, 65 ff., 356 ff., VII, 117, VIII, 153 f.; handbook for Hebrew poetry, VII, 15, 89, 99, 197; *Kitab at-Tamyiz,* dispute over date of, VIII, 203 ff.; linguistic works, VII, 14 f., 33 ff., 234 f.; liturgical poems, VII, 87, 104 f., 141, 219, VIII, 150; methodological treatise, VI, 32; monographs on chronology and calendar, VI, 307; polemical poem against Aaron Ben Asher, VI, 246; polemical poem against Ḥivi, VI, 304; prayer book, V, 150 f., 248, VI, 15, 69, 92, VII, 70, 100 f., 113 ff., 115 f., 140 f., 302; story of the Children of the Hasmoneans, VI, 189; variations on the theme of the Ten Commandments, VII, 141; works neglected by public, VI, 96; *see also* Pseudo-Saadiah

Sabbath: academic joint sessions on, V, 19; association with moon and planets, I, 359, VIII, 184; birth of child on, I, 120; drinking on, V, 245; fasting on, VI, 330 f.; and the Festival of Weeks, V, 195; first, V, 357; Jews not called as witnesses on, I, 245; of Repentance, VI, 165; special lessons, VI, 162, 172 f., 338, VIII, 208

—— observance, I, 71, 153, II, 132, III, 31, 83 f., IV, 26, 156, 183, 268, 283, V, 122, 216, 223, 283, 350, VI, 80, 119 f., 396, 475 f.; carrying objects on, III, 62, IV, 70, VI, 178; censured by Seneca, I, 192; Christians', II, 188; cooking on, VI, 42; eternal law of, V, 91 f.; Graeco-Roman attitude toward, I, 6, 382, II, 107, 109; Jesus' utterance about, II, 67, 69, 356; Karaite rules, V, 217 f., 243 f.; new prominence, I, 143 ff., 359 f.; origin, I, 6, 143, 382; Pharisaic, II, 45, 46, 50; poems devoted to, VII, 90; Saadiah on, VI, 15 f.; violation of, VI, 134

"Sabbath of Sabbaths," I, 144

Sabbatical millennium, II, 318

Sabbatical year, I, 279, II, 271; abolished, II, 263; dating by, II, 116; legal cancellation of debts, I, 261, II, 262, 417; produce of, and betrothals, V, 29

Sabbazius, god, I, 128, II, 24, 25

Sabians, III, 130, VIII, 217; etymology of, VI, 437

Sabionetta, edition of the Targum, VI, 259

Saboraim, VI, 17 ff., 110, 204, 334; and amoraic sayings, VI, 40; liturgical works, VII, 63 ff.; period of, III, 58, 73; rabbinic succession, VI, 426; recension of Babylonian Talmud, VI, 240; source of geonic tradition, VII, 108

Sacrifices, I, 51, 179, 254, 362, VI, 147 f., 300; animal, II, 50, 52, 154, 155, 306, 353; and burnt offering, III, 29; in Christian ceremonies, II, 154; consistent with patriarchal and Mosaic religion, I, 50 f.; ideas underlying Israelitic, I, 315 f.; justification of, VIII, 118; laws of, VI, 95, VIII, 228; limited to Temple at Jerusalem, I, 123, 129, 133; in name of ruler, I, 244, 404, II,

99; obliterated by burning of Temple, I, 179, II, 155, 284; opposition to, I, 123-29 *passim;* Passover (*q.v.*), II, 45; Persian attitude, I, 353; prayer as substitute for, I, 124, 132, 350, II, 125; preeminence of priest in worship, I, 81; of primitive tribes, I, 51, 127; replaced by prayers, VII, 249; and ritual murder (*q.v.*), IV, 135 f.; spiritualization of, II, 308; and temple of Onias, I, 219; for unsolved crime, I, 79
Sadducees and Sadduceeism, I, 142, 221, 234-38, V, 228, 261, VI, 236, VIII, 205; absorbed in mainstream of Judaism, I, 237, 271, II, 129; anti-Syrian revolt, I, 234; and era of Creation, VIII, 208; and Karaites, V, 255; legal code, VI, 78; name, II, 342; priesthood, I, 271 f., 280, II, 46; punishment of, V, 280; rebellions against Rome, II, 90, 99; representatives of priestly and lay aristocracy, II, 35, 36; responsibility for slaves, I, 412; struggle with Pharisees, I, 180, 234, 402, II, 35, 36, 38-46, 343 f.; survival of teachings, II, 117, 129, V, 187 ff., 215, 377 ff.; unable to guide dispersion, II, 55
Sa'd ibn Abu Waqqas, III, 95
Sa'd ibn Manṣur ibn Kammuna, *see* Ibn Kammuna
Ṣafiya, Jewish wife of Mohammed, III, 76, 262
Safra, R., prayer of, VII, 76 f.
Ša-Gaz, *see* Ḥabiru
Sages, ancient, I, 136, 153, 307; innate gifts, VIII, 139; "language of," and the language of Scripture, VII, 56 f.; *see also* Rabbis and rabbinate; Scholars and scholarship
Sahel, *see* Sahl b. Bishr
Sahlal b. Abraham, liturgical poet, VII, 12
Sahl b. Bishr (or Zahel), astrologer, VIII, 148; astronomic works, VIII, 166 ff.; poem on the stars, VIII, 168; variants of name, VIII, 167
Sahl b. Maṣliaḥ, IV, 167, V, 186, 233; biblical interpretation, V, 264; on the calendar, V, 30 f.; charges against rabbinic leadership, V, 236, 238 f., 246; missionary journey, V, 269; on sectarian intermarriage, V, 267
Sahl b. Neṭira, III, 153
Saḥoq b. Esther Israeli, IV, 92
Sa'id ibn Sina al-Mulk, Muslim physician, III, 148, VIII, 250
Saif Dhu Yazan, III, 69
Sailors, Jewish, II, 249
Saint-Denis, Abbey of, IV, 59
Saint Edmundsbury, monastery, IV, 13, 84, 204
Saint Lo, France, IV, 239
Saint Moritz, monastery of, IV, 65
Saint Sophia, *see* Hagia Sophia
Ṣala', meaning, I, 351
Saladin, Seljuk caliph, III, 106; coins, VIII, 255; founder of Nasiri Hospital, VIII, 248; reconquest of Jerusalem, IV, 115 f.; tithe, IV, 81, 279, 297
Salama (Solomon) ibn Mubarak (Meborakh) ibn Raḥamun, *see* Ibn Raḥamun
Salar, term, V, 309
Ṣalat, prayer, VI, 13
Salbit (ancient Shaalbim), synagogue at, II, 29
Salem, *see* Jerusalem
Salerno, Italy: medical school, IV, 24, VIII, 245; population, IV, 244; transfer of Jewish property to archbishop, IV, 22
Salic law, IV, 263
Sallam, interpreter, VII, 12
Salmon b. Yeruḥim, Karaite author, III, 102, 297, V, 363, VII, 16, VIII, 26; vs. 'Ananites, V, 259; biblical commentaries, VII, 27 f., 288; on the exilarchate, V, 236 f.; grave of, V, 408; identified with Ibn Saqawaihi, V, 406; on Karaism, V, 232, 253; liturgical use of Psalms, VII, 70; on Sabbath drinking, V, 245
Salome-Alexandra, I, 223
Salonica, Greece: communal council, V, 55 f.; messianic movement, IV, 107 f., V, 200, VI, 173; taxation of Jews, III, 192
Saltel, Jewish landowner in Spain, IV, 159
Salt mine, IV, 169, 222
Salvation, *see* Redemption
Samael, Rome's angelic "prince," V, 134, VIII, 19
Samareia, village, I, 266, II, 34, 341
Samareitikon, Greek translation of Pentateuch, II, 30
Samaria, I, 72, 99, 167, II, 339; alien in-

Samaria (*Continued*)
flux, II, 27; deportations from, I, 95, 345; fall of, and jubilee years, VIII, 209 f.; fate under foreign rulers, II, 27; high ecclesiastical officers, I, 81; Jewish settlements in postexilic, I, 225, 370; kings assassinated, I, 74; uprising of peasantry of, I, 89; *see also* Israel, Northern
Samaria-Sebaste, I, 280
Samaritans, II, 26-35, 339-42, V, 170-77, 367-73; address king as *theos epiphanes,* I, 229; adoption of Saadiah's translation, VI, 271; alphabet, V, 176; biblical text, II, 30, 32, 340, V, 175, VI, 236, 442; and Caesarea, V, 171; choice of allegiance, II, 30; "contamination" by unbelievers, V, 409; delegation to king of Persia, III, 17, 56; descent, II, 27, 30, 31; Diaspora settlements, II, 34 f., 339, 342, V, 177; edicts, III, 9, 14, 231; Hebrew of, II, 340, VII, 224; heterodox wings, II, 32 ff., 341; historical literature, VI, 212; history of earliest sect, II, 26, 28; and Jewish era of Creation, VIII, 206; and Judaism, I, 162, 167 f., II, 318; and Karaites, V, 261 f.; on levirate, V, 332; liturgy, VI, 372, VII, 64; messianism, V, 170-77, 367-73; observance of biblical laws, V, 173 ff.; physicians, VIII, 248; priesthood, V, 235; rabbinic attitude toward, II, 339; refugees in Persia, III, 255; segregation, V, 172, 174, 219, 409; sources of history and religion, II, 29, 31, 339; sub-sects, V, 369; temple on Mount Gerizim, II, 26 ff., 339, V, 170 f., 367 f.; use of the divine name, II, 434
Samarkand, Persia: Jewish population, III, 110; Muslim defeat at, VI, 434
Samau'al ibn 'Adiyah, Jewish Arabic poet, III, 72, VII, 191
Samau'al ibn Yaḥya al-Maghribi, Jewish convert to Islam, V, 85 ff., 202, VII, 155, VIII, 249; anti-Jewish tract, V, 93, VI, 303; on beauty of the Qur'an, VII, 8; description of *piyyuṭ,* VII, 96; on expansion of knowledge, VIII, 139; interpretation of Scripture, V, 99 f.; and Karaites, III, 112, V, 285; on liturgical changes and Persian persecutions, VII, 82, 255 f.; on melodies for *piyyuṭim,* VII, 125 f.; on Muslim toleration, V, 335; and story of Lot, V, 90
Sambari, Joseph b. Isaac, chronicler, III, 123, V, 38 f., 308
Sambation, mythical river, III, 205
Sambethis, Sibylla, I, 197
Samkartsh, *see* Kertsh
Sampseans, sect, II, 51, 348
Samson, I, 376; as prophet, VIII, 132
Samson, Christian apologist, III, 160
Samuel, prophet (the Seer), I, 317, II, 114; antimonarchical, I, 91; Israelitic unity promoted by, I, 61, 63; prayers at tomb of, VII, 76
—— Books of: authorship, I, 340; interpretation, VIII, 95 f.
Samuel, Armenian scholar, III, 184
Samuel, exilarch of Baghdad, conflict with Samuel b. 'Ali, V, 12, 40
Samuel, Mar (of Nehardea), II, 74, 219, 221, 302, 417, VI, 17 f., 124; on abrogation of a biblical law, II, 262; *Baraita de-Shemu'el,* VIII, 147, 350; formula for solar year, VIII, 198; interpretation of the Mishnah, VII, 13; maxims, II, 208, 313; a Persian patriot, II, 177, 397; on purity of Jewish family, I, 234; school of, II, 207; as scientist, II, 206, 307, 433, VIII, 231; substitute for *'Amidah,* VII, 263
Samuel, R., gaon, V, 15
Samuel b. 'Ali, gaon of Baghdad, III, 217, 222, VI, 119, 224; on appointment of judges, VI, 9 f.; on the exilarchs, V, 10; letter of authorization to Zechariah b. Berakhel, V, 52 f.
Samuel b. David Moses ha-Levi, V, 363
Samuel b. Ḥananiah, V, 42
Samuel b. Ḥofni, gaon of Sura, IV, 212, V, 24, 40, VI, 30, VIII, 287; attitude toward the Aggadah, VI, 176 ff.; correspondence, VI, 42 f.; interpretation of Saul's vision at Endor, VIII, 130; "Introduction to the Talmud," VI, 33; legal monographs, VI, 69 f.; "Letters of Authorization," IV, 217 f.; on miracles, VIII, 128; modes of interpretation, VI, 406 f.; and prohibition of Jewish prayers, VII, 255; prolixity, VI, 94; and Saadiah's Book of Commandments, VI, 93
Samuel b. Hosha'nah the Third, liturgical poet, VII, 100, 167, 262; imitator of Saadiah, VII, 278

Samuel b. Joseph ibn Nagrela, *see* Ibn Nagrela, Samuel
Samuel b. Meir (Rashbam), R., VI, 53, VIII, 371; on meaning of Amen, VI, 130; on opening and closing verses of Scripture, VIII, 192; rational criticism, VI, 294 ff.; student's comment on, VI, 467; supplements to Alfasi's work, VI, 90; on trade with Christians, IV, 220
Samuel b. Naḥmani, R., II, 177
Samuel b. Netanel, II, 117
Samuel b. Palṭiel, IV, 23
Samuel b. Shalom, poet, VII, 167
Samuel di Medina, Salonican rabbi, VI, 136
Samuel ha-Nagid, *see* Ibn Nagrela, Samuel
Samuel of Bemberg, VII, 280
Samuel the Little, *Baraita de-Shemu'el,* VIII, 147, 350
Samuel the Pious, VII, 253
Samuel the Small, II, 220, 275, 421
Sanballat the Horonite, I, 349
Sancha, queen of Aragon, IV, 166
Sancho, king of Leon, III, 156
Sancho I (Sancho Ramirez), king of Aragon, IV, 318
Sancho IV, king of Castile, IV, 160
Sancho VII (the Wise), king of Navarre, IV, 253; protection of Jews of Tudela, IV, 35 f.
Sancho VIII, king of Navarre, IV, 253
Sanctuaries, I, 14, 58, 59, 76, 332; Hebrew, as depositaries and fiscal agencies, I, 333; punishment for desecration, II, 93, 369; Tabernacle in Mosaic age, I, 49, 314; women in, I, 146; *see also* Synagogue; Temple at Jerusalem
Sanctus, VII, 65, 77; Christian, VII, 252; daily recitation, VIII, 12 f.; from Isaiah, VIII, 9; *see also Qadosh; Qedushah*
Sanhedrin, I, 222, 396, 401, V, 315, VI, 24, 132; and the academies, II, 120, 126, 197, 378, V, 19 f.; and ascent of Jewish king, V, 75; proclamation of leap year, VIII, 194, 206; reconstitution of, and calendar reform, VIII, 191
—— tractate: commentaries on, VI, 60, 349, VIII, 64
Sanjari, Isaac, Bulan's teacher, III, 326
Santa Cruz, monastery, Coimbra, III, 160
Santa Maria Maggiore, church, II, 11
Saracens, *see* Muslims
Saragossa, Spain, III, 158, IV, 39; Muslim treaty with Alphonso I, IV, 30
Sarah, I, 58
Sardes, Jewish quarters, I, 188
Sardica, *see* Sofia
Sardinia, I, 246, 248
Sargon, I, 106; inscription, I, 95
Ṣarot, term, II, 225
Sar Shalom Gaon, IV, 187 f.; on late arrivals at services, VII, 250; on Onkelos, VI, 260
Sar Shalom, *nagid, see* Zuṭṭa
Sassanians, dynasty, II, 172 ff., 180, 317; *see also* Persia, Sassanian
Satan (or Asmodaeus), I, 139, II, 19, 43; as Evil principle, VIII, 290; meaning of "delivery unto," II, 85; view of Jew as ally of, IV, 139, V, 132
Satanas, family name, V, 45
Satire, poetical, VII, 149 f.
Saturday, Muslim prejudice re, V, 91; *see also* Sabbath
Saturn, I, 374, 382
Saturnalia, I, 382
Saturninus, C. Sentius, II, 91
Saul, king of ancient Hebrews, I, 63; celebration of double holiday, VIII, 375 f.; vision at Endor, VIII, 130
Saul b. 'Anan, V, 222 f.
Saul of Tarsus, *see* Paul, Saint
Savasorda, *see* Bar Ḥiyya
Sawad, province, III, 163, 168
Ṣawafi, term, III, 163
Saxony, or "As-Skandz" and Ashkenaz, IV, 4
Sayings of the Fathers, VI, 203, VII, 281, VIII, 21, 64
Scaccarium Aronis, IV, 203 f.; *see also* Aaron of Lincoln
Scaevola, Mucius, VI, 232
Schechem-Neapolis, *see* Nablus
Schedia, synagogue inscription, II, 331
Scholars and scholarship, II, 204-8, III, 184, 195; Arabian biographers, VIII, 223; attribution of mystic classics to ancient, VIII, 18; captured by Arab pirate, V, 46 f.; conflict between people and, II, 241; confused by philosophic controversies, VIII, 70 f.; control over community, II, 120, 197, 403, V, 13 ff., 21, 49; dispersal, II, 119, 126; economic position, I, 265, II, 240, 243 f., 256, 269, 277 f.; education, II,

Scholars and scholarship (*Continued*) 117, 306; exemption from taxation, V, 75 f.; Ḥananel on, VI, 47, 83; intellectual debates, VIII, 72; Karaite, V, 233 f., 275; and marriage, II, 221, 235; molders of tradition, VI, 26 f.; and moneylending, IV, 199; posttalmudic biblical learning, VI, 312, VII, 249, 275 ff.; preachers' attitude toward, VI, 172 f.; preferential treatment for students, II, 221; prestige of, II, 201, 235, 276, 279, III, 85, IV, 221, V, 32-38, 75, 305-8, VI, 30; priestly function of, VI, 9; prolixity of style, VI, 94; reaction to criticism, VI, 120 f.; reliance of Christian authors on, IV, 256; talmudic, liturgical poems, VII, 170 f.; titles, II, 120, 201, 419; visits to foreign communities, V, 53 f.; and women, II, 239 f.; *see also* Academies; Education; Rabbis and rabbinate; *and under* respective disciplines

Scholasticism: Christian, VIII, 61 f., 322, 324; Jewish, VIII, 55 ff.; on "natural" and "positive" laws, VI, 144; questions raised by, VIII, 51; *see also* Philosophy

Schools, elementary, and the "new" Torah, VI, 302

Sciences, VI, 169, VIII, 140, 384; classification of, VIII, 121 f., 141-46, 347-49; communities interested in, VI, 422; effect of differences of opinion among scientists, VIII, 172 f.; expanding study of, VIII, 264; Graeco-Roman, VIII, 56 f., 121; handmaiden of law and exegesis, VIII, 218; Ibn Daud's references to, VI, 209; Jewish contribution as intermediary between East and West, VIII, 219 f., 255 f.; Jewish exploration in, VIII, 68, 138-230, 347-87; opposition to, V, 97, 259, 282, VIII, 142; physician's grounding in, VIII, 222; rabbinic training in, II, 306; "seven," VIII, 145; theory vs. practice, VIII, 138 ff., 143, 159, 218 ff.; *see also* Scholars and scholarship; *also under* respective disciplines

Scientia media, VIII, 128

Scina, North Africa, I, 410

Scipio Africanus Minor, I, 176

"Scorched earth" policy, I, 406

Scorpion, symbol of Jew, V, 132

Scribes, ancient: attitude toward state, I, 238; functions of priests taken over by, I, 271; origin, I, 153; Pharisaic, I, 225, 397; *soferim*, VIII, 149; status, I, 142; temple, I, 397

—— professional, I, 334, II, 422, IV, 215, VII, 138; and accuracy of scriptural texts, VI, 237, 254, 441, VII, 150; halakhic works and, VI, 63; important role of, III, 156 f.; school for, I, 315

Script, so-called "Rashi," VI, 345; *see also* Alphabet

Scripture, *see* Bible

Scrolls: of Abiathar, V, 31, 37; Abisha, V, 372; of Fasts (*Megillat Ta'anit*), II, 140, 384, V, 189; "five," VI, 244

—— of law: colophon, IV, 112; in greeting ceremony, IV, 10, 12, V, 39, 41; ransomed from the Crusaders, IV, 111 f.; swearing on, IV, 83; for synagogue services, VII, 73, 286

—— secret: cited by Hai Gaon, VI, 23; Ḥiyya's school's, VI, 41; Nissim b. Jacob's, VI, 33, 335 f.; *see also* Abiathar; Dead Sea Scrolls; Esther; Hasmoneans, Scroll of

Sculptures: barred from temple buildings, II, 9; human and animal figures, II, 9, 10, 13, 15, 154, 402; in synagogues, II, 154, 330

Scythia, I, 99, 338, II, 336

Scythopolis (Beth-shan), I, 225, II, 27; church, II, 392 f.

Seal cylinders, I, 323

"Seal of Prophecy," V, 377

"Seal of Solomon," III, 204

Seals in a Western Semitic alphabet, I, 346

"Sea peoples," invasion of, I, 320

Seasons, and climate, VIII, 200, 216

Sea trade, I, 255 f., II, 249, IV, 175 f., 333 ff.

Ṣebaot, II, 311

Sebaste, I, 225; rebuilt, 236; *see also* Samaria

Sebastes (Augustus, *q.v.*), I, 236

Sebomenoi, *see* Semiproselytes

"Second air," doctrine of, VIII, 342

Sectarianism: Christian, III, 160 f., 216, 220, 259 f., 279, V, 136, 188 f., 374, VIII, 31; Bulgarian, III, 209, 330; in Byzantine Empire, III, 176; Russian, III, 216

—— Jewish, II, 26-56, 339-50, III, 11,

78 f., 220 f., V, 84, 170-285, 367-416, VIII, 66 ff.; Al-Ma'mun's decree, V, 9 f., 222; in Arabia, III, 71 f.; attacked by al-Baqillani, V, 84, 327; and biblical texts, VI, 235 f., 243, 254, 298 ff.; controversies, VI, 5 f., 243, 267, 298 ff., VIII, 203 ff.; Damascus sect (*q.v.*), II, 52-54, 348-50; divisive force among minority groups, III, 57; equalization among, V, 186 f.; Essenes (*q.v.*), II, 48-51, 347 f.; forces shaping ideologies, II, 23-26; independent research, VI, 79; influence on Muslim and Christian, V, 136, 374; and intermarriage, V, 265 ff.; internal conflicts, V, 177-84; in Khazaria, III, 203; legal codes, VI, 78, 108; and magic arts, VIII, 11; and messianism, V, 166 ff., 170 ff.; military and ideological movements, V, 191 ff., 347 ff.; and mystery religions, VIII, 31; names of obscure sects, II, 51, 348; in Persia, III, 254 f., V, 105 f., 183 f., 231; Pharisees and Sadducees (*q.v.*), II, 35-46, 55 f., 342-46; Qirqisani's study of, V, 369, 374 ff., VI, 211; religious importance of grammar to, VII, 4; religious syncretism and, II, 3, *see also* Syncretism; repudiation of oral tradition, V, 188 f., VI, 201, VIII, 57 ff.; Samaritans (*q.v.*), II, 26-35, 339-42, V, 170-77, 367-72; unity within, V, 205 ff.; zealotic faction, II, 47; *see also under* respective sects
—— Muslim, III, 123, 133, 148 f., V, 180, 189; number of sects, V, 374; philosophers' assemblies, VIII, 56; and segregation, III, 145 f.
Security, personal, III, 172; in England, IV, 85 f.; of exilarchs, V, 7; instability of, in era of Crusades, IV, 35, 89 ff., 141; and property, IV, 68 f; under the Caliphate, III, 121-27; under Frankish rule, IV, 50
Ṣedaqah, see Charity
Seder, term, VII, 111
Seder Eliyahu rabbah, VI, 229
Seder 'Olam (World Chronology), II, 141, 376, 384, V, 256, 366; VIII, 203 f.
Seder tanna'im va-amora'im, VI, 21
Sefarad, and Hesperia, IV, 4
Sefardi, Moses, *see* Petrus Alphonsi
Sefardim, *see* Sephardim
Sefer Eliyahu, V, 353
Sefer Gezerata, V, 189
Sefer ha-Bahir, see Bahir
Sefer ha-Ma'asim, Palestinian, II, 283, 422, III, 111 f., VI, 64 f., 355
Sefer ha-Yashar, VI, 197 f.
Sefirat ha-'omer, period of national mourning, IV, 145
Sefirot, ten, VIII, 22 f.
Segregation, ancient, II, 173, 187, 191-214 *passim,* 402; in Byzantine Empire, III, 194 f., VIII, 31; and canon law, IV, 9 f., 42 f., 51, 54, VI, 54, 137; of converts to Islam, III, 126; effect on Jewish and Christian doctors, VIII, 254; and hospitals, VIII, 240; of the "impure," V, 250 f.; integration of Jews in Spain, III, 35; and intellectualization, II, 319; of Jewish quarter, III, 11, 232 f., 301, IV, 35, V, 79 ff., 325; Jews coresponsible for, I, 131, 188, 380, II, 12, 430, V, 79 ff., 100, 131, 186, 219 f., VIII, 49; Karaite, V, 261, 265; occupational, IV, 166, 171; of religious minorities under Islam, III, 97 ff., 142, 144 ff., 300 ff., V, 79 ff.; of Samaritans, V, 172, 174, 219
Se'ir, Palestine, VI, 301
Sejan, councilor, I, 246, II, 368
Sekenoi, I, 410
Selah, VI, 257
Seled, childless, VII, 158
Seleucia, destruction of, II, 174
Seleucid era, II, 118, 376, VIII, 378, 379; and birth of Jesus, VIII, 206; dispute over date, VIII, 203 ff.
Seleucids, dynasty, I, 220, 224, 382, II, 98; charter extended to Jewish subjects, I, 216, 244, 369, 393; Jerusalem under, I, 229, 230; story of ritual murder, I, 193; tax on crops, I, 279
Seleucus, story of, VI, 187
Seleucus of Babylon, VIII, 163 f.
Self-determination, individual, II, 41
Self-government, ancient: under Persia (Achaemenid), I, 166; and citizenship, II, 108 ff., 372, 374; coastal Greek cities, I, 225, 280; communities' local autonomy, I, 228, 231, II, 198-204, 265, 403 f.; Hadrian's attack on, II, 106 ff., 108, 118, 120; individual offices, II, 200; patriarchate and exilarchate (*q.v.*), II, 192-98; Pharisee program, I, 401; protected by imperial legislation, I, 240, 245; segregation and, under

Self-government (*Continued*)
Rome and Persia, II, 187, 191-214 *passim,* 402-7
—— medieval, III, 102, V, 3-81, 293-325; areas of, IV, 86; under Byzantine law, III, 190 ff.; congregational, VII, 131 f.; judicial, V, 62, VI, 135; of local usages, V, 48, VI, 126; for merchants, IV, 260; and the messianic age, V, 118; municipal, influence on communal organization, V, 319; political, VI, 172, 214; ritualistic, IV, 55, VII, 65, 94 f.; state attitudes toward, V, 69 ff.
—— *see also* Civil rights; Communities, Jewish; Rabbis and rabbinate; *also under* respective offices, *e.g.,* Exilarchs and exilarchate
Self-mortification, and Day of Atonement, VII, 122
Self-sacrifice, I, 399; Graeco-Roman emphasis upon, I, 233
Seljuks, III, 106, V, 37, 194; occupation of Jerusalem, III, 104, IV, 94; in Palestine, IV, 285, 295
Ṣemaḥ b. Ḥayyim (?) Gaon, VI, 108; and Eldad's *Halakhot,* VI, 221, 241; and Spanish scholars, VII, 13 f.; support of local customs, VI, 122
Ṣemaḥ b. Joshua, VII, 288
Ṣemaḥ b. Palṭoi Gaon, VI, 23, 27, 28, 31; dictionary of talmudic terms, VII, 13 f.
Ṣemaḥ b. Solomon, VII, 111 ff.; on *piyyuṭ,* VII, 101; prayer book, V, 248
Semaḥot, tractate, VI, 63
Semantics, biblical, VI, 296 ff.
Seminomadic life, I, 55
Semiproselytes, I, 284, 415, II, 149
Semiramis-Astarte, cult, II, 30
Semites, ancient: altars, I, 48; in Egypt, I, 37; influence in Europe and Africa, I, 175; Jewish leadership, I, 210; migration into Palestine, I, 33; monotheism, I, 44; religion expressed in art, I, 14; *see also under* respective nations, *e.g.,* Babylonia
Semitic languages, and Hebrew, VII, 11
Seneca, philosopher, I, 192, 193, II, 16, 170
Sennacherib, king of Assyria, I, 123, 318; campaign against Judah, I, 95; deportees, I, 95, 338; Edomite expansion set in motion by, I, 106
Sennaja, *see* Phanagoria
Sens, France, IV, 61
Senses: internal, VIII, 226; location of, VIII, 79; perception of, VIII, 78 ff.; and the soul, VIII, 108
Separatism, *see* Segregation
Sephardim, VI, 87; and Ashkenazim, IV, 3 f., 43, V, 61, VI, 25 f.; collections of penitential poems, VII, 170; congregational recitation of *Yigdal,* VII, 175; Hebrew pronunciation, VI, 250, VII, 233; New Year's day services, VII, 172; prayer book, VI, 15; talmudic manuals, VI, 34; "Thirteen Principles," VI, 60; *see also* Spain
Sepphoris, II, 99, 108, 123, 164, 175, 179, 224; congregation in, II, 199, 285; Ḥanina's ordination opposed, II, 243; *kohanim* in revered class, I, 413; leadership, V, 179; partial burning of, II, 179, 398; rabbis' struggle for power, II, 242, 413; renamed Diocaesarea, II, 108; theater, I, 401
Septimania, province, III, 245, IV, 52; acquired by the Franks, IV, 43; Jews of, III, 46 f.; Stephen II's letter to prelates of, IV, 47; *see also* Narbonne
Septuagint, I, 186, 187, 196, 199, 379, 383, 384, III, 189, V, 345, VI, 238, 256; antianthropomorphisms, I, 196, 383 f., VI, 258 f.; Arabic translations, VI, 264; Christians' use of, II, 385, III, 12 f., 233; growing hostility of Jews, II, 142, 385; hermeneutic elaboration, VI, 155-63; interpretations of, and the Peshiṭṭa, VI, 257; Latin paraphrase from, II, 143 f.; "translation Greek," VII, 4, 7; *see also* Bible; Old Testament
Sepulveda, Spain, *fuero,* IV, 39
Seraḥ, wife of Bulan, III, 199
Seraphim, V, 142
Serapists, II, 133
Seren, I, 63
Serenus-Severus, *see* Severus, pseudo-Messiah
Serfdom: of Jews, IV, 22, 41, 63, 70 ff., 87, 141, V, 78, 128 f.; *see also* Vassals; Villeins
Sergius, commander of Gaza garrison, III, 87
Sergius, monk of Amida, III, 230 f.

Sergius, patriarch of Constantinople, III, 248
Sergius Paulus, I, 243
Sermon on the Mount, II, 67
Sermons, II, 144, 280, 294, 316, 422; aggadic-halakhic, VI, 36, 169; Christian missionary, forced attendance of Jews, IV, 55, 57; content and development of, VI, 152-75, 399-412; exegetical, VII, 81 f.; poetic, VII, 82; scarcity of compilations, VI, 157; threefold division of, VI, 163 ff.; use of tales and parables, VII, 183; *see also* Homilists and homiletics; Preachers
Serpent: allegorical meaning of, VIII, 86, 339; brazen, I, 66, 322
"Servant of the Lord," I, 157, 365
Servies, term, V, 129
Seth, god, I, 37, 304
Settlements, *see* Communities, Jewish
Set-Typhon, god, I, 382
Seven, number, VIII, 145; cosmic importance, VII, 244
Seven-branch candelabrum, *see* Candelabrum
Seven-day week, I, 6, 120, 192
"Seven times seven years," I, 332
Severan dynasty, II, 187
Severus, patriarch of Antioch, III, 5; "fear of the Jews," III, 17
Severus, pseudo-Messiah, III, 16, V, 182, 184 ff., 193 f.
Severus, Julius, general, II, 98
Severus, Lucius Septimius, Roman emperor, II, 109, 110, 150, 375, 400
Seville, Spain: employment of Muslims by *dhimmis,* III, 146; Jews in, III, 109; Muslims vs. *dhimmi* scientists, V, 97
Sex, VI, 182 f.; abstinence of the Essenes, II, 218; appetites reproved by Paul and rabbis, II, 85, 365; extramarital relations, II, 218, III, 142 f., V, 240 f., VIII, 53; "false" prophet and, VIII, 131 f.; and interfaith rules, III, 142 f.; and Karaites, V, 241 ff.; magic arts and, VIII, 283; menstruating women and, V, 250; morality of Jews, II, 225, V, 133 f., VII, 180; penalties for transgressions, III, 111 f., 143, 300, V, 57; pregnant wife safeguarded, II, 221; relations with foreign women, I, 194; restraints on, I, 146, 147, II, 217, 290, 319; and the Sabbath, V, 217; with slaves, IV, 191, 195, 334; theme in Arabic literature, VII, 187; theme in poetry, VII, 169, 176
Shabbat, designation, I, 143, VI, 267; *see also* Sabbath
Shabbat, talmudic tractate, VI, 41, 80, 382
Shabbata de-rigla, V, 40
Shabbetai, name, I, 6, 120, 121, 349
Shabbetai b. Abraham Donnolo, *see* Donnolo
Shabbetian movement, antinomianism in, VIII, 18
Shabbetit, name, I, 121
"Shabur," generic title, VI, 428
Shaddai, divine name, I, 158, VIII, 179
Shafi'i, Muslim jurist, V, 212 f.; on convert's property, III, 144; Muslim confiscation of property, III, 169; on *sunna* of the Messenger, VI, 330; and *wergeld* of Zoroastrians, III, 295
Shafi'ites, III, 123, 168, VI, 16; in Cairo, V, 268
Shaf ve-Yatib, synagogue, II, 317, 435
Shahrastani, III, 254, V, 327; censure of Ibn Hudail, VIII, 96; on changeability of laws, V, 332; on number of Jewish sects, V, 183, 194 f., 207 f.; religious studies, VIII, 301
Shakespeare, William, V, 348
Shalom, I, 146; *see also* Peace
Shalosh, word, VI, 351
Shalosh regalim, I, 5; *see also* Holidays
Sham'atiyya, V, 84
Shammai, I, 180; controversies with Hillel, V, 255
Shammaite school, I, 114, II, 228, 410
Shapur (Shahpuhr) I, king of Persia, II, 177, 178, 195, 238, 290, 380, 397, 433, III, 55; checked at Palmyra, III, 62
Shapur II, king of Persia, II, 179, 181, 204, 405; and Isfahan, III, 109, 110
Sharecropping, I, 111, II, 258; *coloni* and, III, 31, 244; and concentration of landholdings, III, 163; by *dhimmis,* III, 146
Shari'ah, term, and *halakhah,* VI, 12
Sharon, Valley of, IV, 154
Shaṭbi paper, IV, 169
Sheba, queen of, II, 212
Shebu'ot, tractate, VI, 86

Shechem (Nablus), I, 35, 61; covenant concluded at, I, 308, 325; renamed Flavia Neapolis, II, 123; "sacred town" of Samaritans, II, 28, 31, 35
Shechem Decalogue, II, 29
She'eltot, book, VI, 337 f.; *see also* Aḥai of Shabḥa
Sheep raising, I, 253, 263, 301
Shefaṭiah b. Amittai, Hebrew poet in Italy, III, 180, VIII, 60
Shefelah, Palestine, IV, 153
Sheḥiṭah, ritual slaughtering, VIII, 386; *see also* Slaughter, ritualistic
Shekhinah, I, 389, II, 317
Shelamim, I, 316
Shem, VI, 192
Shema' prayer, I, 186, II, 119, 349, V, 26, 126, 248, VI, 47, VII, 66 ff., 96 f., 120, 244; accuracy of oral transmission, VII, 112; incorporation in the *Qedushah,* II, 182; *piyyuṭim,* VII, 102; prohibition of, VII, 95; recitation of, II, 7, 8, VI, 93, 123, 131, 450, VII, 72
Shemariah, captive scholar, V, 46
Shemaya, ancient sage, II, 203, 346
Shemayah, R., Rashi's pupil, VI, 53 f., 348 f., VII, 281
Shem Ṭob, false claimant to Davidic descent, V, 39
Shem Ṭob b. Joseph ibn Falaquera, *see* Ibn Falaquera
Shemuel, acrostic, VII, 262; *see also* Samuel b. Hosha'nah
Shenazzar, I, 119, 349
Shepherd, messianic connotation, V, 379
Sheqalim, tractate, VI, 336, 349
Sherira Gaon: on Aramaic prayers, VII, 66 f.; on authority of the geonim, V, 23; commentaries on Talmud, VI, 43; on conduct of religious services, VI, 9; Davidic descent, V, 9; "Epistle," VI, 30, 81, 112, 204 f., 233; on geonim and Talmud, VI, 23; loss of pupils, V, 24; on marriage settlement, VI, 24; and Muslim robbers and thieves, III, 122; on "new light on Zion," VII, 116; responsa, III, 111 f., VI, 29 ff.; and R. Yose, VI, 18
Sheshna Gaon, VI, 446; advice re extortion, V, 5
She'ur qomah (Measure of the Divine Stature), VIII, 11 ff., 25 ff., 32 f., 179; Maimonides on, VI, 177 f.
Shi'a, Muslim sect, V, 168, 183 f., 211, VI, 10, 363; accessions among Persians, III, 150; attitude toward Enoch, VI, 437; in Baghdad, III, 123, 133; Idriside dynasty, III, 108; rites, VII, 308; in Tiberias, V, 180
"Shield of David," III, 204
Shilo, identified with messiah, II, 139, 140, V, 118
Shiloh, sanctuary, I, 59
Shimei, I, 324
Ship, as symbol of Israel, V, 361
Shipping: restrictions on Jewish merchants and owners, IV, 183 f.; and shipowners, II, 249, 261; Venetian, exclusive rights to, IV, 24; *see also* Piracy; Trade, international
Shipowners' guild, II, 261
Shirin, Persian wife of Khosroe II, III, 57, 60
Shopkeeping, IV, 179 f.; *see also* Trade
Shoshan-Dukht(?), city built by, II, 204, 404
Shoshenk (Shishak) I, king of Egypt, I, 322, 327
Shouting, congregational, VII, 125 f.
Showbreads, in the Temple, VII, 78
Showfringes, V, 218, 219, VII, 76
Shpsh, god, I, 45
Shrines, Jewish: in Egypt, III, 106; portable, I, 49
Shrouds, II, 273, 287
Shuraiḥ ibn 'Amram, Jewish poet, III, 78
Shureiḥ, Muslim exegete, VI, 471
Shurpu, I, 50
Sibawaihi, Baṣran philologist, VII, 34
Sibylline Oracles, I, 204, 385, 390, II, 397, III, 15, 234
Sicarii (assassins) of Zealotic faction, II, 47, 347
Sichardus, John, editor of pseudo-Philo apocryphon, VI, 196 f.
Sicily, III, 24, IV, 24, 115; Graeco-Byzantine tradition, VIII, 256; Jewish communities, III, 109, IV, 20-24, 242 f.; Jewish converts, III, 28; Jewish landowners, IV, 160; languages, IV, 21; service of fleet in the Crusades, IV, 298; synagogues, III, 30, 175
Sicut Judaeis, IV, 7 f., 235 f., 240; *see also Constitutio pro Judaeis;* Papacy
Siddur, term, VII, 274; *see also* Prayer books

Sidonians, I, 162, 176, 374 f.;
blockade, I, 277
ollinaris, V, 125 f.
IV, 338
Africa, IV, 170
I, 156, 400
rency, IV, 347; industry, II,
58 f.; trade, IV, 169, 183
6; artificial production of,
mines, IV, 211; standard,

orite, IV, 245
eth Arsham, III, 67 f.
es the Elder, III, 6
muel, R., of Vitry, VI, 75,
turgical works, VII, 122 ff.,
on Qalir's poems, VII, 103
I, 162, 278; Mosaic com-
VI, 90 f.
rch, I, 39; tribe of, I, 317,
III, 208
Simon, R., and Hai, VI, 364; on individual prayer, VII, 74
Simon, Richard, VI, 306
Simon, son of Boethos, I, 216
Simon, son of Giyoras, I, 231, 268, 412, II, 347
Simon an der Pfort, R., VI, 162
Simon b. Abba, R., II, 253
Simon Bar-Jona, II, 74
Simon b. Eleazar, II, 419
Simon b. Gamaliel, R., II, 14, 15, 117, 141, 237, 253, 408, 430, VI, 31; academy head, II, 126, 127; as patriarch, II, 193, 403; on translation of Torah, II, 143
Simon b. Isaac "the Great," cantor of Mayence, VII, 144
Simon b. Laqish, R., II, 44, 148, 194, 206, 237, 283, 305, 392, VI, 181, VII, 62; epigrams, II, 276; on eternity of Jewish law, II, 161; homily against separateness, II, 241; pun on the law, II, 277; quoted, II, 172, 184, 246
Simon b. Megas the Priest, VII, 92
Simon b. Menasya, R., II, 67, 356
Simon b. Ṣemaḥ Duran, *see* Duran
Simon b. Shetaḥ, I, 219, 221, 395, II, 21, 236, 409, 421, 422, V, 255, VI, 207
Simon b. Yoḥai, II, 96, 124, 125, 185, 265, 309, 426, IV, 157, VIII, 283; book of "Mysteries," V, 148 f.; on Islam, III, 93; legends, I, 9, V, 140; prayer, III, 274, IV, 296, V, 353; tomb, II, 279; on Torah vs. economic endeavors, II, 251
Simon b. Zoma, R., II, 218, 248
Simonias, Palestinian community, VI, 36, VII, 81
Simon Maccabee, Jewish ruler, I, 220, 222, 223, 229, 235, 255, 368, II, 98; numismatic sovereignty, I, 369, *see also* Coins and coinage, Maccabean; political sovereignty recaptured by, I, 166
Simon Magus, II, 32, 341
Simon the Hasmonean, *see* Simon Maccabee
Simon the Just (or the Pious), II, 120, 421, VI, 155; encounter with Alexander the Great, VI, 207
Simony, II, 268; Church legislation vs., III, 249
Simon Zealotes, II, 74, 346
Simson b. Abraham of Sens, VI, 54 f., 349 f.
Sin, Babylonian moon deity, I, 44; worship, in Arabia, III, 64
Sin, desert, I, 45
Sinai, Mount, I, 45, 48, II, 139, 161, V, 92; Moses on, V, 93, VI, 8, 91, 100, 228, 232, 269, 300, VIII, 6, 41, 294; *see also* Revelation
Sinaitic Peninsula, I, 36
Sinaitic slaves, I, 36
Sinan, Sabian medical commissioner, III, 146; vizier's order to, VIII, 240
Sindbad, Parables of, VII, 189
Sind b. 'Ali, Arab astronomer, VIII, 167 f.
Singers: among returning exiles, I, 124; prophesy, I, 153
Singing: in synagogue and church, I, 125, II, 8, 155, 330, 389, VIII, 3; in Temple, I, 123; *see also* Music
"Singing girls," VII, 205
Sins: avoidance of, as preventive medicine, VIII, 261; biblical synonyms for, VI, 296; Crusades as expiation for, IV, 101; doctrine of original, II, 433; exile and, V, 100 f.; extinction of, in messianic era, V, 165 f.; forgiveness of, II, 308, V, 17, VII, 92; interrelated origins of death and, I, 139; and penitence, VIII, 52, 105; and punishment, I, 136, *see also* Punishments; remedy, I, 294; responsibility for, I, 135, II, 41, 346; and transmigration of souls, VIII, 36; *see also* Confession of sin; Redemption

Siqariqon, law of, II, 104, 372
Sirach, Jesus, I, 6, 151, 185, 198, 228, 252, 255, 265, 272, 386, 397, II, 34, 222, 228, 313, V, 188, VII, 66; beliefs of, II, 19, 38, 44, 45, 346; epigram on the physician, VIII, 221; medieval knowledge of works of, VII, 260; prayer, II, 342; quoted, II, 129, 379, 420
Siroe, son of Khosroe II, III, 239
Sisebut, king of the Visigoths: anti-Jewish decrees, III, 37, IV, 5, 155 f.; effect of intolerance of, in France, III, 47
Sivan 20, fast of, IV, 138, 145, V, 217
Sixth century, I, 103-5, 341-44
Skeletons, at Montjuich, IV, 33, 249
Skepticism, VIII, 79; Jewish spokesmen for, V, 104 f.; religious, VIII, 66 f.; *see also* Philosophy; Rationalism
Slaughter, ritualistic, II, 306, IV, 104, V, 93, 249, VI, 70, 359, VIII, 227; of half cow, half dog, VI, 183 f.; house, IV, 39; monopoly on, IV, 244; nonsacrificial, I, 148, 150; poems on, VII, 192; regulations, IV, 60 f., VI, 70, 359, VIII, 386
Slaves and slavery: children of bastards and, II, 223; circumcision of, IV, 188, V, 219; conversion, III, 179, IV, 49, 52, V, 219; of converts to Islam, III, 126; and debts or fines, II, 257, 258, 303; decree on clothing, III, 139; Egyptian, I, 259, 260; employment, IV, 196; Ethiopian, II, 238; female, I, 71, 85, 112, 259, 269, 324, II, 224, 230, III, 89, *see also* Concubines and concubinage; freedom of, through baptism, III, 14; and free workers, I, 267-71, 412; fugitive, I, 71, 85, 324; Gentile, I, 70, 71, 268, 269, 324, II, 259; in industry, II, 247; Jewish ownership, I, 110, 181, II, 259; laws affecting, I, 70, 85, 88, 267, 324, II, 259, III, 89, VI, 84; Muslim attitude toward, III, 302 f., IV, 195; Negro, mother of Mustanṣir, III, 158; Pharisaic-rabbinic aversion toward, I, 269; prisoners of war sold as, I, 95, II, 102, IV, 110; ransom of, I, 259, 268, 281, III, 200, IV, 188 f., 255; reference to, in Jewish prayer of thanksgiving, VII, 109; religious instruction, IV, 190, VI, 12; responsibility for damages inflicted by, I, 269; runaway, IV, 190; Sabbath observance by, IV, 156; Sinaitic, I, 36; Slavs as, III, 214, IV, 172, 194; state, I, 324; Syrian, I, 409; taxation, II, 105; tax receipt as mark of, III, 168; temple, I, 324; treatment on basis of equality, II, 258; treatment of freed, I, 269, II, 223, 286, *see also* Freedmen; unrest of, II, 57
—— Christian, III, 32, 36, 51; Arian, in North Africa, III, 234; circumcision, IV, 188; owned by Jews, III, 30 f., 188, 219, 243, 252 f., IV, 19, 154 ff.
—— Jewish, II, 258 ff., 416, III, 45; accretions to community through, III, 110; 'Anan on, V, 219; Hebrew, I, 57, 69, 70, 85, 267, II, 114; and Israelites, I, 57; perpetual slavery, III, 43
Slave trade and traders, I, 70, II, 259, 262, III, 30 f., IV, 187-96; ban on sales to Jews, IV, 9; fraudulent, IV, 192 f.; and labor shortage, IV, 172; Phoenician, I, 176; prices, I, 268, 324, IV, 188 f., 255; self-sales, I, 324
Slavonic countries: Jewish merchant traders, IV, 175 f.; source of slavery, IV, 194
Slavonic dialect, Old, IV, 177; Christian writings in, III, 211; *see also* Josephus
Slavs: and "Canaan," III, 214 f., IV, 177, VI, 437; contributions to Christian literature, III, 211; Jewish settlers among, III, 206 ff., 330 ff.; legal codes, III, 187; as slaves, III, 214, IV, 172, 194; in Syria, III, 98
Smallpox, VIII, 242 f.
Smiths, Palestinian, I, 60
Snake bite, verbal charms for, VIII, 234
Snake symbol, I, 66, 322
Ṣobah, *see* Aleppo
Social classes, *see* Classes, social
Social justice, I, 25, 332; Essenes' preoccupation with, II, 48; an essential of religion, I, 88; preachment of Islam on racial equality, III, 98
Social science, VIII, 121 f.
Social unrest, I, 67-72, 322-25; Graeco-Roman period, I, 250-85, 406-15; and prophecy, I, 73, 84-91, 332-36; *see also* Revolts
Social welfare: in talmudic age, II, 269-74; 420; pietism and, VIII, 48 f.; *see also* Charity
Societies, friendly, II, 288, 289, 424

Society: cleavages in Israelitic, I, 275; moral foundation, I, 50, 319; primacy over individual, IV, 222, VIII, 120; and religion, I, 3-31, 189, 277, 293-97
Socioeconomic conditions, IV, 150-226, 312-52; and changes in law, VI, 63, 146 f.; class distinctions in Muslim society, III, 148 f.; effect on aggadic study, VI, 152 ff.; in England and Normandy, IV, 76 ff.; interfaith, III, 50, 147, IV, 14 f., V, 95 ff.; Karaites and, V, 238 f., 400 f.; leisure class, VIII, 72; medical practice and, VIII, 254; Paul's acceptance of, II, 77; and pessimism under Rome, II, 57; protection of rights by papacy, IV, 7 ff.; and rabbis' insistence upon procreation, II, 210; regional variations, IV, 158-64; and religious propaganda, I, 174; reported by Benjamin of Tudela, VI, 223 f.; and sectarianism, V, 177 ff.; and type of occupation, IV, 167, 179 f.
Socrates, Greek philosopher, I, 233, II, 259
Socrates, Byzantine chronicler, V, 167 f., 366 f.
Sodom, punishment of, VI, 482
Soferim (scribes), VIII, 149
Soferim, tractate, II, 143, VI, 34 f., 238 f.
Sofia (Sardica), Bulgaria, III, 210
Soklos, Pannonia, III, 207
Soldiers, *see* Military service
Solomon, Hebrew king, I, 22, 67, II, 212, III, 244 f., VIII, 77; authorship of biblical books, II, 145, VI, 285, 308; breach of law of succession, I, 149; centralized controls, I, 74 f., 326; collaboration with Tyre, I, 64, 321; *corvée,* I, 70, 84, 324; eulogized as king of magicians, II, 17, 21, VIII, 223 f., 283; expeditions, VII, 16; figures in palace and Temple decoration, II, 15; foreign gods served by, I, 65, II, 160; harem, III, 201; identification with Agur b. Jakel, VI, 160; industrial and commercial undertakings, I, 326; influenced by earthly trigon, VIII, 180; knowledge of natural sciences, VIII, 387; mystical midrash, VIII, 18 f.; Northern Israel as continuation of kingdom of, I, 73; and Palmyra, II, 407, III, 62; population under, I, 29, 320; prayer, II, 60; as prophet, VIII, 132; seal of, III, 204; splendor of court, I, 77; taxes and payments in kind, I, 318; wives, I, 65, II, 226, III, 201
Solomon, governor of Africa, III, 230
"Solomon," acrostic used by Saadiah, VII, 141, 144
Solomon, Song of, *see* Song of Songs
Solomon, Testament of, VIII, 283
Solomon Abu'l Munajja ibn Sha'ya, constructor of Nile canal, III, 155
Solomon b. Aaron of Troki, V, 272
Solomon b. ha-Yatom, VI, 62
Solomon b. Ḥisdai, exilarch: and academy of Sura, V, 9; appointments to gaonate of Sura, V, 15
Solomon b. Isaac or Yiṣḥaqi, *see* Rashi
Solomon b. Kuji, V, 203
Solomon b. Saron, apologist for Karaism, V, 229
Solomon b. Simson, chronicler of First Crusade, IV, 94 ff., 285 ff., V, 199 f., VI, 193, 217 f.; vs. Christians, IV, 143; and forced converts, IV, 106; on Jewish martyrs, IV, 96 f., 144 f.
Solomon b. Yehudah, Palestinian gaon and poet, III, 295, V, 33, 48, 233, VII, 268; career, V, 34; and Karaites, V, 280; Nathan b. Abraham's campaign against, V, 274; prayer for fellow Jews, III, 104
Solomon ha-Kohen, messianic pretender, V, 202, 260
Solomon ibn Adret, *see* Ibn Adret
Solomon ibn Parḥon, *see* Ibn Parḥon
Solomon's Temple, *see* Temple at Jerusalem, First
Solomon-Sulaiman, of Sanjar, liturgical poet, VII, 100, 268
Solomon the "Babylonian," IV, 14
Solomon the Egyptian, Jewish court physician, III, 185
Song, synonyms for, VIII, 279
Song of Deborah, I, 141, 317, 318, VI, 261
Song of Moses, II, 330; pronunciation, VI, 250
Song of Songs, I, 336, 340, II, 145, 386, V, 282, VII, 158, 213; eschatological interpretation of, V, 156 f.; Judeo-Christian controversy, VI, 161; Midrash on, VII, 81; Targum of, VI, 160, 403
Songs, secular, VII, 203

Sons, younger, in biblical legend, I, 22
Sonzolo, Shem-Ṭob, IV, 12
Sophism, VIII, 78 f.
Sophronius, patriarch of Jerusalem, III, 87, 277
Sopron (Oldenburg), Hungary, III, 211
Sorcery: prohibition of, VIII, 276; *see also* Magic arts
Soul, I, 390 f., VIII, 318 f.; and Adam's body, I, 52; ascent to heaven, VIII, 21 f., 23, 105, 284 f.; and body, VIII, 36 f., 226; faculties of, VIII, 82 ff., 105 ff., 117, 331 f.; Greek concept, I, 208; Hebrew synonyms for, VIII, 338; hygiene of, VIII, 339; immortality of, VIII, 104; location, VIII, 107; meaning of words as, VII, 51; prophetic, transmission of, VIII, 134; well-being of, VI, 142; *see also* Immortality of the soul; Resurrection
Sovereignty of the people, I, 91
Space: four ells in, V, 303; philosophic discussions of, VIII, 88 ff.
Spain, I, 169, 170, III, 33-46, 244-50, IV, 27-43, 245-56; Alfasi in, VI, 86 f.; apocalyptic tract, V, 145 f.; Arab conquest, III, 91 f., 272; Babylonian Talmud in, V, 47, VI, 332; biblical commentaries, VI, 277, 284 f., 309; capital punishment in, VI, 45, 134; Christian-Muslim relations, IV, 93 f.; Council of Elvira, II, 188, 210; court poets, VII, 146 ff.; Crusades against Jews and Muslims, IV, 131 f., 148; emigrés to Italy, IV, 21; evolution of Jewish calendar, VIII, 199 f., 204; *ghubar* numerals, VIII, 150; Golden Age of Jewish literature, VI, 188, VII, 136 ff., VIII, 263; identification with Sefarad, IV, 4; international trade, III, 156; Jewish agriculture, IV, 158 ff.; Jewish communities, II, 210, III, 27-43, 33 ff., 108 f., IV, 44 ff., 148, V, 51, 58; Karaites, V, 241, 271, VII, 228; liturgy, VII, 107 f., 116, 118, 272 f.; manuscript of Aḥimaaz' chronicle, VI, 432; massacre and pillage, IV, 39 f.; medical science, VIII, 248; merchants, IV, 179 f.; mishnaic commentaries, VI, 61 f.; Mohammed's decrees of religious toleration, III, 124; moneylending, IV, 206 f.; Muslim prohibition re slaves, IV, 194; New Christians, III, 176 f.; paper manufacture, IV, 169; philosophic speculation, VIII, 39, 63 f., 135, 311; Phoenician ghettos, I, 176; recitation of Aramaic version, VI, 262; record of postgeonic century, VI, 208; responsa collections, VI, 117; rise of Jewish influence and power, III, 155 ff.; slaves in, IV, 194 f., 337; spread of influence of Muslim Golden Age, IV, 3 ff.; taxation of Jews, III, 169; Tosafists, VI, 56; use of Hebrew language, VII, 47, 54 f.; and vernaculars of east and west, VIII, 229; vineyards and orchards, IV, 162
—— Visigothic, III, 33-46, 244-50; Babylonian influence on Jewry of, V, 61; laws on Jews, III, 33 ff.; number of Jews, III, 245; weakness of the monarchy, III, 44
Sparta and Spartans: affinities with Jews, I, 185, 377; delegation to St. Nicon Metanoites, III, 184, 318
Spartianus, II, 109
Speculations, metaphysical, II, 314; attitude toward, VIII, 68 f.; vs. revelation, VIII, 85
Speculations: regulations against economic excesses, II, 254; *see also* Business transactions; Economic conditions
Speech: Aramaic supplanted by Arabic, VII, 67; divine, VIII, 129; "levantinization" of, VII, 10; purity of, and environment, VII, 3, 223
Spelling: in biblical texts, VI, 238; in the Masorah, VI, 293; and pronunciation, VI, 243 f.
Spheres, celestial, VIII, 93 ff., 163, 213; and the Hereafter, VIII, 105; influence on man, VIII, 111
Spices, Book of, VIII, 235
Spice trade, IV, 44
Spinoza, Baruch: *scientia intuitiva,* VIII, 131; and Trinitarian creed, VIII, 96
Spires, Germany: Jewish community, IV, 67, 68, 74, 96, 134, VI, 345; Jewish quarter, IV, 275, 347, V, 79
Spirits, world of, VIII, 180; *see also* Demonology
Spiritual exercises, II, 315, 316
Sports and games, II, 421
Spring, miraculous, V, 367
Staff called Graciousness, V, 264
Stars: Abraham's knowledge of, II, 16; Hebrew names of, VIII, 358; influence

of, VI, 231, VIII, 94, 111, 175; movements of, VIII, 169; trepidation of, VIII, 164 f., 173; *see also* Astrology; Astronomy; Planets
State: artificial, I, 122; attitudes of Jews toward, I, 4, 16-25, 27, 235; coercion vs. Jews, V, 70 f.; vs. communal autonomy, V, 69 ff.; Jesus and, II, 69, 73; loyalty to, V, 77 f., VIII, 263; and nationality, I, 17-25, 93-96, 234, 338; Sadducees and, II, 99; scholastic theory of, V, 71 ff.; *see also* Political power; Rights, legal; Self-government
Steer, eschatological monster, VIII, 10
Status: of burghers, IV, 23; of farmers in Byzantium, IV, 153; of Muslims in foreign lands, III, 129; change in socioeconomic, V, 126 f.; *see also* Rights, legal; Socioeconomic conditions
Stephen, Saint, II, 74, 83
Stephen III (IV), pope, IV, 42, 47
Stephen V (VI), pope, IV, 260
Stephen VI (VII), pope, IV, 260
Stephen, king of England, IV, 81
Stilicho, Teuton ruler of Rome, III, 234
Stobi (Yugoslavia), II, 210, III, 207; synagogue, II, 10
Stone quarries, I, 257
Stone structures, built by English Jewry, IV, 85, 170
Stoning, V, 241
Stories and storytelling, VI, 168-74, 181-88, 408-16; art of, III, 71; intermingled with history, VI, 233; popularity of, VI, 167; in synagogue and mosque, VI, 154; types of, VI, 180 f.
Strabo, I, 180, 252, 255, 262, 266, 396, II, 13, 266
"Strange woman" of the Proverbs, I, 151, 363
Straton of Gorgippia, III, 200
Strikes and strike breakers, I, 270
Strongbow, Richard (Richard de Clare, 2d earl of Pembroke), IV, 82
Strophe, Hebrew, VII, 199
Students: books supplied to, VII, 137 ff.
Study: time for, and employment, IV, 221, 223; *see also* Education
Style, Hebrew, purification of, VII, 50 f., 54
Subotniki, Russian sect, III, 216
Suetonius, Paulinus, I, 178, II, 57, 104, 105 f.
Suez, Isthmus of, IV, 173
Suffering: divine compensation for, VIII, 103; of Israel, V, 144, 160; values in, I, 257, II, 215, IV, 146 f., V, 101 f., VI, 439, VIII, 126 f.
Ṣufism, Muslim, VI, 143, VIII, 51, 112; and alchemy, VIII, 225; influence on Judaism, VII, 78; *see also* Mystics and mysticism
Suftaja, draft, IV, 213
Sugyot, lessons, VI, 20
Suicide, V, 241; as alternative to enforced baptism, IV, 96; exhortation vs., VI, 193 f.; funeral rites, II, 287
—— mass: in England, IV, 125 f.; in Mayence, IV, 104; public reaction to, IV, 144
Suidas, VIII, 57; on Agapios, VIII, 241
Sulaiman, caliph, III, 102
Sulaiman al-Sanjari, *see* Solomon-Sulaiman
Sulaiman of Andalusia, III, 115
Sumer, Jewish fiscal expert, III, 150
Sumerian law codes, I, 327
Sun: creation of, VIII, 203, 368; position, VIII, 201; rotation, VIII, 163; size, VIII, 162 f., 360; worship of, I, 45, II, 50, 51
Sunday, II, 134, 380; Judeo-Christian trade on, IV, 220; observance of, IV, 60 f., 157, V, 123 f.
Sun goddess, I, 311
Sunna: in Fez, V, 79; and Jewish *halakhah,* VI, 7; judicial summaries, VI, 363
Superman, doctrine of, VIII, 344 f.
Supernatural: attraction of, VII, 76 ff.; formulas for control of, VIII, 8 ff.; and man, VIII, 27; *see also* Angels; Demonology; God; Intermediaries; Magic arts; Miracles
Superstition: Karaites on, V, 258; religious, VIII, 26
Supreme Being, I, 174; *see also* God
Sura, Babylonia, II, 207, 405, III, 114; discriminatory rules on medical treatment, III, 146, VIII, 240; Jewish majority, III, 99; synagogue, VII, 108
—— academy, III, 59, 154, V, 9, 13 ff., 276, VI, 201 f., 425, 455; adherence to Judaean custom, VI, 124 ff.; archives, VI, 112 f.; Babylonian Talmud, VI, 17 f.; enrollment, V, 19; and the exilarchate, V, 14 f.; Palestinian traditions, VI, 24; revenue, V, 14; superiority over Pumbedita, VI, 430; weaver

Sura (*Continued*)
as presiding officer, V, 74 f.; *see also* Amoraim; Geonim and gaonate
Surgeons and surgery, VIII, 238, 260
Surveyors, methods of mensuration, VIII, 157
Survival, after death, VIII, 104; *see also* Immortality of the soul
Survival of Jews, I, 9, 105, II, 215; dependent upon fulfillment of covenant, I, 90
Susa: exiles at royal court, I, 115, 132; Ezra and Nehemiah in, I, 116; rebuilding of, II, 204
Suyuti, Arab historian, III, 153; history of Qur'anic exegesis, VI, 468
Sviastoslav, duke of Kiev, III, 205 f.
Sviatopluk, duke of Prague, IV, 118
Swastika, emblem, II, 11
Swiatopolk II, of Kiev, III, 216
Swinthila, king of the Visigoths, III, 39 f.
Switzerland: multilingualism, VII, 223; outlawry of *sheḥiṭah,* VIII, 386
"Sword of Moses," VIII, 11, 281
Symbolism, VIII, 284; of letters, VIII, 15; numerical symbolism, VI, 157 f.; phonetic, VI, 249 ff.; and tombstone inscriptions, IV, 33; *see also* Images and symbols
Symmachus, Bible translation, II, 143
Synagogé (Johannes Scholasticus), III, 187
Synagogue, I, 351, 410, II, 280-86, 422 f.; architecture, II, 9, 284 f.; benefactors, II, 187, 191, 242, 333, 338, 402; benefactresses, II, 24, 240, 338, 413; books discarded, VII, 139; Caesarea, II, 423; chief works on, II, 423; churches converted into, III, 280; communal life in, I, 15, 126, 133, 214, II, 45, 285 f., 291, VI, 154, VII, 62 ff.; construction, III, 232; converted into churches, III, 8, 30, 136, 296; customs concerning, VI, 123 f.; decorated with signs of Zodiac, VIII, 184; dedication to pagan dignitaries, II, 4; destruction of, II, 189, 284, III, 6; at Dura-Europos, I, 14, II, 241, 346; equality with church and mosque, I, 24; exemption from billeting of soldiers, III, 192; Galilean, in which Jesus taught, II, 67, 355; and Graeco-Oriental arts, II, 6 ff., 9 ff., 146, 285, 330 ff., 402; hospice and, I, 214, VIII, 239 f.; Karaite, V, 247 ff.; location and autonomy, II, 199, 403 f., IV, 266 f.; oldest known, II, 10; orientation toward Jerusalem, II, 285, *see also* Jerusalem; origins, I, 351, VI, 392; outlawed in North Africa, III, 8 f.; papal attitude toward, III, 29 f.; pre-Islamic, II, 175, 242, III, 136; prohibition of new, II, 181, 192, 398, III, 9, 10, 134-39, 188, 230; preparation of scrolls, VII, 73, 286; professional readers, VI, 237, *see also* Cantor; protective laws for property, II, 189, 192; rebuilt, III, 175; Samaritan, V, 174, 177; segregation of sexes, II, 241; separate, of Palestinian and Babylonian rituals, V, 28, *see also* Ritual; and Temple, I, 132, II, 125, VII, 128, 274; use of, to denounce Islam, III, 123; violation classified, I, 245; woman's role within, II, 240, 413; worship of Christians in, II, 188, VII, 84, 128
—— Great, Men of the, VI, 203 f., 206, 230, VII, 65 f., 101, 251, VIII, 21
—— services, II, 280 ff., III, 72, VII, 128; attendance and length of, VI, 139 f., VII, 69, 71, 130 f., 246 f.; books necessary for recitation, VII, 135; cantillation of weekly lessons, VII, 126; congregational leader, VII, 79-85; congregational responsoria and singing, VII, 125 ff., 284; educational and devotional aspects, II, 280, 281, VII, 73 f., 271 f.; interruption by public appeal, V, 66 f., VI, 139; music, II, 8, 155, 330, 389, VII, 125-31, 281-85; procedure, VI, 41 f.; recitation of Aramaic version, VI, 262; regional autonomy in use of *piyyuṭim,* VII, 104; scriptural lessons, VI, 257, 262, VII, 81, 94; sermons in, IV, 55, V, 112; *see also* Liturgy; Preachers; Rabbis and rabbinate; Worship
"Synagogue Greek," I, 186
Syncretism, II, 292; astrology, magic, and ritual, II, 15-23, 334, 336 f.; bridges between Jewish and Gentile worlds, II, 3-6; geographical centers, II, 24 f.; Graeco-Oriental art, II, 6-15, 330-34, 402; Islamic, III, 80-86, 265-68; Israelitic, I, 349; Judeo-Christian, V, 367; Khazar Judaism, III, 200-206; Mishawayh's, V, 196 f.; and Second Commonwealth, II, 23-26, 54-56, 338 f.; and

sectarianism (*q.v.*), II, 3, V, 179; shaping forces, II, 23-26, 338
Synods, Catholic, *see* Councils, Church
Synods, communal, V, 64 ff., 70 f.; of Usha, II, 126, 271, 378, 420
Synonyms, biblical, VII, 12; multiplication of, VIII, 14
Syracuse, Sicily, III, 175
Syria and Syrians, I, 217; ancient Christians in, II, 83, 164, 165, 393; antisemitism, I, 176, 283, II, 89; apotheosis of royal power, I, 398; army's desertion of Jews, I, 218; bronze, I, 318; Byzantine campaign, III, 317; concentration of landholdings, III, 163; Crusaders in, IV, 297; ethnic and racial groups in, III, 98; extortions of Ventidius, I, 264; industry, II, 248 f.; Jews in, I, 169, 170, 283, 393, III, 103 ff., 279, IV, 108 f.; Maccabean uprising, VI, 189; merchants, I, 260; migrations to, II, 210; Palestine a province, II, 94; political stupor of ancient Jewish communities, I, 247, II, 96, 99; proselytes, I, 183, 283; religion, I, 229, II, 3, 165 f.; Sadducees leaders of revolt against, I, 234; *see also* Seleucids
Syriac Christians, VIII, 76; Al-Muqammiṣ and, VIII, 97 f.; doctrine of divine attributes, V, 120 f.; emphasis on ceremonial laws, VIII, 17; influence of religious philosophy of, V, 120 f., VIII, 58; in international trade, III, 49, 53, IV, 44; law codes, II, 432, VI, 4 ff., 321 f.; liturgy, VII, 65; poetry related to current events, VII, 99; Trinitarian creed, VIII, 96; version of Bible, VI, 241, 263, 454; works of translation, VIII, 64; *see also Peshiṭṭa*
Syriac language, II, 146, VI, 256, 453, VII, 4, 84, VIII, 393; church use of, VII, 68; medical works, VIII, 242; poems in, VII, 196; *see also* Aramaic
Syria Palaestina, official name for Judaea, II, 123, 380
Syro-Roman Code, VI, 4
Syrus, Michael, III, 177, V, 8
Szabolcs, Council of, III, 212

T

Ta'abod, term, V, 129
Taanach, I, 313
Ṭabari, 'Ali b. Rabban al-, I, 341; interpretation of biblical prophecy, V, 87; "Paradise of Wisdom," medical work, VIII, 243; self-appraisal as controversialist, V, 88; use of Syriac version, VI, 263
Ṭabari, Mohammed ibn Jarir aṭ-, V, 86, VI, 170; commentary on the Qur'an, VI, 282; on ordinary meaning of scriptures, VI, 463
Tabeel, I, 348
Tabernacle, I, 49, 314, VI, 147, VIII, 147; in desert, VIII, 7, 94; Moses' building of, IV, 167, VI, 163
Ṭabit ibn Qurra, *see* Ibn Qurra
Tables of testimony, I, 314
Tabrizi, at-, VIII, 346
Tacitus, I, 193, 248, 262, 372; anti-Jewish bias, I, 175, 181, 183, 191, 194, II, 170; despair of Roman future, II, 57; on Great War and after, II, 90, 92, 102, 106, 368, 372; ignorance of Israel's preexilic history, I, 192; on Jews, I, 382, 411, II, 5, 109, 219, 223, 394
Tadmor, *see* Palmyra
Taḥpanḥes, Egypt, I, 111
Ta'if, Arabia, introduction of viticulture, III, 70
Tajo, bishop of Saragossa, III, 248
Taku (of Tachau), Moses b. Ḥisdai, VIII, 39, 286; report of legend re Ibn Ezra's death, VIII, 368
Tales, fantastic, II, 306, 433; *see also* Stories
Talismans, protective, II, 20; used during childbirth, I, 329; *see also* Magic arts
Talmidim, term, VI, 342
Talmud: II, 207, 215-321, 408-36; on agriculture, IV, 157; allusions to moon's nativities, VIII, 161; on *'am ha-areṣ* (*q.v.*), IV, 167, V, 178; anatomical observations, VIII, 228; antitalmudic movements, II, 264; on appointment of officials and judges, V, 71; on asceticism, II, 435; and astrological approach, VIII, 176, 178; on bans imposed by *nasi,* V, 48; biographical material, VI, 24; borrowings from the Persian, II, 206, 405; bulwark against forces of nature, II, 293 f., 319-21, VI, 19 f.; burning and suppression of, VI, 90; capital punishment, V, 45, 57; cemeteries, II, 286-90, 423 f.; and Christianity, II, 130, 297, 427, V, 110;

Talmud (*Continued*)
chronology, II, 297; circumcision of slaves, IV, 187 f., 189; community, II, 290-92; concentration of study on, VI, 236; on consumption of butter, IV, 315; on darkness and light, VIII, 34; "days of the Messiah," V, 148; designation of Meṭaṭron, VIII, 281; deviations from, V, 52, 59; discussions of ritual, VII, 108 f.; distinction between theoretical and practical laws, VI, 77; economic trends and policies, II, 241-55, 262, 264, 413-18, IV, 209, 217; education, II, 274-79, 421 f.; eugenics, II, 229-35, 411; exegetes, VI, 50, 347, *see also* Exegetes and exegesis; few anthropomorphisms, VIII, 100; few anti-Gentile polemics, II, 111, V, 110; Gemara, II, 295, 305; Gentile prophets, VIII, 133; geographic references, VIII, 215; Gnosticism opposed, II, 314-18, 434-36; Graeco-Roman words used, II, 300, 302; "great things," VIII, 71; *Hekhalot rabbati* on, VIII, 17; and Hellenism, I, 388; and history, II, 296, 320; ignorance of Khazar Jews, III, 202; intellectualization, II, 319-20, 436; "introductions" to, VI, 32 f.; judiciary, II, 265-69, 418 f.; *jus divinum,* V, 78; Karaite study of, V, 253; Karaites vs. supporters of, V, 230 f.; labor, appreciation of, II, 256-60, 416; language of, II, 147, 387, VI, 27 ff., 256, VII, 28-32, 56 ff., 60, 192 f., VIII, 263; law and religion, II, 293-321, 425-36; list of preexistent things, V, 147; literature, II, 294-98, 425-29; on liturgy, VII, 69 ff., 170 f.; logic, II, 297; magic formula from, VIII, 9; manuscripts, editions, and translations of, II, 297, 427 ff.; marriage, II, 217-23, 408 f.; and martyrdom, IV, 96; on medical fees, VIII, 232; messianic folklore, V, 165; monogamous trends, II, 223-29, 409 f.; on music, VII, 206, 283; on mutilation of slaves, IV, 191; names of plants and animals, VIII, 226 f.; number of bones in body, VIII, 230; number of communal officials, V, 60; obscure literary allusions to, VII, 142; Pharisaic doctrines elaborated, II, 310-14, 434; on pilgrimages, I, 213, 214; prohibition of tax stamp, III, 168; protection of tradesmen, V, 68; reason for supplying biblical names, VI, 281; references to God's love, VIII, 114; references to older halakhic works, VI, 63; regimentation, II, 260-65, 417 f.; on rights of settlers, V, 68 f.; ritual and moral law, II, 307-9, 433; rules concerning debates, VI, 30, *see also* Debates, talmudic; on sale of slaves to non-Jews, IV, 193; scarcity of copies, VI, 21, 111 f., 201; Sirach quoted in, II, 129; situation out of which born, II, 214; social welfare, II, 269-74, 420; study of, V, 3, VI, 34 f., VII, 71, VIII, 219; supremacy of law, II, 298-307, 429-33; synagogues, II, 280-86, 422 f.; tanning, IV, 166; tax legislation, V, 65 f.; urban vs. farm property, IV, 316; warning on pronunciation, VI, 240; women's status, II, 223, 235-41, 412 f.

Talmud: Babylonian, II, 294, 295, 297, 302, 316, 320, III, 3, 99, VI, 230; circulation of, VI, 441; commentaries on, VI, 35-56, 336-50, 352; geonim and, V, 212; lexicon, VII, 29; oral transmission, VI, 19, VIII, 7; Saboraic recension, III, 54, 73, VI, 240; in Spain, V, 47; supremacy, V, 22, 25 f., VI, 17, 34, 100, 242 ff., VII, 29; text, VI, 237 f.; translation into Arabic, VI, 264; uniform recension, VII, 28; unifying influence, V, 180 f.

—— Palestinian, I, 376, II, 13, 294 ff., 302, 333, 426, VI, 331; Arabic translation, VII, 29; area of dissemination, VI, 346; commentaries on, VI, 88 f.; Ḥananel and, VI, 47; Maimonides' reliance on, VI, 104 f.

—— *see also* Aggadah; Amoraim; Law; Mishnah; Rabbis and rabbinate; Religion; Tannaim

Tam, Jacob b. Meir, R., of Rameru, France, III, 217, IV, 48, 119, 162, V, 70, VI, 295, VII, 47, VIII, 43; on ban of settlement, V, 68; collection of northern responsa, VI, 117 f., 121; on early halakhic works, VI, 63 f.; on escape of slaves to Palestine, IV, 190; on geonic teachings, VI, 133, 332; on lack of door-post inscriptions, V, 59; and local customs, VI, 129; on Menaḥem-Dunash controversy, VII, 228; on purchase of land, VI, 147; reaction to criticism, VI, 121; on R. Simḥah's work, VII, 123; on study of the Tal-

mud, VI, 34, 55; on synagogue attendance by workers, IV, 155; on use of dairy products, IV, 315
Tamid, offering, I, 316, 404
Tamim Abu Ḥarb, leader of Palestinian peasant revolt, III, 166
Tana de-be Eliyyahu, III, 198
Tancred, IV, 110
Tanganyika, Lake, III, 116
Tanḥuma, Midrash, V, 217, VI, 40
Tanḥum b. Ḥanilai, VI, 164
Tanḥum Yerushalmi, Egyptian scholar: lexicographic works, VII, 31 f.; mistaken historical views, VII, 242
Tanis, I, 35
Tanit, deity, I, 374
Tannaim, I, 386, II, 295, 425, VI, 19, 30, 334, VIII, 147; agricultural controls, II, 263; and Amoraim, VI, 29, 201; ban on written recensions, VI, 454; controversy over intercalations, VIII, 371; economic controls, IV, 219 f.; on emigration from Palestine, IV, 221; Hai on, VI, 176 f.; interest in masoretic problems, VIII, 280; law on acquisition of books, VII, 135 f.; literary allusions to lives of, VII, 142; prophecy re end of age, VI, 17; R. 'Aqiba's compilation of law, VI, 107; sayings in halakhic works, VI, 63; teachings re number of commandments, VI, 91; works ascribed to, VI, 159, VIII, 18; *see also* Mishnah; Rabbis and rabbinate; Talmud; Tosefta; *and under* names of teachers
Tannaitic and Amoraic Sages, Order of, VI, 201 f.
Tanners and tanning, I, 275, IV, 166 f.
Tarfon, R., II, 117 f., 205, 222, 227, 409; quoted, II, 133
Targum, Aramaic (Onkelos): V, 159, 213, VI, 239, 264 f., 421, 444, VII, 17, 249; Babylonian revision, VI, 256; Masorah for, VI, 259 f.; replaced by Saadiah's translation, VI, 270; use of, by synagogue reader, VI, 257; *see also* Onkelos
—— Jonathan, II, 146, 387, 411, VI, 260 f., 456
—— Palestinian, VI, 160, 261 f., VII, 94, 263; aggadic accretions, VII, 82; dates of, VI, 456; and Onkelos, VI, 262
—— Samaritan, VI, 455
—— *sheni:* of the Book of Esther, VI, 188
Tarichaea, I, 255, 407
Tarragona, Spain, IV, 34; "city of Jews," III, 109
Tarshish, III, 34; location of, VII, 16; ships of, I, 321
Tarsus, and Tarshish, VII, 16
Tartar dialect, V, 247
Tartessus, Phoenician colony, I, 321, III, 34
Tashlikh ceremony, III, 241
Taurus, constellation, VIII, 177 f.
Taxation: ancient Israelitic, I, 76, 160, 326; Byzantine, III, 190-94, 320 f.; in Caliphate, III, 96 f., 150, 161-70, 308-12, VI, 112; collectors and farmers of taxes, I, 190, 274, 275, 279, 414, II, 105, 110, 184, 185 f., 194, 373, III, 152, 165 f., IV, 151, 201 f., V, 5 f., 18, 65 f.; communal responsibility for, II, 243, 245; concessions to converts, III, 242, 295; in England, IV, 81; evaders, II, 243; and flight from land, II, 245; indirect, III, 192 f.; in Jerusalem, III, 101; land tax, III, 162 f., 274 f., IV, 152, 214; in Latin Kingdom of Jerusalem, IV, 114 f.; loss of land by defaulters, II, 242; Norman system, IV, 23; paid in kind, I, 318; patriarchate's collection of, II, 193 ff.; of peasants, II, 245, 414, IV, 151 f.; poor tax, III, 274; property tax, IV, 81; punishment for default, III, 309 f., 312; resources of Jewish communities, I, 175; receipt stamped on neck of taxpayer, III, 168; revenue sources for religion and charity, II, 194; on sales at fairs, IV, 325; Temple tax, I, 394, II, 105, 118; under Persia, II, 180, 184 ff., III, 56; under Rome, I, 248, 262 ff., 279, 411, 415, II, 100, 104, 105 f., 183 ff., 263, 373, 375, 399; *see also* Poll tax
—— exemptions from: I, 263, III, 164, 179 f., IV, 38 f., 67 f., V, 75 ff.; for officials, I, 397; for priests, II, 413; for rabbis, II, 243 f., 277, 413
Taxo, of tribe of Levi, II, 59, 346
Tchernichovsky, Saul, Hebrew poet, III, 79, 264
Teachers and teaching, II, 278, IV, 215; *see also* Education; Rabbis and rabbinate
Tebtunis, I, 266; papyrus, I, 261
Technical progress, II, 248

Ṭeharot: geonic commentary on, VI, 42, 340; introduction by Maimonides, VI, 60 f.

Teima, Arabia, I, 349; identification of, III, 257; Jewish settlement, III, 63 f., VII, 191

Teleology, and the existence of God, VIII, 324

Tella, defense of, II, 179, 398

Tell al-Yahudia, Heliopolis: inscriptions, I, 394; temple, I, 219, 394

Tell Beit Mirsim, I, 115

Tell el-Amarna, *see* El-Amarna

Tell en-Nasbeh, I, 326

Tell Halaf (Gozan), I, 345

Temple at Jerusalem: First (Solomon's), I, 48, 83; abominations worshiped, I, 88, 335; building of, I, 14, 66; date of founding, I, 321; destruction, I, 102, 126, II, 87, 131, III, 62; Ezekiel on gates of, I, 122, 350; as fiscal agency, I, 333; incense (*q.v.*), I, 352; music, I, 123; orientation toward, I, 213; orientation within, I, 392; sacrificial worship, I, 123-29 *passim*, 148, 219, 352; symbol of freedom and power, I, 126

—— Second, III, 23, VIII, 125, 211, 273; Caligula's statue ordered, I, 219, 231; computations based upon, V, 366, VIII, 205; conflicting views of, II, 44 f., 74, 82, 305; construction, I, 258, VIII, 372; correctors of biblical books, VI, 235; Day of Atonement worship, VI, 390; desecration, I, 192, 217, II, 34; elaborate ceremonies, II, 6; figures in decoration, I, 238, 402, II, 13, 15; focus of Jewish intellectual life, I, 161 f.; gates, I, 262, 263; Gentiles excluded, I, 157, 239, 258, 402; gratitude for rebuilding dissipated, I, 237; Greek influence, II, 9 f.; *heqdesh*, VIII, 240; high priesthood of Hyrcanus denounced, I, 227; high priest's confession, VII, 79; holiness of, II, 28; Jesus' reference to himself as temple, II, 83, 364; Julian's promise to rebuild, II, 154, 160, 392; Maccabean rededication of, VI, 163, *see also* Ḥanukkah, festival of; and messianic age, V, 147 ff., VIII, 40; and Mosque of the Rock, III, 272; pilgrims in, I, 213, 392; plan to rename temple of Zeus, I, 229; poems on the "watches," VII, 90; position of implements in, VII, 78; restoration, I, 160, 161, 367; revenue, I, 272, 273, 413, II, 82, 194; sacrificial system, I, 271, II, 33, 284, V, 218, VII, 72, VIII, 41; scribes, VI, 441; separation of sexes, II, 240; special privileges for property of, II, 252; site of, III, 277 f., VI, 228; state's main exchequer, I, 215, 333, II, 44, 82; and synagogue (*q.v.*), II, 282, V, 247, VII, 62, 293; tax, I, 215, 393, 394, II, 105, 118; tables in outer and inner courts, III, 29; world marvel, II, 9; yearly gathering at Wailing Wall, II, 108

—— destruction of, I, 166, II, 131, III, 62, IV, 283 f., VI, 447, VIII, 379; antecedents to, II, 34, 341; and Christians, II, 74, 83, 364; dating events by, II, 116, 376, III, 237, IV, 283 f.; as homiletical theme, VI, 167; long-lasting effects, II, 90; loot from, I, 217, II, 113, 375, III, 11, 232; mourning over, II, 8, 111 ff., 375 f.; people's beliefs about, II, 112, 113 f.; responsibility for, II, 93, 369; vision of Third, V, 140 f.

Temples: Greek, in Palestine, II, 8; of Jupiter Capitolinus, II, 13, 106, 373; pagan, II, 6, 7, 24; Parsee, I, 353; and private banking in Assyria, I, 108; Samaritan, II, 26, 29, 30, III, 9, V, 173; *see also* Gerizim, Mount

—— Jewish, I, 132; in Elephantine (*q.v.*), I, 129

Temuda, Arab official, III, 63 f.

Tenan, term, VI, 65

Tenancy, *see under* Landlords

Ten Cities, I, 225

Ten Commandments, *see* Decalogue

Ten Days of Repentance, VIII, 74

"Ten horns," V, 158

Ten Martyrs, I, 231, II, 370, IV, 285

Ten plagues, I, 189

Ten Tribes, III, 117, 205, 329, VI, 434; cause of loss, II, 338; redemption of, II, 61, V, 144, 151, 200; *see also* Israel, Northern

Tents, I, 72

Terah, Abraham's father, I, 33, 302, 311

Teraḥ, word, I, 302

Terahites, I, 311

Ṭerefot, term, VIII, 387
Terminology, biblical: requisite for exegesis, VII, 12; grammatical, lists of, VII, 51; legal, VIII, 338; Rashi's work on, VI, 52, VII, 31; scientific, difficulty with equivalents in translation, VII, 6 ff., 220 ff., VIII, 75 ff., 227, 245; talmudic, VI, 27-35, 332-36; *see also* Words
Terracina: religious rights of Jews in, III, 29 f.; synagogue, III, 31
Territory: attempt to reconquer minimum of, I, 164; clan society and territorial society, I, 55; Jewish attitudes toward, I, 4, 16-25 *passim;* and nationalism, I, 53-61
Tertullian, II, 136, 396; on Christian officials, I, 243, 404; on history of Israel, II, 80; on prayer, VII, 79
Teruel, Spain, *fuero,* IV, 41
Teshubah, see Repentance
Testamentary dispositions, II, 253
Testament of Abraham, II, 4
Testaments of the Twelve Patriarchs, II, 345, 351
Testimonies against the Jews, II, 386; compilations of, V, 345; messianic, V, 157
Tetragrammaton, V, 120, VI, 249, 409, VIII, 275; in incantations, VIII, 281; meaning of the two *he*'s in, VIII, 36; misspelling and mispronunciation of, VI, 449; numerical value, VIII, 152; ritualistic repetition of, VIII, 284; *see also* Yahweh
Teutons, as mercenaries, II, 238
Textile industry, I, 257, 408, II, 248, 249; growth of, IV, 165; and international trade, IV, 327; *see also* respective branches, *e.g.* Linen
Thanksgiving, formula for daily, VII, 109
Theater: Greek, I, 189, II, 9; Jewish attitude toward, II, 9
Thebes, Greece, communal council, V, 55 f.; silk industry, IV, 168 f.
Theobald, count of Champagne, *see* Thibaut
Theobald, tale of martyred children, IV, 135 f.
Theocracy, I, 163, 165, 167; vs. old aristocracy, II, 279; regime, I, 130, 152, 221-27, 395-97; term coined by Josephus, I, 152, 223, 271
Theodicy, I, 136, 356 f.
Theodora, wife of Justinian II, III, 7, 198
Theodore of Mopsuestia, Syriac author, VI, 257, VII, 136; exegetical works, VI, 282
Theodoret of Cyrrhus, II, 434, V, 133, 338, VI, 271, 304
Theodoric the Great, king of the Ostrogoths, II, 398, III, 25 f.; *Edictum Theoderici,* III, 25 f.; policy toward Jews, III, 240
Theodorus, Byzantine commander, III, 23
Theodosian Code, II, 192, 398, III, 13, 187, 243; domination of, in western Europe, III, 25; Jewish status under, III, 49, IV, 50 f.
Theodosians, Coptic sect, III, 9
Theodosius, abbot of Petcherskii Monastery, III, 215
Theodosius I, Roman emperor of the East, II, 193, 399; Ambrose's victory over, II, 189, 401; economic moves, II, 250, 254, 261; legal decrees, II, 266, 267, 419, III, 8; quoted, II, 192
Theodosius II, Roman emperor of the East, II, 180, 186, 398, III, 11; on Nestorians and Jews, III, 229; *Novella* 439, III, 35
Theodosius of Alexandria, III, 17
Theodotion, Greek translator, II, 143; and Targum Jonathan, VI, 261
Theodotos, son of Vettenos, I, 214, II, 202, 285
Theodotus, poet, II, 31
Theodulf of Orléans, IV, 257
Theology: Christian controversies re, III, 21; interfaith debates, V, 83 ff.; and medicine, VIII, 259 f.; and messianism, V, 163 ff.; attributes of God in Muslim, VIII, 96; and politics, VIII, 349; rank of, as science, VIII, 142 f., 160; *see also* Philosophy; Religion
Theophanes: on forced conversion, III, 176; on Jews in Jerusalem, III, 103; on tax stamps, III, 168
Theophilus, Christian missionary, in Ḥimyara, III, 65 f.
Theophilus of Antioch, II, 73, 136, 138
Theophrastus, I, 377, 404
Theophylactus Simocatta, III, 58 f.

Theophylaktos, son of Romanos I, III, 182

Theosophy, pietism and, VIII, 50 f.

Theotonio, founder of monastery of Santa Cruz, III, 160, 308

Therapeutae, sect, II, 347, 349; compared with Essenes (*q.v.*), II, 51

Theriak the Great, VIII, 257

Thessalonica, Paul in, II, 79; *see also* Salonica

Theudas, false messiah, I, 221, 395, II, 36, 61

Theudas of Laodicea, VIII, 241

Thibaut, count of Champagne, IV, 62 f., 269

Thietmar, IV, 271

Thieves, I, 268

"Third communion," Jews as, II, 173, 396

"Third order": claim of Christians to be, II, 396; term, II, 366

Third Wall, Jerusalem, II, 369

Thomas à Becket, Saint, IV, 280 f.; loan for flight to France, IV, 82

Thomas Aquinas, Saint: on imposition of taxes on Jews, V, 77 f.; on royal alliance with Jews, V, 348

"Three imposters," VI, 301

Throne of Glory, VIII, 6, 82, 273; preexistence of, VIII, 125 f.; song of, VIII, 13

Thucydides, I, 25

Thutmes III, king of Egypt, I, 38

Tibbonide family: "translation Hebrew," developed by, VII, 7; *see also* Ibn Tibbon

Tiberias, city, II, 99, 108, 123, 164, 175, IV, 113, 169, V, 180; academy, II, 196, III, 102, V, 32 ff., VI, 245, 446; aid to Persian army, III, 21; Byzantine commander and, III, 23; vs. Christians of Ḥimyara, III, 67 f.; center of masoretic research, VI, 239, 245; congregations, II, 199, 404; exilarchate, VI, 200; guardian of Hebrew language, VI, 245, VII, 33, 47; Ḥimyarites and, III, 67 f., 260, V, 180; leadership of Jewish communities, III, 20; rabbis' struggle for power, I, 242; riot against ordination of Ḥanina, II, 277; Saladin's conquest of, IV, 298; starvation in, II, 245; textile industry, IV, 323

Tiberius, Roman emperor, I, 178, 264; and Jews of Rome, I, 246, 248

Tiberius Alexander, II, 91, 93, 110, 368, 369

Tiberius Claudius Balbillus, II, 369

Tiberius Claudius Fatalis, II, 368

Ticino, Council of, IV, 26

Tiflis, Armenia, III, 110

Tiflisites, V, 182, 195, 219

Tigranes I, king of Armenia, I, 169

Timagenes, I, 396

Time, II, 158, VI, 469; philosophic discussions of, I, 295, VIII, 88 ff.; *see also* Chronology

Timothy I, patriarch, V, 378

Timothy III, patriarch of Alexandria, III, 68

Tiridates, king of Armenia, II, 165

Tishre, month, I, 294, V, 224, VIII, 184

Tithes: for academies, V, 14; of animals, V, 399; charitable, II, 241, 271; ecclesiastical, IV, 13, 43, 58, 153 f., 239, 256; *ḥomesh,* V, 14; Karaite, V, 235; priestly, I, 272, II, 118, IV, 13, 313; Saladin, IV, 81, 279, 297

Titles: honorary, V, 48, 59, 60, 283, 313, 314; princely, V, 311; used by Jewish leaders, III, 233

Titus, Roman emperor, II, 92-93, 102, 108, 113, 120; love affair, II, 92, 369; policy toward Jews, I, 248

Tmutarakan, duchy of, III, 205

Ṭob 'Elem (Bonfils), Joseph b. Eliezer, VIII, 362 f.

Ṭob 'Elem (Bonfils), Joseph b. Samuel, IV, 157, V, 62, VI, 48; on communal responsibility, V, 65; collection of responsa, VI, 113; copy of *Seder tanna'im,* VI, 34, 202; on intercommunal noninterference, VI, 393; liturgical works, VII, 121

Tobiah b. Eliezer, Jewish scholar, III, 210, V, 200; aggadic learning, VI, 173; mystical teachings, VIII, 30; works, VI, 174 f., VII, 82

Tobiah b. Moses of Constantinople, translator, III, 195, V, 233 f., 252 f., VI, 173, VIII, 301; on conversion to Karaism, V, 274; similarity of original work and translations, VII, 220; translation of Arabic works into Hebrew, VII, 7, 48

Tohu va-bohu, VI, 302

Toledo, Spain, IV, 28, 132; Arabic documents on moneylending, IV, 206; collaboration of Jews in Arab capture of,

III, 92; Councils of, III, 36-46, 246-50, IV, 241, V, 129; Jews of, III, 34; Mozarabs, III, 127; privilege to Mozarabs, Castilians, and Franks, IV, 40
—— Third Council of, IV, 19; on circumcision of Christian slaves, III, 36; on clergy and temporal powers, III, 41; on mixed marriages, III, 36
—— Fourth Council of, III, 41; on converts, III, 43, 248; on forced conversion, III, 39
—— Sixth Council of, III, 41, 54, IV, 241
—— Eighth Council of, III, 41; on sale of slaves to Jews, IV, 188
—— Eleventh Council of, III, 43
—— Twelfth Council of, IV, 19; Erwig's appeal to, III, 44
—— Sixteenth Council of: on property of Jews, III, 45
—— Seventeenth Council of, III, 43, IV, 41
Toledot Adam, VI, 197 f.
Toledot Yeshu (Life of Jesus), II, 140, 384, V, 348
Toleration, religious, IV, 114 f., V, 103 ff., VI, 6, VIII, 136; abrogated by Philip Augustus, IV, 61 f.; 'Anan and, V, 218 f.; in Byzantine legal codes, III, 187 f.; Church policy of, IV, 53 f., 56, 121, 141; equality in Spain, IV, 28; in Italy, III, 29 f.; of Jewish observances, III, 148, V, 124; juristic interpretation of, III, 124; in Khazaria, III, 200; Mohammed's decree, III, 124, 131; and nationalist revival, V, 186; separate ethnic-religious groups, IV, 86; under Theodoric, III, 26; Theodosius I and, III, 8; treaties, III, 130 f.; under the Caliphate, III, 123 f., 133, 171 f., V, 82, 210, 264, 335; under the Sassanians, III, 57, 128 f.; *see also* Persecutions; Religious liberty
Tolls, Roman, I, 279, 415
Tombs: decorative motifs and inscriptions, II, 11 ff., 14, 63, 146, 331, 353, 376; psyche, II, 14; of rabbis, II, 279; studies of ancient, II, 333; violation of, I, 410; *see also* Cemeteries and catacombs
Torah: contradictory biblical statements on, VI, 305; on economic matters, IV, 162; equality of parts, VIII, 318; eternity of, II, 319, 320, V, 91 f., 130, 229; VI, 146; fenced around by elaboration, II, 319, 436; festival of Rejoicing, V, 26; *Ḥuqqe ha-torah* (Laws of the Torah), VI, 140 f.; *jus divinum,* V, 78; Karaite concept of, V, 251 f.; language, VI, 248; Midrash *Sar Torah,* VIII, 19 ff.; neglect of, VI, 100 f.; new, VI, 302; preexistence, VI, 228, VIII, 6, 19 f., 125 f.; rejected by Esau and Ishmael, V, 134; as revelation, VI, 307 f.; study of, IV, 221, 223, V, 162 f.; Western Jewry and, III, 173; *see also* Bible; Law; Old Testament; Pentateuch
Torat kohanim, I, 150; *see also* Priestly Code
Torlonia, Villa: tombs, II, 11, 146, 331
Tortosa, Spain, IV, 132; Jewish community, IV, 332; Judeo-Christian debate, VI, 172; Muslim treaty with Ramon Berenger IV, IV, 30
Tosafists and *Tosafot,* V, 61, 78, VI, 53-56, 88, 172, 202, 278, 348 ff., 363; compilers of, VI, 350; on conclusion of Torah scroll, VI, 253; on dairy products, IV, 315; on division of earth's surface, VIII, 214; measuring circular field, VIII, 157; and talmudic methodology, VI, 34
Toscana, Berta di, IV, 245
Tosefta, I, 273, II, 123 f., 294, 295, 425, VI, 53 f., 104; ancient, VI, 413; compilation of, II, 301, VI, 76, 204; concordance to, VII, 29; on physician's responsibility, VIII, 238
Tota, queen of Navarre, III, 155 f., IV, 29
Ṭoṭafot, term, VII, 21; *see also* Phylacteries
Totalitarianism, I, 325
Totressia, and Tetragrammaton (*q.v.*), VIII, 284
Toulouse, IV, 55
Tours, battle of, III, 91
Town, Israelitic, I, 71, 325; responsibility for unsolved crimes, I, 327; *see also* Cities; Urbanization
Toys, mechanical, VIII, 356
Trachonitis, I, 172
Tracts, controversial, V, 83 ff.; *see also* Apologetics; Controversies, socioreligious
Trade: ancient, I, 60, 64 f., 69, 255-58,

Trade (*Continued*)
318, 323, 360, II, 262; advance of, II, 247, 249-51, 260, 414; anti-Jewish regulations, IV, 13, 24 f.; associations, IV, 185, *see also* Guilds; barter, IV, 214; charters, IV, 48 f.; Jews attracted to, I, 108, II, 123; laws of sales and purchases, VI, 67 f.; local, VI, 126; Muslim law on, III, 126, IV, 351; in Near East, III, 339; in Palestine, II, 244; rabbinic restrictions on, II, 262, IV, 219 ff., 351; and Sabbath observance, I, 360; in Spain, III, 156; taxes, IV, 152; women engaged in, I, 113, II, 237; *see also* Business transactions
—— international, III, 49, 284 f.; effect on family relationships of traders, VI, 395; effect on Jewish unification, VII, 136; elimination of Jews from, V, 25; influence on geographic knowledge, VIII, 212 f.; Italian republics and, IV, 4 f., 186; Jewish settlement on routes, IV, 175, 266 f., *see also* Routes, trade; legal aspects, IV, 176 f.; as medium of cultural exchange between East and West, VIII, 256 f.; military aspects, IV, 186; rabbinic control of Palestine's export trade, II, 262; restrictions on Jewish shipping and shipowners, IV, 183 f.; role of Jews in, IV, 44, 171-96, 322-36; routes (*q.v.*), IV, 172 f., 175, 180 f., 266 f.; Russo-Norman, IV, 181; talmudic law and, V, 27
Trades: and manufactures, II, 248 ff.; specialization, I, 257; *see also* Crafts and craftsmen
Tradition: adherence to, and scientific progress, VIII, 138 f.; agnostics and, VIII, 90; historic continuity, VIII, 31; vs. innovations, V, 109 f.; and medical science, VIII, 234 f.; as source of knowledge, VIII, 80 ff.
—— Jewish, V, 188; adjusted to new demands, VII, 131 ff.; chain of, VI, 205, 230, VIII, 20 ff.; conservatives and, VIII, 68; departure from, in legal codes, VI, 77 ff.; historical accuracy of oral, I, 305; Karaites and, V, 235, 251 ff., 261; legal, VI, 16-27, 327-32; Mosaic, VI, 8, 334; mystic roots in, VIII, 20 ff., 25; preservation of, by Franco-German Jewry, VIII, 42 ff.; proof of, by reasoning, VIII, 82; and Scripture, V, 209 f., VI, 460; sources of, VI, 267; talmudic vs. posttalmudic, VI, 100 f., 210; proponents of written, VI, 427; *see also* Oral Law
—— Muslim, VI, 7; collections, VI, 26 f.; historic validity and, III, 308 f.; oral, III, 273
Trajan, Roman emperor, II, 121, 156; outlawry of Judaism in Cyprus, III, 19 f.; revolt against, II, 94-97, 100, 370 f.
Trance, ecstatic, II, 315
Trani, Italy, Spanish refugees in, IV, 21, VI, 167
Transjordan: cattle raising, I, 57, 72, 253; cities in hands of Greeks, I, 224 f.; conquest of, I, 250, 308; historic intermissions, I, 33; iron in, I, 320; Jewish settlements, I, 167, 370; modern, I, 307; Nabatean-Roman domination, III, 61
Translation: of Arabic classics, IV, 3, 32; of entire literature, I, 187; free vs. literal, VII, 7; of philosophic works, VIII, 64 f., 75 ff.; and transliteration of names and terms, VIII, 172, 174; use of like-sounding words, VII, 8
"Translation Hebrew," VII, 7, VIII, 316
Translations, biblical: Jewish and Catholic collaboration in, VIII, 265 f.; *see also under* Bible *and* respective versions
Transmigration of the soul, V, 211, 228, 259, VIII, 36, 104 f.
Transmission, oral, VI, 37, 194, 205, 426 f., VII, 87, VIII, 7; Decalogue, VI, 427; generations of transmitters, VIII, 210 f.; of historical chronicles, VI, 433; of learning, Jewish role in, VIII, 256; of linguistic material, VII, 243; mnemotechnic aids, VII, 88, VIII, 149; and opposition to written, VI, 37, 110 f., 205, 426 f., 454, VII, 107, 124; of prayers, VII, 85 ff., 112, 124
Transport associations, II, 257, 261, 417
Transportation, II, 249; difficulties caused by famines, II, 245; by sea, II, 249
Transport workers, I, 275
Trapezite banking, I, 410; *see also* Banking; Moneylenders and moneylending
Traveler: conditional divorce of, VI, 139; role in cultural exchange, VIII, 256

Travelogues, VI, 219-26, 433-37, VIII, 211 f.; value of, VI, 225 ff.
Treason: charges of, vs. Jewish converts, III, 46; political, in Visigothic Spain, III, 40 f., *see also* Loyalty; religious, VIII, 263, *see also* Heretics and heresies
Treasures, concealed, IV, 211
Treaties: between city and conqueror, IV, 30; between city and Jews, IV, 27; between Rome and Judaea, I, 218; extradition, IV, 80, 204; with merchants, IV, 63; Muslim, of religious toleration, III, 97, 130 ff., 161 ff., 269, 293 f.; peace, IV, 70 f., 89 f., 141, 236; regional, IV, 63; royal, re Jews, IV, 62 f.
Trebonian, III, 13
Tree of knowledge, I, 253; size of, VIII, 26
"Tree of Life," I, 363; size of, VIII, 26
Trees: in Jewish iconography, I, 253; symbolism, II, 13, 332, 333
Trent, Council of, IV, 19
Treuga Dei, IV, 236
Treves: burning of effigy of bishop, IV, 283; early Jewish settlers in, II, 406; expulsion of Jews, IV, 92, 283; forced baptism, IV, 106, 293, 310
Triangle, equilateral, VIII, 157
Tribes, Arabian: I, 41; and Abraham, V, 137, *see also* Ishmael; desert, I, 46; *see also* Kenites; Midianites
—— Hellenic, amphictyony of, I, 61
—— Israelitic, I, 41, 47, 61, 317; ethnic unity, I, 39 ff., 55, 61; God of, I, 47, 313; groups, I, 317; led by Joshua, I, 53; racial mixtures, I, 39; role in messianism, V, 144, 355; sacrifices, I, 51; seminomadic, I, 33, 41, 315; seven-year redistribution of land, I, 333; system of twelve, I, 61, 319; ten lost: II, 61, 338, III, 117, 205, 208; *see also* Ten Tribes
—— Jewish: in Arabia, III, 64, V, 168; exiled from Medina, III, 78 f.; Jeraua in North Africa, III, 91, 271 f.
—— Slavonic, in Poland, III, 206 ff., 213 ff., 330 ff., 333 ff.
—— Turkic, V, 162, VI, 226
Tribute, I, 263; payment of, for protection, IV, 38 f., 55 f., 74, 81, 99, 102 f., 142 f., 152; to escape discrimination, III, 147; *see also* Taxation
Trigon, earthly, conjunctions of, VIII, 180 f.
Trilingualism, dictionaries, VII, 17
Triliterality, VII, 41 ff., 48
Trinity, doctrine of, II, 161, V, 26, VI, 5 f., 303, VII, 179, VIII, 30, 95 ff., 279; Maimonidean view, V, 365; Mohammed's view, III, 83; religious debate over, V, 120 f.; separation of God the Father, VIII, 42
Tripolis, Syria, IV, 113; Jewish community, III, 104; treatment of prisoners of war, III, 150
Tripolitania: Jewish settlement, III, 107 f.; and Roman synagogue, I, 410
Trito-Isaiah, I, 103
Troki, Karaite settlement, V, 285
Troubadour, in Spain and Provence, VII, 151; *see also* Poetry
Troyes, France: Rashi's school in, VI, 49, VII, 121 f.; synods, IV, 48, V, 64 f.; tanneries, IV, 319
Trullan Council, III, 175; anti-Jewish canons, III, 194; on bathing in public places, III, 142; canon re traditional interpretation of Bible, V, 109; injunction on preaching, VI, 154, 159
Truth, quest of scientists and philosophers, VIII, 173
Tryphon, R., *see* Tarfon, R.
Tryphon, name, II, 380
Tryphon, of Justin's dialogue, II, 133
Tubal-Cain, first smith, I, 60
Tübat (Tibet?), tribe, III, 115
Tudela, Spain, IV, 248; privilege from Sancho VII, IV, 35 f.; treaty with Alphonso I, IV, 30; *see also* Benjamin of Tudela
Tulunides, rulers of Palestine, V, 222 f.
Tumai, Egypt, III, 23, 105
Tummim, I, 49, 82
Tunes: Jewish aversion to foreign, VII, 205; as mnemotechnical aid, VII, 125 ff.; secular, for religious poems, VII, 204
Tunis, and Tarshish, VII, 16
Turbo, Marcius, II, 95, 96
Turkestan, I, 322
Turkey: law on forced conversion, III, 132; public officials, III, 151; treatment of minorities, III, 137, 160; tribes, V, 162, VI, 226
Turkish language, III, 324
Tustar, III, 165

Tyrannos, I, 63, 320
Tyre, I, 162, 176, 322, 375; alliance with Solomon, I, 64, 321; economic blockade, I, 277; glassblowers, IV, 168; Jerusalem academy transferred to, V, 37; Jewish community, III, 104, IV, 113; Jewish "siege" of, III, 19 f., 236; relationship with Delos, I, 377; surrender to the Crusaders, IV, 113

U

'Ubaid-Allah al-Azdi, VI, 165
Ucles, battle of, IV, 36
Ugarit, *see* Ras Shamra
Ugrians, III, 204; *see also* Hungary
'Ukbari, Isma'i al-, V, 182, 262, VI, 299; biblical interpretation, V, 195 f.; tombstone inscription, V, 195
'Ukbarites, V, 182, 195 f., VI, 475
Ulpian (Domitius Ulpianus), VI, 55; quoted, II, 110, 375
'Umar I, caliph: career of world conquest, III, 86 ff., 94; disposition of captured lands, III, 95 f.; on inheritance rights, III, 144; mosque of, III, 103, 134, 269, 272; revival of exilarchate, V, 141; successors in the Caliphate, III, 152; supported by Jews and Nestorians, III, 89 f.; suppression of Arabian Jews, III, 76, 80, 274; treaties, III, 97, 101, 269, 293 f.; violent death, III, 122
—— Covenant of 'Umar, III, 97, 129, 131, 269; ban on unbelievers in public office, III, 151; injunction re family names, III, 148; provisions restored under the Latin Kingdom, IV, 115 f.
'Umar II, caliph: and the Covenant of 'Umar, III, 131, 294; decree against infidels, III, 97, 176; discharge of *dhimmi* officials, III, 151 f.; and Jewish medical writings, VIII, 236; on price fixing, IV, 223
'Umayyad dynasty, III, 88; and Byzantium, III, 198; dissolution of, VII, 147; period of transition to 'Abassids, III, 121 ff.; status of Jewish minority under, III, 120; status of judges, VI, 9; support of fatalism, VIII, 109; *see also under* names of caliphs, *e.g.,* Mu'awiya
Ummi, term, III, 263
Understanding, gates of, VIII, 294
Unemployment, I, 70, 412
Unitarianism, VIII, 98
Unity: absolute character of, VIII, 152; ideological, of Jews, V, 198; in Jewish sectarianism, V, 205 ff.; *see also* Ethnic unity
Universalism, I, 23; and nationalism (*q.v.*), I, 31, 158; and particularism, I, 96-99, 339; prophetic, in Exile, I, 157
Universe: divine government of, VII, 172, 174; duration of, VI, 146, 232; image of, VIII, 160-66, 313-15; plural nature of, I, 202, II, 310, 311; *see also* World
Unleavened bread, I, 148
Unmoved Mover, VIII, 90 f.
'Uqba, Mar, ancient exilarch, II, 198, 272
'Uqba, Mar, medieval exilarch, III, 107, V, 40, 213; controversy with Pumbedita academy, V, 10 ff.; in Kairuwan, V, 39
Ur, city, I, 33, 44
Urban II, pope, IV, 94, 97 ff.
Urbanization: under the Caliphate, IV, 152 f.; and changes in Jewish law, VI, 147; growth of, VI, 132, V, 177; of Jewish population, IV, 274; rise of leisure class, VII, 69; role in ethnic-religious conflicts, I, 372; *see also* Cities; Town, Israelitic
Uriah, prophet, I, 79, 324, 327
Uriah the Hittite, I, 326
Urim, I, 49, 82
Urine, VIII, 244
Urraca, daughter of Alphonso VI, IV, 38, 252 f.
Usama ibn Munqidh, Muslim emir, VIII, 398
Usatges, custumal of Barcelona, IV, 41
Usha academy, V, 14; synod at, II, 126, 271, 378, 420
Usury, I, 20, 194, 265, II, 250, 302, IV, 75 ff., 88, V, 128; bans on, IV, 79, 197 ff.; charge of, against Jews, IV, 121; and foreigners, I, 156; interest considered as, I, 109; Jewish aversion to, I, 85 f., 261, 409; Meir b. Simon on, IV, 224; "open" vs. "concealed," IV, 205; Saadiah's tract on, VI, 69; *see also* Banking; Interest; Loans; Moneylenders and moneylending
'Uthman, caliph: efforts re Qur'anic text, VI, 243; violent death, III, 122

Utopian thinking, II, 58
'Uzziel, R., viceroy of Ḥamat, III, 159

V

Valens, Roman emperor, II, 188
Valerian, Roman emperor, II, 177, 380
Vandalism, sepulchral, IV, 236
Vandals, III, 7
Vannes, Council of, III, 50
Varro, Marcus Terentius, I, 251, 254
Varuna, ethical deity, I, 45
Vassals: Christian and Jewish, IV, 163; status of, IV, 49 f.; *see also* Serfdom
Vecelin, clerical convert to Judaism, IV, 9, 66
Vegetables, names of, VIII, 229
Vegetative power, VIII, 107
Ve-hizhir, midrash, VI, 23, 40
Veil, wearing of, III, 142, 283, 299
Venafro, church of, III, 31
Venereal disease, V, 250
Vengeance, I, 134, 135; motive of Crusaders, IV, 102; and Day of Recompense, II, 31, 341
Venice: ban on Jews in shipping trade, IV, 183; Jewish community, IV, 25; shipping rights in Byzantium, IV, 24
Venosa: inscriptions, IV, 20, VIII, 204; itinerant preacher, VI, 156
Ventidius Cumanus, I, 239, 264
Venus, I, 311; planet, I, 57
Veracity, consent of masses as proof of, VI, 145 f.
Verbs, Hebrew: doctrine of paradigms, VII, 53; forms of, VII, 35 ff., 49; triliterality of, VII, 42 f.
Verdun, Treaty of 843, IV, 43, 64
Verona, Italy, IV, 26
Verses, biblical: hermeneutic elaboration of, VI, 164 f.; in prayers, VII, 69; number and division of, VI, 238; *see also* Bible
Vespasian, Roman emperor, I, 391, II, 57, 103, 131, 369; all land taken over by, I, 265; campaign in Palestine, II, 91 f., 245; Commentaries of, II, 372; coronation, VI, 420; execution of all who claimed Davidic descent, II, 121; Jewish fiscal tax enacted by, I, 266, II, 106, 186, 373, III, 191; Jewish rights under, I, 248, II, 100, 108; R. Johanan's demand of, II, 120, 377; sympathy for Jewish faith, II, 92; Temple of Onias closed by, II, 93; witticism, I, 244
Vestal priestesses, I, 146
Vetus Latina, Bible version, II, 144, 385 f., VI, 272 f., 462 f.; *see also* Bible; Jerome, Saint
Ve-yitqales, usage of, VII, 246
Vibia, wife of Vincentius, II, 25
Vienna, Austria, IV, 72
Villages: agricultural, IV, 157; celebration of High Holidays, VII, 79; collective tax responsibility, IV, 152; contrasted with towns, I, 325; owned by Jews, IV, 161 f., 163
Villa judaica, IV, 29
Villa Torlonia tombs, II, 11, 146, 331
Villeins and villeinage, II, 258; and Jewish "serfdom" (*q.v.*), IV, 63 f., 70 ff.; labor, IV, 155; *see also* Peasants
Vincentius, tomb, II, 25, 338
Vine: productiveness, I, 251; symbolism, I, 253, II, 13
Vineyards: royal and ecclesiastical, IV, 317; talmudic innovation, IV, 163; work in, on half holidays, IV, 315
Violence, outlawry of, IV, 70
Viper, flesh of, VIII, 247
Virgil: "messianic" eclogue, II, 5; indebtedness to Judaism, II, 329
Virginity, V, 241 f.; of bride, V, 29, VI, 59
Virtue, I, 201
Vishehrad, Czechoslovakia, IV, 103
Visigoths: in Spain and Gaul, III, 33-46, 127, 176, 244-50, IV, 5; anti-Jewish legislation, III, 33 ff., 127; areas of influence in Christian Spain, IV, 27 ff.; "bigotry," IV, 19; Byzantine influence, III, 246; vs. forced conversion, IV, 5; Jewish collaboration with Arab invaders, III, 91 f.; laws, on land tenure, IV, 155 f.; *Leges Visigothorum,* III, 36, 42, 44; *Lex Romana Visigothorum,* III, 35, 49; and Mozarabs, III, 127
Visions: apocalyptic, V, 149 f., 353; of Daniel, III, 179, 183, 315; prophetic, VIII, 129 f., 133; Ibn Gabirol on, VIII, 333
Vitalism, VIII, 226
Vital power, VIII, 107
Vitellius, Lucius, I, 238-39, II, 10
Viticulture, IV, 162; in Arabia, III, 70; in France, IV, 317; *see also* Grape culture; Vineyards

Vivisection, VIII, 203 f.
Vladimir I, duke of Kiev, III, 215
Vladimir II (Monomakh), duke of Kiev, III, 216, 217
Volkmar, *see* Dithmar
Vowels, Hebrew: analysis of, VII, 36; antiquity of, VII, 60; in Arabic and Hebrew, VII, 194 f.; points, VI, 260; pronunciation of, VI, 250; ratio of, to consonants, VII, 314; slurring over, VI, 248; symbolism of, VIII, 35 f.; tenfold division, VII, 52 f.
Vows: Aḥai on, VI, 39; "All Vows and Abnegations," VI, 125; dissolution of, V, 249; laws on, VI, 95 f.; unwittingly broken, VII, 78
Vratislav, duke, of Prague, IV, 118
Vulgate, II, 144, 385 f., VI, 272 f., 462 f.; *see also* Bible; Jerome, Saint

W

Wadi Tumilat, I, 37
Wages, I, 270, 325, 412; community regulation, II, 261; of Jewish labor, I, 270, IV, 170, 321; *see also* Labor and laborers
Wahb ibn Ya'ish of Raqqa, VIII, 310
Wailing Wall, at Jerusalem, III, 101, 278, V, 236; sole remnant of Temple, II, 108
Walcher, abbot of Malvern, England, VIII, 174
Walking, on the Sabbath, VI, 80
Wamba, king of the Visigoths, III, 41, 46, IV, 47
Waqidi, library, VII, 138
War: in behalf of a commandment, II, 100, 372; Jewish leaders, III, 157; Judeo-Roman, I, 212, II, 89-102, 106, 121, 368-71, *see also* Bar Kocheba; Great War; Hadrian; Roman Empire; Trajan; mass participation, I, 332; messianic, V, 144 ff., 191 ff., 353; purchase of booty, V, 317; *see also* Crusades; Military service; Revolts
Warjalan (Ouargela), African Karaite community, VII, 226
Warmth, loss of natural, VIII, 259
Warning, poems of, VI, 372
War of Investiture, IV, 73, 95
"War of the Children of Light with the Children of Darkness," II, 53
Wasit, Egypt, VIII, 168
Waṣiyya, term, V, 7
Water: in biblical cosmology, VIII, 6, 22 f., 336; proportion of earth's surface, VIII, 214; significance, I, 407; and wind, VIII, 217
Water Drinkers, II, 51
"Water of bitterness" ordeal, II, 222, 409
Way of life, and reproofs of instruction, VIII, 37
Wealth: acquisition of, VIII, 48 f.; a motive for joining the Crusade, IV, 101; Muslim jeweler's, IV, 214; rabbinic attitude toward, II, 256, 276 f., 278, IV, 220 f., 347; short-lived, of Romans and Jews, II, 420; term, II, 422
— of Jews, I, 262-67, 410-11, II, 242, 247, IV, 118, 203, 214; communal, IV, 82, 85; debate re source of, IV, 211; envy of, IV, 85, 126 f., 142; of exilarchs, V, 8; expropriation of, by Vratislav, IV, 118; funerals, II, 287; Isaiah's warning, I, 68; sectarian, V, 258; short-lived, II, 420; *see also* Poverty
Weapons: ban on carrying, III, 62, IV, 70, 141, 303; lack of, in Jewish communities, IV, 126
Weavers and weaving, I, 408, IV, 167 f.; head of Sura academy, V, 74 f.; *see also* Textile industry
Wedding: Baghdad ordinance re, VI, 140; choice of day, V, 29, VI, 123, 130; customs, II, 231, VI, 75; poems for, VII, 143, 176, 180
Week, "cosmic," VI, 232, 440; seven-day, I, 6, 120, 192
Week days, designation of, I, 144
Weights and measures, I, 85, II, 254, 255
Welfare, medical, VIII, 238, 404
Weli worship, III, 137, V, 308, VII, 76
Wends, German Crusades against, IV, 131
Wergeld, III, 295, IV, 35, 39, 41, 253 f.; *see also* Fines; Punishments
West-Semitic dialect, I, 36
Wheat, I, 251, 252
WHWH, *see* Yahweh
Wicked Priest, II, 53 f., 349
Widows, V, 321; distribution of estate among, VI, 85; *ḥaliṣah,* V, 299; pre-

scribed settlement for, IV, 345; support of, VI, 124; *see also* Women
Wieselburg, Germany, IV, 106 f.
Will, divine, VIII, 101, 328; changeability of, VI, 145; Christian and Muslim contention re, VI, 482; media of revelation of, VIII, 342; mediation through, VIII, 91 ff.; medical practice and, VIII, 231; and miracles (*q.v.*), VIII, 129; *see also* Prophets and prophecy
Will, freedom of, *see* Free will
William, Saint, IV, 135 f.
William, archbishop of Tyre, IV, 109 f.
William I, king of Sicily, IV, 27
William II, king of England: and forced converts, IV, 106, V, 113; policy toward Jews, IV, 77
William III, count of Montpellier, IV, 63
William of Auvergne, VIII, 101; on Jewish philosophy, VIII, 72
William of Malmesbury, IV, 76
William of Newbury, IV, 76, 124, 140; on crimes of Crusaders in England, IV, 127 f.; on Jews of England, IV, 87
William Rufus, *see* William II, king of England
Wills, II, 253
Winchester, England, IV, 125, 136 f.
Wind, and water, VIII, 217
Wine, I, 251, 252; 'Ananites' consumption of, V, 218; blessing over, V, 245, VI, 123; funerary, II, 288, 424; fifth cup, VII, 116; inspirational effect, VII, 200; law re Gentiles and, IV, 162, V, 281; Muslim ban on, IV, 164; Palestinian and foreign, II, 246; payment in, by Gentile debtors, VI, 128 f.; poems to drinking, VII, 158 ff.; ritualistic requirement, IV, 158, 165; and song, VII, 203; *see also* Vineyards; Viticulture
Wisdom: beginning of, VIII, 176; and divine will, VIII, 91 f., 328; literature, I, 150, 377; religious and national heritage, I, 151, 363; schools of, I, 141, 150 f.; "seven pillars" of, VIII, 145; *see also* Education
Wisdom of Solomon, The, I, 141, 198, 204, 386, II, 222
Witches, II, 21
Witnesses: formula for, VI, 67; illiteracy of, VI, 255; in Judeo-Christian litigations, IV, 15 ff., 41 f., 49, 78; requirements, IV, 69, V, 56; warning to, II, 137
Wojtech, *see* Adalbert, of Prague
Wolf, and Joseph, story of, VI, 170
Women: agents of religious conversion, V, 267 f.; antifeminism, VII, 309; banned at public baths, III, 142; beauty, II, 237 f., 412; benefactresses, II, 24, 240, 338, 413; community of, II, 183, 222, 251; *dhimmi*, III, 142, V, 202; duties, II, 237, 239; employment of Christian, IV, 15; exclusion from public office, V, 74; freedom of, V, 224, VI, 64; in harems, III, 201, 283; intellectual pursuits, II, 239, V, 323; levirate marriage (*q.v.*), I, 79, II, 231, 411; magic arts, I, 347, II, 21; marriage of captive, V, 8 f.; menstruating, V, 250, VI, 69; Moses' Ethiopian wife, I, 38; "obstreperous," VI, 64, 133 ff., 138; pregnant, V, 283, 349; preponderance of men over, I, 113 f.; and procreation, II, 218; profanation of, V, 240; proselytes, I, 177, II, 233; reference to, in Jewish prayer of thanksgiving, VII, 109; rights, III, 283, V, 243, VI, 68; role in the Crusades, IV, 96; Roman, I, 191, 405, II, 239, 240; rules of conduct, II, 222, 228, III, 111, 139 f., 142, VI, 182 f.; in sanctuaries, I, 146; secondary wives, II, 224; "singing girls," VII, 205; status, I, 58, 111-14, 146, 191, 347-48, II, 235-41, 303 f., 306, 412 f., 421, V, 221 f., VII, 188; status in Mazdakite movement, III, 55; sufferings, I, 265; in synagogue, II, 240, 413; veils, III, 142, 283, 299; widows (*q.v.*), I, 275, II, 271, 303, 304, 420; *see also* Concubines and concubinage; Marriage; Slaves and slavery
Wool industry, I, 257, 408
"Word," divine, and *logos* (*q.v.*), V, 121
Words: biliteral and triliteral, VII, 38; as body and soul, VII, 50 f.; foreign, in Hebrew commentaries, VI, 52 f., 347, 349, VII, 31; implications of correct interpretation, VI, 166, VII, 13, 68; like-sounding, VI, 288, VII, 8, 145, 223; power of, II, 22, VII, 87, VIII, 8, 12, 14; significance of correct spelling, VI, 166, VII, 12 f.; vocabulary, and comparative linguistics, VII, 12

Words: biblical, VII, 25; alphabetical listing, VI, 252; controversy based on numerical value of, V, 86 ff.; derived from same root, VII, 25; plural forms, V, 120; substitution, VI, 293 ff.; *see also* Grammar; Lexicography
Workers, *see* Labor and laborers
World: divine government, V, 259, VIII, 16, 18, 23, 34 ff., 86, 101; duration of, VIII, 78 f., 81, 87 ff., 191 f., 372; end of, III, 15, 97, 176, V, 142 f., 360, VIII, 191, *see also* End of days; five worlds of Bar Ḥiyya, VIII, 94 f.; sublunary, VIII, 94, 102, 103, 128, 222 f.; superlunary, VIII, 162, 165; *see also* Creation; Universe
World Chronology (*Seder 'Olam*), II, 141, 376, 384; aggadic scheme of, V, 147 ff.; in messianism, V, 148 ff.
World government, I, 209
World history, VI, 198-204, 210, 423-25, 429 f.; "devolutionary" views, VI, 229 f., VII, 56; dividing point, VI, 227 f.; Judeo-Christian view, VI, 209, 227 ff.; Yeraḥmeel, VI, 195 ff.
World Intellect, VIII, 333
World Orders, VI, 200, 233
World Soul, VIII, 115, 333
World-to-come, *see* Hereafter; Immortality of the soul
World War, Second, I, 293
Worms, Germany: Jewish community, VI, 48 f.; privilege granted by Henry IV, IV, 67 f., 71; siege of, IV, 70
Worship, VII, 62-134, 244-85; ban on public, III, 14; daily participation in, VII, 62; imperial, I, 244, 404, II, 5, 99, 109; inwardness of, VII, 73 ff., 179, VIII, 3; linguistic problem, VII, 66 ff.; mystic union in, VII, 212 f.; private, I, 352, VII, 120 f., 168; proper behavior in, I, 351, VIII, 3; ritualistic dynamism, VII, 131 ff.; sacrificial, V, 173, *see also* Sacrifices; *see also* God; Liturgy; Prayers; Ritual
Writing, I, 334; Arabic calligraphy, IV, 36 f.; knowledge of, in Arabia, III, 82; knowledge of ancient art of, I, 314; Mohammed on Jews' method of, III, 85; preexilic, I, 305; Slavs' learning of, III, 208; *see also* Alphabet
Written transmission, *see under* Transmission, oral
Würzburg, Germany, IV, 120
Wydobycz, *see* Kiev

X

Xerxes I, king of Persia, I, 341, 348

Y

Yabneh (Jamnia): academy of, II, 115, 120, 126, 377, VIII, 193; debate on charities, II, 270, 420; Greek attack on Jews, I, 219
Yaho and Ḥnub, I, 352
Yahu, names compounded with, I, 78, 327
Yahweh: awe of name, I, 128, II, 17; and Baal, I, 349; image of, I, 322; kingship of, I, 93; and mercy, I, 46, II, 311; name (the holy Tetragrammaton), I, 13, 59, 138, 309, II, 18; substitute names, I, 128, 312, II, 28, 335; as tribal god, I, 39; WHWH, archaic form, II, 18; *see also* God; Tetragrammaton
Yahwism, I, 44, 64, 78; and demonology, I, 358; pure, against eclectic, I, 61
Yahwist, I, 42
Yaḥya, of Antioch, III, 103
Yaḥya b. Adam, III, 163
Yaḥya b. Yaḥya, Idrisite ruler, III, 142
Yaḥya ibn Matruḥ, vizier of Damascus, VIII, 249
Yaḥya ibn Sa'id, chronicler, III, 137
Yaḥya ibn Suleiman, *see* Zechariah b. Solomon
Yahziel, angel, VIII, 8 f.
Yalta, II, 239
Yannai, R., Amora, II, 263; and a peddler, VI, 154; suspension of years of fallowness, VIII, 209
Yannai, R., liturgical poet, VI, 248, VII, 84; acrostic of name, VII, 260, 262; halakhic content of poems, VII, 103, 262; legend on death of Qalir, VII, 270; liturgical poems, V, 276, VII, 93 ff., 261 f.; and Palestinian Targum, VII, 263
Yao (or Iao), divine name, VIII, 9
Ya'qubi, al-, *Tariḥ*, IV, 226
Ya'qub ibn Killis, vizier, III, 154
Ya'qub ibn Musa al-Nigrisi, VIII, 370
Yaqut, Muslim geographer, III, 109, VII, 14, VIII, 153, 212

Yashar, Sefer ha- (Book of the Just), VI, 197 f., 212 f., 423
Yashar b. Ḥesed at-Tustari, V, 233 f.
Yassin, Anbal, Kievan Jew, III, 216
"Yasu'," Arabic name of Jesus, III, 258
Yathrib, *see* Medina
Yaukin, king of Judah, I, 115, 348
Yazdegerd I, king of Persia: and Isfahan, III, 109, VI, 427; and Jewish wife, II, 181, 204, 404
Yazdegerd II, king of Persia, II, 181, 213
Yazdegerd III, king of Persia, III, 60, 89
Year: intercalation of lunar months, VIII, 188; length of, VIII, 189 ff., 198 f., 204, 376; lunar and solar, V, 191 f., 201, VIII, 185 ff., 188, 368 ff.; in messianic computations, V, 201; One, VIII, 202; and religious observance, V, 191 f.; seasons, VIII, 201 f.; *see also* Calendar; Chronology; Jubilee year; Sabbatical year
Yebamot, tractate, VI, 81 f.
Yedaiah b. Abraham ha-Penini, of Béziers, VII, 188, 204, 240; defense of scientific study, VIII, 264
Yeḥiel Ashkenazi, VI, 136
Yehoel (Jaoel), angel, VIII, 9
Yehudah, I, 397; *see also* Judaea
Yehudah, exilarch, VI, 214
Yehudah b. Barzillai al-Barceloni, II, 262, III, 202, VI, 113, VIII, 24, 287; and Bar Ḥiyya, VI, 149, 439, VIII, 266; "Book of Deeds," IV, 34; *Commentary on Yeṣirah,* VIII, 38, 58, 142, 279, 327, 353; compilation of halakhic works, VI, 73, 75, 89, 361; computations re Messiah, VIII, 361; linking of persecutions with literary activity, VII, 83; liturgical monograph, VI, 73, VII, 118; possible influence of Saadiah, VI, 211; on rabbinic view of *piyyuṭim,* VII, 102; on recitation of Targum, VI, 262 f.; and Simon Qayyara, VI, 365; sources for geonic period, VI, 73, 208; on traits of a local leader, VI, 324
Yehudah b. Isaac Shabbetai, mysogynist, VII, 188
Yehudah b. Joseph ibn abi'l Thanna, VIII, 243
Yehudah b. Joseph of Kairuwan, V, 309
Yehudah b. Meir ha-Kohen, VI, 48
Yehudah b. Nathan, R., VI, 53; commentary on Sanhedrin, VI, 349
Yehudah b. Saadiah, founder of Egyptian *negidim* dynasty, V, 41 f.
Yehudah b. Samuel ha-Levi, *see* Halevi, Yehudah b. Samuel
Yehudah b. Samuel he-Ḥasid (the Pious), German pietist, VI, 140, VIII, 42; attitude toward forced converts, IV, 146; "Book of Divine Glory," VIII, 45, 293; "Book of the Pious," VI, 404, VIII, 46 ff., 258, 261, 265, 294 f.; on magic practices, VIII, 46 f.; Petaḥiah and, VI, 436
Yehudah b. Solomon al-Ḥarizi, *see* Al-Ḥarizi
Yehudah Gaon on marriage customs, VI, 122, 395
Yehudah ha-Kohen, R., rabbi of Mayence, III, 219
Yehudah ibn Tibbon, *see* Ibn Tibbon, Yehudah
Yehudai b. Naḥman Gaon, head of Sura academy, V, 15, 25, 210, 212; liturgical comments, VII, 70 f.; and the Palestinian Talmud, VI, 22; on qualifications of a cantor, VII, 129; recodification of Jewish law, VI, 78 ff., 363 f.; and scholar, VI, 9
Yehudi b. Sheshet, VII, 23
Yelamdenu midrashim, VI, 182
Yeluatshi, ruler of the Kerait, VI, 434
Yemen, Arabia: Jews of, III, 69, V, 49; liturgical synthesis, VII, 120; Maimonides' "Epistle" to, III, 291, V, 78, 198, 204 f., VIII, 64, 180 f.; messianic movement, V, 198, 204 f.; midrashim, VI, 401, VII, 83; "Mourners for Zion," V, 376; reception of Saadiah's translation, VI, 270; regional Jewish chiefs, V, 43 f.; romances in sacred literature, VI, 181; route to, opened, I, 64; use of Aramaic, VII, 67; use of Babylonian punctuation, VI, 253; variations in pronunciation and meaning of talmudic terms, VII, 28
Yequtiel ibn Ḥassan, Jewish grandee, VII, 152, 159, VIII, 69
Yeraḥmeel b. Solomon, VI, 170, 195 ff., 422, VIII, 43
Yerahmeëlites, I, 57
Yerushalmi, *see* Talmud, Palestinian
Yeshu'a b. Yehudah (Abu'l Faraj Furqan

Yeshu'a b. Yehudah (*Continued*) ibn Asad), Karaite theologian, V, 159, 231, 233, VI, 83, VIII, 60
Yeshubokht, archbishop, VI, 4
Yeṣirah, Sefer, *see* Creation, Book of
YHWH, YHW, YHH, *see* Yahweh
Yiddish, I, 19, 27, 186, VII, 9; biblical renditions, VI, 272; literature, VI, 187
Yinnon, reputed name of the Messiah, V, 153
Yiṣḥaqi, *see* Rashi
Yissakhar, tribe, VI, 247
Ym, god, I, 45
Yobel, I, 349
Yoma, tractate, VI, 86
Yom Ṭob b. Isaac, R., IV, 125
Yom Ṭob Kohen, V, 74
York, England: martyrdom of Jews, IV, 124, 125 ff.; Jewish community, IV, 148
Yose, R., head of Pumbedita academy, VI, 18
Yose b. Yose, R., liturgical poet, VII, 40, 90 ff.; quoted by Ibn Janaḥ, VII, 261; use of acrostics, VII, 88, 257, 261
Yosephon or Yosippon: aggadic collection, II, 384, III, 240, VI, 188 ff., 233, 417 ff., VIII, 43; discussion of ethnology, VI, 226; sources, VI, 194 f.
Yoṣer ra'ash shebi'i, IV, 153
Yotabe, Jewish colony, III, 69 f.
Yudghan (Yehudah) and Yudghanites, V, 182; messianic movement, V, 185, 191 f., 219
Yugoslavia: Jewish communities, II, 210, III, 210 f.; synagogue, II, 10
Yusuf ibn Tashfin, Almoravid ruler of Morocco, III, 124
Yusuf Rabban, II, 212, 407, III, 114
YW, son of El, I, 309

Z

Zacuto, Abraham, scientist-chronicler, VII, 29; use of Ṣemaḥ's dictionary, VII, 224
Zadok, David's priest, I, 149, 330, II, 203; house of, II, 342, 343; *see also* Sadducees
Zadok, gaon, VI, 131
Zadok, R., II, 111, 117
"Zadokite" documents, II, 53, V, 187 f.; *see also* Damascus sect
Za'frani, Musa al-, III, 110, V, 182 f., 196, VI, 299
Zahalon, Jacob b. Isaac, VIII, 239
Zahel, misspelling of Sahl b. Bishr's (*q.v.*) name, VIII, 167
Zahir, ar-, caliph, V, 271, 280
Zahirites, Muslim, VI, 463
Zaid b. 'Ali, *Madjmu'a,* VI, 363
Zakat, poor tax, III, 274
Zakkai b. Akhunai, exilarch, V, 9
Zakkai b. Azariah, branch dynasty in Mosul, V, 43
Zakkai b. Ḥabibai, V, 15
Zakkai b. Joseph, V, 311
Zalaqa, battle of, IV, 36
Zangi, Imad ad-Din, V, 203
Zaradusht, Mazdakite founder, III, 55
Zarqali, al-, *see* Al-Zarqali
Zealots: iconoclastic fervor, II, 15, 47, 346; and Judeo-Roman conflicts, II, 94, 101, 372, 423; messianism, II, 58, 126; origins of, II, 47; Peter a member? II, 74
Zebaḥ, I, 353
Zechariah, patriarch, III, 22, V, 141, 264
Zechariah, prophet, I, 130, 158, 354, 364, VI, 405; and "third communion," II, 173, 396
Zechariah b. Berekhel, V, 52 f., VI, 17
Zechariah b. Solomon (Yaḥya ibn Suleiman), *Midrash ha-Ḥefes,* VI, 411
Zedek, god, I, 45
Zedekiah, king of Judah, I, 115
Zedekiah, Jewish sage, VI, 161
Zedekiah Anav degli Mansi, VII, 107
Ze'era, R., II, 182, 208
Ze'iri, R., II, 16
Zekhut abot, I, 135, II, 42, 346
Zeno, Roman emperor, I, 392, II, 189, 286, 339, III, 6
Zenobia, queen of Palmyra, II, 211, 407, III, 63
Zenodorus, II, 14
Zenon papyri, I, 106, 255, 344, 392, 408, 409
Zephaniah b. Cushi, prophet, I, 86, 118
Zera, R., wonder worker, VIII, 21; *see also* Ze'era
Zerah, Asa's victory over, I, 322
Zeraḥiah b. Isaac ha-Levi: Book of Light, VI, 87 f., 368 f.; correspondence with Abraham b. David, VI, 119
Zerahiah b. Isaac of Rome, translator of Maimonides, VIII, 402

Zerubbabel, governor of Jerusalem, I, 106, 119, 354, VIII, 125, 278; restoration under, I, 103, 110, 125, 161, 367; Temple of, I, 238
—— Book of, III, 20, 239, V, 140 f., 152, VIII, 179
Zeus, I, 374; identification of Antiochus with, I, 229, 398
Zeus Xenios, II, 30
Zindiq, III, 143, V, 104, 106, VI, 482, VIII, 296; equated with Manichaean, V, 337
Zion: belief in restoration of, III, 204, VII, 97; Karaite references to, V, 260; light shining upon, VII, 115 f.; "Mourners" for, V, 32, 185, 257, 258, 271, 376; odes to, VII, 154, 168, 197; *see also* Jerusalem
Zionism, I, 27 f., 297, II, 296
Zirids, Moroccan dynasty, III, 108
Ziv, V, 148
Zodiac, signs of, VIII, 184
Zohar, V, 134, VIII, 278; origin of, VIII, 274; theosophy of, VIII, 51
Zoology, studies in, VIII, 226 ff.
Zoroaster and Zoroastrianism, I, 102, 315, 341; II, 173, 180, 183, 313, III, 130, V, 105 f., 183, VI, 3, 19, 299, 438, VIII, 16; burial tradition, III, 22, 297; dualism, VI, 305 f.; in Fez, III, 145; heavenly family concept, II, 317; Jewish idea re, III, 17; Ka'aba of, II, 397; on light and darkness, VIII, 34; marital unions, II, 231; relations with Judaism, II, 317 f., 436; religion of Sassanian dynasty, II, 213; Saadiah and, VI, 479; taxation of, III, 191, 193; *wergeld,* III, 295; *see also* Parsees and Parsiism; Persia
Zuṭra, Abraham, *see* Abraham Zuṭra
Zuṭra, Mar, II, exilarch, II, 182, 196, 213, 399, VI, 200; date of execution, VI, 424
Zuṭra, Mar, III, exilarch, II, 196, III, 20, 63, V, 32, VI, 199 ff.; emigration to Palestine, VI, 424, 446; founder of Tiberian academy, VI, 239, 243; generations of descendants, V, 305; liturgical changes in period of, VII, 255
Zuṭṭa (or Sar Shalom), VI, 110; Scroll of, VI, 215
Żydowo, Poland, III, 218